TEXAS WOMAN'S UNIVERSITY LIBRARY
Date Due
AUG 4 1970
MAY 12 2017
JUN 14 2017
Demco 38-297
282407
D0369033

THACKERAY
A Personality

BY THE SAME AUTHOR

THE PLAYGOER'S HANDBOOK TO RESTORATION DRAMA

CHARLES READE: A BIOGRAPHY

THACKERAY IN 1852
From a portrait by Samuel Laurence

THACKERAY

A Personality

BY

MALCOLM ELWIN

'*What care I to appear to future ages (who will be deeply interested in discussing the subject) as other than I really am?*'

THACKERAY, in a letter of September 1856.

NEW YORK / RUSSELL & RUSSELL

FIRST PUBLISHED 1932
REISSUED, 1966, BY RUSSELL & RUSSELL
A DIVISION OF ATHENEUM HOUSE, INC.
BY ARRANGEMENT WITH MALCOLM ELWIN
L. C. CATALOG CARD NO: 66—15427

PRINTED IN THE UNITED STATES OF AMERICA

CONTENTS

LIST OF ILLUSTRATIONS

PREFATORY NOTE

ON BEGINNING this book, I applied to the publishing house of John Murray, as the owners of Thackeray's copyrights, for permission to quote copyright material. I was referred to their literary adviser, Leonard Huxley, who was an old friend of Thackeray's family and proposed to mediate on my behalf with Thackeray's grand-daughter, Mrs. Hester Fuller, though he emphasised that she and her mother, Lady Ritchie, had always refused to countenance any biography in accordance with what they considered to have been Thackeray's wish. He later informed me regretfully that Mrs. Fuller declined co-operation because she was herself contemplating a book about her grandfather, but asked that my book should be submitted to her in proof.

I possess two bound page-proof copies of the book—one marked with Huxley's helpful marginal comments, the other scoured by Mrs. Fuller, who demanded the deletion of many quotations, including the extracts from Thackeray's letters to Mrs. Brookfield. On Huxley's advice the house of John Murray declined to enforce Mrs. Fuller's proposed suppressions, and the book was published as I had written it.

There were still critics who believed that Thackeray's family refused to countenance a biography because they had something disgraceful to hide—even if there might be little worse than such suspected philanderings with governesses as had been suggested by Charlotte Brontë's dedication of

Jane Eyre. Thus Michael Sadleir wrote in reviewing this book, "The 'lights' he has painted firmly and well; the 'darks' he tries to convince us are not there."

But the book forced Mrs. Fuller to revise her policy of suppression. She never published her own contemplated biography, but she did release the family collection of Thackeray's letters for the use of Professor Gordon N. Ray in his four massive volumes of *The Letters and Private Papers of W. M. Thackeray,* 1945-46. This abundant material serves to emphasise the 'lights' as they are painted here, and shows that the "darks" existed only in the imaginations of those whose suspicions had been excited by the mistaken policy of suppression.

MALCOLM ELWIN.

THACKERAY
A Personality

CHAPTER I

§ I

WEARING a military great-coat and a three-cornered hat, a short, thick-set man was taking a morning walk in his garden. His chin was sunk upon his chest, one hand was hidden within the front of his coat, his blue eyes brooded hopelessly, for they saw nothing of the man's immediate surroundings, the garden which he himself had planned and helped to plant. They were the eyes of a man existing upon memories, the bitter-sweet diet of those approaching the end of life's journey.

Unseen, from the rocky hills overlooking the garden, two pairs of eyes were watching, eagerly observing every movement of the man in the garden. They belonged to a little English boy and his black servant, travelling from India to England on a ship which touched for a few hours at the island of St. Helena.

'That is he,' said the black man, 'that is Bonaparte! He eats three sheep every day, and all the little children he can lay hands on!'

The ignorant Calcutta servant probably believed his own words, for the name of the Emperor Napoleon was execrated throughout the world in those days, when foolish mothers and nurses frightened refractory children with the threat that 'Bony' would come for them if they were not good. Doubtless the little boy was duly impressed and drew upon the resilience of a vivid imagination a picture of the Corsican ogre regaling himself upon a banquet of baby flesh. But, perhaps also, other thoughts entered his mind as he gazed upon the bent head of the captive emperor.

Perhaps he wondered a little at the feelings of the man who, after riding roughshod over the civilised world, receiving the plaudits of the populace, the homage of kings and princes, and the languishing glances of lovely women, was doomed to the sad solitude of this rocky, unhealthy island. Few children of six years old would so have wondered, but this one might.

For he was William Makepeace Thackeray, possessed of the divine gift of sympathy, which enabled him to look deep into the human heart and evoke laughter from which tears were rarely far removed.

§ 2

The Thackerays of Hampsthwaite might have been expected to procreate a physically big man, but hardly a writer of genius. They were Yorkshire yeomen, descended from a Thackwa or Thackwra who held thirty acres and a dwelling-house under the Abbot of St. Mary of Fountains in 1336. In the reign of James I one branch settled at Hampsthwaite, near Knaresborough; the last of the direct line died there on his small holding in 1804. But while the eldest sons stayed at home to till the family heritage, their juniors ventured into the outer world to shift for themselves. One of these was a certain Thomas, who, at the age of twelve, gained a scholarship at Eton in 1706. Five years later he won a further scholarship at King's, of which college he eventually became a fellow. As an Eton master he married well in 1729, his wife being the daughter of a landed proprietor in Warwickshire. He became headmaster of Harrow in 1746, chaplain to the Prince of Wales, and died, an archdeacon, in 1760.

He had sixteen children, the youngest of whom, William Makepeace—the Makepeace a family name supposed to have belonged to a Thackeray martyred by Bloody Mary—was born in 1749. His widowed mother obtained for him a writership in the service of the East India Company, and he sailed for Calcutta early in 1766. There were plenty of plums for the picking in India after the Seven Years' War, members of the administrative service regarding their profits from private trading almost as a perquisite accompanying their official salaries. Young Thackeray utilised his position in the counting-house of the Governor of Bengal to excellent advantage, though not so flagrantly as to incur the displeasure of his superiors. Consequently, after five years, he was promoted to be factor at Dacca and enabled to relieve his mother of the care of two of his sisters, Jane and Henrietta. Both quickly found husbands in a country where white women were scarce, Henrietta marrying her brother's chief at Dacca, James Harris, while Jane became the wife of Major James Rennell, the celebrated geographer.

With the appearance of Warren Hastings as governor-general, Thackeray, at twenty-three, was appointed 'collector,' or chief administrator, of the province of Sylhet, on the north-eastern frontier of Bengal. It was a post which offered to its holder, besides considerable financial rewards, exceptional discomfort and danger. It was pioneer work, for the province was largely inhabited by rebellious natives, who combined with the beasts of the vast tracts of jungle to render precarious the security of peaceful settlements. Thackeray and his successor 'converted what had been a wild borderland into a British province,'[1] and 'Thackeray's House' remained an historic landmark for succeeding generations of empire builders. His principal sources of revenue were the destruction of tigers, for which the government paid so much a head—an annual bag being sixty or seventy—and the capture of elephants, which the government purchased for the purpose of military transport. His fortunes prospered so well that, on visiting Calcutta in 1775, falling in love with Amelia Richmond

[1] *The Thackerays in India*, by Sir William Wilson Hunter. London, 1897.

Webb, and contemplating marriage, he could make immediate arrangements for retirement from the service. He was not yet twenty-seven years of age and had been in India rather less than ten years, but he preferred to return to England with his health, a moderate income, and a greater part of his life before him, rather than remain to amass a splendid fortune at the expense of his physical constitution.

Married at Calcutta on 31st January 1776, he soon afterwards sailed for England with his wife. She was one of the four daughters of Colonel Richmond Webb, a kinsman of that hero of Wynendael who is so picturesquely portrayed in *Esmond.* Her sister Sarah did even better for herself by marrying Peter Moore, who created a spectacular career for himself in the same service as Thackeray. But while the latter was hunting elephants, Moore became so expert in the juggling of figures at Calcutta that he became Warren Hastings' ablest revenue officer and profited so well that he was able to retire after fourteen years' service, returning to England with great wealth at the age of thirty, to make a new career as a Member of Parliament, company promoter, and man about town. He took a country house at Hadley Green, near Chipping Barnet, where his nearest neighbour was his wife's brother-in-law, the elephant-hunter, who had settled there, within easy reach of his aged mother at Harrow, seven years earlier.

But while Moore busied himself with politics and high finance, Makepeace Thackeray pursued the tranquil existence of a small country squire, living on 'a quiet mead, with here and there fresh pools of water shining beneath clusters of fair lime trees.' After those few adventurous years in India, rendered necessary by the absence of worldly means, he reverted to type and lived, on a slightly more exalted social plane, the same sort of life as his Hampsthwaite cousins. He had 'a generous, good-humoured face, with kind eyes, well-cut features, and a fresh colour.' When he died in 1813, the local oracle lamented the passing of one whose 'benevolence, integrity, and genial humanity' had rendered him beloved by the neighbourhood.

Upon this solid shire-horse blood was grafted the nobler race-horse strain of the Richmond Webbs. The elephant-hunter's wife bore him twelve children over a period of twenty years; she died in 1810, aged only fifty-three. Seven sons and four daughters lived to maturity. The latter all married well.[1] Of the sons, no fewer than six sought careers in India, probably on account of the influence wielded by their father and Peter Moore upon their erstwhile employers, but, unlike their father and uncle, none of them lived to bring home a fortune. Their generation found fortunes not so easily made as in the days of Clive and Hastings. William, the eldest, enjoyed a brilliant career in the administrative government of Madras, becoming a High Court judge and president of the Board of Revenue, before the climate completed the destruction of his constitution, and he died in 1823, in his forty-fifth year. The two brothers who followed him to Madras enjoyed even shorter careers, Webb, the third brother, dying at the age of nineteen within a year of his arrival, while St. John, the fifth, showed brilliant promise in the political department of the service before, at thirty-five, he was killed by Maratha rebels when approaching them to arbitrate under cover of a flag of truce.

Francis Thackeray, the only one to stay at home, took

[1] Augusta, the eldest, married Dr. Halliday of the East India Company and died at Paris in 1849. Charlotte, who married John Ritchie and died in 1854, was the mother of William Ritchie and grandmother of Sir Richmond Thackeray Ritchie, K.C.B., who married the novelist's elder daughter. Emily, who died of cholera in India in 1824, married John Talbot Shakespear, by whom she had Colonel John Dowdeswell Shakespear, who is said to have borne some resemblance to Colonel Newcome, Colonel Sir Richmond Shakespear, and a daughter Augusta, the wife of General Sir John Low. The fourth sister, Sarah, married Robert Langslow, sometime attorney-general at Malta and Ceylon, and died in 1847.

orders and retired to the scholarly seclusion of a country parsonage. He was the author of a biography of Chatham, reviewed by Macaulay, and the father of Colonel Edward Thackeray, V.C., and the Rev. St. John Thackeray. Charles, the youngest brother, was called to the Bar before he went to India to practise in Calcutta. Apparently the most brilliant of the brothers, he developed a weakness for drink and eked out a living in journalism, before sinking, 'about 1846, into an obscure grave.' He was one of the first leader-writers on the Calcutta *Englishman*.

The other brothers entered the Bengal service, like their father before them. Both showed signs of making names for themselves if they had lived longer. Thomas, the younger, an infantry officer, would have forestalled his nephew in winning the Victoria Cross if the order had then existed. In the Nepal War of 1814, though already wounded, he volunteered to cover the retreat before the advancing rebels. His company charged eight times, each time driving back the enemy, but at the ninth attempt the little force was surrounded and its commander killed. He was only twenty-five.

Richmond Thackeray was the elephant-hunter's second son. He was born on 1st September 1781 (though his tombstone suggests a date more than a year later), and after five years at Eton, he sailed for Calcutta as a Writer in the Company's Civil Service. In some respects his career was curiously like his father's. Like him, he was sent to a rebellious and dangerous district in the hills, like him, he gained rapid promotion, and like him again, he was joined by two of his sisters, who quickly found husbands. But he enjoyed none of his father's opportunities for making a fortune. India under the Marquis Wellesley was not the India of Warren Hastings. There were no profits to be obtained from tigers and elephants; private trading was prohibited for the Company's servants. After a period of apprenticeship as a district officer at the turbulent frontier station of Midnapur and a short spell in the capital, he was appointed, in 1803, Collector at Birbhum, another wild and dangerous frontier district. There he ruled alone for four years, with such success that he was rewarded with an important post in the revenue department at Calcutta.

He now occupied 'a considerable place in the official and social life of the capital.' He was as handsome as he was eligible. His granddaughter described his portrait as 'that of a very young man in an old-fashioned dress and brass buttons, and a white handkerchief round his neck; with brown hair falling loose, with bright soft hazel eyes and arched black eyebrows. The face is long and narrow, the nose is long, the complexion is clear, the mouth delicate and yet not without a certain determination and humour. The eyes have a peculiar out-looking depth of expression which I remember in my father. He looks simple and good and sensitive.' In his face there was a refinement lacking in the heavy brows, truculent mouth, and square chin of the elephant-hunter,[1] revealing a legacy of the Richmond Webbs. He might have been a scholar, like his clerical brother Francis, if his destiny had not taken him to India. With his brother William he shared a gift for acquiring languages, for, on his arrival in India, when studying at Fort William, he took a first-class in Arabic, with distinction in Persian.

He must have cut an attractive figure among potential husbands in Calcutta society, and it is no matter for wonder that he wooed and won a reigning beauty for his wife. Anne, the fatherless daughter of John Harman Becher, of an illustrious Anglo-Indian family, is revealed by her portrait as vivaciously lovely—tall and slender, with great dark eyes, raven curls, a sweet, tender mouth,

[1] A portrait of the elephant-hunter, together with one of 'Richmond Thackeray, his wife, and child,' drawn in 1814, is reproduced in *Ballads and Miscellanies* (Biographical Edition).

and beautiful features. She was only seventeen when she married Richmond Thackeray at Calcutta Cathedral on 13th October 1810. Some nine months later, on 18th July 1811, her only child, William Makepeace Thackeray, was born at Calcutta.

Shortly after the birth of his son, Richmond Thackeray was appointed Collector of the district surrounding the capital, 'then considered one of the prizes of the Bengal Service.' His official residence at Alipur had been the country lodge of Sir Philip Francis some thirty-five years before. He was entirely responsible for the administration of the district, combining the functions of magistrate, judge, chief of police, minister of public works, of revenue and commerce, and inspector of education. He was the supreme local potentate. His period of administration was remembered principally for the improvement of the roads, gravel being first used in the streets of Calcutta on his recommendation.

His young wife, with her exceptional beauty and charm, made a brilliant figure in Calcutta society. Together they faced life joyously, for they possessed all the accessories to perfect happiness—love, beauty, success, prosperity. It was too good to last long. India ruthlessly claimed Richmond Thackeray as it had already claimed two of his brothers and was soon to claim three more. He died on 13th September 1815.

§ 3

At his father's death Richmond Thackeray's son was too young to be separated from his mother. He remained for nearly two more years under her eye, and, remembering one of his parents only as 'a very tall man, rising out of a bath,' he lavished the sum of his childish affections upon the lovely survivor. He adored her for her beauty and her tender love of himself. Tall, graceful, gentle, leaving him with a seductive rustle of silk and a faintly fragrant perfume, she created in the heart of an impressionable child an ideal of womanood which was never supplanted. It was she who, with her sweet sympathy and understanding frankness, encouraged in him the habit of confiding his thoughts, his humours and impressions to feminine ears, with the result that he ever resorted to his pen to unburden his emotions, writing whimsical, often pathetic, letters, not only to his mother, but to Mrs. Brookfield, Kate Perry and her sister, Lucy Baxter and her mother—those women with whom he sought the solace of sympathy after the tragedy of his married life. In none of the novelist's heroines was there absent some suggestion of his childhood's idol and in Helen Pendennis there is an attempt to portray her as she appeared to him in his youth.

At the age of six, in the autumn of 1817, he embarked for home to commence his education. Within two years of the end of his life he was reminded of the parting from his young mother by the death of Sir Richmond Shakespear, who accompanied him on the voyage, remembering 'a ghaut, or river-stair, at Calcutta, and a day when, down those steps, to a boat which was in waiting, came two children whose mothers remained on the shore. One of those ladies was never to see her boy more, and he, too, is just dead in India. . . . We were first-cousins; had been little playmates and friends from the time of our birth; and the first house in London to which I was taken, was that of our aunt.'[1]

This aunt was Richmond Thackeray's sister, Charlotte, the wife of John Ritchie. Her most auspicious attention to her nephew resulted in a visit to a specialist. She was alarmed to observe that his head exactly fitted his uncle's hat, which he had put on in play, but the physician assured her that there was no cause for worry—'he has a large head, but there is a great deal in it.' More picturesque were his mother's grandmother and the unmarried daughter who lived with her. Grandmama Becher was the 'most

[1] *Roundabout Papers*, 'On Letts's Diary.'

lovely and picturesque old lady, with a long tortoiseshell cane, with a little puff or *tour* of snow-white (or was it powdered?) hair under her cap, with the prettiest little black velvet slippers and high heels you ever saw,' who figures in the *Roundabout Papers*. She lived in the sleepy little town of Fareham, 'inhabited by the wives, widows, daughters of navy captains, admirals, lieutenants.' The widow of a naval captain, who must have sailed under Rodney, she was a little old lady of dignity; her great-grandson, writing to assure his mother that he does not allow his uncle Charles Becher to kiss him, as he only takes such favours from ladies, adds with piquancy, 'I don't have many from grandmama.'

Great-aunt Becher, whom her mother always called 'Miss Becher,' lived long enough to witness the little boy's rise to fame. Thus she who had made a home successively for her brother's orphan daughter and that daughter's little son, also knew the childish embraces of her great-nephew's daughters. One of the latter remembers her at least thirty years later, as 'a little dignified old lady, in a flaxen front, with apple cheeks and a blue shawl.'[1] She was 'strict and outspoken, but very kind.' She sat for the portrait of Miss Martha Honeyman, and her relations with her great-nephew may be supposed to have been not unlike those of that good lady with young Clive Newcome.

At Fareham, Thackeray spent many happy hours, but he had no pleasant recollections of his schooldays. His first school, 'somewhere in Hampshire,' to which he was sent along with Richmond Shakespear, is described in the *Roundabout Papers* as 'a school of which our deluded parents had heard favourable reports, but which was governed by a horrible tyrant, who made our young lives so miserable that I remember kneeling by my little bed of a night, and saying, "Pray God, I may dream of my mother." '

[1] Biographical introduction to *The Newcomes*, which contains Thackeray's boyish letters.

More than thirty years afterwards he told his daughters of 'when I was a miserable little beggar, at school at the Polygon, under an olivey little blackguard who used to starve and cane us.'[1]

His mother's memory acquired only an added sweetness from her absence. When he heard of her approaching marriage to Captain Henry Carmichael-Smyth, he evinced no resentment at the idea of a stepfather, but rather grasped at fresh hopes that his mother would be restored to him. In his first letter to her, written on 12th February 1818, obviously under the supervision of his Aunt Ritchie, who is declared to be 'very good to me,' he politely expresses the hope that 'Captain Smyth is well,' adding fervently, 'give my love to him, and tell him he must bring you home to your affectionate son, William Thackeray.' His great-aunt Becher, to whom he sent this letter to be forwarded, tells her niece that 'he drew me your house in Calcutta, not omitting his monkey looking out of the window and black Betty at the top drying towels, and he told me of the numbers you collected on his birthdays in that large room he pointed out to us!'

Sent to another school at Chiswick, he was kindly treated but little happier. Once he ran away, but, having penetrated as far as the Hammersmith Road, he was appalled at the vastness of a friendless world and ran back again before he was missed. In April, when he writes again under evident supervision, he has been learning geography 'a long time, and have begun Latin and ciphering, which I like very much.' Then, in June, after some childish ailment, he is sent down to Fareham to recuperate, and writes:

'MY DEAREST OF ALL MAMAS,—I have much pleasure in writing to you again from Fareham, to tell you how happy I am. . . . I should like you to have such another pretty

[1] *Letters of Anne Thackeray Ritchie, with Forty-two Additional Letters from her Father, William Makepeace Thackeray.* Selected and edited by her daughter, Hester Ritchie. London, 1924.

home as Mrs. O'Brien's, there is such a beautiful garden. I am grown a great boy; I am three feet eleven inches high. I learn some poems, which you was very fond of, such as the "Ode to Music." I shall go on Monday to Chiswick and hear the boys speak; I intend to be one of those heroes in time. . . . I have lost my cough, and am quite well, strong, saucy and hearty, and can eat grandmama's gooseberry-pyes famously, after which I drink yours and my papa's good health and speedy return.'

In due course his mother returned to England with her husband. Writing to her sister in India of her reunion with her son, she said:

'He had a perfect recollection of me; he could not speak, but kissed me, and looked at me again and again, and I could almost have said, "Lord, now lettest Thou Thy servant depart in peace." He is the living image of his father, and God in heaven send that he may resemble him in all but his too short life! He is tall, stout, and sturdy. His eyes are become darker, but there is still the same dear expression. His drawing is wonderful.'[1]

Thackeray's mother's words are echoed by Colonel Newcome. 'The boy's talent for drawing is wonderful, sir, wonderful,' he tells Dr. McTaggart of little Clive, and Martha Honeyman wrote to the colonel, just as Great-aunt Becher wrote to her niece, to describe the little boy's achievements in draughtsmanship. Clive Newcome caricatured his aunts and uncles, and Martin Tupper, Thackeray's senior at Charterhouse, recalled how the younger boy 'used to caricature Bob Watki and the other masters on the fly-leaves of his class-books to the scandal of myself and other responsible monitors.'[2] The display of this early talent, fondly extolled by his mother and his aunt, doubtless settled in their minds and his, that, like Clive Newcome, he was destined for an artistic career.

[1] Biographical introduction to *Vanity Fair*.
[2] *My Life as an Author*, by Martin Farquhar Tupper. London, 1886.

From his preparatory school at Chiswick, Thackeray proceeded to Charterhouse in January 1822, when still six months short of his eleventh year. Probably he went as young because of his persistently expressed dislike of the other school, his parents hoping that he would be happier in a fresh environment. But he hated school to the end. Sensitive and imaginative, he was not the type to become acclimatised to the robust atmosphere of a public school. Moreover, he was no good at games—an impediment as fatal to popularity then as now. Throughout his life, despite his titanic physique, he never cared for outdoor sports, nor even took physical exercise beyond an occasional ride on horseback, which, in his day, was a means of transport as well as a recreation. If motor cars had existed, he might not even have bothered about riding. He was, however, incapable of ball games, for he suffered always from shortness of sight; he once told his daughter how the disability had handicapped him at school, remarking that he could not even see the balls which he was made to field at cricket.

For the first half of his time at Charterhouse, he boarded at the house of Mr. Penny, but, in 1825, an event occurred which decided his parents upon the advisability of his becoming a day boy. This was the fight with George Stovin Venables, which resulted in the permanent deformity of his nose. The house monitor, Roupell, relates:

> 'It was a wet half-holiday when a boy named Glossip asked leave for Thackeray and Venables to fight. We wanted some amusement so I let them fight it out in Penny's room, with the important result to Thackeray's nasal organ. Thackeray bled so profusely as to stop the fight, but he and Venables remained friends for life.'[1]

After this disaster, he lodged in Charterhouse with a Mrs. Boyes, who kept some kind of a hostel for boys at the school.

[1] Cf. *Notes and Queries,* index to Eleventh Series. London, 1920.

The headmaster, Dr. Russell, belonged to the race of schoolmasters which believed in preparing pupils by means of methodical grinding at the classics, vigorous physical training, and rigorous discipline, for proconsular careers. He subscribed to the system which inspired Wellington to observe that Waterloo was won on the playing-fields of Eton. It is a system admirably suited to the equipment of empire builders, but responsible for the infliction of incalculable misery upon the sensitive and highly strung in their most impressionable years. Venables told Trollope that he imagined Russell's character, 'which was vigorous, unsympathetic, and stern, though not severe,'[1] was uncongenial with Thackeray's. But Venables possessed a disposition sufficiently robust to be impervious to the headmaster's harsh jeers and vituperative sarcasm. The effect of violent treatment upon a more nervous temperament is instanced by Martin Tupper, who accused Russell of having 'worked so upon an over-sensitive nature to force a boy beyond his powers, as to fix for many years the infirmity of stammering, which was my affliction until past middle life.' The reverend doctor probably succeeded in intimidating the little boy of eleven and twelve, when, like little Pendennis, he was informed that, if he 'did not know his Horace, or could not construe his Greek play,' he 'was a disgrace to the school, a candidate for ruin in this world, and perdition in the next'; but, as Thackeray grew older and approached the end of his subjection to the hated domination, he affected a sullen indifference worthy of the 'lordly Pen.' 'I have got four hours of delightful Doctor Russell to-day before me,' he tells his mother during his last half, 'is it not felicitous? Every day he begins at me, "Thackeray, Thackeray, you are an idle, profligate, shuffling boy" (because your friends are going to take you away in May).'

Though never popular, on account of his ineptitude for

[1] *Thackeray*, by Anthony Trollope, English Men of Letters Series.

games, he was generally liked by his schoolfellows, for he did not commit the fatal error of revealing any outstanding brilliance as a scholar. Venables implied that the 'scholar-like knowledge of Latin,' which he afterwards possessed, was acquired after leaving Charterhouse, and Dean Liddell, of Liddell and Scott fame, declared that, when he sat beside him in school, 'we spent our time mostly in drawing.'[1] In the *Roundabout Paper*, 'De Juventute,' there is a glimpse of a boy:

'A boy in a jacket. He is at a desk; he has great books before him, Latin and Greek books and dictionaries. Yes, but behind the great books, which he pretends to read, is a little one, with pictures, which he is really reading. It is —yes, I can read now—it is the *Heart of Midlothian*, by the author of *Waverley*—or, no, it is *Life in London, or the Adventures of Corinthian Tom, Jeremiah Hawthorn, and their friends Bob Logic*, by Pierce Egan; and it has pictures—oh! such funny pictures! As he reads, there comes behind the boy, a man, a dervish, in a black gown, like a woman, and a black square cap, and he has a book in each hand, and he seizes the boy who is reading the picture-book, and lays his head upon one of the books, and smacks it with the other. The boy makes faces, and so that picture disappears.'

He seems to have made some effort to suppress his appetite for romances, for he tells his mother when, in his seventeenth year, he had become a monitor, 'I have not read any novel this term except one by the author of *Granby*, not so good as *Granby*. I have read a curious book on the Inquisition, with plates delineating faithfully the various methods of torture.'[2]

While still at school, he evinced an inclination to write and the unfortunate ambition to establish periodicals,

[1] *Henry George Liddell: A Memoir*, by Rev. H. L. Thompson. London, 1899.
[2] The author of *Granby* was T. H. Lister. The other novel was probably his *Herbert Lacy*. Colburn, 3 vols., 1828.

which pursued him through life and plunged himself and his stepfather into disaster. Venables relates how he 'took part in a scheme, which came to nothing, for a school magazine, and he wrote verses for it, of which I only remember that they were good of their kind.' Mentioning this project to his mother, he observes: 'The *Carthusian* does not come on at all; they seem to have dropped all idea of it; the novelty of the thing has perhaps gone off as well, for it strikes me that we should make but poor work of it.' Venables remembered the first line of a parody he perpetrated upon a poem by L. E. L.—then vying with Mrs. Hemans as claimant to Byron's crown in Mr. Jerdan's *Literary Gazette*—in which 'Violets, dark blue violets' was rendered as 'Cabbages, bright green cabbages.'[1] He tried his hand at fiction, too, for, in February 1828 he tells his mother: 'I have not yet drawn out a plan for my stories, but certain germs thereof are budding in my mind, which I hope by assiduous application will flourish yet and bring forth fruit. I always feel as if I were at home when I am writing; and although it may give you very little amusement, it is certainly very amusing to me—that is to say, when once I begin.' He often began but rarely persevered; that was the tale of how he came to be left behind in the race for fame by Dickens. His precocity equalled that of Dickens, Ainsworth, even Bulwer and Disraeli, but only when sheer necessity drove him to 'assiduous application' did he eventually harness his genius to the wagon which bore him to the stage he shared alone with Dickens.

His holidays were mainly spent with his mother and his stepfather, who proved a staunch, affectionate, and sympathetic friend to his wife's only son. His nobility and eccentricity are immortalised in Colonel Newcome. But the calamity which overtook the colonel was partially described from another impression. His great-aunt's

[1] The poem and the parody are quoted at length in *The Life of William Makepeace Thackeray*, by Lewis Melville. 2 vols., 1899.

husband, Peter Moore, was his guardian, and the boy frequently visited the manor house at Hadley. Moore had enjoyed many triumphs in the forty years since his retirement from the East India Company's service. He had been the chief projector of the Highgate Tunnel, sat with Byron on the commission for the rebuilding of Drury Lane Theatre, and championed the cause of coal-gas against oil-gas, emerging in triumph because his opponents had to pay costs amounting to £30,000, while he dropped only £15,000. He was considered 'one of the most adroit and successful men ever known' in negotiating a Company's Bill through the Commons. But his luck turned, as the luck of all speculators does turn sooner or later. In 1824 he lost his seat at Coventry because the weavers suspected him of siding with their masters in a trade dispute. A year later, he was made 'the scapegoat for a multitude of Jobbers' in some such inflated speculation as the Bundelcund Bank. Like Colonel Newcome, he 'gave up all his property (except a small maintenance) for the benefit of persons who had lost money in companies with which he was associated,'[1] and retired to Dieppe, dying at Abbeville three years later.

Major Carmichael-Smyth received the appointment as governor of the training college at Addiscombe some months after his stepson's entry at Charterhouse. He remained there till 1825, when he retired to Larkbeare, near Ottery St. Mary, in South Devon, which he rented from the local potentate, Sir John Kennaway, setting up as a small country squire or gentleman-farmer, as the elephant-hunting Thackeray had done fifty years before. There he reaped his crops, brewed cider, and shot partridges, while his wife drove in her carriage with a footman on the box, to visit the neighbours. Larkbeare was the Fairoaks, Ottery St. Mary the Clavering St. Mary, and Exeter the Chatteris of *Pendennis*. All the characters were

[1] *Dictionary of National Biography.*

there, except Colonel Newcome, and a little girl who visited Larkbeare afterwards informed Lady Ritchie that 'when I think of that rather rough lawn, with its homely beds of stocks and wallflowers, I always see your grandmother, tall, stately, and graceful, standing there on a calm summer's evening, looking with her wide, beautiful grey eyes at the sunset.' Dr. Portman lived in the local vicar, Dr. Sidney Cornish, who, in his *Short Notes on the Church and Parish of Ottery St. Mary, Devon*, relates how he himself sent to the *Western Luminary* (the prototype of the *County Chronicle and Chatteris Champion*) Thackeray's parody of an intended speech of Lalor Sheil's upon Penenden Heath, called 'Irish Melody.'[1]

§ 4

Leaving Charterhouse in April 1828 Thackeray went up to Trinity College, Cambridge, in the February following, though still several months short of his eighteenth year. Thus, most of his contemporaries were slightly his senior, W. H. Brookfield, for instance, who was nearly two years older, coming up as a freshman a term later. Edward FitzGerald, however, having gone up as young as Thackeray was nearing the end of his third year; James Spedding, Monckton Milnes, and Frederick Tennyson were little junior, while John Allen, Charles and Alfred Tennyson had just completed their first year. Among others at Trinity whom Thackeray knew in later life were his schoolfellow Venables, Richard Trench, and J. M. Kemble, the Anglo-Saxon scholar and historian.

Even as young Pendennis was escorted to Oxbridge by his uncle, the major, Thackeray travelled from Larkbeare to Cambridge with his stepfather, who coached him during the months following his farewell to Charterhouse for his 'Little-go.' At Charterhouse he had developed the habit of

[1] Cf. *Life of W. M. Thackeray*, by Herman Merivale and Frank T. Marzials. London, 1891.

writing to his mother in the form of a diary, writing a little each day and dispatching the letter at the end of the week. This practice he continued at Cambridge. In his *Life of Dickens*, Forster quotes Thackeray as saying of Steerforth's character in his mother's eyes, 'My letters to my mother are like this, but then she likes 'em—like Mrs. Steerforth.' The first letter from Cambridge, dated 28th February, begins: 'After father left me, I went in rather low spirits to my room, and found myself just too late for lecture. I was employed all the morning in nailing, hammering, and such-like delectable occupations.' Like all freshmen from a big public school, he immediately sought refuge from solitude and the cold stares of strangers in the society of old schoolfellows, even though they were members of other colleges. James Reynold Young of Caius, afterwards a Warwickshire parson, renewed a close schoolboy friendship,[1] but his most intimate companion was a certain Carne, who bore some resemblance to Pen's Bloundell-Bloundell. His mother did not approve of Carne, thinking him 'too fond of open air and adventures,' but Thackeray continued the intimacy during the first part of his time at Cambridge. With him he wined, rode, and ran beside the college boats in the Lent races. It was Carne who first induced him to 'spout' at the Union.

'Carne had just been speaking before me, and went on in a fluent and easy manner, but it was all flam. As for me, I got up and stuck in the midst of the first footstep, and then, in endeavouring to extricate myself from my dilemma, I went deeper and deeper still, till at last, with one desperate sentence, to wit, that "Napoleon as a captain, a lawgiver, and a king, merited and received the esteem and gratitude of France," I rushed out of the quagmire into which I had so foolishly plunged myself, and stood down, like Lucifer, never to rise again with open mouth in that august assembly. So much for the Union.'

[1] Cf. *A Book of Recollections*, by John Cordy Jeaffreson. London, 2 vols., 1894.

The same story might be told of almost every effort at public speaking ever made by Thackeray. Twenty years later he tells Mrs. Brookfield of the 'awful smash' he made at a dinner of the Literary Fund, and writing to Macready from America in 1855 to apologise for something he had said at the dinner given in his honour before his departure from England, he says: 'If I lose my head when I try speech-making, all is up with me. I say what I don't mean, what I don't know afterwards the Lord forgive me.'[1] When he sent to Manchester to speak at the founding of the Free Library there, he enthusiastically informed James T. Fields that he had composed for the occasion a remarkably telling speech, which he expected to surpass in impressiveness those of Dickens and Bulwer, both eloquent speakers, who were to precede him. For three minutes he spoke perfectly; then, 'in the middle of a most earnest and elaborate sentence he suddenly stopped, gave a look of comic despair at the ceiling, crammed both hands into his trouser-pockets, and deliberately sat down. 'Everybody,' said Fields, 'seemed to understand that it was one of Thackeray's unfinished speeches and there were no signs of surprise or discontent among his audience.'[2] Sala tells a similarly amusing story of his collapse at the first *Cornhill* dinner,[3] and Thackeray expresses the hope in *Philip* that 'a day will soon arrive (but I own, mind you, that I do not carve well) when we shall have the speeches done by a skilled waiter at the side-table, as we now have the carving. Don't you find that you splash the gravy, that you mangle the meat, that you can't nick the joint in helping the company to a dinner-speech? I, for my part, own that I am in a state of tremor and absence of mind before the operation: in a condition of imbecility during

[1] *Thackeray in the United States*, by James Grant Wilson. London, 2 vols., 1904.
[2] *Yesterdays with Authors*, by James T. Fields. London, 1872.
[3] *Things I have seen and People I have known*, by George Augustus Sala. London, 2 vols., 1894.

the business; and that I am sure of a headache and indigestion the next morning.'

A letter of introduction from his Aunt Ritchie secured him the acquaintance of the Thackeray settlement at Cambridge, including a sister-in-law of the elephant-hunter, aged over ninety. Young, of Caius, introduced him to a circle far removed from the society of the ebullient Carne, and, by the end of April, Thackeray's mother is informed that 'we are going to establish an Essay Club. There are as yet but four of us, Browne, Moody, Young, and myself, all Carthusians. We want no more Charter-house men; if we get ten we shall scarely have to write three essays a year, so that it will take up little of our time.' The society was supplemented by W. H. Thompson, subsequently Master of Trinity, John Allen, Henry Alford, and Robert Groome, all of whom became ecclesiastical dignitaries. Like all such societies, it lasted not long, but his connection with these literary aspirants probably gained him an intimacy with the set which had just established a weekly paper called the *Snob*. The first number of this periodical appeared on 9th April, and, at the end of the month, he tells his mother that 'a "poem of mine" hath appeared in a weekly periodical published, and called the *Snob*.' His contribution, 'Timbuctoo,' a parody of Alfred Tennyson's prize poem of that name, earned for him some little reputation.

'Young had a pleasant wine-party,' he writes, 'at which for a short time I attended. "Timbuctoo" received much laud. I could not help finding out that I was very fond of this same praise. The men knew not the author, but praised the poem; how eagerly I sucked it in! "All is vanity!" '

Evidently he was welcomed as a capable contributor, for a few days later he writes: 'the *Snob* goeth on prosperously. I have put "Genevieve" into it with a little alteration,' and then again:

'On Monday night, myself and the Editor of the *Snob* sat down to write the *Snob* of the next Thursday. We began at nine and concluded at two, but I was afflicted with such laughter during our attempts that I came away quite ill and went to bed immediately.'

The *Snob* died with the end of the term, but between 21st May and 18th June appeared four papers concerned with a mythical Dorothea Julia Ramsbottom, which foreshadow the character of the author's future contributions to *Fraser's Magazine* and *Punch*. In the following autumn, he conceived the idea of a more serious sort of paper to be called the *Chimera*, for which he wrote an essay on Shelley, whose poetry he had been reading the previous term, but the project found no favour. When the *Snob* was reborn in November as the *Gownsman*, he contributed the dedication, another Ramsbottom letter, and two pieces of verse.

He took a fourth class in the May examination, having previously warned his mother that he would be lucky to get a fifth. Having gone up in the middle of an academic year instead of at the beginning, he had the choice of taking schools in company with those having half a year's advantage of him, or of waiting till the following year. He decided to take the bold course rather than remain at the university longer than he had intended, but the result decided himself and his parents that the odds were too heavy against his chance of taking a good degree and consequently there would be no motive in his completing the usual period of residence. Thus, his college career lasted little more than a year, and he left Cambridge as he had both entered and left Charterhouse, exceptionally young.

Possibly the knowledge that he would not be working for a degree inspired carelessness of the prescribed routine, for, except for an effort to appreciate the beauties of Greek tragedy by refusing to use a word of English, he appears to have neglected serious study—at any rate, after the

May examination. In the character of Mr. Batchelor in *Lovel the Widower*, he reflects: 'Perhaps I misspent my time as an undergraduate. Perhaps I read too many novels, occupied myself too much with 'elegant literature' (that used to be our phrase), and spoke too often at the Union.' At least, he crowded into a single year quite as much of college life as many undergraduates experience in a full course. And he enjoyed the good fortune, so rare at school and college, of laying the foundation of more than one lasting friendship.

CHAPTER 2

§ 1

On 5th October 1829 Fanny Kemble made her début at Covent Garden. 'We all of us,' Thackeray told her on the last occasion they ever met, 'were in love with you, and had your portrait by Lawrence in our rooms.'[1] She was the daughter of Charles Kemble, lessee of Covent Garden, and sister of John Mitchell Kemble, a contemporary of Edward FitzGerald at Cambridge. It is characteristic of Thackeray's youthful habit of always being a year or two in advance of his precise contemporaries that he struck up a friendship with these men so much his senior at the university. Perhaps his parody on 'Timbuctoo' excited their curiosity in the young freshman, but their acquaintance with him, rapidly ripening into intimacy, presents an early example of Thackeray's lifelong sociability. FitzGerald, though at Trinity with Alfred Tennyson half a year before Thackeray went up, did not make his acquaintance at Cambridge, yet Thackeray came to know them both in the space of a term or so. Perhaps John Kemble's actress sister served as an attraction, but Thackeray frequently visited the Kembles' house in town during the autumn and winter of 1829. There he met Charles Buller, who had gone down from Cambridge before Thackeray went up, and the seeds of another lasting friendship were sown.

In the *Roundabout Papers* he tells of how, going down for the Easter vacation of 1830 with twenty pounds in his

[1] *Records of Later Life,* by Frances Anne Kemble. London, 3 vols., 1882.

pocket, he went 'for a lark to Paris, where my friend Edwards was staying.' Edwards was FitzGerald, who had taken his degree in the previous January, and with him Thackeray enjoyed his first sight of the city which, in years to come, became to him as familiar as London. He inherited nothing of the Thackeray habit of taking root in a place; the blood of much-travelled Bechers and Richmond Webbs flowed in his veins, and this taste of Continental life whetted his appetite for more. He returned home suddenly, evidently to plead with his parents for permission to leave Cambridge and complete his education abroad. W. G. Lettsom, the editor of the *Snob*, had gone down with FitzGerald, and was completing his preparation for the diplomatic service by making the grand tour. Thackeray, having commenced his cosmopolitan adventures at Coblenz in July, came across him at Weimar towards the end of September, studying German under Dr. Weissenborn along with Norman Macleod, who thirty years later became the exemplary editor of *Good Words*. Accepting Lettsom's assurance that 'the place was exactly suited for me,' he enlisted the services of 'good old Weissenborn,' and settled down to gather those impressions which inspired the Pumpernickel of *Vanity Fair*. He has a pair of trousers cut into breeches to be presented to the old Grand Duke; sees at the theatre a translation of *Hernani*, 'the tragedy by Victor Hugo which made so much noise in Paris'; secures an introduction to Devrient, 'the Kean of Germany, who in several particulars resembles his illustrious brother of the buskin'; actually obtains an audience of the great Goethe, whose eyes, 'extraordinarily dark, piercing, and brilliant,' remind him of Maturin's *Melmoth*, as he told G. H. Lewes years afterwards, when the latter was preparing his *Life of Goethe*; and falls in love with the Princess of Weimar, 'who is unluckily married to Prince Charles of Prussia.' Apologetically he asks 'a very absurd favour' of his mother:

'I want a cornetcy in Sir John Kennaway's yeomanry. The men here are all in some uniform, and if hereafter I go to other Courts in Germany, or in any other part of Europe, something of this sort is necessary as a Court dress. It is true that here I can do without it, but in case of my going elsewhere I must have some dress or other; and a yeomanry dress is always a handsome and respectable one. As it is, I have to air my legs in black breeches, and to sport a black coat, black waistcoat, and cocked hat; looking something like a cross between a footman and a Methodist parson.'

How mercilessly he satirises his youthful conceits in *Pendennis*! 'A tall, thin, large-eyed, full and ruddy-faced man with an eye-glass fixed *en permanence*—' so Thompson of Trinity remembered him and so he may be seen in Maclise's sketch of 'The Fraserians,' some four years later. Not unlike the elegant Pen, except for the unfortunately misshapen nose and the fact that Pen rarely gratified his fond mother with such long and anecdotal letters. Nor did his sense of humour, allied with the self-conscious habit of introspection which became so painful with the passing years, allow him to take himself quite so seriously as the youthful Pen.

In the new year, still pursuing a butterfly life at Weimar, his conscience begins to impede his flutterings. Realising that he is wasting valuable time, he feels it necessary to choose a profession. At Cambridge and Weimar the boyish idea of becoming an artist has assumed absurdity with the acquisition of supercilious indifference and cheap cynicism, common in undergraduates of no illusions; he sees others, with apparent artistic gifts, consigning such unprofitable attainments to the background of a conventional career. Lettsom, for instance, in spite of his brilliant efforts as editor of the *Snob*, is preparing himself for the diplomatic service. Art and letters were decorative playthings providing pleasant relaxation from the serious business of a gentleman's life. In those days, not Bulwer and Disraeli only, but innumerable scions of the nobility, as a glance at the old annuals reveals, found the reputation of being literary or artistic an admirable recommendation to political and social consideration. So Thackeray, following the fashion, decides to read for the Bar, thinking, perhaps, to become a Brougham or a Jeffrey, and writes home on 25th January 1831 a perfectly Pendennisian letter:

'I do believe, mother, that it is not merely an appetite for novelty which prompts me, but really a desire to enter a profession and do my duty in it. I am nearly twenty years old—at that time, my father had been for five years engaged on his. I am fully aware how difficult and disagreeable my task must be for the first four years, but I have an end in view and an independence to gain; and if I can steadily keep this before me, I shall not, I trust, flinch from the pursuit of them.'[1]

Thus the grand tour comes to an end, and Thackeray, in due course, establishes himself at No. 1 Hare Court, Temple, to read in chambers with a Mr. Taprell.

§ 2

Like many literary men, from Congreve to 'Christopher North,' Thackeray found the law an unattractive study. 'This lawyer's preparatory education is certainly one of the most cold-blooded, prejudiced pieces of invention that ever a man was slave to,' he told his stepfather after a few months. But, at first, he settled down with the same sanguine zeal which had prompted him to tackle the May examination at the end of his first term at Cambridge, though he did not allow his exertions to hinder his enjoyment of the attractions offered about town.

'I go pretty regularly to my pleader's,' he told his stepfather in December, 'and sit with him till past five; then

[1] Biographical Introduction to *Yellowplush Papers.*

I come home and read and dine till about nine or past, when I am glad enough to go out for an hour and look at the world. As for the theatre, I scarcely go there more than once a week, which is moderate indeed for me. In a few days come the Pantomimes! Huzza! . . . I find this work really very pleasant: one's day is agreeably occupied; there is a newspaper and a fire and just enough to do. Mr. Taprell has plenty of business, and I should think would be glad of another assistant, whom I hope to provide for him, in my friend Kemble, with whom I am very thick. . . . I have been employed on a long pedigree case, and find myself very tolerably amused, only it is difficult to read dry law-books and to attend to them. I sit at home a good deal, but proceed very slowly. I have to lay out nearly £5 to-day for these same ugly books.'

Mr. Taprell did not take advantage of the offer of John Kemble's services: probably he recoiled in horror from the prospect of two lordly young Cantabs fraternising in his office. Thackeray shared his chambers with no Warrington, who represented the mental attitude of the author at the time of writing the novel, just as Pendennis depicted him as he remembered himself in these carefree days.

He went down to Cambridge, spending four days 'feasting on my old friends, so hearty and hospitable.' His uncle, Francis Thackeray, was kind and hospitable, but asked him to dinner too often. Like Pendennis, he did not lack invitations. He was a frequent visitor at both the Kembles' and the Bullers'; at the latter house he met John Stuart Mill and Harriet Martineau, who formed of him 'no clear notion in any way, except that he seemed cynical.'[1] There also he met A. W. Kinglake, who, with Arthur Buller, dined with him one night 'at the Bedford,' after which they went 'canvassing for Percy and Reform . . . a silly prank, but has shown me how easy it is to talk men over.' On another evening, after he had dined in

[1] *Harriet Martineau's Autobiography*. London, 3 vols., 3rd ed., 1877.

hall, Kemble and Arthur Hallam called on him, leaving him to read 'Christopher North's' article in *Blackwood* on Alfred Tennyson's first book of poems, 'abusing Hallam for his essay in the *Englishman*.'

Charles Buller, enjoying a reputation for brilliance among his friends only rivalled by Alfred Tennyson, aroused in Thackeray an admiration mingled with some antagonism and envy, afflicting a wakeful conscience. 'I wish to God I could take advantage of my time and opportunities as C. Buller has done,' he exclaims. 'It is very well to possess talents, but using them better still.' Discussing him with a mutual friend who denies that Buller has taken full advantage of his opportunities, he consoles himself with the reflection that, 'as to advancement, society, and talent, he has had greater advantages than most men, not the least of them that Carlyle was his tutor.' FitzGerald, always a good influence on Thackeray, was keeping up a regular correspondence with him; they sent each other copies of verse along with accounts of their daily doings, which, on Thackeray's side, were always illustrated with sketches and caricatures. After having written to 'E. F. G.' 'a letter as from Herrick' and reflecting that it might have been done much better, he asks himself: 'How can a man know his own capabilities? . . . Buller has a high reputation for talent, and yet I always find myself competing with him.' Here is none of young Pen's fluent self-satisfaction. Conscious of ambition, he fears to gauge his aspirations, lest his powers might prove inadequate for their fulfilment. Lacking a balance on which to weigh his own capacity, he apologises to his own intelligence for even involuntarily venturing to vie with a man of acknowledged parts. Later in life, when he eagerly sought opinions upon his work, so exposing himself to the charge of vanity, he was only endeavouring to satisfy his eternal craving for conviction that he did not over-estimate in his secret judgment the quality of his achievements. He had none of the confident artist's complacency, for none lacked more profoundly the faculty of accurately valuing his own work.

In his intimacy with Buller he shows himself susceptible to the slightest impressions of his friend's mentality. Mistrust of himself again assails him when he discovers that 'C. B. and I did not at all agree about poetry,' and the instinct of emulation recurs in the remark that 'C. B. is a clever fellow, at any rate, and makes money by magazine writing, in which I should much desire to follow his example.' The opportunity was not far to seek. Probably in Paris during the previous year he had made the acquaintance of the Irish Jesuit, Francis Mahony, who, resigning his priestly avocation as inconsistent with convivial inclination, came to London at this time to earn a living in journalism. It was he who introduced Thackeray to the Irish element of literary Bohemia so picturesquely portrayed in *Pendennis*, and to the great lion of literary journalism, the indefatigable, intransigent Dr. Maginn.

Pendennis's introduction to Captain Shandon occurs in the Fleet Prison, but Maginn had not yet made his way to that lodging. Impecunious he had always been from the days when, more than a dozen years before, as a schoolmaster at Cork, he had addressed anonymously to *Blackwood* the trenchant articles which had made him the most brilliant and indispensable coadjutor of Lockhart and 'Christopher North,' but now he was the editor of the newly founded *Fraser's Magazine*, rivalling in brilliance and notoriety the illustrious *Blackwood* itself. He held a position in the literary world absolutely unique in those days. Possessed of palpable genius, he flung its seeds to the winds, and most of those which took root are to be found flourishing only on the stony ground of ephemeral journalism, like wild flowers among weeds. Lightheartedly adopting literature as a trade, his pen, like the sword of a soldier of fortune, was at the service of the highest bidder. When Pendennis gallantly declares that he 'would rather starve, by Jove, and never earn another penny by my pen . . . than strike an opponent an unfair blow, or, if called upon to place him, rank him below his honest desert,' the experienced Shandon shakes his head indulgently, thinking within himself that 'a few years hence, perhaps, the young gentleman won't be so squeamish.'

Thackeray's portrait of Captain Shandon hardly does justice to Maginn's brilliance, but it was a more generous tribute to his memory than most of his contemporaries accorded. There were few gouty toes upon which Maginn had not trodden in his truculent progress through two literary decades, when death claimed him, at the age of forty-nine, in 1842. No secrets were secure from his ready ear; every pseudonym or anonymity appeared transparent to his shrewd eye. With dexterous dagger-thrusts in the daily Press or the formidable array of his organised batteries in the monthlies, he dealt murderous havoc among literary reputations. As Wilson lashed and Lockhart stung, Maginn ravaged and plundered with ruthless butchery; his death removed the scourge of the literary world. Socially, his ready wit and engaging manner gained him the liking of everybody, but his improvidence and hopeless fondness for the bottle robbed him of all respect. Yet all his delinquencies did not lose him the affection of Lockhart, who established a pension fund for his widow and children, and combined humour with pathos in the epitaph ending:

'Barring drink and the girls, I ne'er heard of a sin:
Many worse, better few, than bright broken Maginn.'

This remarkable man wielded a marked influence upon Thackeray's early career. Not merely was he the editor of the magazine in which Thackeray's first important writings appeared, but he was largely responsible for the early manner of his work. His first appearance upon Thackeray's horizon occurred on 2nd May 1832, when 'Dr. Maginn called and took me to the *Standard*, showing me the mysteries of printing and writing leading articles. With him all day till four. Dined at the Sablonnière.' Maginn eagerly cultivated his new acquaintance, for as Mahony remarked, 'Thackeray was a young buck in those days,' and unlikely to refuse an occasional loan to a person so distinguished as the celebrated doctor. They dined together the following day in company with 'a dull party of low literary men'; Thackeray's first impressions of Bohemia made no suggestion of his future celebrity in such society. But his opinion of Maginn was unaffected.

'Maginn with me all the morning, one of the pleasantest I ever passed. Maginn read Homer to me, and he made me admire it as I had never done before. . . . His remarks were extraordinarily intelligent and beautiful, mingled with much learning, a great deal of wit, and no ordinary poetical feeling.'

With Maginn, 'whom I like for his wit and good feeling,' Thackeray learned to appreciate much besides Homer. It is said that Dr. Cornish at Ottery first taught him to judge a good glass of port, but in Maginn's company he not only learned to drink heavily but to carry his wine 'like a gentleman.' Though he described himself as 'a two-bottle man,' as Jeaffreson declares, nobody ever saw him under the influence of 'a glass too much.'

While he was meeting Maginn at the Somerset Coffee House, dining with Buller or Kemble at the Bedford, and following the social round, the country was in the throes of the Reform Bill agitation. Subsequently professing Radical opinions far in advance of his time, Thackeray never bothered about practical politics and regarded the Reform excitement merely as a joyous adventure. He was a reformer, of course, but no rabid partisan; walking with Kemble in the park, he 'met the Duke looking like an old hero.' Obtaining an order of admission to the Commons debate, he reflects that 'it will soon, I suppose, be a house of delegates,' and buys 'a big stick wherewith to resist all parties in case of an attack.' At the dissolution of Parliament he leaves Mr. Taprell alone with his special pleading and conveyancing, travelling down to Cornwall to assist Charles Buller in his candidature for Liskeard. Memories of this electoral campaign, with the speaking and canvassing, vague pledges and promises, their arrival at the wrong inn, the feasting and processions, and the dragging of the candidate's carriage by enthusiastic supporters, all of which he describes with ironical humour in letters to his mother and the aloof FitzGerald,[1] furnished the material for the election episode in *The Newcomes*. He has 'grand fun' for a fortnight, canvassing, publishing addresses, and writing 'awfully satirical songs,' making the Tory opponent's canvasser, 'a very shabby fellow,' confess his nefarious practices when drunk, and making many new friends, including some attractive ladies. In his spare moments he reads *Wallenstein* and Irving's orations, and does some sketching. In the midst of the merry turmoil, dissatisfaction creeps upon him, and he asks FitzGerald:

'My dear Teddikin,—will you come with me to Paris in a month? We will first take a walk in Normandy, and then go for a fortnight or so to Paris. I have a strange idea that I shall be in Italy before the autumn is over, and if my dear old Teddibus would but come with me, we will be happy in a paradise of pictures.'

On 18th July he comes of age and writes: 'Here is the day for which I have been panting so long.' Shaking the dust

[1] Cf. the Biographical Introduction to *Yellowplush Papers* and *Christmas Books*.

of Mr. Taprell's documents from his fingers for ever, he travelled direct from Cornwall to France.

§ 3

Though rumour exaggerated the amount of Thackeray's patrimony in fabulous figures, he seems to have inherited a capital producing, as Trollope stated, an income of about five hundred a year. On entering upon his inheritance he informed his mother of his intention to keep his little chambers in the Temple and to take 'a regular monthly income which I will never exceed.' Being convinced by Maginn that art and letters were by no means beyond the sphere of a gentleman's serious consideration, he proposed to pursue a similarly studious and philosophical life as FitzGerald was leading, at the same time augmenting his income by such literary efforts as Maginn would accept.[1]

In Paris he read widely—Voltaire, Victor Hugo, Balzac, Gibbon, and Montaigne. *La Peau de Chagrin* he described as possessing many of the faults and beauties of the new romantic school: 'plenty of light and shade, good colouring and costumes, but no character.' He made friends as freely there as in England; his figure soon became as familiar to Parisians of that day as that of R. L. Stevenson towards the end of the century. He saw Mademoiselle Mars as Hazlitt had seen her only a few years before. On reading Victor Cousin, he remarks, 'The excitement of metaphysics must equal almost that of gambling.' Pendennis, remaining

[1] *Elizabeth Brownrigge: A Tale*, appearing in *Fraser* for August and September of this year, is generally ascribed to Thackeray, because it seems to be a juvenile effort in the same vein as *Catherine*, and the subject of its satire is Bulwer. A notice of the Annuals for 1832, appearing in December, may possibly be Thackeray's, as it is the sort of work an editor might offer to a 'prentice hand. But there is no evidence for ascribing to him the two reviews of 'Novels of the Season,' appearing in February and August of 1831 (cf. *A Thackeray Library*, collected by Henry Sayre van Duzer. New York, privately printed, 1919), for he had not then made Maginn's acquaintance.

longer at Oxbridge than Thackeray at Cambridge, falls a victim to dicing and *vingt-et-un*, and Harry Warrington runs the gamut of the 'Rake's Progress' in *The Virginians*. Thackeray fell in with a gambling set at Paris, part of his patrimony passing into the pockets of those who supplied him with material for the Hon. Deuceace and Barry Lyndon. Years later he pointed out the figure of a broken roué at a Rhineland watering-place as the original Deuceace.

He returned home for Christmas, FitzGerald writing to John Allen early in December:

'The news of the week is that Thackeray has come to London, but is going to leave it again for Devonshire directly. He came very opportunely to divert my Blue Devils: notwithstanding, we do not see very much of each other: and he has now so many friends (especially the Bullers) that he has no such wish for my society. He is as full of good humour and kindness as ever.'[1]

It was his last Christmas at Larkbeare. The failure of an Indian bank depleted his stepfather's comfortable income, absorbing also some of Thackeray's own capital. The major decided that he must seek an investment productive of bigger dividends than the cultivation of his farm afforded, and, thinking at the same time to offer an opportunity to his stepson, he acquired an interest in the *National Standard and Journal of Literature, Science, Music, Theatricals, and the Fine Arts*, the first number of which appeared on 5th January 1833. Probably he was persuaded into the enterprise by the representations of Thackeray, who may have been influenced by a third party. In *Lovel the Widower* Mr. Batchelor relates:

'Had I been Moses Primrose purchasing green spectacles, I could scarcely have been more taken in. *My* Jenkinson was an old College acquaintance, whom I was idiot enough

[1] *Letters of Edward FitzGerald*, ed. W. Aldis Wright. London, 2 vols., 1894.

to imagine a respectable man. . . . He, and a queer wine-merchant and bill-discounter, Sherrick by name, had somehow got possession of that neat little literary paper, the *Museum*, which, perhaps, you remember; and this eligible literary property my friend Honeyman, with his wheedling tongue, induced me to purchase. . . . He was in dreadful straits for money when he sold me the *Museum*. He began crying when I told him some short time afterwards that he was a swindler, and from behind his pocket-handkerchief sobbed a prayer that I should one day think better of him; whereas my remarks to the same effect produced an exactly contrary impression upon his accomplice, Sherrick, who burst out laughing in my face, said, "The more fool you!" Mr. Sherrick was right. . . . I daresay I gave myself airs as editor of that confounded *Museum*, and proposed to educate the public taste, to diffuse morality and sound literature throughout the nation, and to pocket a liberal salary in return for my services. I daresay I printed my own sonnets, my own tragedy, my own verses. . . . I daresay I wrote satirical articles, in which I piqued myself upon the fineness of my wit, and criticisms, got up for the nonce out of encyclopædias and biographical dictionaries. . . . I daresay I made a gaby out of myself to the world. . . .'

Mahony told Blanchard Jerrold thirty years later that it was at this time, when Thackeray needed an editor for his magazine, that he introduced him to Maginn, who would not go into the matter before he had received five hundred pounds. But Father Prout's memory was obviously at fault; if Slumley, like Shandon, was sketched from Maginn, it was he 'who first showed me how grievously I had been cheated in the newspaper matter.' The *National Standard* carried no such guns as Maginn brought to any vessel he boarded. Nevertheless, he certainly borrowed money extensively from Thackeray as is shown by a letter from the latter to the publisher of *Fraser's Magazine*, written from Boulogne in February 1838:

'I have seen the doctor, who has given me his commands about the hundredth number. . . . He reiterates his determination to write monthly for you, and to deliver over the proceeds to me. Will you, therefore, have the goodness to give the bearer a check (in my wife's name) for the amount of his contributions for the two last months? . . . You have already Maginn's authority.'[1]

Poor Maginn by that time was nearing the end of his tether, and, though still directing the policy of *Fraser*, residing on the other side of the Channel to avoid his creditors.

The editor and founder of the *National Standard* was F. W. N. Bayley—'Initial' or 'Alphabet' Bayley, as he was called, to distinguish him from Thomas Haynes Bayly, the song-writer, generally known as 'Butterfly' Bayly on account of his popular lyric, 'I'd be a butterfly.'[2] Of 'low literary men,' there were few who sank beneath his level. From serving Theodore Hook on *John Bull* as a scavenger of scandal, he became successively editor of three short-lived papers, of which the *National Standard* was the second, before proceeding to the position of fashionable reporter on the *Morning Post* and receiving some employment upon the foundation of the *Illustrated London News*. Modelling himself on Maginn, even to the extent of mimicking his manner of speech, he possessed none of the Irishman's characteristics except a weakness for drink, which brought him, like Maginn, to poverty and an untimely death. He occupied the editorial chair of the *National Standard* for barely four months, just long enough to impose a hopeless handicap upon its chances of ultimate success. Apparently Thackeray and his stepfather then bought him out, for in the issue of 11th May

[1] *Thackeray in the United States*, by James Grant Wilson. London, 2 vols., 1904.

[2] Writing in 1829, Barham, author of the *Ingoldsby Legends*, refers to him as 'Old Bailey' when differentiating him from 'Butterfly' Bayly. Cf. *Life and Remains of Theodore Edward Hook*, by Rev. R. H. D. Barham. London, 2 vols., 1849.

there appeared an address, evidently written by Thackeray, announcing that 'we still retain the assistance of a host of literary talent, but Frederick William Naylor Bayley has gone. We have got free of the Old Bailey, and changed the Governor.' The new governor was Thackeray, but it does not appear what talent he had at his command besides his own. In the first week of his new office, he wrote:

'I have been wanting very much to see you, dearest mother, but this paper has kept me so busily at work, that I really and truly had no time.

'I have made a woodcut for it of Louis Philippe, which is pretty good; but have only written nonsense, in the shape of reviews. The paper comes out to-morrow afternoon, and then I will come up to you with a copy thereof. I have been obliged to put off the play and everything else, having actually done nothing except work the paper. I send a boy with this, for I thought you would be glad to know what my proceedings are. God bless you, my dearest mother! I send you a couple of magazines I have received in my new capacity.'

After six weeks, during which time he contributed, besides caricatures and verse, a vitriolic review of 'Satan' Montgomery's *Woman*, an essay in dramatic criticism, and a parody of Cowper's 'Lines to Mary Unwin' on the Lord Mayor, he handed his duties to a deputy and departed for Paris, whence he wrote to his mother on 6th July:

'It looks well to have a Parisian correspondent, and I think that in a month more I may get together stuff enough for the next six months. I have been thinking very seriously of turning artist; I think I can draw better than do anything else, and certainly like it better than any other occupation; why shouldn't I? It requires a three years' apprenticeship, however, which is not agreeable, and afterwards the way is clear and pleasant enough. An artist in this town is by far a more distinguished person than a lawyer, and a great deal more so than a clergyman.'

Already the monotonous drudgery of running a weekly newspaper was beginning to pall. Mentally and morally, he was unsuited to the anxious, restless task of an editor. He had no method or talent for organisation, little discriminative judgment, and no idea of pursuing a definite policy. His almost comical attitude to contributors impressed everybody who came into contact with him during his editorship of the *Cornhill*.

For four weeks he sent over a letter from Paris for publication, after which his contributions appeared only at irregular intervals. Infatuated with the glamour of Parisian life, he eagerly entertained the prospect of studying art in such agreeable surroundings. In September, when in London, he wrote:

'I am wanting very much to leave this dismal city, dear mother, but I must stay for some time longer, being occupied in writing, puffing, &c., and other delightful employments for the *Standard*. I have had an offer made for a partner, which I think I shall accept, but the business cannot be settled for a week or ten days. . . . I find a great change between this and Paris, where one makes friends; here, though for the last three years I have lived, I have not positively a single female acquaintance. I shall go back to Paris, I think, and marry somebody. There is another evil which I complain of, that this system of newspaper writing spoils one for every other kind of writing. I am unwilling, now more than ever, to write letters to my friends, and always find myself attempting to make a pert, critical point at the end of a sentence. . . . I have been thinking of going out of town, but *les affaires!*—as for the theatres, they are tedious beyond all bearing, and a solitary evening in chambers is more dismal still. One has no resource but the Club, where, however, there is a tolerably good library of reviews and a pleasant enough society—

of artists of all kinds, and gentlemen who drop their absurd English aristocratical notions. . . . FitzGerald has been in town for a day or two, and I have plenty of his acquaintances. There are a number of *littérateurs* who frequent this Club, and the *National Standard* is, I am happy to say, growing into repute, though I know it is poor stuff.'

The letter concludes with three caricatures, one of James Smith, of *Rejected Addresses*, a foundation member and prominent figure at the Garrick Club, to which Thackeray had been elected apparently on the strength of his connection with the *National Standard*.

Evidently the tender worries of Helen Pendennis on account of her wayward son were not without foundation in fact. Having left Cambridge without waiting for a degree and then dallied for a year with the idea of reading for the Bar, he was now, when presented with the opportunity, which he had always desired, of editing a paper, manifesting a marked desire to desert a sinking ship. Fluttering from one foible to another, he evinced no inclination to perseverance with any particular ambition. He was as far from realising his capabilities as he had been a couple of years before. Moreover there were many among those numerous Parisian acquaintances whom Mrs. Carmichael-Smyth cannot have deemed entirely desirable. Most likely the flippant mention of marriage was inspired by some gentle hints from his mother, who thought that a suitable wife might impose some restraint and sense of responsibility upon a too mercurial temperament.

A month later he is in Paris, drawing at the Atelier and careless of his literary obligations in London. 'I think,' he writes, 'that in a year, were I to work hard, I might paint something worth looking at.' The prospect of working hard appears only a possibility, not a determination, and he goes on to observe that 'the other men at the Atelier are merry fellows enough, always singing, smoking, fencing and painting very industriously besides.' Meeting him in

Paris about this time, Planché, the playwright, found him 'a slim young man, rather taciturn, and not displaying any particular love or talent for literature,' and remarked that 'drawing appeared to be his favourite amusement; and he often sat by my side while I was reading or writing, covering any scrap of paper lying about with the most spirited sketches and amusing caricatures.'[1]

Back in London in December he finds affairs with the *National Standard* in no state to permit his absence at Larkbeare for Christmas. The paper and his Parisian playmates have finally relieved him of the remnant of his patrimony remaining from unlucky investments, but he is undismayed at its loss.

'I am anxious that the first number for the year should be a particularly good one, and I am going to change the name to the *Literary Standard*, and increase the price to 3d., with which alteration I hope to do better. I am sure we shall be as merry in the new house as possible. I believe I ought to thank Heaven for making me poor—it has made me much happier than I should have been with the money. But this is a selfish wish, for I shall now have to palm myself on you and my father just at the time when I ought to be independent.'

In some respects his mother may have felt relief at his loss of independence, for now that retrenchment of expenses and the necessity for her husband's presence in the city compelled them to live in London, her son would be under her eye, while his lack of means caused him to seek a lodging in Paris with his maternal grandmother, Mrs. Butler.

The last number of the *National Standard* duly appeared with an address announcing the change in price and promising a series of tales and translations 'by the most popular English authors,' the first of which, a short story

[1] *Recollections and Reflections of J. R. Planché.* London, 2 vols., 1872.

from the German, figured the following week in the newly christened *Literary Standard*, most likely from the anonymous pen of Thackeray himself. But, as might have been expected, the alteration in the price and title affected the paper's sales rather adversely than otherwise, and the last number was issued on 1st February.

§ 4

Maginn appears to have proved a kind friend after the failing of the *National Standard*. Doubtless he owed money to Thackeray, for, while a well held water, it was impossible for him to refrain from filling his pitcher as often as possible. But nobody who knew Maginn ever expected him to pay back his borrowings, and his financial obligations to Thackeray were no more than he owed to half his acquaintance. Men of so little morality in money matters customarily avoid their creditors, especially if they become as needy as themselves. But Maginn did not belong to that breed, for it was now that Thackeray properly commenced his long connection with *Fraser's Magazine*. From March to June there appeared each month a contribution almost certainly from his pen; if only one may be definitely identified as his, it is because the others possessed only an ephemeral interest and so were unworthy of acknowledgment by being subsequently reprinted. In Daniel Maclise's famous sketch of *The Fraserians*, published during this year, he figures between Percival Bankes and Jack Churchill, with his monocle, high cravat, and hair carefully curled. Not far away, ncxt to Coleridge, to whom there remained only a few months of life, sits the extraordinarily handsome Harrison Ainsworth, whose *Rookwood* had just taken the town by storm and occasioned the article 'Highways and Low-ways,' probably by Thackeray, 'puffing' him at the expense of Bulwer.

THE FRASERIANS

From a Drawing by Daniel Maclise, 1834

Maginn's influence upon Thackeray's writing, like everything else except his drinking and debts, has never been adequately recognised.[1] During the 'thirties his literary influence preponderated over that of Jeffrey, Carlyle, Macaulay, or even Lockhart. Under his editorship, *Fraser* sustained the tradition of militant criticism engendered by Jeffrey in the early days of the *Edinburgh Review* and exaggerated to the utmost excess of violence by Wilson, Lockhart, and Maginn himself in *Blackwood*, and by Hazlitt. As Jeffrey vindictively assailed the romantic poets, and *Blackwood* vented vituperative scorn upon the 'Cockney school,' the writers in *Fraser*, at Maginn's dictation, selected the fashionable novelists as butts for their satire and ridicule. The typical reviewer of the day appears in *Pendennis* as Mr. Bludyer, who 'smashed and trampled down the poor spring flowers with no more mercy than a bull would have on a pasture.' The pseudonymous habit, contrasting picturesquely with the austere anonymity of the *Edinburgh* and the *Quarterly*, was fostered by Maginn, who remembered the formidable power reposing in the mysterious identity of 'Christopher North.' He himself assumed the *alias* of Sir Morgan O'Doherty, Mahony achieved such celebrity under the pseudonym of 'Father Prout' that even his intimates knew him better by that name than his own, and Thackeray, imaginatively expanding the idea, created for himself a host of fictitious personalities. Assimilating the sardonic humour and caustic wit characteristic of both Maginn and Mahony, Thackeray developed that style of satirical irony which earned him a reputation for cynicism.

A redeeming feature of *Fraser*, though enhancing the scope of its scurrility, was its independence. Unlike its

[1] Ignorance of Maginn's proper position in literary history remains an anomaly of modern criticism. A signal instance of victimisation by early Victorian prejudice, his merits received no recognition after Lockhart's death until the publication of Mr. Michael Sadleir's *Bulwer: A Panorama—Edward and Rosina, 1803-1836* (London, 1931), which contains a bibliography of his works.

contemporaries in being controlled by a publisher unconcerned with other interests, it was under no obligation to 'puff' books bearing any particular imprint and free to commit assault and battery as fancy willed. For years Bulwer was a favourite butt. Thackeray bore him no personal grudge—before the publication of *Vanity Fair* they met on only one occasion, at Harrison Ainsworth's, probably in 1837—but, as he told Lady Blessington, 'there are sentiments in his writing which always anger me, big words which make me furious, and a premeditated fine writing against which I can't help rebelling.'[1] From *Elizabeth Brownrigge* in 1832 to *George de Barnwell*, the first of *Punch's Prize Novelists*, published fifteen years later, Thackeray continued to issue skits and quips at Bulwer's expense. No wonder Bulwer was one of those who, after Thackeray's rise to fame, encouraged the hostility between the rival camps of the two great novelists, expressing 'the highest admiration' for Dickens, while his opinion of his opponent was 'almost wholly adverse!' In his autobiography he expressed bitter consciousness of Thackeray's hostilities and, according to one of his biographers,[2] eagerly related any anecdote to his disadvantage. In later life Thackeray declared his regret for those juvenile ferocities, not only in conversation with Forster and James Hannay, but in his preface to Appleton's edition of his works, written at New York in December 1852, to which he called Bulwer's attention in a courteous letter. According to Escott, a reconciliation between them was arranged by the efforts of Kinglake and Forster, the quartette dining together at the Athenæum Club not long before Thackeray's death.

[1] *The Life of Edward Bulwer, First Lord Lytton*, by his grandson. London, 2 vols., 1913.

[2] *Edward Bulwer, First Baron Lytton of Knebworth*, by T. H. S. Escott. London, 1910.

CHAPTER 3

§ 1

DURING the summer of 1834 Thackeray divided his time between London and Paris. Though definitely determined upon studying art, he did not settle long in Paris before he was running across the Channel for short stays with his mother or his friends. He found himself not altogether comfortable in his grandmother's household, repeatedly hinting that he would be able to work better in a lodging of his own, and eventually his fond parents were prevailed upon to augment his allowance sufficiently to enable him to rent a small apartment in the Rue des Beaux Arts, 'where I intend to work hard, and lead a most pious, sober, and godly life.' He saw a good deal of FitzGerald, who, having allowed him to illustrate his *Undine* 'in about fourteen little coloured drawings very nicely,' formed an idea of publishing a volume containing all the papers in the *Spectator* relating to Sir Roger de Coverley, with illustrations by Thackeray. Informing John Allen in September of Thackeray's imminent departure for France, he said: 'I shall miss him much.'

In Paris he spent much of his time copying at the Louvre. Henry Reeve, whom he had met at the Bullers', on looking over his sketch-book, declared his drawing to be 'as pure and accurate as any I have seen,' adding that 'he is a man whom I would willingly set to copy a picture of Raphael's, as far at least as the drawing goes.'[1] He worked with a painter named John Brine, with whom he

[1] *Memoirs of the Life and Correspondence of Henry Reeve*, by J. K. Laughton. London, 2 vols., 1898.

became a frequent visitor at the house of Eyre Evans Crowe, the Paris correspondent of the *Morning Chronicle.* Crowe's wife was Irish, and many Irishmen, including John Sheehan, a friend of Mahony's and the celebrated Thomas Moore, frequented her drawing-room, where she entertained her guests to musical evenings, 'the supreme enjoyment being a song from Thackeray.'[1] The Crowes remained his lifelong friends, Thackeray afterwards assisting the two eldest sons in their careers and receiving one of the daughters into his household almost as his own child. His capacity for friendship is a tribute to his character; the making of many friends bespeaks congenial charm, but the keeping of them connotes selfless sympathy and a sensitive understanding.

Throughout the year 1835 he remained in Paris, drawing and painting. In March Henry Reeve dined with him and his grandmother; in June he was one of a picnic party with Tom Trollope to the woods of Montmorenci.[2] Restless as ever, he applied, probably with an introduction from Evans Crowe, for the post of correspondent at Constantinople! His sole reasons for this extraordinary departure were, as he told FitzGerald, that it would afford 'a handsome income for a year, and fill my sketch-book into the bargain.' Trying to persuade his cousin, young William Ritchie, who was just going up to the university, to join his expedition, he says:

'I purpose going from Marseilles to Venice by what I hear is the most magnificent road in the world, then from Venice—if I can effect the thing—I will pass over for a week or so into Turkey, just to be able to say in a book I am going to make that I have been there, after which I will go to Rome, Naples, Florence, &c. . . . Then I will go to England, book in hand—I will get three hundred

[1] *Reminiscences of Thirty-five Years of My Life*, by Sir Joseph Crowe. London, 1895.

[2] *What I remember*, by Thomas Adolphus Trollope. London, 3 vols., 1887-89.

guineas for my book; then I will exhibit at the Water-Colour Society, and sell my ten drawings forthwith. . . .'[1]

The *Morning Chronicle* was not disposed to finance the expedition, and no funds being forthcoming elsewhere, the project fell through. FitzGerald, writing the following month, asks: 'What has become of these Eastern plans? For my part, I am glad you stay at Paris and work at your art. But you tell me that my letters are rather too sensible, and I know well what that means, so I will write in a loose way.' And he proceeds to praise Raphael, whose work Thackeray had compared unfavourably with Rubens and Paul Veronese. His irresponsible friend had reproached 'old Fitz' for seeming to reprove him; contenting himself with this rejoinder, the older man held his peace. He proved his affection with deeds as well as words.

§ 2

The harvest of wild oats was nearly reaped. In January 1836 Henry Reeve wrote in his diary:

'I have seen a good deal of Thackeray this last week. That excellent and facetious being is at the present moment editing an English paper here, in opposition to Galignani's.[2] But what is more ominous, he has fallen in love, and talks of being married in less than twenty years. . . . I dined yesterday with his object, who is a nice, simple, girlish girl; a niece of that old Colonel Shawe whom one always meets at the Sterlings'.'

Possibly Thackeray came to know her through the old uncle, for he also frequently visited the Sterlings, whom he

[1] Biographical Introduction to *Sketch Books*.

[2] Reeve is usually supposed to have been mistaken in this assertion, and it may be that he misunderstood the rumour of a projected paper by Thackeray for actual fact. But Thackeray is described by one authority as 'scribbling "feuilletons," in the *London and Paris Courier*, the best of these pen-sketches to be afterwards collected in a volume under the title of *The Paris Sketch-Book*.' Cf. *A Jorum of 'Punch,'* by Athol Mayhew. London, 1895.

had met at the Bullers'. Her father was a retired colonel of infantry, her mother, who supplied the character of the Campaigner in *The Newcomes*, belonged to the ancient Irish family of Creagh. Both hailed from County Cork and contributed to the Irish element preponderating at Mrs. Crowe's musical evenings, where Thackeray, as he related to his children, fell in love with their mother on hearing her sing. Small and slight, she seems to have been a pretty, gentle creature, much in love with the brilliant, erratic young man whose personality entirely overwhelmed her own, but awakening in him a tender, protective passion by her sweetness, freshness, and girlish charm.

She possessed nothing beyond her personal attractions, for her father doubtless belonged to the great regiment of retired officers living on the Continent for reasons of economy, but her mother, if faithfully described as the Campaigner, would regard this circumstance only as intensifying the necessity for worldly advantages in a prospective husband. Enthusiastic and impulsive, Thackeray can have been no patient lover, and Reeve's announcement of his attachment is followed by a burst of energy. He renewed his connection with *Fraser* in addition to the journalistic activities to which Reeve refers, and on 1st March issued his first book simultaneously in London and Paris, a quarto brochure containing nine plates, signed with pseudonym 'Théophile Wagstaffe,' and no letterpress, entitled *Flore et Zéphyr—Ballet Mythologique*. He published this probably at his own expense and to serve as a credential, to which he could refer when applying for commissions as an illustrator.

Within a month of its publication he crossed to London in search of this sort of work. The first shilling number of the *Pickwick Papers* appeared on 31st March, and a few days afterwards, its illustrator, Seymour, committed suicide. A successor had to be appointed without delay and Thackeray lost no time in applying for the job, going himself to Dickens's chambers in Furnival's Inn with two or three specimen sketches in his portfolio, which, unfortunately, were considered unsuitable. Six months younger than Thackeray, Dickens was then a working journalist, newly married, and known to a small public under the pseudonym of 'Boz.' Apparently this occasion was the first encounter between the two novelists who rivalled each other for supremacy in popular estimation during their lives and whose names ever since have been indissolubly linked in critical comparison and partisan appreciation.

Unsuccessful in his efforts to obtain any commissions for illustrations except from the generous FitzGerald, he returned to Paris at the end of April. Going to the Garrick Club on the 26th, the actor Macready 'met Thackeray, who has spent all his fortune and is now about to settle at Paris, I believe, as an artist.'[1] Speedily realising that the task of making a living by brush and pencil was likely to occupy a long and painful period of waiting, Thackeray had to appeal to his parents for the means to marry. His stepfather's fortunes were now in no condition to increase his allowance, but, with a cheerful optimism reflected in his stepson, he was prepared to risk the remnants of his once considerable capital in an effort to recoup his losses in unlucky investments and defaulting Indian banks, which would at the same time provide his stepson with a fixed occupation and assured income.

Among Thackeray's artistic friends in Paris was John Barnett, a composer already attracting notice of his talent, at whose lodgings he became intimate with Henry Mayhew and Douglas Jerrold. Mayhew, perhaps the truest type of Victorian Bohemian, was living in Paris for the sake of cheapness on a meagre allowance from a wealthy father,

[1] *The Diaries of William Charles Macready*, ed. William Toynbee. London, 2 vols., 1912. *Macready's Reminiscences, and Selections from his Diaries and Letters*, ed. Sir Frederick Pollock. London, 1876.

who disapproved of his son's reckless decision to discard the prospect of succession to a flourishing solicitor's practice for vague notions of a literary career. Jerrold, an older man by nearly ten years, possessed considerable reputation as a playwright besides having been concerned in several journalistic ventures; a truculently assertive, combative, and fiery little man, endowed with a fertile imagination, sarcastic wit, and a fluent, facile pen, but lacking the intellectual nobility of genius, he successfully expressed his personality upon paper in his periodical writings, especially in *Punch*. Impressed by the popularity of the Paris *Charivari*, Mayhew suggested the plan of a similar paper under the same name in London. Both Thackeray and Jerrold welcomed the idea and promptly selected members of their acquaintance suitable for forming a staff. Thackeray proposed John Poole, author of *Paul Pry* and a prominent member of the Garrick Club, and John Leech, his junior at Charterhouse and also an unsuccessful applicant for Seymour's vacant post as illustrator of *Pickwick*, who introduced his friend and fellow medical student at Bart's, Percival Leigh. Jerrold nominated his old friends and associates, Laman Blanchard and Kenny Meadows. The scheme is said to have advanced so far that the first pages were actually in type when it was suddenly abandoned 'through a mistaken notion of Thackeray's that each co-partner—there being no "capitalist" thought of—would be liable for the private debts of his colleagues.'[1] This objection, easily obviated by the insertion of a clause in the partnership agreement, seems a flimsy pretext for the quashing of an enterprise so far advanced and suggests a financial prudence inconsistent with Thackeray's character. More probably the venture collapsed for lack of capital. Mayhew and Thackeray were equally impecunious, Leech and Leigh possessed no more than a student's usual allowance, Meadows and

[1] *The History of 'Punch,'* by M. H. Spielmann. London, 1895.

Blanchard depended upon their professional earnings for a livelihood, and Jerrold was living in Paris as a convenient refuge from persistent creditors.

This incident, occurring probably in the winter of 1835–6, was attended by a sequel in the following autumn, when Major Carmichael-Smyth became chairman of the Metropolitan Newspaper Company, with a capital of £60,000 in six thousand shares of ten pounds each. Charles Buller and his friend, Sir William Molesworth, were both interested, and the company, having purchased a struggling but established property called the *Public Ledger*, proposed to take advantage of the reduction of stamp duty on newspapers from fourpence to a penny, introduced in the Budget of the previous May, to found a fully fledged Radical daily paper. Thackeray's initiative, visible in securing the support of Buller's political circle, is equally evident in selecting the staff of the journal, Laman Blanchard being appointed editor, and Douglas Jerrold dramatic critic, while he himself became Paris correspondent at a salary of eight guineas a week.

The first number of the *Constitutional and Public Ledger* appeared on Thursday, 15th September 1836, and on the prospect of his weekly salary Thackeray married Isabella Gethin Creagh Shawe, 'of the Parish of Donerail in the County of Cork Spinster and a Minor,' with the consent and in the presence of her mother at the British Embassy in Paris. According to Jeaffreson, the 'Campaigner' promised to allow her daughter fifty pounds a year for pin-money, which represented the sole subsidy of Thackeray's salary. Writing to congratulate a friend on his marriage during his first American tour he said:

'I married at your age with £400 paid by a newspaper, which failed six months afterwards, and always love to hear of a young fellow testing his fortune bravely in that way. And although my own marriage was a wreck as you know, I would do it once again, for behold love is the crown and completion of all earthly good. The man who is afraid of his fortune never deserved one.'

He had been afraid of his fortune throughout the youthful years when he was frittering away his patrimony, ever since he had lamented his inability to emulate Charles Buller in making use of his opportunities and wondered how he was to measure the scope of his capabilities. He knew himself no better now, for he still anticipated an artistic career, regarding this journalistic occupation only as a makeshift, supplying a source of necessary income while he found a market for his drawings. With his habit of mistrustful introspection, his incapacity for application, and lack of self-confidence, he might never have known himself if sheer necessity had not subordinated his inclinations and driven him desperately to undertake anything within his power likely to prove productive of money. Marriage, attended by the birth of children and financial disaster, assured the salvation of his abilities. Oblivious of responsibility for a few careless years, its burden was flung suddenly upon his shoulders with crushing force, and, on the record of his adolescent career, he might have been expected to wilt beneath its weight. Instead, he sustained its pressure to the end of his life, which was shortened by the strain of incessant effort, the continual striving to regain the loss of his patrimony and provide adequately for his children. Nobody ever paid dearer for an early crop of wild oats.

§ 3

The life of the *Constitutional* lasted little more than nine months. Its failure was due to neither incompetence nor mismanagement, but rather to an excess of quality. As in the case of John Murray's *Representative* a few years earlier, its staff consisted of reputable writers, accustomed to work on literary periodicals, whose weapons were wit, humour, and reasoned argument. They were incapable of competition with the scurrilous scribblers contributing to the popular newspapers like the *Age*, the *Satirist*, *John Bull*, and the *Morning Post*. Moreover, by advocating the principles of the extreme Radical group, they alienated the cultured class of reader which might have responded to an attempt at wholesome journalism, and directed their appeal to a class which, though parliamentarily powerful since the Reform Act, did not exist as a reading public, because most of its members had never learned to read.

Thackeray, regularly contributing a Paris letter under the signature 'T. T.,' seems soon to have lost faith in the paper's chances of success, for he began eagerly to seek other work. On 13th December he wrote to John Kemble from his new home, 15 bis, Rue Neuve St. Augustin:

'I write from the most interested motives. Mr. Beaumont is about to bring forth an Evening Paper I hear; and you must be aware how much he will need a Paris Correspondent. Pray give me your vote and interest, should the worthy Member for Northumberland persist in his intention.

I suppose you know how I exercise the same office for a Radical Morning Paper, the *Constitutional*—who in fact, has not heard of T. T.? but I have plenty of time for another similar duty; and plenty of employment for the additional weekly guineas it might bring—My dear fellow, do your best for me, for our friendship is old, our life is short, and our fortune uncertain: also as you know, I am a married man (and you can understand my situation), and have an alarming prospect before me of many additions to the race of Roaldus de Richmond. You also are probably in a similar state—wife, children coming, and nothing in three per cents. . . . do your best for me: if you encourage me perhaps I will send an article for the review (we want lightness, to my thinking) so that you see this note is, as all letters from married men should be, entirely about my own pocket and interest, which I want you to support.

I have nothing to tell you, except that I am grown strangely fat, and am the happiest man in the neighbourhood; I have a good wife, good dinners, plenty of work, and good pay—Can a man want more? . . . Write to me if you have got anything good to give me in the review, or if you have not and are disposed to write, or what style of article you want.'

Kemble was then engaged on the *British and Foreign Review*, owned by Wentworth Beaumont, and it seems probable that Thackeray contributed to the periodical something besides the review of Brougham's *Speeches* in the number for April 1839. He obtained regular work on *Galignani's Messenger* at a salary of 'ten francs a day,' as he afterwards informed Mrs. Brookfield,[1] but this connection presumably ceased when, his last letter from Paris having appeared in the *Constitutional* on 18th February, he returned to England to reside temporarily with his parents at No. 18 Albion Street, Hyde Park. This move, though convenient on account of his wife's condition, was probably occasioned by a policy of retrenchment on the part of the paper, the Paris correspondent's services being required at headquarters to fill vacancies created by a cutting-down of staff. Moreover Paris offered only limited opportunities, and the state of the *Constitutional's* fortunes threatened an urgent necessity for finding more work.

He commenced a heart-breaking search for employment. His offer to illustrate Ainsworth's *Crichton* was rejected, because, as in the case of Dickens and *Pickwick*, the author did not approve the designs submitted. He obtained a commission to execute three drawings for a one-act play, *King Glumpus*, of which a hundred copies were privately printed for the author, John Barrow, an old schoolfellow

[1] *A Collection of Letters of W. M. Thackeray, 1847-1855*. London, 1887.

at Charterhouse, for whom he illustrated a similar production, *The Exquisites*, two years later. He made the acquaintance of George Cruikshank, who claimed to have taught him etching, and frequently dined with him in the company of other literary Bohemians. But no more work came his way before the last number of the *Constitutional*, with a farewell address from his pen, was issued on 1st July.

His stepfather's ruin was completed by the paper's failure. Probably he had suffered from the delinquencies of joint-stock banks, the conduct of which was the subject of a parliamentary inquiry at this time. He found it convenient to retire to Paris, where he and Thackeray's mother established their home, while arrangements were made for the liquidation of his liabilities. Both he and his stepson adopted the honourable course of Colonel Newcome, insisting upon the payment of all claims, which remained a millstone about Thackeray's neck for more than ten years. As late as the summer of 1848, when *Vanity Fair* had sealed his fame, he wrote asking his publisher for an advance payment on account of his forthcoming Christmas book, so that he could pay off the last outstanding claim against his stepfather as a birthday present.

Vacating his parents' house in Albion Street, where his wife had given birth to their eldest daughter on 9th June, he went to live at No. 13 Great Coram Street, Brunswick Square, where the remainder of his brief married life was spent. He refused an offer of the editorship of the *Carlisle Patriot*, as he afterwards said, 'because it was too Tory for me,'[1] though more probably because he was unwilling to bury himself with small hope of advancement in a remote provincial town. His friendship with the Sterlings obtained him occasional work on *The Times*, to which his first contribution was a review of Carlyle's

[1] Biographical Introduction to *Esmond*.

French Revolution, published 3rd August, of which Carlyle wrote to his brother:

'The writer is one Thackeray, a half-monstrous Cornish giant, kind of painter, Cambridge man, and Paris newspaper correspondent, who is now writing for his life in London. I have seen him at the Bullers' and at Sterling's. His article is rather like him, and I suppose calculated to do the book good.'[1]

In common with many others of his generation, Thackeray felt a reverential admiration for Carlyle, who was some fourteen years his senior, but as yet recognised as a great writer only by a select band of critics. He did his utmost in these years to popularise Carlyle's work, and the latter wrote to his brother Alexander on 10th January 1838:

'A man in *The Times* newspaper, for the last ten days, is writing diligently a series of Papers called *Old England* extravagantly in my manner; so that several friends actually thought it was I! I did not see them till last night; and had a loud laugh over them then. It is that dog Thackeray (my Reviewer on *The Times* . . .); he, I am persuaded and no other: I take it as a help and compliment in these circumstances; and bid it welcome so far as it will go.'[2]

Again, on 1st May following, speaking to his sister of his first lecture, he wrote:

'*The Times* I spoke of above contains a very kind notice of it (written, I understand, by the man who reviewed my Book there).'

Thackeray's connection with *The Times* continued till the death in 1841 of its editor, Thomas Barnes; after the

[1] *Letters of Thomas Carlyle to His Youngest Sister*, ed. C. T. Copeland. London, 1899.

[2] *New Letters of Thomas Carlyle*, ed. and annotated by Alexander Carlyle. London, 2 vols., 1904.

succession of the celebrated Delane to the editorial chair, he went over to the principal opposing paper, the *Morning Chronicle*. Through Charles Buller he established a footing on the *London and Westminster Review*, then conducted by John Stuart Mill, and owned by Sir William Molesworth, to which he contributed a paper on Dickens in July. The same month Macready met him at the Bullers' house in company with both Mill and Dickens. Dickens was then editing *Bentley's Miscellany*, in the September number of which appeared 'The Professor: A Tale of Sentiment, by Goliah Gahagan,' the first of Thackeray's writings under that pseudonym.

Thackeray was never an intimate friend of Dickens, with whose circle he had little in common. But their acquaintance was far more familiar than is popularly supposed. In his *Life of Dickens* John Forster jealously suppressed as many references as possible to any intimacies between his subject and anybody besides himself. Harrison Ainsworth, for instance, maintained a familiar friendship with both Dickens and Forster throughout the 'forties, and Wilkie Collins, at a later date, developed closer relations with Dickens than Forster himself enjoyed at that time, yet neither received more than casual mention in the official biography. For ten years, from Thackeray's settlement at Great Coram Street to his sudden elevation to the position of Dickens's only considerable rival in public estimation, cordial relations existed between them, and the subsequent constraint prevailing till shortly before Thackeray's death arose from no ill will on either side, but from the effect upon the sensitive, self-conscious pride of both created by persistent comparisons and the consequent partisan attitude of their separate friends. Thus, though Thackeray expressed his admiration for the description of Paul Dombey's death, a minority of critics rightly deprecated the sickly sentiment of the scene, and Dickens, irritated by their criticism and unfair comparison with his rival's work, disparaged the death of Colonel Newcome on the same grounds. Memoir writers, who revelled in recording their impressions of the feelings entertained by either towards the other, had obviously enjoyed equal delight in deriving their impressions by malicious hints dropped in casual conversation.

John Forster was not of the hint-dropping cattle; there was nothing mean or petty about him. It is ironical that he should be mainly remembered as a Boswell, for he was the most Johnsonian figure of his generation. Energetic, enthusiastic, shrewd but impulsive, he was quick-tempered and domineering; though brusque in his manner to a point of rudeness and often offending his most intimate friends, he was susceptible to the slightest affront from another and would wreak unreasonable mischief to satisfy his resentment. His character was described with lucid brevity by a discomfited London cabman, who was heard to refer to his fare as a very 'harbitrary gent.' Possessed of sound literary judgment and a practical aptitude for affairs, he won the confidential esteem of such different personalities as Dickens, Landor, Bulwer, and Macready, to whom, by means of his downright honesty and fidelity, together with his capacity for management, his friendship became indispensable. His personality was a dominant power in the literary world; Bulwer remarked, 'more than any living critic, he has served to establish reputations.'

This extraordinary man met Thackeray, like Dickens, at Harrison Ainsworth's hospitable house on the Harrow Road. They never became really friendly. The valued friend of men of established reputation, Forster was prepared to patronise, and when Thackeray, proud and sensitive, declined to be patronised, he became irritated by a sense that the struggling, if talented, writer inclined to give himself airs. Moreover, being himself concerned only with serious literary criticism, he despised and depreciated Thackeray's affiliation to the Maginn school of flippant swashbuckling. Thackeray, on his side, aware of the other's aggressiveness, conceived his energy and earnestness as meddling pomposity and assumed a defensive attitude of careless banter, thereby convincing Forster, as he convinced others, of his insincerity and cynical levity. He was too thin-skinned to row easily in the same galley with men like Forster.

At this time Forster, besides being literary editor of the *Examiner*, virtually controlled the *New Monthly Magazine* in his capacity of confidential adviser to its publisher Colburn, for Theodore Hook—the Wagg of *Pendennis*—though nominally editor, did little more than lend the already tarnished lustre of his name to the publication. With his usual unerring judgment he recognised Thackeray's ability and apparently snatched him up under Dickens's nose to contribute the exploits of Major Goliah Gahagan to the pages of Bentley's principal competitor. Sooner or later he also admitted Thackeray to the columns of the *Examiner*, to which the latter contributed till 1844, establishing during that time a cordial friendship with the paper's principal editor, Albany Fonblanque. During the latter part of this connection, at least, he received a regular weekly salary or retaining fee of four pounds.

Obviously Thackeray made the best possible use of his friends in obtaining employment following the crisis in his fortunes. Cruikshank, the most popular illustrator of the day, for whose *Comic Almanack* he wrote 'Stubbs's Calendar, or, The Fatal Boots,' seems to have dropped him some crumbs from a table creaking beneath the weight of lucrative commissions. He received twenty pounds for eighteen illustrations to a book of travels issued by Bentley—*Damascus and Palmyra: A Journey to the East*, by Charles G. Addison—and executed twelve drawings for Douglas Jerrold's *Men of Character*, published in three volumes by Colburn. Reviewing the latter on 24th February 1838, the *Athenæum* cruelly observed: 'According to the prevailing fashion the work is illustrated by etchings *after* Cruikshank, which are only remarkable for the badness of the drawing, and the total absence of humour.' In defiance of pious Thackerayan enthusiasts, it is impossible to deny that he was, at his best, a talented amateur as a draughtsman. His execution is sketchy, lacking finish and polish, his expressions are wooden, and his attempts at the ridiculous usually achieve the grotesque. When he came to illustrate his own written works, his opportunity for perfect illustration was obvious, for none could be expected to portray more accurately the appearance of the characters than the author of their conception. Charlotte Brontë appreciated the advantage when she made an unsatisfactory attempt to illustrate *Jane Eyre*.

'How he can render, with a few black lines and dots, shades of expression so fine, so real; traits of character so minute, so subtle, so difficult to seize and fix, I cannot tell —I can only wonder and admire. Thackeray may not be a painter, but he is a wizard of a draughtsman; touched with his pencil, paper lives. And then his drawing is so refreshing; after the wooden limbs one is accustomed to see pourtrayed by common-place illustrators, his shapes of bone and muscle clothed with flesh, correct in proportion and anatomy, are a real relief. All is true in Thackeray. If Truth were again a goddess, Thackeray should be her high priest.'[1]

The maiden author, when she indulged in that extravagant eulogy, was in the first ecstatic flush of her admiration for *Vanity Fair*; in her present orgy of rapture she would have hailed its author as the herald of truth if he had sworn an affidavit that the exploits of Major Gahagan had been founded upon fact. Moreover, in the seclusion of her remote parsonage she had experienced few opportunities for arriving at an adequate appreciation of the

[1] *Charlotte Brontë and Her Circle*, by Clement K. Shorter. London, 1896.

illustrator's art. Perhaps it is unfair to compare Thackeray's efforts with the work of such masters as Keene and Frederick Walker, but place his illustrations for *Pendennis* beside those of Doyle—a second-rate draughtsman by comparison with the others—for *The Newcomes*! The result will arouse no wonder that he failed to make income or reputation as an illustrator.

Apart from his work for *The Times*, his most remunerative as well as his most important writings were contributed to *Fraser's Magazine*. In November 1837 appeared the first paper by 'Charles Yellowplush,' which immediately caught the fancy of the magazine's readers and secured for Thackeray a commission to continue Mr. Yellowplush's memoirs till further notice. The extent of their success and the author's value to the magazine is testified by a letter written in February by Thackeray to the publisher, in which, having stated the arrangement by which Maginn agreed to liquidate his debt to him with his earnings as a contributor, he says:

'I hereby give notice that I shall strike for wages. You pay more to others, I find, than to me: and so I intend to make some fresh conditions about Yellow-plush. I shall write no more of that gentleman's remarks except at the rate of twelve guineas a sheet, and with a drawing for such number in which his story appears—the drawing two guineas. Pray do not be angry at this decision on my part: it is simply a bargain, which it is my duty to make. Bad as he is, Mr. Yellow-plush is the most popular contributor to your magazine, and ought to be paid accordingly: if he does not deserve more than the monthly nurse or the Blue Friars, I am a Dutchman. I have been at work upon his adventures to-day, and will send them to you or not as you like, but in common regard for myself, I won't work under price.'

The publisher agreed to his terms, for the papers appeared monthly from January to August of 1838, and were succeeded by the less successful *Diary of Dolly Duster*. Thenceforward, for several years, with an occasional break of a month or two, Thackeray was one of the most valued and consistent contributors to the magazine, which afforded a considerable part of his annual income.

The most famous of his pseudonyms, Michael Angelo Titmarsh, suggested, it is said, by the fact that the famous Florentine also owned a broken nose, first figured in *Fraser* for June 1838, as the author of *Strictures on Pictures*, a review of the Royal Academy's exhibition for the year. Titmarsh's activities quickly extended beyond the confines of art criticism, but his humorously satirical commentary on the Academy became an annual event and a nightmare of dread to the unfortunate exhibitors. In June 1845, FitzGerald informed Frederick Tennyson:

'If you want to know something of the Exhibition . . . read *Fraser's Magazine* for this month; there Thackeray has a paper on the matter full of fun. I met Stone in the street the other day; he took me by the button, and told me in perfect sincerity, and with increasing warmth, how, though he loved old Thackeray, yet these yearly outspeakings of his sorely tried him; not on account of himself (Stone), but on account of some of his friends, Charles Landseer, Maclise, etc. Stone worked himself up to such a pitch under the pressure of forced calmness that he at last said Thackeray would get himself horse-whipped one day by one of these infuriated Apelleses.'

In the spring of 1838 *The Times* sent him over to Paris to review the *Salon*. Having broken his journey at Boulogne to interview Maginn, he wrote to his wife on 20th March:

'There is a chance of £350 a year here. Poor B. is dying, and his place is worth as much; but then I throw away a very good position in London, where I can make as much, and a little fame into the bargain. My game, as far as I can see it, is to stick to *The Times*. . . . I have been writing all day, and finished and despatched an article for *The Times*. My next visit will be to the Spanish pictures, the next to Versailles, and on Monday week, please God, I will be home.'

He declined the chance of this post, possibly as a Paris correspondent, as he had refused the offer from Carlisle, because he felt rightly that in London lay his only hopes of advancement. With his work on *The Times* and *Fraser*, he was earning a sufficient livelihood; the occasional commissions obtained elsewhere afforded assistance to his parents in their penurious struggle to pay off the major's heavy liabilities.

Thackeray was happy in harness. He had now no leisure for moods of dubious introspection; whatever the extent of his capabilities, necessity now compelled him to concentrate upon the opportunities offered. Possessing youth, health, and happiness, he disdained the unambitious security of a sinecure and flung himself recklessly into a whirlwind of work. It was these busy years—when even a slight illness, incapacitating him for a few short weeks, might have deprived him of valuable connections and the sources of his income, when he was scribbling against the clock to fulfil accepted commissions, yet dared never to refuse the chance of a new connection lest an old one should fail—which played havoc with his constitution and wore out his vitality in middle life. The pace began to tell when he got himself called to the Bar in the hope of obtaining a metropolitan magistracy, but that was only after years of tremendous exertion which would have exhausted the most elastic energies. At the outset, only a year after ruin had overtaken his family, he faced his fortune gaily. Responding to his enthusiasm, the steady FitzGerald wrote in November: 'I am very glad you are engaged in a way of life that you like: that is a good thing indeed, which most people miss.' To his wife he exclaimed: 'Here have we been two years married and not a single unhappy day. Oh, I do bless God for all this happiness which He has given me.' Then, with a trace of the old pessimism which ever oppressed his reflections, he added: 'It is so great that I almost tremble for the future.' He had reason. As if enraged by the gay courage with which he had faced financial disaster, the Fates reserved for him the cruellest of human calamities.

CHAPTER 4

§ 1

IN the midst of his varied and exhausting labours, Thackeray found plenty of time for social pleasure. Thus early, he acquired the habit of burning the candle at both ends which pursued him inexorably to the end of his life. 'Old Thackeray,' said FitzGerald to Frederick Tennyson in 1845, 'goes on in his own way; writing hard for half a dozen Reviews and Newspapers all the morning; dining, drinking, and talking of a night; managing to preserve a fresh colour and perpetual flow of spirits under a wear-and-tear of thinking and feeding that would have knocked up any other man I know two years ago, at least.' Though he had not yet embarked upon the racketing about clubs and taverns with which he relieved his subsequent loneliness, he sought recreation from his work in good company and conversation. After a good dinner he liked to spread his bulk in a comfortable chair, yarning and smoking cigars into the small hours. A heavy smoker, he expresses in *Philip* a hatred of fashionable houses where smoking was barred, and James Payn relates how, excusing himself on the score of a particular engagement immediately after dinner, he was asked if he would not stay for a cigar before leaving, whereupon he exclaimed, 'Oh, they smoke here, do they? Well, to tell you the truth, that *was* my engagement,' and he remained for the rest of the evening.[1]

Though not one of Spedding's list of prospective members of the Sterling Club, he joined that select circle soon after its foundation. Intimate with the Sterlings and Bullers,

[1] *Some Literary Recollections*, by James Payn. London, 1884.

he had known Spedding at Cambridge and came to know Carlyle well. Though they were never more than casual friends, he felt respect and admiration for Carlyle, who, he once observed, when expressing the hope that 'we shall begin ere long to love art for art's sake,' had 'worked more than any other to give it its independence.' He dined in the company of Carlyle, Sydney Smith, and George Grote at the house of Henry Reeve, who was living with H. F. Chorley, the musical critic of the *Athenæum*, at this time. He was frequently invited to Dickens's Twickenham home and belonged to the Shakespeare Club, of which Dickens and Forster were the leading lights. Macready describes in his diary the club dinner on 30th March 1839. Dickens was in the chair. William Jerdan and Laman Blanchard were the vice-presidents, Leigh Hunt was a guest of the evening, Clarkson Stanfield and Forster were prominent speakers, and 'Barry Cornwall' fell asleep under the influence of the excellent dinner. Thackeray is merely mentioned as being present, pushed in between Jerrold and Samuel Lover. Charles Knight, the publisher, found himself 'at a side table with a remarkable-looking young man opposite to me, who I was told was the Michael Angelo Titmarsh of *Fraser's Magazine*.'[1] Thackeray was a nonentity; as Titmarsh, he could sit at a side table in the company of celebrities.

Knight's remark is significant. Thackeray's tall, broad-shouldered figure, with his thick, waving hair, striking features, and spectacles perilously balanced on his dab of a nose, became a familiar, readily recognised sight about the clubs and streets, but passers-by pointed him out as Titmarsh or Yellowplush. George Hodder declared that he enthusiastically admired the writings of Titmarsh long before he knew that Thackeray was the author. There is no doubt that pseudonymous disguise hindered his name from getting known to the general public, and there were

[1] *Passages of a Working Life*, by Charles Knight. London, 3 vols., 1865.

many of his own profession well acquainted with the brilliance of his writings and yet unaware of his identity. The Rev. James White, a contributor to *Blackwood*, having promised to introduce him to the Edinburgh publishers, wrote:

'He is the cleverest of all the London writers, I think—his name is Thackeray; a gentleman, a Cambridge man. I told him he had better not waste his time with the inferior magazines when he writes the best things (he is the Yellow Plush of *Fraser*, and the Major Gahagan of the *New Monthly*), but go at once to you. He is shy, I suppose, for he said he wished you would *invite* him to contribute. If you will let me know whether you wish to hear from him, I will communicate your reply; or if you wish to see him, he lives No. 13 Great Coram Street, Russell Square. He is also literary reviewer in *The Times*.'[1]

Blackwood, with a competent staff of regular contributors, was not disposed to offer a commission, but Thackeray was informed that he might submit something for consideration. He sent *The Great Hoggarty Diamond*, which was rejected.

Of this story he afterwards remarked that 'it was written at a time of great affliction, when my heart was very soft and humble.' His second child, another daughter, died in infancy during the early spring of 1839. Of this bereavement, which remained an always painful memory to Thackeray and probably an enduring affliction upon his wife, he wrote to his mother:

'What shall I say to you about our little darling who is gone?—I don't feel sorrow for her, and think of her only as something charming that for a season we were allowed to enjoy: When Anny was very ill, dying as I almost

[1] *William Blackwood and His Sons*, by Mrs. Oliphant and Mrs. Gerald Porter. Edinburgh, 3 vols., 1897-98.

thought, it seemed to me wrong to pray for her life, for specific requests to God are impertinences, I think, and all we should ask from him is to learn how to acquiesce, and now I would be almost sorry—no that is not true—but I would not ask to have the child back again and subject her to the degradation of life and pain.'[1]

His religious feeling represented a curious mixture of simplicity and scepticism. Having learned from his mother and his aunts in childhood to accept the idea of God as a matter beyond argument, in the same way as he accepted the facts of his parentage, he never entertained any controversial dogma except for the inquisitive phase inevitably experienced at the university. Realising the futility of speculation, he resigned himself to an agnostic philosophy tending to fatalism; he believed in God, but not as a despotic potentate susceptible to the blandishments of canting services and self-seeking prayers. 'Happiness is as good as prayers,' he said once to his wife, conceiving happiness as a compliment to God. Looking upon life as a trial through which those came best who made the most of their opportunities, he did not concern himself with timid theories of eternity. His attitude to death, as expressed in his bereavement, remained the same throughout his life. Fifteen years later, he said:

'I don't pity anybody who leaves the world, not even a fair young girl in her prime; I pity those remaining. On her journey, if it pleases God to send her, depend on it there's no cause for grief, that's but an earthly condition. Out of our stormy life, and brought nearer the Divine light and warmth, there must be a serene climate. Can't you fancy sailing into the calm? Would you care about going on the voyage, only for the dear souls left on the other shore? but we shan't be parted from them no doubt though they are from us. Add a little more intelligence

[1] *Letters of Anne Thackeray Ritchie: with Forty-two Additional Letters from her Father, William Makepeace Thackeray*, ed. Hester Ritchie. London, 1924.

to that which we possess even as we are, and why shouldn't we be with our friends though ever so far off?'

Those critics who discover an excess of sentiment in his books rarely remark his consistent contempt for hypocrisy in an age when sanctimony was the fashion. He loathed Pecksniffery and Chadbandism with more personal sincerity than Dickens, though he merely flicked its face with the whip of humorous satire instead of pelting it in the pillory of malicious ridicule. 'The modern fanaticism,' wrote F. D. Maurice in 1852, 'will drive hundreds of literary men far from ill-affected to Christianity (such as Thackeray) into positive hatred of Christianity.'[1] If he had lived, how he would have loathed the legend of Charles Kingsley!

But he could admire a man confident and content in his faith, sincere in his professions, and superior to prosy posing and preaching. John Allen, his old Cambridge friend, now his neighbour in Coram Street, was the first to offer condolence on the loss of his child. Thackeray wrote to his mother:

'If you were here and could be intimate with John Allen, how you would respect him. The man is just a perfect saint, not more nor less, and not the least dogmatical or presumptuous; but working, striving, yearning day and night in the most intense efforts to gain Christian perfection —and yet the world would not be as good a world as it is, were all men like him; it would be but a timid, ascetic place, in which many of the finest fancies of the soul would not dare to exercise themselves. No man can, however, escape from his influence, which is perfectly magnetic.'[2]

Allen was the original of Dobbin in *Vanity Fair*, that faithful, solid, reliable fellow, so felicitously named. The

[1] *Life of F. D. Maurice*, by Sir J. F. Maurice. London, 2 vols., 1884.
[2] Biographical Introduction to *Barry Lyndon*.

Dobbins of the world are born to befriend the George Osbornes and Amelias, to illustrate the worth of decent mediocrity, but who would not rather meet the Beckys and the Rawdon Crawleys?

§ 2

Unable to afford a more expensive holiday, Thackeray took his wife to Gravesend to recover from the first shock of their bereavement. 'I wish I could afford more frequent trips,' he told his mother, 'one to Paris above all for profit as well as for pleasure, but it is not improbable that something may turn up to keep me in London for the whole of the summer.' He had a variety of work on hand. Besides his work on *The Times*, articles appeared in the *London and Westminster* and *British and Foreign Reviews*, and he contributed three articles to *Heads of the People*, a publication in monthly parts, illustrated by Kenny Meadows. He is believed to have written *The Loving Ballad of Lord Bateman*, which contained illustrations by Cruikshank and a preface attributed to Dickens, and he obtained a useful commission for cartoons in the *Anti-Corn Law Circular*. Of the latter, Henry Cole, the secretary of the Anti-Corn Law League, wrote to Richard Cobden:

'The artist is a genius, both with his pencil and his pen. His vocation is literary. He is full of humour and feeling. Hitherto he has not had occasion to think much on the subject of Corn Laws, and therefore wants the stuff to work upon. He would like to combine both writing and drawing when sufficiently primed, and then he would write and illustrate ballads, or tales, or anything. I think you would find him a most effective auxiliary, and perhaps the best way to fill him with matter for illustrations, would be to invite him to see the weavers, their mills, shuttles, et cetera. If you like the sketch, perhaps you will return it me, and I will put it in the way of being engraved. He will set about Lord Ashley when we have heard your opinion of the present sketch. Thackeray is the writer of an article in the last number of the *Westminster Review* on French caricatures, and many other things. For some time he managed the *Constitutional* newspaper. He is a college friend of Charles Buller.'[1]

Apart from two woodcuts, drawn in accordance with Cobden's directions and reproduced by Cole in his memoirs, it is impossible certainly to identify Thackeray's contributions, but he is believed to have contributed both articles and drawings to the circular at intervals for a year. For the *Comic Almanack* for 1840 he wrote 'Barber Cox, and the Cutting of His Comb,' subsequently reprinted as *Cox's Diary*.

During the summer he established a new and curious connection. The American poet, Nathaniel Parker Willis, came on a visit to England and secured his services as London correspondent of a New York literary weekly called the *Corsair*. To his partner, Willis wrote on 26th July:

'I have engaged a contributor to the *Corsair*. Who do you think? The author of *Yellowplush* and *Major Gahagan*. I have mentioned it in my jottings, that our readers may know all about it. He has gone to Paris and will write letters from there, and afterwards from London, for a guinea a *close column* of the *Corsair*—cheaper than I ever did anything in my life. I will see that he is paid for a while to see how you like him. For myself, I think him the very best periodical writer alive. He is a royal, daring, fine creature, too.'

In the 'jottings' intended for publication, Willis continued:

'I have been delighted to find that the authors of the two best periodical series of papers that have appeared for twenty years are one and the same person. One of my first

[1] *Fifty Years of Public Work*, by Sir Henry Cole. London, 2 vols., 1884.

enquiries in London was touching the authorship of *The Yellowplush Papers* and *The Reminiscences of Major Gahagan*—the only things in periodical literature, except *The Pickwick Papers*, for which I looked with any interest or eagerness. The author, Mr. Thackeray, breakfasted with me yesterday, and the readers of the *Corsair* will be delighted, I am sure, to hear that I have engaged this cleverest and most gifted of the magazine writers of London to become a *regular correspondent* of the *Corsair*. . . . Thackeray is a tall, athletic man of about thirty-five with a look of talent that could never be mistaken. He has taken to literature after having spent a very large inheritance, but in throwing away the gifts of fortune, he has cultivated his natural talents very highly and is one of the most accomplished draughtsmen in England as well as the cleverest and most brilliant of periodical writers. He has been the principal critic for *The Times* and writes for *Fraser* and *Blackwood*. You will hear from him by the first steamer after he arrives in Paris and thenceforward regularly.'

The first of the 'Letters from London, Paris, Pekin, Petersburgh, &c. By the Author of "The Yellowplush Correspondence," "The Memoirs of Major Gahagan," &c.,' signed, as on the *Constitutional*, with the initials 'T. T.,' appeared on 24th August, and were continued weekly or bi-weekly till the end of October. Three letters straggled across the Atlantic between then and the following March, when the correspondence finally ceased, probably because Willis's payment 'for a while' was exhausted and no further remuneration was forthcoming for a feature which had completed its purpose as a 'stunt.'

Meanwhile, *Catherine, A Story, by Ikey Solomons, Esq., Junior*,[1] had begun its run in *Fraser* for May. The Newgate fashion in fiction—corresponding in some respects to the 'detective story' craze of the years 1925 to 1930—was then at its height. Following Bulwer's *Paul Clifford* and *Eugene Aram*, Ainsworth had sprung into the front rank of best-

[1] The original Ikey Solomons was a notorious receiver of stolen goods.

selling novelists with *Rookwood*. Then Dickens had introduced Bill Sikes's housebreaking and Fagin's trade of 'cly-faking' into *Oliver Twist*, which was succeeded in the pages of *Bentley's Miscellany*, commencing in January 1839, by the most popular of all Newgate novels, Ainsworth's *Jack Sheppard*. The success of this story staggered the critics. Everybody was reading it, and eight different adaptations of the book were presented simultaneously in the London theatres. Conceiving that a satire on such a theme would take the popular fancy, Thackeray followed Ainsworth's example in consulting the *Newgate Calendar* and selected for his heroine a murderess named Catherine Hayes,[1] who had flourished about the same time as Sheppard.

The story failed to make any popular appeal. The callous ruthlessness of the heroine and the gruesome horror of the murder revolted the sensibilities of readers who were sentimentally thrilled by the dashing Turpin and the bold, bad, sadly betrayed Jack Sheppard. Its splendid irony and Defoe-like realism were wasted on them. 'Carlyle says it is wonderful,' Thackeray told his mother, 'and many more laud it highly, but it is a disgusting subject and no mistake. I wish I had taken a pleasanter one.' The intelligentsia appreciated the cleverness and point of the satire, but the ordinary reader was not impressed and no publisher considered the story a profitable proposition for book-issue on its completion as a serial. Bitterly dis-

[1] Some eleven years later, Thackeray's reference to the murderess, Catherine Hayes, in one of the monthly parts of *Pendennis* evoked a storm of newspaper vituperation. There happened to be a young and beautiful *prima donna* named Catherine Hayes, then charming the opera lovers of Dublin. The Irish press, seizing upon a pretext to vent its indignation against the author of the *Irish Sketch Book*, reviled him as 'the Big Blubberman' and 'the hugest humbug ever thrust on the public,' accusing him of malicious intent to ruin the innocent singer, while a question was even asked in the House of Commons. Thackeray pricked the bubble with an amusing letter of explanation, entitled 'Capers and Anchovies,' appearing in the *Morning Chronicle* of 12th April 1850. Apart from this connection with Thackeray, Catherine Hayes's claim to be remembered is based upon Forster's story of her compliment to Dickens's wife on having had for her father so clever a painter as Mr. Hogarth!

appointed, Thackeray declared the idea was 'a mistake all through,' actually attributing its lack of success to the fact that 'it was not made disgusting enough . . . the triumph of it would have been to make readers so horribly horrified as to cause them to give up or rather throw up the book and all its kind; whereas you see the author had a sneaking kindness for his heroine, and did not like to make her quite worthless.'

It seems likely that he cherished secret hopes that *Catherine* might prove to be his *Joseph Andrews*. He admired Fielding, whose works he reviewed in *The Times* during the following year, beyond all other writers; *Amelia* he considered 'the most delightful portrait of a woman that surely ever was painted,' and he once remarked that 'my English would have been very much better if I had read Fielding before I was ten.' He modelled his style upon Fielding as Dickens received inspiration from Smollett, and the idea of becoming a metropolitan magistrate was possibly suggested by Fielding having held such an office. Remembering that Fielding had commenced *Joseph Andrews* with no more ambition than to satirise *Pamela*, the possibility of *Catherine* proving the key to fame and fortune excited his highest hopes. After all, Ainsworth had reached celebrity at a bound with a Newgate romance and Dickens had created the most popular book of the day out of a commission to supply suitable letterpress to a series of sporting pictures.

The comparative failure of *Catherine* and the rejection of *The Great Hoggarty Diamond* by *Blackwood* disappointed but did not dishearten him. 'I have just turned off a thundering article against Bulwer,' he told his mother at the beginning of December, 'and yesterday had the misfortune to read the *Comic Almanack*—anything worse or more paltry cannot well be imagined—it is as bad, very nearly, as the prints which illustrate it. . . . Cruikshank, I suppose, is tired of the thing and bends all his energies to the illustrations of *Jack Sheppard*.' Willis, regardless of veracity in detail when composing an attractive advertisement, described him as a contributor to *Blackwood* on the strength of a story submitted and not yet rejected, for nothing of his ever appeared in the pages of that magazine, though he made a second effort to establish a connection with it. On 29th January he wrote suggesting a series of London letters on similar lines to those sent to *Fraser* occasionally by Titmarsh from Paris:

'No politics, as much fun and satire as I can muster, literary lath and criticism of a spicy nature, and general gossip. I belong to a couple of clubs in this village, and can get together plenty of rambling stuff. For instance, for next month Courvoisier's hanging (I'll go on purpose), strictures on C. Phillip's speech, the London Library, Tom Carlyle and *The Times*, Bunn's new book, of which great fun may be made, and an account of Willis that may be racy enough.'

The bill of fare should have tempted the appetite, for it was precisely the type of article with which Maginn had delighted his principals twenty years ago, when they were waging war against Hazlitt and the Cockney school. But old William Blackwood was dead and the magazine grew steadily more sedate under the direction of his sons. Perhaps, too, in spite of his tactful suggestions of 'no politics,' they were reluctant to employ an avowed Cobdenite, who was writing for the Radical *London and Westminster Review* and the *Anti-Corn Law Circular*.

His Liberalism was confirmed by election to the Reform Club early in this year. Under the influence of Carlyle, Buller, and the friends of Cobden, he developed a keen interest in Radical politics. He saw in industrial conditions the flagrant injustice which ultimately created trades-unionism, and abominated the new commercial bureaucracy, which is always subjected to satirical ridicule in his books. Perhaps if his destiny had been differently cast, he might have pursued his sociological principles, not as a parliamentarian, for which his incapacity for public speaking would have denied any success, but as an intellectual thinker and teacher, like Mill and Carlyle. As it was, politics played no prominent part in his career and he introduced his views into his novels far less than most of his contemporaries. Speaking to his mother of 'the rascally Whigs and Tories,' he wonders when 'those two humbugs are to disappear,' adding, 'I'm not a Chartist, only a Republican. I would like to see all men equal, and this bloated aristocracy blasted to the wings of all the winds.' He admitted that the aristocracy had been, and still was, useful to a degree, and depreciated all coercive violence—'the bigotry of that and of the present Chartist leaders is greater than the bigotry we suffer under.' These sentiments would have served him equally well nearly a century later. Like intelligent observers before and since, he saw all too clearly the evils of both sides, yet could visualise no practical system under which fresh parasites could not creep over the corpses of the old and fasten their poisonous fangs into the flesh of the State. His problem retains its freshness a century after the Reform Act.

The humanitarian views which he developed at this time are reflected in the curious article appearing in *Fraser* for August, 'Going to See a Man Hanged.' Nowhere may be found a more vivid impression of the mentality of the mob. The extraordinary phenomenon of respectable citizens, in the company of their modest wives, flocking at an inconveniently early hour to a public execution receives comment upon all its aspects. Here there is evident the peculiar insight and observation which equipped the social satirist. Yet again he utters thoughts far in advance of his time, when he passionately pleads for the abolition of capital punishment.

Monckton Milnes was the friend who, having voted in the House of Commons for the abolition of the death penalty and being 'anxious to see the effect on the public mind of an execution,' invited Thackeray to accompany him to the execution of Courvoisier. Milnes wanted to follow the usual fashion in making a night of it before proceeding to the hanging, but Thackeray excused himself on the ground that he must have sleep in order to be fit for work on the morrow. Milnes, the Mæcenas of his age and almost the last of the great patrons of literature, provides another example of Thackeray's faculty for enduring friendship. Commencing at Cambridge, their cordial relations continued till the younger man's death, and Thackeray thrice visited Fryston, the famous Yorkshire house where Milnes welcomed men of letters with a hospitality equal to that of Cobham or Halifax in the days of Congreve and Addison.

His social engagements at this time were as numerous as his literary undertakings. To his mother he wrote early in February:

> 'We have been on a sweet trip to Clapham to see my friend Cattermole, who has married a charming little wife, and has a beautiful place, and on another to Chelsea to see Carlyle and Mrs. C. Pleasanter, more high-minded people I don't know. Leigh Hunt has produced a charming play, and my lady is going with the Kembles in their private box. Fitz is to come too, and I intend to stop at home and work.'

He saw Leigh Hunt's *Legend of Florence* a week or two later, for the Queen, returning from her honeymoon, ordered a command performance, for which the playwright Planché obtained a couple of tickets for Thackeray and his wife. FitzGerald stayed at Coram Street when he came up to town from his country seclusion, and Thackeray found it 'delightful to have him in the house, but I'm afraid his society makes me idle; we sit and talk too much about books and pictures and smoke too many cigars.'

With the memory of last year's bereavement less painfully present and the pressure of financial embarrassment relieved by abundant employment, he was settling down to his new life of happy domesticity and hard work. Still the gay adventurer, in spite of the overwhelming crash of the *Constitutional*, he now meditated some modest little periodical on the lines of Cruikshank's subsequent *Omnibus*. The first number was to contain *The Veracious History of Dionysius Diddler*, a humorous skit in pictures at the expense of Dr. Dionysius Lardner, editor of the encyclopædia bearing his name, and the inevitable Bulwer, who figures as 'Sir Henry Pelham.' His wife wrote to his mother on 20th April:

'William is full of his *Dionysius*. I want him to run no risks and be content with half profits, for it has yet to be proved that there will be profits. He says I am a *coward*, but I think we are properly balanced. The engravers spoilt his designs in the most cruel manner. They are something in the style of M. Vieuxbois, and he proposes bringing twelve out for sixpence. I do not like to send you any until they are properly got up. It is a kind of pastime for William, for you know it gives him no trouble to sketch.'

The wifely caution was wasted on Thackeray in his present state of optimism. John Macrone, a young publisher who was intimate with Ainsworth and had issued the *Sketches by Boz*, undertook to publish two volumes of Titmarsh's Parisian articles. 'I am in a ceaseless whirl and whizz from morning to night, now with the book, now with the drawings, now with articles for *The Times*, *Fraser*, here and there,' he tells his mother on 30th April.

'The days pass away to me like half-hours. . . . I have just done a huge article on G. Cruikshank for the *L. and W.*

which I will send you when it appears. And furthermore, am bringing out on my own account a weekly paper, the *Foolscap Library*. I think it will take: and the profits of it are so enormous if successful that I don't like to share them with a bookseller: there is no reason why I should not make a big lump of money by it. . . . You will see in the Cruikshank article some remarks against myself: I fail by sneering too much: but I think *Foolscap* will succeed; it begins with the adventures of *Dionysius Diddler*, all in pictures like M. Vieuxbois, quite fabulous, but a good likeness of Lardner and Bulwer introduced. . . . I don't know that I shan't have to borrow from Father for the *Foolscap*: the thing is a fortune, but wants about £30 to start it: however, I have some and shan't want yet. Why shouldn't I sell 5000, 10,000 copies?—they will pay me 40 or 80 a week: 80 a week is 4000 a year of which I would put by 3 at the very least per an.'

The project never matured sufficiently to frustrate or fulfil his hopes; the first number of thc *Whitey-Brown Paper Magazine*, as the *Foolscap* came to be called, went to press, but never appeared on sale. The terrible calamity which dispelled his happiness and cast a lasting blight upon his life now loomed over him, distracting his attention from all except the most urgent affairs.

§ 3

His third and younger surviving daughter was born on 28th May 1840.[1] His wife was in delicate health at the time and he had taken her to Leamington for the few weeks preceding her confinement. Her condition continued unsatisfactory, occasioning uneasy concern, though manifesting no immediate symptoms of the awful malady so rapidly developing. They were still at home in Coram Street on 24th June when his old Cambridge friend,

[1] Harriet Marian, called 'Minnie,' became the first wife of Leslie Stephen, and died 27th November 1875.

Brookfield, dined with them.[1] In August they went to Margate in the hope that the sea air would restore his wife's health. But it was here that his eyes were opened to a realisation of the terrible truth. He was working on *A Shabby Genteel Story* for *Fraser* and a review of Fielding's work for *The Times*.

'I . . . used to walk out three miles to a little bowling-green, and write there in an arbour—coming home and wondering what was the melancholy oppressing the poor little woman. *The Times* gave me five guineas for the article. I recollect I thought it rather shabby pay, and twelve days after it appeared in the paper, my poor little wife's malady showed itself.'

The scene revives in shadows of sombre sadness. The penniless journalist, pressed by necessity to write hard for the means to pay the cost of medical attention and their present holiday, tears himself away from the invalid's side and goes off by himself for the day to work, knowing that, if he remains, his anxious solicitude will not allow him to concentrate on his task. In the evening he returns to find her forlorn little figure seated alone, her eyes staring sightlessly, vacantly, out over the sparkling sea. As he takes her hand and she looks up, he sees in her glance a haunted, frightened, wondering look. He asks her, with a laugh, what she has been doing with herself all day and talks cheerfully about his work. But all the time he is darting covert, questioning glances at her, anxiety gripping his heart and causing him to catch his breath. And then, on one such evening, all doubt is dispelled. . . .

The article on Fielding appeared in *The Times* of 2nd September. As soon as he was aware of his wife's affliction, Thackeray took her to see her mother at Cork, probably hoping that the familiar surroundings of her childhood

[1] *Mrs. Brookfield and Her Circle*, by Charles and Frances Brookfield. London, 2 vols., 1905.

and the society of her family would restore her mental balance. On 19th September 1848 he wrote to his sister-in-law:

'It is about this time eight years that the *Jupiter* came into Cork with our poor little woman on board. My dear, I can't forget how tenderly you always loved her: and look over often in my mind that gap of time since she has been dead to us all and see that dear artless sweet creature who charmed us both so. What a whirl of life I've seen since then! but never her better, I think. "N'est-ce pas mourir tous les jours"—don't you recollect her singing and her sweet, sweet voice? Her anxious little soul would have been alarmed at my prosperities such as they are. She was always afraid of people flattering me: and I get a deal of that sort of meat nowadays.'

Jeaffreson expressed the opinion that the removal of his wife's restraining influence accounted for Thackeray's irregular habits and reckless abuse of his health, resulting in his early death. It accounted for more than that. The tenor of his entire life and temperament was altered. No man more urgently required the complement of a wife's companionship. The vanity of which he was frequently accused in the days of his celebrity and success was no more than eagerness for honest criticism such as a wife might have offered. Accustomed from childhood to confide in his fond mother, he experienced in those few short years of married life the happy solace of perfect communion with feminine sympathy. After the loss of his wife's society he always sought sympathy from his female friends, unburdening his heart to them, almost apologetically, and covering each outburst of feeling with a humorous sally or playful description of some casual incident. 'I can't live without the tenderness of some woman,' he cried in anguish, writing to Jane Brookfield during his first American visit, and adds, with a typically self-conscious touch of pathetic humour, 'when I am sixty I shall be marrying a girl of eleven or twelve, innocent, barley-sugar-loving, in a pinafore.' The gay irresponsibility of his early life vanished for ever in the first months of his wife's illness, to be replaced by a reflective melancholy, ever harking wistfully back to happy memories of the past. At forty he was not merely prematurely old in body and appearance; his mental outlook was that of an old man, reminiscent, contemplative, brooding sentimentally over the past without any speculative interest in the future. Still short of his thirtieth year, Thackeray appears henceforward essentially a figure of tragedy.

After the first few months, his hopes of his wife's recovery must have been only the fever of despair. For a time he nursed her himself with the assistance of a faithful servant, a Scotswoman, who deferred her own marriage rather than forsake her master in his distress. From Ireland he took her to the Continent, first for hydropathic treatment in Germany and then to a private asylum in Paris, where she remained some four or five years, until she was brought back to England and placed in the care of respectable and reliable hands at Epsom, whence she was later removed to Leigh in Essex. In 1846, he told his mother that she was 'so well and calm' that he hoped she would be able to return to their home when the children were 'of an age sufft.' But she never sufficiently recovered for the advisability of her return to be seriously considered. Thackeray never relaxed his tender care, going regularly to visit her and even writing to her affectionate letters describing his doings, couched in simple, playful language such as he used when addressing their children.[1] Nathaniel Hawthorne, visiting London in 1856, was told by a third person that Thackeray was 'most beautifully tender and devoted to

[1] Such a letter, dated from Constantinople, 17th September 1844, and addressed to 'Mrs. Thackeray, chez M. le Docteur Purin, Rue des Batailles, Chaillot, Paris,' appears in *Unpublished Letters by W. M. Thackeray*, of which twenty-five copies were privately printed by Clement Shorter. London, 1916.

his wife, whenever she can be sensible of his attentions.'[1] Surviving her husband by more than thirty years, the poor lady died on 11th January 1894. Her eldest and only surviving daughter, who continued her father's devoted care of her after his death, remarked at the time: 'I should like to think the children could feel as little sorrow and as much love, when I go from them and their father.'

[1] *Passages from the English Note Books of Nathaniel Hawthorne.* London, 2 vols., 1870.

CHAPTER 5

§ 1

THE expenses of his wife's illness reduced Thackeray to a degree of poverty beyond the mere necessity for economy with which he had commenced his married life. Literally, he lived from hand to mouth, feverishly scribbling articles and stories, for which he had to pester publishers and editors for immediate payment. The memory of these years remained a nightmare for the rest of his life. He told his children how, one day, his servant interrupting him at work to ask him for money, he changed the last five pounds he possessed, and only eighteen months before his death, when he was describing in *Philip* the story of his own early struggles, he reminded his mother:

'Think of the beginning of the story of the "Little Sister" in the *Shabby Genteel Story* twenty years ago, and the wife ill, and the publisher refusing me £15, who owed me £13 10s., and *The Times*, to which I applied for a little more than five guineas for a week's work, refusing to give me more—and all that money difficulty ended, God be praised, and an old gentleman sitting in a fine house like the hero at the end of the story!'[1]

The proof-sheets of the *Whitey-Brown Paper Magazine* were flung heedlessly aside; he had no money to pay for the printing, far less the capital to risk in such a speculative enterprise. When Macrone issued the *Paris Sketch Book* during July 1840, a few copies were specially bound for the author, some for presentation to friends like FitzGerald,

[1] Biographical Introduction to *Philip*.

but most for sending to influential acquaintances who might review the book. To James Wilson, editor of the *Anti-Corn Law Circular*,[1] he wrote on 12th July:

'I don't ask you to treat this book according to its merits for I know very well that in a Government newspaper gentlemen do not take impartial views of things; but I do solemnly and pathetically adjure you to give poor Titmarsh a puff, for surely no man ever wanted one more than him.'

Six days later he told H. F. Chorley to 'name anything you wish as a proof of my gratitude. . . . Never was such a good-natured puff as that in the *Athenæum* of "Titmarsh." '[2] The book enjoyed no success, however, the publisher's announcement of a second edition being a subterfuge calculated to stimulate interest by the suggestion of a ready sale. Thackeray himself expressed the belief some years later that there might be found a number of unsold copies still in the publisher's stock.

His *Essay on the Genius of George Cruikshank*, having appeared in the June number of the *London and Westminster Review*, was published in volume form a month or two later on the responsibility of Henry Cole, who commissioned the article for the review. On sending him the manuscript in May, Thackeray remarked that, thinking over 'the hours of toil which have been spent in its composition I cannot but give it as my candid opinion that you have had all things considered a pretty good bargain for your money,' and when he was informed of the projection of its separate publication, he wrote to Cole on 31st July, suggesting that 'the author, who was paid ½ price in the first instance, should be paid something for his name and his permission to use his writing.' In the light of modern literary custom,

[1] *The Anti-Corn Law Circular* was converted by Wilson into the *Economist*, which was subsequently edited by his son-in-law, Walter Bagehot.

[2] *Henry Fothergill Chorley: Autobiography, Memoir, and Letters*, ed. H. G. Hewlett. London, 2 vols., 1873.

the claim appears legitimate, but apparently Thackeray derived no profit from the reprint, for he wrote again to Cole on returning from Margate: 'I suppose *Cruikshank* is useless by this time—but I was out of town—and only came back to be in great trouble and anxiety.'

From his parents he could expect no financial assistance, though the warning that he might borrow from his stepfather for the *Whitey-Brown Paper Magazine* suggests the possibility of a small occasional loan from that source. Major Carmichael-Smyth's financial losses, except for the crash of the *Constitutional*, are shrouded in mystery, but it is possible that his circumstances, sufficiently straitened to compel his retirement to Paris in 1837, were still further reduced in November 1841, when a bank, of which John Ritchie was a director, failed, causing Thackeray's Aunt Ritchie and her family to take up their residence in Paris also for reasons of economy.[1] After that time the income of Thackeray's parents amounted to no more than £200 a year, and witnessing their happiness and cheerfulness in adversity, he reflected sadly on this 'dismal end' to the careers of 'a famous beauty and a soldier who had been in twenty battles and led a half dozen of storming parties!' Besides assisting in the liquidation of his stepfather's liabilities, he had to sustain the expenses of his wife's maintenance under surveyance and the upbringing of his two little children. 'I wanted money sadly,' he told James T. Fields in 1859, 'but how little I got for my work! It makes me laugh at what *The Times* pays me now, when I think of the old days, and how much better I wrote for them then, and got a shilling where I now get ten.'

He placed the children in the charge of his mother, who, as he remarked nine years later, supplied to them the place of their own. Doubtless he chose an asylum in Paris for the treatment of his wife, because his parents would be able to keep him informed of her progress, while his work detained

[1] Cf. *The Ritchies in India*, by Gerald Ritchie. London, 1920.

him in London. Remaining there over Christmas and the New Year, he witnessed, in the company of Monckton Milnes, the state funeral of Napoleon, whose remains had been removed from St. Helena by order of Louis Philippe's government. In four days he wrote the fine example of graphically descriptive writing called *The Second Funeral of Napoleon*, which was promptly published at half a crown, with the ballad of 'The Chronicle of the Drum' appended, by Macrone's successor, Hugh Cunningham. The little book was well reviewed in the press, Thackeray expressing himself especially pleased with the notice in *The Times*, because he thought it would 'make people curious to get the book,' but it enjoyed a very limited sale, the sum of its royalties amounting to little more than the price of a magazine article. Writing in February to W. H. Thompson, FitzGerald asks:

'Have you read Thackeray's little book—*The Second Funeral of Napoleon*? If not, pray do; and buy it, and ask others to buy it: as each copy sold puts 7½d. in T.'s pocket: which is very empty just now, I take it. I think this book is the best thing he has done.'

FitzGerald, always the friend in need, unobtrusively offering sympathy and practical encouragement, was Thackeray's most intimate companion and counsellor in these dark days. After the failure of the *National Standard* and the loss of Thackeray's patrimony, he had commissioned drawings to encourage the hopeful artist; now he was canvassing his acquaintances to buy his friend's books and striving to comfort him in his calamity. After Thackeray's death he destroyed quantities of his letters, preserving only the innumerable sketches with which they were illustrated, and presenting them to his friend's daughter, for whose eyes he considered the letters themselves too intimate and painful. To him Thackeray confided his misery and despair, receiving in return the consolation of a serene philosophy or cheerful attempts to distract his mind, as when they had 'great laughing' together in the desolation of the Coram Street house over their speculations about James Spedding's forehead.

The foundation of an enduring friendship was laid by the generous sympathy of the Procters. Everybody in any way connected with literature and art sooner or later became a guest at their hospitable house in Upper Harley Street. Procter attained eminence as a poet and playwright in the 'twenties under the pseudonym of 'Barry Cornwall,' but he lives in the memory of posterity as having secured the affection of innumerable literary men from Lamb and Hazlitt to Carlyle and Coventry Patmore. 'An excellent man, whom everybody loves,' Crabb Robinson called him. His wife, who was Anne Skepper, a stepdaughter of Basil Montagu, and a brilliantly accomplished woman, became the first of those feminine correspondents, besides his mother, to whom Thackeray addressed long and intimate letters recounting his thoughts and daily doings. Like FitzGerald, she did her best to push the sales of *The Second Funeral of Napoleon*, though at the time she was troubled by private misfortune. Writing to thank her, Thackeray said:

'I found my letter, when half done, did not contain a word of sympathy for you, and only a long, selfish account of my own particular sorrows, and so tore it up. Don't be angry if I tell you that on reading your letter I felt glad that somebody else was miserable and lonely.'

In another letter, some months later, he reverts to this morbid mood:

'Please, when you write, not to give me any account whatever of any gaieties in which you indulge, or any sort of happiness falling to the share of you or anybody else. But if anybody meets with an accident, is arrested, ruined, has a wife run away with, if C. falls ill and is marked with the smallpox, do be so kind as to write me off word immediately.'

Then follows, inevitably upon any involuntary revelation of feeling, the self-deprecatory touch of sardonic humour: 'Despair, madam, is the word. Byronish, I hate mankind, and wear my shirt-collar turned down.' Apologising for some such outburst, he says:

> 'It was written by a very miserable fellow, who was quite unaccustomed to that kind of mood, and is not a whit happier now, only he bears his griefs more composedly. What won't a man bear with a little practice?—ruin, blindness, his legs off, dishonour, death of dearest friend, and what not.'

With the practice now experienced, he learned to bear every vicissitude with fortitude, for all his trials seemed trivial after the crushing blow of his wife's tragedy. In the last year of his life, when Jeaffreson published his novel called *Live It Down*, he remarked sadly it would be the very title for the story of his own life.

§ 2

His regular connection with *The Times* probably ceased with the death of its editor, Barnes, in May 1841, but he very soon replaced this loss of income by a similar engagement with the *Morning Chronicle*. He had also, in February, become a regular contributor to *Britannia*, a weekly paper, of which Samuel Carter Hall was the editor and the Rev. George Croly, author of *Salathiel*, the principal leader-writer. Hugh Cunningham advertised the publication of *Dinner Reminiscences*, but does not appear to have issued such a book, probably because he was disappointed with the sales of *The Second Funeral of Napoleon*, and

Thackeray succeeded in placing the manuscript with *Fraser*, in the June number of which it appeared as *Memorials of Gormandising*. As a working journalist, he now adopted the practice of keeping note-books, in which he jotted down ideas for articles and stories, notes on the books he was reading, and suggestive extracts from them. It was an effort to effect a working system of the sort laboriously perfected by Charles Reade, but he lacked Reade's dogged perseverance and persistent application, and, on one occasion, confesses that he 'found in my portfolio an article written two months ago, of which the existence was completely forgotten, and saw more and more the utility of keeping some memorandum.' Unmethodical and procrastinating, he was conscious of his defects and developed an almost fanatical habit of self-discipline, which pursued him to the last, for he confessed, when working on *Denis Duval*, to a superstition that whether well or ill, he must write at least one line every day.

His sole object was the making of money. So long as it paid, he welcomed any class of literary work. When somebody suspected him of being the author of Mrs. Gore's newly published novel, *Cecil*, he said to Mrs. Procter: 'How I wish I had written it, not for the book's sake, but for the filthy money, which I love better than fame. The fact is, I am about a wonderful romance, and I long for the day when the three volumes shall be completed.' He commenced this romance at the suggestion of 'Ingoldsby' Barham, who, early in the year, wrote to Richard Bentley, the publisher:

'Thackeray called here yesterday; wants to be busy, so I recommended him to treat with you for a three vol. historical novel, which he is very well inclined to do. From his reading I think he would succeed, especially if, as I suggested, it were of the Queen-Hoo Hall style, illustrated by his own woodcuts of costume, caricature,

&c., in the livelier parts. Turn this over in your mind.'[1]

Either Bentley turned it over without effect, or Thackeray himself rejected the idea, finding that the labour entailed by a three-volume novel would occupy too much valuable time. With every payment received immediately swallowed by his many expenses, he could not afford to wait six months or more for his money, and consequently concentrated upon work for magazines and newspapers, which provided a ready turn-over.

In May, Hugh Cunningham issued *Comic Tales and Sketches* in two volumes, the first containing the *Yellowplush Papers* from *Fraser*, with a preface dated 'Paris, 1 April 1841,' while the second consisted of *Major Gahagan* and *The Bedford Row Conspiracy* from the *New Monthly*, *The Professor* from *Bentley's Miscellany*, and *Stubbs's Calendar* from the *Comic Almanack*. Described on the title-page as 'edited and illustrated by Mr. Michael Angelo Titmarsh, Author of the *Paris Sketch Book*,' this publication, containing the pick of his periodical writings to date, represented an effort to identify himself in the eyes of the general reading public. Just as he subsequently regretted the carelessly vituperative character of his early satirical writings, he already lamented his exuberant adoption of Maginn's pseudonymous fashion. Readers who revelled in *Yellowplush* knew nothing of *Gahagan*, and neither had heard of Titmarsh. Seeing his friends, Dickens and Ainsworth, commanding a huge public for everything they chose to write, he revolted from the prospect of degenerating, like the brilliantly gifted Maginn, into a mere periodical writer, dependent upon the readers of an individual magazine. Assuming that he could enlist the readers of each magazine under the banner of Titmarsh as soon as

[1] *Life and Letters of the Rev. Richard Harris Barham,* by his son. London, 2 vols., 1870.

he was identified with the other pseudonyms, he calculated on a considerable sale, forgetting that a volume of magazine miscellanies offers little attraction, unless by an author already established in general estimation. When he approached *Fraser* for permission to reprint the *Yellowplush Papers*, it was given, he said, 'with a smile—almost an ironical one, as much as to say, "Much good may you get out of them." '[1] He got little enough, as he told his mother:

' "Titmarsh" has sold 140 copies, and be hanged to it—the donkeys of a public don't know a good thing when they get it. It has, however, been highly praised by the Press, and will serve to keep my name up, though a failure.'

The financial returns proved as negligible as in the case of the *Paris Sketch Book*, and surplus copies of this edition were sold in 1848, embellished with a new title-page, describing Mr. Titmarsh as the 'author of *Our Street*, *Vanity Fair*, etc.'

Rejected by *Blackwood*, *The Great Hoggarty Diamond* appeared serially in *Fraser* from September to December of this year. According to one authority,[2] Thackeray received a command from the editor to curtail the story,

[1] *Personal Recollections*, by H. Sutherland Edwards. London, 1900.

[2] *Personal Remembrances of Sir Frederick Pollock*. London, 2 vols., 1887. Pollock, who was the eldest son and heir of Lord Chief Baron Pollock, first baronet of that name, proves himself, though an eminent lawyer and 'sometime Queen's Remembrancer,' unfortunately careless of accuracy. He asserts that he dined with Thackeray in Coram Street, when his wife was present, the only other guest being Henry Reeve, 'early in 1842.' Probably the dinner actually took place two years earlier when Pollock was newly arrived in London from apprenticeship on the Northern Circuit. A casual acquaintance of some of Thackeray's intimate friends, he never knew the novelist well and provides an example of the minority, of which too much notice has been taken, which professed dislike of his character. In Pollock's case the reason is obvious. A model of respectable pomposity, he possessed a typically legal or judicial sense of humour. Having felt the rough edge of Carlyle's tongue, he comforted himself with the placid conviction that Carlyle did not mean half he said! He was incapable of realising when Thackeray was joking or in earnest. As Macready's executor he became the first editor of the actor's diaries, a task he characteristically accomplished with decorum, but without distinction.

because it failed to please the readers of the magazine, but probably it was submitted in the form originally written for *Blackwood* and required compression to conform with the less ample style of *Fraser*. John Sterling read the first two instalments 'with extreme delight,' exclaiming to his mother:

'What is there better in Fielding or Goldsmith? The man is a true genius; and, with quiet and comfort, might produce masterpieces that would last as long as any we have, and delight millions of unborn readers. There is more truth and nature in one of these papers than in all [Dickens]'s Novels together.'[1]

Sterling expressed an opinion shared in different degrees of enthusiasm by many of Thackeray's friends and a minority of discerning critics. They recognised his genius, as they recognised Carlyle's, though his work continually failed to attract general attention. Even when he eventually achieved success, he never attained the popularity of Dickens or Ainsworth, or even Bulwer or Lever; like Meredith and D. H. Lawrence in succeeding generations, his art appealed to the more cultured and intellectual class, which, being necessarily more critical and less impulsive than the indiscriminating masses, awakens less quickly and unanimously to enthusiasm and then affords a narrower though usually more enduring fame. A significant comment upon contemporary popularity is provided by the story of how, on his first visit to America, Thackeray asked the New York publisher, Harper, who was the most popular novelist of the day, and, hoping to hear his own name but expecting that of Dickens, he was astounded to learn that G. P. R. James easily headed the list of sales.

Besides *The Great Hoggarty Diamond*, Thackeray contributed to *Fraser* articles on 'Men and Pictures' in July,

[1] *Life of John Sterling*, by Thomas Carlyle. London, 1851.

'Men and Coats' in August, and almost certainly the 'Notes on the North What-D'Ye-Callem Election' in September and October, though none of the bibliographers has ever numbered this item among his writings. During the general election of July 1841 Thackeray visited the north to support the candidature of a Parisian friend, John Bowes, of Streatlam Castle and Gibside Park, County Durham, one of the two sitting members for the southern division of that county. On his return southwards, he was invited to break the journey at Fryston by Monckton Milnes, the Tory candidate for Pontefract, but the latter, having been called away to fulfil an engagement at York, asked him to defer his visit for a day or two. Thackeray replied on 10th July from Stockton-on-Tees:

'I had hoped to come to you on Monday, staying Tuesday and be-offing Wednesday; for I must have two days in London, and be back in Paris on Sunday. I shall look out for you Monday at the Grand Jury room at York, and regret heartily that I am not allowed to have a couple of days' quiet talk with you in your paternal groves, after the cursed racket of this infernal election. I shall not of course, conceal from you that the Tories in this Division have met with a heavy blow and great discouragement.'[1]

Milnes persuaded him to return from York to Fryston, where he spent several days before departing for town on his way to Paris. He wrote one day in September:

'Drew all the morning, or else read Marryat's *Joseph Rushbrook*, a good-natured, manly sort of book. Walked with Isabella by the Park de Monceaux, looking green and pretty, and on the plain of Monceaux, hearing the steam-engines. After dinner talked to my wife, and read article on Bowes' election.'

[1] *Life, Letters, and Friendships of Richard Monckton Milnes, First Lord Houghton*, by T. Wemyss Reid. London, 2 vols., 1891.

This article, consisting of four letters purporting to be written by Napoleon Putnam Wiggins, of Passimaquoddy Bay, to an aunt in Babylon, Kentucky, to whom he is 'under considerable pecuniary obligations, which he wishes naturally to increase,' contains all the humours of an election, narrated in Thackeray's best style of humorous satire and based upon his own experiences at Stockton—or 'Stuffington,' as Mr. Wiggins names the town. The laugh at N. P. Willis's expense lends credence to the probability of Thackeray's connection with the *Corsair* being terminated by some shabby treatment, most likely the absence of any further remittance beyond Willis's first payment on account.

Though spending much of his time in Paris in order to be with his wife, he retained the house in Great Coram Street in the hope that she might soon be well enough to return. Realising at length that there was no immediate, if eventual, prospect of her recovery, he finally vacated the house in 1843. Meanwhile, however, he resided there whenever affairs took him to London, and FitzGerald stayed with him whenever they were in town together. He went little into society at this time, but dined out occasionally at the Bullers', the Sterlings', the Carlyles', and Harrison Ainsworth's. With Ainsworth he always maintained cordial relations, in spite of occasional professional differences, and at his house he received a warm welcome in these years, not only from his host, but from the latter's motherless young daughters, in whom he visualised his own girls as they might be after the passing of a few years. Having broken with Bentley, whose *Miscellany* he had edited since Dickens's resignation, Ainsworth started his own magazine in February 1842, and Major Gahagan reappeared in the first number as the author of *Sultan Stork*. The story concluded in May and *An Exhibition Gossip* by Titmarsh appeared in June, after which Thackeray seems to have discontinued this connection.

In the spring of 1842 he applied for the vacant editorship

of the *Foreign Quarterly Review*, writing on 15th March to Chapman and Hall, who had recently acquired the proprietorship of the periodical:

'If you have a new editor, as you will no doubt, and unless you have a great man like Carlyle at the head of your undertaking, please to remember your humble servant. . . . I know a couple of languages, French and German, and could have Italian in another month, having already a smattering; and if your intention is not to have a pompous review, but a smart and lively one, I believe I should make as good an editor as another.'

In spite of an assurance in a postscript to the effect that he could be grave as well as gay in his writings, the publishers assumed that Titmarsh might be too 'smart and lively' as an editor, and appointed John Forster to the post. Thackeray's services, however, were enlisted as a regular contributor, his first article, a review of Victor Hugo's *Le Rhin*, appearing in the April number, while various others are ascribed to him during the next two years. It was possibly at this time that he obtained a post, perhaps as sub-editor, on the *Examiner* under Fonblanque and Forster, for which he received four pounds a week. This income, together with that derived from regular work on the *Morning Chronicle*, somewhat relieved his financial anxiety, and consequently his magazine activities became less miscellaneous. Of his former connections, that with *Fraser* alone continued; Fitz-Boodle made his bow in June, while, in March, appeared an amusing article on 'Dickens in France,' prompted by a dramatic version of *Nicholas Nickleby* on the Paris stage and poking fun at Jules Janin, the dramatic critic of the *Journal des Débats*, with whom he was familiarly acquainted.

His only other occasional work for periodicals during 1842 comprised his first contributions to *Punch*. Douglas Jerrold and Henry Mayhew had succeeded, during the previous year, in persuading a number of their Fleet Street acquaintances, including an engraver and a printer, to establish a paper on the lines of the Paris *Charivari*, according to the plan conceived by them in company with Thackeray in Paris some six years earlier. Except Jerrold,[1] none of the writers engaged yet possessed any reputation, and as Titmarsh would have been a valuable acquisition, the collaborators naturally approached Thackeray, thinking that he would the more readily join them since he had participated in the original proposition. Mayhew was particularly eager to secure his services, but, the paper's financial stability being very insecure during the first eighteen months of its existence, Thackeray hesitated to waste time on work which might prove unprofitable. Moreover, his friends advised him against entering upon a connection which, being unassociated with any reputable writers, might discredit him, in the event of the paper's failure, with the better-class periodicals. As late as 22nd May, FitzGerald asked Pollock to 'tell Thackeray not to go into *Punch* yet.' Presumably he had heard rumours that Thackeray was in danger of succumbing to Mayhew's persuasions and these were quickly confirmed, for *The Legend of Jawbrahim-Heraudee*, ascribed to Thackeray, appeared on 18th June, and the first of *Miss Tickletoby's Lectures on English History* on 2nd July. *Miss Tickletoby*, which supplied the idea of *The Comic History of England*, subsequently devised by Leech and Gilbert à Beckett, did not please the contributors of *Punch*, at whose desire the series was discontinued at the eleventh number. On 27th September Thackeray wrote to them from Ireland:

[1] Maginn, who died 21st August 1842, was an inmate of the Fleet Prison during the autumn of 1841. Mayhew is said to have visited him there and even to have resided for a week within the walls to assist Maginn and H. P. Grattan, another resident, in the writing of the first *Punch Almanac*. The scene in *Pendennis* where Shandon compiles the prospectus of the *Pall Mall Gazette* probably owes its origin to this story.

'Your letter, containing an enclosure of £25, has been forwarded to me, and I am obliged to you for the remittance. Mr. Lemon has previously written to me to explain the delay, and I had also received a letter from Mr. Landells, who told me, what I was sorry to learn, that you were dissatisfied with my contributions to *Punch.* I wish that my writings had the good fortune to please everyone; but all I can do, however, is to do my best, which has been done in this case, just as much as if I had been writing for any more dignified periodical.

But I have no wish to continue the original agreement made between us, as it is dissatisfactory to you, and, possibly, injurious to your work; and shall gladly cease "Mrs. Tickletoby's Lectures," hoping that you will be able to supply her place with some more amusing and lively correspondent.

I shall pass the winter either in Paris or in London where, very probably, I may find some other matter more suitable to the paper, in which case I shall make another attempt upon *Punch.*'

During the following year he contributed half a dozen trivial features at fitful intervals, but only in the new year of 1844 commenced his regular connection with *Punch.*

§ 3

When applying for the editorship of the *Foreign Quarterly* in March, Thackeray offered to defer a projected trip to Ireland if he received the appointment. Interest in the Irish question was then at its height, the agitation for repeal of the union combining with the Chartist movement to provide the most anxious problems confronting Sir Robert Peel's newly established government. Threats of rebellion in Ireland were ultimately defied by the arrest of Daniel O'Connell in November 1843, an event occurring some six months after the publication of the *Irish Sketch Book.* The idea of an Englishman visiting the disaffected country to examine, with an open mind, the social conditions, character, and feelings of the people, and to describe impressions obtained by personal observation, appealed to the publishers as an attractive proposition, and, as few writers possessed better qualifications than the most popular author of magazine articles on Paris and Parisian affairs, Chapman and Hall commissioned Titmarsh to undertake the task.

Armed with letters of introduction, mostly supplied by FitzGerald, he set out in the middle of June, travelling by a pleasantly devious route through Wales and arriving in Dublin at the beginning of July. Writing to FitzGerald, who lamented his laziness for not accompanying him, he says:

'What the deuce are you in the dumps for? Don't flatter yourself but that I'll get on very well without you. Such a place as this hotel is itself enough to make a chapter about, such filth and liberality. O my dear friend, pray heaven on bended knee that to-night when I go to bed I find no * * * Turn over. Have you ever remarked that the little ones of all sting worst?'

The itinerary of his journey, with the sights he saw and the deductions he drew, is inimitably described in his book. He stayed with FitzGerald's uncle, Peter Purcell, an eminent adversary of the agitators for repeal, at Halverstown, Kildare, whose home and estate he describes in Chapter II of the *Sketch Book*. He highly enjoyed his stay with the Purcells: 'Nothing but laughing and sunshine from morning till night along the road,' he told his mother, 'and when I parted from them, I felt as if I had known them all my life,' who, having entertained him with the sights and society of the neighbourhood, escorted him to Cork and introduced him to Father Theobald Mathew, the celebrated apostle of temperance, 'a fine fellow, simple, straightforward, manly, and with one idea,' who figures in the fifth chapter. Proceeding west alone through Bantry, Limerick, and Galway, he returned to the Purcells in Kildare (Chapter xxv) before going on to Dundalk, where he introduced himself to a distant cousin, the Rev. Elias Thackeray, whose parochial affairs he describes in the next chapter. From Dublin he made solitary excursions to Belfast, to Donegal, and to Bantry Bay, confessing to feelings of homesickness on visiting the lonely grandeur of the Giant's Causeway, both in a letter to his mother and in the relative published passage. Reserving his last chapter for Dublin, he remained there for some weeks to write a considerable part of the book, enjoying the hospitality of several friends, among whom were Anthony Sterling, then attached to the Lord-Lieutenant's staff, and Charles Lever.

To Lever, then living at Templeogue House, just outside Dublin, Thackeray received a letter of introduction from a mutual friend. Already celebrated as the author of *Harry Lorrequer* and *Charles O'Malley*, Lever was the lion of literary Dublin and entertained on a lavish scale in a manner becoming a *bon vivant*. He invited Thackeray to dinner in company with two military men, Captain Siborne and Major Dwyer, the latter of whom wrote his reminiscences of the evening.[1] Being informed by their host that Thackeray 'wrote under the *nom de plume* of Michael Angelo Titmarsh, that he was what is called a humorist, had been a good deal on the Continent, and meant to write about Ireland,' Dwyer was disappointed to find him 'at first reserved, earnest, and quiet,' evidently expecting him to behave like a pantomime comedian, ebullient,

[1] 'Reminiscences of Lever and Thackeray, by Major D—' appear in an appendix to *The Life of Charles Lever*, by W. J. Fitzpatrick. London, 2 vols., 1879. This book upholds the tradition of mid-Victorian biography for careless inaccuracy, rambling irrelevance, and disingenuous partiality. Realising something of its shortcomings, Fitzpatrick issued a revised edition in one volume (London, 1896) in which he incorporated the gist of Dwyer's reminiscences with his text and included some fresh information about Lever's relations with Thackeray, mainly derived from letters lent to him by Frederick Chapman, of Chapman and Hall, which, unfortunately, he omitted to print at length.

loquacious, and loud in 'some external manifestation of his supposed humoristic proclivities.' The good major, in fact, regarded the visitor rather as a curious animal, being both a tourist and a journalist, and felt disgruntled by his courteous manners in declining to talk about himself and studiously seeking to converse upon subjects agreeable to his host. The confession, occurring casually in the course of conversation, that he was a member of the Reform Club, completed Thackeray's degradation in the estimation of the major, whose politics conformed with military convention. He immediately conceived that Thackeray's mission was 'to write up something in the interests of his party,' and considered all his opinions as characteristic of Radical tendencies. Nevertheless, he exhibits an occasional flash of shrewd perception:

'He abhorred boasting and exaggeration to such an extent as to be very frequently tempted to disbelieve the naked truth and to substitute for it something which, although not exactly fictitious, was but a clipped and shorn distortion of reality; this was one of his weaknesses in so far as it constantly jarred with the great kindliness of his heart; on the other hand, it incontestably strengthened the poignancy of his satire and rendered it perhaps more acceptable to the general public.'

Here Dwyer tries to express his consciousness of Thackeray's invariable habit of tempering his enthusiasm with humorously satirical reflections in self-conscious deprecation of an excessive display of genuine feeling, a characteristic which, both in his writings and his conversation, adverse critics condemned as cynicism, and, contrary to Dwyer's conjecture, antagonised popular opinion against his novels.

Acting in accordance with the wishes of Lever, who lost no opportunity of assisting his brother-writer in the acquisition of data for his task, Dwyer accompanied Thackeray on several excursions as a guide and mentor.

His heavy turn of humour never suspected Thackeray's sense of fun when, on visiting Phœnix Park to watch a military review, he affected terror of being ridden down in a cavalry charge, like Mr. Pickwick by the infantry of Colonel Bulder, and of the approach of an officer of dragoons, lest he came to warn them off a place where they should not have been. The whole scene presents a Pickwickian aspect, of which the major reveals himself serenely unconscious. He describes how, 'thinking that my office of cicerone, which Lever imposed on me, entailed the duty of pointing out the general object and nature of the movements that were being carried out, I endeavoured to do so in few words,' and Thackeray listened with polite attention until, at last, he 'begged of me not to take any more trouble on the subject, as he felt that he should never understand the least about these matters,' so off they go to see the ladies instead. With Lever, he accompanied Thackeray to Maynooth, and, observing his 'sardonic smile of utter derision and contempt' when contemplating the sordid squalor of the place, he ventured to remark that 'Maynooth certainly was most desolate-looking,' and felt pain and disappointment when 'Thackeray shut me up, by replying that Trinity College was not a whit better in respect of cleanliness.' Imputing to him 'dislike of Protestant ascendancy and Saxon supremacy in Ireland,' 'distrust of the Celt,' and a tendency to rate too highly the Roman Catholics, Dwyer declares him 'unable to conceal his contempt for the Irish,' and believed that his feelings reflected 'more of antagonism to one side than of sympathy with the other.' Dwyer confesses that he never read the *Sketch Book*, which, he fancied, must have betrayed 'too strong evidence of its author's scepticism,' and 'could hardly have been written *con amore*.' He would have been surprised if he had done so, for, as the reviewer in *Ainsworth's Magazine* remarked, the book reveals 'a man of acute observation, of warm sympathies, and excellent humour.'

Necessarily void of temporary political bias, it discloses a mind of liberal principles, practical philosophy, and lucid vision; in later times Thackeray would certainly have been a rabid advocate of Home Rule.

With Lever he established a friendly intimacy. They had much in common—both were convivial, loving good food and wine, lively conversation and provocative argument, both had a highly developed sense of humour and a fondness for spirited fun. Dwyer relates how he and Siborne sat entranced, while each of the novelists exerted himself to entertain the other, how they were convulsed with laughter at Thackeray's talent for mimicry, and how 'he was fond of exhibiting his French pronunciation' and of 'caricaturing very cleverly that of his own countrymen, the English.' They discussed together the battle of Waterloo, Lever's treatment of which, in *Charles O'Malley*, Thackeray thought 'too imaginative and high-flown,' and Dwyer remembered him remarking that 'something might be made of Waterloo,' adding his belief that he acquired much of the materials for the Brussels scenes of *Vanity Fair* from his friendly relations with the regimental mess at Newry. Lever told his cousin that Thackeray was 'the most good-natured man alive,' and Thackeray, impressed with Lever's brilliance, tried to persuade him to leave Dublin and settle in London, pointing out that he was at present surrounded by men of inferior ability and that he would find greater scope for his attainments at the hub of affairs. He offered every assistance within his power, but Lever, while appreciating his generosity, remarked privately that he was 'like a man struggling to keep his head over water, and who offers to teach his friend to swim.' Thackeray advised him with sincerity, for he himself had steadily refused, even in the face of poverty, to accept a sinecure outside London, believing that his chances of success lay in maintaining close touch with affairs in the capital. They parted on excellent terms, and the *Irish Sketch Book*, the first of Thackeray's works to appear with his own name, was dedicated to Lever, 'a friend from whom I have received a hundred acts of kindness and cordial hospitality.' Like a subsequent compliment to himself, the dedication was not attended by entirely pleasant consequences to its recipient, for Lever was credited with having suggested many of the conceptions which offended both parties in Ireland, each of which found much in the book reflecting unfavourably upon themselves.

Published in May 1843, the book received favourable notices in most of the magazines. The long and laudatory notice in *Fraser* for June was apparently written by Percival Leigh, one of the *Punch* fraternity, to whom Thackeray wrote:

'Did Leech impart to you the modest service I want of you? A notice of half a dozen pages for *Fraser* will be accepted and acceptable. Not a puff, you understand—hit as hard as you like, but in a good-natured way, and so as not to break bones.'

He had no illusions about the impartiality or integrity of reviewers, having learned to fly as a fledgeling from the nest of Maginn, who, on the publication of Lockhart's *Spanish Ballads*, confiding the information that his influence with Croker and the *Quarterly* was such that the periodical would accept any article he offered, regretted that he himself possessed insufficient knowledge of Spanish literature to deal adequately with the book, and suggested that Lockhart might write the review himself! To his mother, he wrote:

'The book is going pretty well. The Irish are in a rage about it. . . . "Boz" has written me a letter of compliments, and the literary people like it generally very much; not, I am afraid, White, who promises to review it in *Blackwood*, and pulled a very long face the other day when I met him.'

FitzGerald, who had himself gone to Ireland the year after his friend's visit, did his best, as usual, to advertise the book among his friends, and wrote from Dublin to the painter, Samuel Laurence:

'The first volume of Titmarsh's *Ireland* is at 39 Portland Place. . . . I wish you would ask for it there and get it. . . . It is all true. I ordered a bath here when I got in: the waiter said it was heated to ninety degrees, but it was scalding: he next locked me up in the room instead of my locking him out.'

But, though attended by more success than his previous books, the *Irish Sketch Book* aroused only the casual interest generally accorded to a volume of travels, heightened a little by topical curiosity about a subject attracting much attention in parliament and the press. Such a book might add to his credit as a magazine-writer, but advanced him no further towards a place in popular estimation.

CHAPTER 6

§ 1

THIRTY years afterwards, FitzGerald told Fanny Kemble that he remembered her sister, Adelaide Sartoris, coming in her brougham to bid Thackeray to dinner when he was staying with him in Coram Street—'*Jorum* Street, he called it'—in 1843.[1] It must have been very early in the year, if FitzGerald's memory for dates was not at fault, for Henry Vizetelly found him in March, living over a shop in Jermyn Street, 'eight or ten doors from Regent-street, and within a few doors of the present Museum of Geology.'[2]

'Knocking at the private entrance, a young lodging-house slavey in answer to my inquiries bade me follow her upstairs. I did so, to the very top of the house, and after my card had been handed in, I was asked to enter the front apartment, where a tall slim individual between thirty and thirty-five years of age, with a pleasant smiling countenance and a bridgeless nose, and clad in a dressing-gown of decided Parisian cut, rose to receive me. When he stood up, the low pitch of the room caused him to look even taller than he really was, and his actual height was well over six feet. This, then, was Michael Angelo Titmarsh. . . . The apartment was an exceedingly plainly furnished bedroom, with common rush-seated chairs and painted French bedstead, and with neither looking-glass nor prints on the bare, cold, cheerless-looking walls. On the table from which Mr. Thackeray had risen, a white cloth was spread, on which was a frugal breakfast-tray—

[1] *Letters of Edward Fitzgerald to Fanny Kemble,* ed. W. Aldis Wright. London, 1895.

[2] *Glances Back Through Seventy Years,* by Henry Vizetelly. London, 2 vols., 1893.

a cup of chocolate and some dry toast—and huddled together at the other end were writing materials, two or three numbers of *Fraser's Magazine*, and a few slips of manuscript.'

Vizetelly came, with an introduction from G. W. Nickisson, James Fraser's successor as publisher of *Fraser's Magazine*, to secure his services as art critic and literary reviewer to the *Pictorial Times*, an illustrated weekly he was starting in opposition to the newly established *Illustrated London News*. Thackeray agreed to 'write upon art, to review such books as he might fancy, and to contribute an occasional article on the opera,' eagerly embracing an offer of three guineas for a couple of columns weekly.

This connection continued from the first number of the paper, published on 18th March 1843, until he left England for the Near East in August of the following year. His last identified contribution, a review of Disraeli's *Coningsby*, appeared on 25th May 1844. This short notice of about a thousand words fairly represents Thackeray as a reviewer. Caustic and concise, he contrives to deride both the author and the novel, while describing the salient features of the story in a manner so informative and provocative that the reader of the review must eagerly seek the book. He reveals himself an apt pupil of Maginn in the playful art of back-handed puffing. Calling the author a coxcomb, he shows how the reader may think and laugh at him, as well as with him, before proceeding to point out the piquant personalities of the characterisation—the Marquis of Monmouth being a caricature of Lord Hertford, Lord Eskdale of Lord Lonsdale, Lord Henry Sydney of Lord John Manners, Beaumanoir of Belvoir, and so on. Identifying Mr. Rigby with John Wilson 'Joker,' he declares that 'a better portrait of a parasite has never been written since Juvenal's days.' Thackeray on *Coningsby* has the curiosity of an antique gem, equally valuable as a contemporary commentary upon the novel and for its biographical significance in regard to the reviewer. In *Vanity Fair*, Lord Hertford reappears as the Marquis of Steyne, Lord Lonsdale as Lord Colchicum, and Croker as the sycophant Wenham: so much of its conception germinated from the seed of *Coningsby*. The recognisable caricatures of actual personalities, subsequently considered an odious feature of Thackeray's fiction, owed their origin to Disraeli. Seeking a saleable proposition for a novel, Thackeray may have remembered the busy gossip in the clubs when, as he himself describes, the volumes of *Coningsby* were eagerly devoured and 'everybody recognises everybody's portrait.'

Disraeli and Thackeray were nodding acquaintances; they may have met at Ainsworth's or in company with Monckton Milnes. Though the review in the *Pictorial Times* may have been reckoned commercially advantageous to *Coningsby*, the personal remarks were scarcely calculated to recommend the reviewer kindly to the novelist. When, three years afterwards, *Punch* published the inimitable parody of *Codlingsby*, Disraeli accepted an affront which, having rankled for thirty years, was avenged by the character of St. Barbe in *Endymion*. He is said never to have addressed Thackeray voluntarily again, and John Hollingshead saw them pass each other without acknowledgment at the Exhibition of 1862.

Associated with the *Pictorial Times* were several of the *Punch* staff, notably Douglas Jerrold, Mark Lemon, and Gilbert à Beckett, who thus enjoyed ample opportunities for appreciating Thackeray's qualities as a colleague. By this time Bradbury and Evans had acquired the proprietary rights of *Punch*, and, having established the paper on a sound commercial basis, were able to offer attractive terms to their contributors. At Christmas 1843 Thackeray was finally persuaded to join the staff, succeeding to the seat of Albert Smith, whose contributions had been for some time considered unsatisfactory, and for seven years few of *Punch's* weekly numbers appeared without an article from his pen. 'It was a good day for himself, the journal, and the world,' said Shirley Brooks, a subsequent editor of the paper, 'when Thackeray found *Punch.*' As Mr. Spielmann remarks, his work covered every corner of *Punch's* field—'burlesque of history and parodies of literature, ballads and songs, stories and jokes, papers and paragraphs, pleasantry and pathos, criticisms and conundrums, travels in the East and raillery in the West, political skits and social satire.' He possessed an unique value to the paper by his equal facility with pencil and pen, illustrating his own writings and occasionally supplying cartoons, and shared with Leech and Jerrold in the major honours of *Punch's* rapid rise to popularity and unparalleled success.

Every week the staff assembled for dinner, the principal object of the gathering being the selection of a subject for the political cartoon. In the summer the dinners took place at Greenwich; in the winter they were usually held at the *Punch* office, but occasionally at a chosen hotel or tavern, notably the Bedford in Covent Garden, a favourite resort of Thackeray's. An eighteenth-century atmosphere pervaded these gatherings, at which the viperish Jerrold and the scholarly Taylor exchanged conversation with Mark Lemon, serene, shrewd, and inscrutable, à Beckett of the nimble wit, and Percival Leigh, while Thackeray beamed humorously through his spectacles, interpolating provocative comments and playful jokes. As the evening waned and the acerbity of Jerrold's wit became aggravated by wine, the revellers sought refuge in song and Thackeray invariably rendered his ballad of 'The Three Sailors' and 'The Mahogany Tree.' Even after the termination of his active connection with the paper, he frequently attended these convivial evenings, at which a seat, latterly on the presiding publisher's right hand, was always reserved for him.

The Bohemian character of the early *Punch* dinners

represented the type of entertainment in which Thackeray habitually indulged. Deprived of domestic amenities by his wife's affliction, he sought amusement and recreation in clubs and taverns. Essentially gregarious, he loved good company, and would sit up to any hour rather than break up a convivial party. 'Solitude,' he once told his mother, 'creates a muzziness and incoherency in me.' In these days, when his impecuniosity and uncertain position denied him the *entrée* to the society for which birth and culture had designed him, he derived consolation from the company of journalistic Bohemians, the Hoolans and Doolans of *Pendennis*. Jeaffreson observed that he was probably 'the last greatly eminent man of letters who preferred the old-world tavern to the modern club-house,' a preference undoubtedly fostered by romantic notions accruing from his study of the eighteenth century. He was at his best in the smoke-laden atmosphere of snug coffee-rooms after a good dinner, exchanging anecdotes of travel and reminiscences of early literary and artistic life over wine and cigars. Most of the memoir-writers who recorded their impressions of his personality in this environment knew him only in the latter years of his life, and consequently regarded him with the respectful admiration of youthful aspirants for an established celebrity. These, like Jeaffreson, were charmed by 'his genial manner, his conversational communicativeness, and social kindness.' Vizetelly, however, speaking of the time when Thackeray was working for the *Pictorial Times*, found him an equally agreeable companion:

'He never appeared to me to shine in conversation, and he most certainly made no kind of effort to do so—never in fact talked for effect, and, indeed, never usurped any large share of the conversation. Ordinarily, he would interpose occasional quaint humorous comments, and would show himself far more tolerant than men of his capacity usually are of bores. Whenever the talk grew dull and wearying, he would content himself by filliping it up with some witty or shrewd satirical remark, and turn it into a new channel. None of the little aside sermons which he preached in his books by any chance fell from his lips. At this period of his career his placid temper and pleasant courtesy, in spite of the mild sarcasms in which he indulged, charmed all who came in contact with him.'

At the height of his celebrity, impartial hearers discovered little alteration in his manner. Describing how he poured out anecdote after anecdote from his 'treasures of wit and sarcasm,' Max Müller observed that, though 'he used plenty of vinegar and cayenne pepper . . . there was always a flavour of kindness and good-nature, even in his most cutting remarks.'[1] Soon after the appearance of *Vanity Fair*, Albert Smith wrote:

'Last night I met Thackeray at the Cyder Cellars, and we stayed there until three in the morning. He is a very jolly fellow, and no "High Art" about him.'[2]

Yet Thackeray disliked Smith for his bumptious self-assertion and boisterous manner, and Vizetelly remarked that, in his company, 'he treated him with contemptuous toleration, showing him outward civility, but the occasional sarcastic observations which he permitted to escape him, disclosed his true sentiments respecting Albert's mountebank ways.'

The Cyder Cellars, where Smith encountered him, was a favourite resort of Thackeray's and figures in *Pendennis* as the 'Back Kitchen.' Situated next to the stage-door of the Adelphi Theatre in Maiden Lane, its proprietor in Thackeray's early days was a certain Evans, who subsequently moved to Evans's Supper-Rooms in the basement of an hotel on the Piazza in Covent Garden. The

[1] *Auld Lang Syne*, by F. Max Müller. London, 1898.
[2] *Memories of My Time*, by George Hodder. London, 1870.

latter resort furnished the original of 'The Cave of Harmony' in *The Newcomes*, but 'little Nadab' belonged to the Cyder Cellars, his prototype being a Jew named Sloman, who receives mention in the parody of Wordsworth, addressed to the opera-singer Braham, in the *National Standard* for 11th May 1833. Maginn and Mahony introduced Thackeray to the Cyder Cellars as Warrington introduced Pendennis to the Back Kitchen, and frequenters of the tavern in the 'forties regarded him, though little more than thirty, almost as a veteran, on account of his former intimacy with men whose names already received the homage of fabulous legend. His habit of wistful reminiscence, nourished by melancholy reflection, thus received encouragement even in moments of recreation and revelry, and gathering irresistible force with the passage of time, like the influence of a narcotic drug, ultimately found expression in the painful pathos which shed soft lights of human tenderness in the *Roundabout Papers* and cast gloomy shadows, irritatingly tedious, upon *Philip* and *Lovel the Widower*.

As Dr. John Brown remarked,[1] he was never morose—he loved life with all its pleasures, whims, and oddities too well for that. His sense of humour saved him equally from maudlin self-pity and savage misanthropy. Calamity and disappointment affected him rather as they affected Charles Lamb than Swift. Never morbid nor bitter, his absence of illusions and susceptibility of understanding engendered a capacity for tender sympathy almost womanly, and he laughs and cries with the subjects of his satire rather than at them. In the selfless devotion of his life, his fortitude calls for comparison with that of Lamb, from whose example he may have derived some comfort, for he once exclaimed to FitzGerald, putting a letter of Lamb's to his forehead, 'Saint Charles!' Of all writers only Lamb might have

[1] *John Leech and Other Papers* (*Horæ Subsecivæ*, Third Series), by John Brown, M.D. Edinburgh, 1882.

written, at the age of thirty-five, a lyric so mournfully sentimental as 'The Ballad of Bouillabaisse,' replete with the melancholy reminiscence of a lonely old man revisiting a haunt of his happy youth.

§ 2

Spending as much of his time as possible in Paris, where, living with his parents and his children, he was able to visit his wife regularly, his lodgings at 27 Jermyn Street served merely as an anchorage during his fleeting visits to London. He dined out at his clubs or a tavern, where he returned the hospitality of those friends who invited him to their houses. To one such dinner he invited Dickens, Ainsworth, and Maclise, but neither Dickens nor Ainsworth could attend and Thackeray wrote to the latter that 'as I can't have it without my two roaring animals . . . the great Titmarsh banquet is hereby postponed.' To Maclise he wrote:

'From the lamentable state in which I left you on Sunday evening you have probably quite forgotten your engagement to dine with me. . . . Ainsworth and Boz won't come and press for delay. Well, then, though I know from the state of the banker's account at present that next week there won't probably be five shillings wherewith to buy dinner—yet let them have their will.'

On another occasion his guests at a tavern dinner included Maclise, Forster, Emerson Tennent, Evans Crowe, Saville Morton, and Tennyson, while Samuel Lover, the Irish novelist and ballad-writer looked in, and being introduced to Tennyson, expressed his delight in meeting a brother-poet. Tennyson, like Thackeray, was at that time recognised as a genius only by a select minority of critics, and his financial and social position was rather inferior, for he lacked the numerous friends in the literary world possessed by Thackeray. Forster omitted to mention how he and Dickens became acquainted with Tennyson, but it was possibly by means of Thackeray's introduction. On the evidence of Morton, who was equally the friend of Tennyson and Thackeray, Maclise at least had never before met the poet, and the personnel of the party suggests that Thackeray good-naturedly selected his guests from those likely to be of some service to Tennyson.

Perhaps it was on this occasion that, on Tennyson launching an enthusiastic eulogy of Catullus, Thackeray impatiently remarked, 'I do not rate him highly; I could do better myself,' and then wrote the next morning:

'My dear Alfred,—'I woke at two o'clock, and in a sort of terror at a certain speech I had made about Catullus. When I have dined, sometimes I believe myself to be equal to the greatest painters and poets. That delusion goes off; and then I know what a small fiddle mine is and what small tunes I play upon it. It was very generous of you to give me an opportunity of recalling a silly speech; but at the time I thought I was making a perfectly simple and satisfactory observation. Thus far I must unbus'm myself: though why should I be so uneasy at having made a conceited speech? It is conceited not to wish to seem conceited.'[1]

Tennyson's comment was: 'It was impossible to have written in a more generous spirit. No one but a noble-hearted man could have written such a letter.' It might equally well be construed that none but a supremely self-conscious man would write such a letter. Nor was this an isolated instance of his remorse for a rash utterance; he wrote to Macready during his second trip to America, explaining how he had intended, in his speech at the dinner given in honour of his departure, to pay a compliment to the actor in a phrase which might have been otherwise

[1] *Alfred Lord Tennyson: A Memoir*, by his son. London, 2 vols., 1897.

interpreted. Painfully aware of his own faults, he mercilessly depicted them in the character of Pendennis, showing him cynical, conceited, and self-opinionated, as he conceived himself to have been in his youth.

An incident illustrative of his excessive sensitiveness, providing a curious parallel with the notorious affair of Yates and the Garrick Club near the end of his life, occurred at this time. In *Fraser* for April 1843 appeared an article entitled *Illustrations of Discount*, containing the following unmistakable caricature:

'The first person we met in the coffee-room was Bill Crackaway, one whom we have always looked upon as a bird of ill omen. His long ungainly person is crowned with a face which Dame Nature must have fashioned just after making a bad debt, and therefore, in the worst of tempers. A countenance of preternatural longitude is imperfectly relieved by a nose on which the partial hand of Nature has lavished every bounty—length, breadth, thickness, all but a—bridge; a mouth that seemed suddenly arrested in the act of whistling, and from its conformation could only eliminate a sinister sneer, but was physically incapable of the candour of an honest laugh, which, with a most inhuman squint, gave a rare finish to the *os frontis* of this Corinthian capital of our club.'

The writer proceeds to refer in an uncomplimentary manner to the faint lisp which characterised Thackeray's pronunciation, and to ascribe to him, apparently without foundation, the editorship of 'a pseudo-philosophical magazine' and the business of a bill-broker in the city. Thackeray wrote on 8th April to Nickisson, the publisher of *Fraser*, demanding that the author of the article, whom he identified as Deady Keane, should be compelled to discontinue his contributions, or he himself, 'one of the oldest and I believe one of the best of your contributors,' would sever his connection with the magazine.

*

'As in a private house or an inn,' he wrote, 'if any person with no other provocation but that of drunkenness or natural malice should take a fancy to call me by foul names, I should have a right to appeal to the host and request him to have the individual so offending put out of doors—I may similarly complain to you that I have been grossly insulted in your magazine.'[1]

He declared that his demand was intended 'not in the least as an act of retaliation against Mr. Keane, but as an act of justice I owe to myself and which is forced upon me.' The reflections upon his conduct in the Yates case might be applied only less aptly in this instance. He had pursued Bulwer with ridicule for years and was soon to call Disraeli a coxcomb; why then should he object to a taste of similar medicine? His answer appears in the extract quoted from his letter to Nickisson; he would not suffer personalities at his expense under the roof which sheltered himself and his vilifier. He attacked Bulwer in *Fraser* and *Punch*, both of which periodicals presented a generally hostile attitude to that author, who had no connection with either. Moreover, he had no friendship with Bulwer, whereas Deady Keane had shaken hands with him, as he informs Nickisson, only a fortnight before the appearance of the article. His conduct towards Yates fifteen years later was entirely consistent; he resented the aspersions of a fellow-clubman as he resented those of a journalistic colleague, conceiving them an act of treachery and a breach of etiquette. The *tu quoque* argument of Yates's adherents that Thackeray himself offended in the same way by caricaturing Andrew Arcedeckne, a member of the Garrick Club, as Foker in *Pendennis* scarcely applied, for, so far from being his friend, Arcedeckne irritated Thackeray by his familiarity, cheerfully hailing him as 'Thack,' although he received repeated

[1] Reprinted from the *Bookworm* for May 1890, this letter, dated 'April 8, 1843,' appears in *The Life of William Makepeace Thackeray*, by Lewis Melville. London, 2 vols., 1899.

rebuffs from the sharp edge of Thackeray's tongue. A pupil of Maginn might hardly have been expected to insist upon such niceties, but Maginn was only his literary master. His moral upbringing was received from the Anglo-Indian circle of his family, particularly from his stepfather, whose quixotically punctilious ideas of honour were rehabilitated in Colonel Newcome.

His attitude achieved an effect similar to the later case; Keane apparently contributed no more while Thackeray wrote regularly for *Fraser*. His connection with the magazine continued to January 1847, by which time nearly all the original contributors had long since faded from its pages. The main prop of his career as a periodical writer, *Fraser* published, among other articles, the *Fitz-Boodle Papers* during 1843 and *Barry Lyndon* in the following year, finally losing its valuable contributor only when he became fully occupied with the issue of novels in monthly parts.

He appears to have spent most of the spring of 1843 in London, from his engagement by Vizetelly early in March to the date of the Greenwich dinner on 20th May, given in honour of John Black, the retiring editor of the *Morning Chronicle*, on which occasion he acted as host in company with Dickens, Forster, Fonblanque, Maclise, Macready, Charles Buller, and others. He spent the remainder of the year in Paris, except for a visit to London in November 'to have his eyes doctored,' when FitzGerald came up to town from the country to stay ten days with him. In October he was alone at his grandmother's house in the Champs Élysées, his family being away at Montmorenci.

'As I go thither once or twice a week, and lose a whole day in the journey to and fro,' he tells his Aunt Ritchie, 'I can't afford to give up more of my precious time, but am obliged to remain at home for the rest of the week working, or pretending to work. I believe I am writing a novel, and shall be delighted when the day arrives when you shall be able to read this remarkable production.'

The mediæval romance, proposed by Barham, had long been laid aside, but the idea of an historical novel remained in his mind, though he eventually decided upon the more attractive period of the eighteenth century. Doubtless he began with some intention of imitating Ainsworth, whose habit of absorbing the atmosphere of his period by diligent reading he emulated, not only in this instance, but when he came to write *Esmond*, *The Virginians*, and *Denis Duval*. Eighteen months before, when he was reviewing Victor Hugo for the *Foreign Quarterly*, he told FitzGerald that he had 'read no good books or novels to talk of, but scores of volumes of history.' Failing to interest Bentley in the projected novel, he allowed it to lapse until he persuaded the proprietor of *Fraser* to undertake the publication of monthly instalments written up to the time for press. By this arrangement he hoped to complete a novel suitable for volume publication while receiving payment at magazine rates, as if he was expending the time and labour upon occasional articles.

Under the title of *The Luck of Barry Lyndon* the story occupied eleven numbers in *Fraser*, commencing in January and ending in December 1844, the October issue being omitted. In a note-book he jotted down a fitful diary of his work:

'Jan. 12. . . . Wrote for *Fraser* till 5, and went to see Arnal in *L'homme blasé*. Quite tired and weary with writing, which the evening's amusement did not cure. Wrote "Barry Lyndon" for *Fraser* again—beginning, however, to flag. . . . Jan. 20.—In these days got through the fag-end of chap. iv. of "Barry Lyndon" with a great deal of dulness, unwillingness, and labour. Feb. 2.—Wrote all day for *Punch*. "The Next Revolution." Feb. 21.—Wrote all day "Barry Lyndon," at five went out very tired, and came back still more tired at 9½ . . . continual labour annoys and excites me too much.'

Accustomed to dashing off a sketch or a story in a few days, the sustained effort of writing a novel sorely tried his patience. After eight numbers had appeared, he wrote one day in August: 'At home all day drawing and dawdling, with "B. L." lying like a nightmare on my mind.' Conscious of the pressing need to work, he would sit down at his table, pen in hand, and spend hours in vain attempts to concentrate upon his task, meanwhile covering every scrap of paper within reach with careless drawings and sketches. In his conscientious determination to devote his energies to work, he was subject to such spells of unwilling idleness throughout his life, for Holman Hunt, who knew him in his latter years, related how he once refused to join such a dinner-party at Richmond as he always loved, pleading that he had work to do, and some of the revellers, calling at his house on their return to town, found that he had written only a line and a half during the evening.

The satire on the Irish braggadocio in the character of Barry Lyndon revived the spleen of those Irish who had expressed indignation at the *Irish Sketch Book*. Lever, still irritated by the discomfort innocently invoked by the compliment of Thackeray's dedication, fell into a fever of righteous wrath and wrote in April to Ainsworth violent expressions of his opinion of 'Thackeray's rascality,' apparently on the grounds that he had abused the privileges of hospitality by utilising the fruits of his observation as a subject for satire. There can have been no cause for personal complaint, for the review of *Tom Burke*, which Thackeray contributed to *Fraser* in February, though containing characteristic touches of satirical humour, could hardly be interpreted otherwise than as an appreciation of Lever's work. Lever's attitude induced a coolness between them, which continued until Thackeray again provoked the Irishman's pugnacious hostility by the inclusion of *Phil Fogarty* in *Punch's Prize Novelists*. The ill-feeling resulting lent colour to such assertions as Sutherland Edwards's, that Lever was 'no friend of Thackeray,' although their friendly relations were subsequently renewed.

Like *Catherine*, *Barry Lyndon* proved a bitter disappointment. The public, which indulged in raptures over *Jack Sheppard* and *Eugene Aram*, failed to appreciate a hero whose rogueries were described with satirical irony instead of sentimental sympathy. But the historical realism and delicate artistry of the story impressed those critics among his friends who were convinced of his genius. 'If compliments can serve a man,' he remarked to his mother in July, 'they are to be had in plenty, and a great deal of small flattery at tea and dinner parties.' He was also rapidly acquiring a reputation on *Punch*, rivalling Jerrold as the most popular purveyor of the wit and humour for which the paper was already celebrated. Of his first notable contribution, the 'History of the Next French Revolution,' which appeared between February and April, he wrote to the proprietors, 'I am glad that the "Revolution" is approved of, and thank you for the remittance.'

Early in March he crossed from Paris to resume his 'comfortable old quarters in Jermyn Street.' One of his first affairs of business was the conclusion of his connection with the *Examiner*. His success on *Punch* being now assured, he welcomed the opportunity of quitting a less profitable and agreeable class of journalism. 'The *Examiner* and I have parted company in the best humour possible,' he told his mother, 'for it took more time than I could afford to give for four sovereigns, and I was much too clever a fellow to do it well; making omissions, blunders, &c., which any honest, plodding clerk would never have fallen into; so that chain is off my leg, but there are plenty of other little ones.' In July he wrote regretfully that he could not join his mother and the children on their summer holiday in Belgium because he had 'some awful work on hand, which presses severely this month. . . . *Fraser* and the *Chronicle*, and the mighty *Punch* above all, would tie me here for many days to come.' Earlier in the summer, however, he paid fleeting visits to them at Chaudfontaine, near Liège, sometimes staying with them at their villa, sometimes at a neighbouring inn. 'He never remained very long with us,' declared his daughter, 'he came and went suddenly.' His movements were those of a bird of passage, snatching momentary fragments of pleasure in the brief intervals of the busy round of toil. FitzGerald wrote on 11th April of being 'indignant with this nasty place London,' as 'Thackeray, whom I came up to see, went off to Brighton the night after I arrived, and has not reappeared.' He expressed his intention of awaiting his return, however, and saw a good deal of Thackeray during the summer. Some six weeks later, he wrote to Frederick Tennyson:

'I see in *Punch* a humorous catalogue of supposed pictures; Prince Albert's favourite spaniel and boot-jack, the Queen's Macaw with a Muffin, etc., by Landseer, etc., in which I recognise Thackeray's fancy. He is in full vigour play and pay in London, writing in a dozen reviews, and a score of Newspapers: and while health lasts he sails before the wind.'

Sanguine as ever, though overwhelmed with literary work, he mooted the idea of a new weekly periodical, 'a paper which should have a decided air of white kid gloves,' containing sound articles and reviews by first-rate writers. 'I have begged and implored my friends, Chapman & Hall, on the subject,' he declared, 'and to have the papers signed, and by good men—Buller, Carlyle, Forster; and I could take the fine arts, the light literature and theatres under my charge.' No publisher was prepared to risk capital in such a venture, nor could any be persuaded to issue 'a good stout book full of tales, reprints from *Fraser*—literary articles with illustrations by myself.' Chapman and Hall, however, commissioned him to write a life of Talleyrand, a task for which he hoped to obtain material from Talleyrand's former secretary, Colmache, who had married a Parisian friend of his mother's.[1] Though he read omnivorously during the summer for this work, which the publishers actually advertised for publication, he never proceeded with it on account of his other multifarious undertakings.

In the intervals between his varied labours, he found time for many social engagements, the Procters especially inviting him frequently to their house. In the midst of all his busy occupations he still looked forward to the possibility of his wife's return. To the elder of his little daughters he wrote in June: 'Mamma I hope will soon come and live with me in England, at a very pretty village called Twickenham which is by the river Thames.' He formed no preconception of a visit to the East; it occurred with the suddenness characteristic of all his movements at this time. On 19th August he wrote: 'Wrote all day "Barry Lyndon." Dined with Bevan at the Reform Club, where I met Emerson Tennent and had much talk about a trip to the east.' Bevan and Tennent proposed that he should accompany them on a trip to Palestine, via Constantinople and Egypt, and Thackeray immediately embraced the proposal, providing he could make the necessary arrangements. The following day he was 'in the City again to arrange about the Eastern Trip; wrote a little "Barry Lyndon"; dined with [Dr. Frederick Hervey Foster] Quin at a party where FitzGerald was in wonderful cue, but I was too much flustered myself thinking about the great voyage to enjoy the fun much.' The conductors of *Punch* welcomed the idea of receiving some humorous skits on his travels, and Chapman and Hall agreed to publish a similar account of his experiences as the *Irish Sketch Book*. On the 21st he wrote to his mother:

'I am going to write to you the great news, but my heart fails me as I send it, and I wish it weren't true. I have just,

[1] A series of *Talleyrand Papers* appeared in the *New Monthly Magazine* during 1844, largely based upon information supplied by a certain 'C—,' most likely Thackeray's friend Colmache.

only yesterday, had an offer to go passage-free by the Oriental Company to Lisbon, Cadiz, Gibraltar, Tangier, Athens, Constantinople, Smyrna, Jericho, Syria, and Jerusalem, in ten weeks, and I thought the chance so great, that I have accepted. The book, of course, is ordered, and go I do to-morrow. I am to write a book for C. & H. for £200 on the East, or that Cockney part which I shall see. Then to Talleyrand.'

Emerson Tennent, a Member of Parliament and a man of influence, obtained for him the free passage from the ship-owners, a beneficence which angered Carlyle, who 'compared the transaction to the practice of a blind fiddler going to and fro on a penny ferry-boat in Scotland, and playing tunes to the passengers for half-pence.'[1] Informing Thackeray of Carlyle's opinion, Charles Buller confessed that he himself concurred, believing that 'out of respect for himself and his profession, a man like him ought not to have gone fiddling for half-pence or otherwise in any steamboat under the sky.' Thackeray bore no malice, but accepted Carlyle's rebuke with humility, for he always respected his implacable care for the dignity of the literary profession. Praising Carlyle to a Philadelphian during his American lecturing tour, he remarked: '*He* would not go round making a show of himself as I am doing.' The more human FitzGerald took a lighter view. 'Titmarsh at Jerusalem,' he remarked, 'will certainly be an era in Christianity.'

§ 3

On 22nd August, only three days after his dinner at the Reform Club with Bevan and Tennent, Thackeray, as he confessed in the preface to *Notes of a Journey from Cornhill to Grand Cairo*, was 'astonished to find himself one of the passengers on board' the *Lady Mary Wood* in Southampton Water. The details of the voyage are recorded with

[1] *Conversations with Carlyle*, by Charles Gavan Duffy. London, 1892.

picturesque fidelity in *Cornhill to Cairo*, which ranks, by reason of its descriptive eloquence, discriminating observation and rapid narrative, among the classics of travel literature. If its author had not attained subsequent celebrity as a novelist, this book, usually relegated as a 'minor work' of Thackeray's nonage, might now be more widely read, although, of all branches of literature, the booksellers consider books of travel to possess the most ephemeral interest. The voyage was a trip, as distinct from a tour; he did not, as in Ireland, take his own time in gathering impressions, lingering at leisure in pleasant surroundings and hastily departing from places lacking attraction. His movements were governed by the ship's time-table, and he went ashore at each port for the prescribed period, like a Cook's tourist. Bearing this fact in mind, the extent of his observation and the picturesque clarity of his impressions must arouse amazement and admiration.

Touching at Lisbon and Cadiz, he reached Gibraltar in a week, proceeding thence to Malta, Athens, Smyrna, and Constantinople, whence he wrote to his wife, mentioning the Turkish bath described in his seventh chapter and recording his impression of Athens as 'filthy, beggarly, rockety, lousy, buggy, full of dogs, donkeys and other vermin—a beggarly place with the most noble hills round about it.' Having visited Rhodes and Beyrout, he travelled by caravan from Jaffa to Jerusalem and back again, an excursion rather with a flavour of Sterne. On board the boat he read *Hajji Baba* and *Eothen* in the intervals between making notes on his experiences, writing for *Punch* and working on *Barry Lyndon*. Under the pseudonym of 'the Fat Contributor' he wrote for *Punch* his *Wanderings*, *Travelling Notes*, and papers called *Punch in the East*, which constituted his second signal success on the paper. By 18th September, when he was at Constantinople, he had 'finished four letters of the F. C.' The journey to Jerusalem occupied the first week of October; he then sailed from Jaffa to Alexandria, where he did no work, 'but sketching a little, and wonderment everywhere.' After Cairo came the period of quarantine at Malta, during which he devoted himself entirely to work. On 3rd November he finally finished *Barry Lyndon* 'after great throes late at night,' and during the following days 'did scarcely anything but work and design the characters for *Mrs. Perkins's Ball.*'

At one time he had some notion of spending the winter at Malta, but he travelled home by the overland route by way of Naples and Rome as soon as he was released from quarantine. One of his companions, Samuel Bevan, in his book *Sand and Canvas*, published in 1849, tells of 'Titmarsh' taking the chair at a convivial dinner at Rome, and being called upon for a song, begged for a few minutes' grace, during which he composed his ballad of 'The Three Sailors,' or 'Little Billee,' of which 'he soon after delivered himself in a fittingly lugubrious tone of voice.' Calling at Paris to spend a few days with his family, he arrived in England early in December.

He spent the winter between Brighton and an inn at Chelsea, in Cheyne Row, a few doors from Carlyle's house. From this year onwards he frequently visited Brighton, as a resort within convenient reach of London for change of air and the uninterrupted quiet his work demanded. A considerable literary settlement welcomed him to its pleasant society. With the family of Horace Smith, the surviving brother of *Rejected Addresses* fame, a man of many friends, whose reputation for sincerity and benevolence corresponded with that of Procter, he developed a familiar friendship, and he frequently dined with James Morier, the author of *Hajji Baba*. Each of these two veteran men of letters, who belonged to the vanishing generation which had included Scott and Lamb, Shelley and Byron among its contemporaries, died within a few months of the other in 1849, and on the death of Smith, Thackeray wrote to Mrs. Brookfield:

'Dear old Horace Smith, that good serene old man, who went out of the world in charity with all in it, and having shown through his life, as far as I knew it, quite a delightful love of God's works and creatures—a true, loyal, Christian man. So was Morier, of a different order, but possessing that precious natural quality of love, which is awarded to some lucky minds such as these, Charles Lambs, and one or two more in our trade . . . to a friend of yours by the name of Makepeace, perhaps, but not unalloyed to this one.'

At Brighton he first met Kate Perry, a daughter of the former proprietor of the *Morning Chronicle*, who, with her sister, shared a most intimate and affectionate friendship with him in the latter part of his life.

After the hurry and bustle of travel, his yearning for domestic comfort revived with eager impatience. 'I wish I had a home, and all of you here,' he wrote from Brighton to his mother, 'it is the merriest place.' And a little later from the Chelsea inn, whither he had retired for seclusion to write up the account of his travels:

'When I get the book out of hand, please God I shall see the dear, dear little and big faces again. I have fond visions of double cottages in the Hammersmith or Hampstead districts, where we could be all together, and yet each independent. What a blessing it would be to have a home once more!'

He still cherished hopes that his wife might soon be sufficiently well to rejoin her husband and children, though henceforth always a delicate invalid, unfit for family and social responsibilities. Apparently her medical attendants, with characteristic professional caution, declined as yet to commit themselves on the prospect of the disorder and the possibility of her recovery, shaking their heads with dubious gravity while dropping tentative hints for hope of a change in her condition sooner or later, but definitely declaring her removal from their charge as yet impossible. His last hope flickering, Thackeray momentarily abandoned his plan of making a home, and settling to wait a little longer with the patience of despair, he took lodgings at 88 St James's Street, in the spring of 1845.

CHAPTER 7

§ 1

HIS intimacy with the Brookfields now began. William Henry Brookfield, after a brilliant career at Cambridge, contrived, by means of engaging manners and facile talents, to acquire influential patrons and a fashionable reputation as a preacher. His faculty for friendship compared even with Forster's, though he lacked the latter's literary advantages, for he ranked high in the affectionate esteem of all his old Cambridge acquaintances, Frederick and Alfred Tennyson, Spedding, Kinglake, Milnes, Buller, and Venables. As a parson he represented a very different type from John Allen, following rather the model of 'Ingoldsby' Barham in his fondness for the company of the wits, for fashionable literary society, for dining out, gossip, and fun. Kinglake said of him, 'Ever generous, indulgent, large-minded, Brookfield was never in the least demoralised by taking Holy Orders.'

During years of exile in country curacies, he kept up a close correspondence with Thackeray, as with others of his Cambridge friends, until he came to London in 1840, secured election to the Sterling Club, and became a familiar figure at the evenings of literary hostesses. In November 1841 he married Jane Octavia Elton, a beautiful and accomplished girl of twenty, youngest daughter of a Somerset baronet and niece by marriage of the historian Hallam. Their first home was at lodgings in Jermyn Street, and Brookfield lost no time in introducing Thackeray to his wife, bringing him in unexpectedly to dinner:

'There was, fortunately, a good plain dinner, but I was young and shy enough to feel embarrassed because we had no sweets, and I privately sent my maid to the nearest confectioner's to buy a dish of tartlets, which I thought would give a finish to our simple meal. When they were placed before me, I timidly offered our guest a small one, saying, "Will you have a tartlet, Mr. Thackeray?" "I will, but I'll have a two-penny one, if you please," he answered, so beamingly, that we all laughed, and my shyness disappeared.'

Such was Thackeray's first meeting with the woman who wielded a dominant influence upon the most important years of his life. A similar instance of Thackeray's happy knack of placing people at their ease with a joke or playful remark is recorded by Max Müller, who was present at a dinner-party of awe-stricken Oxford dons collected to meet the author of *Esmond*.

At Christmas 1842 Thackeray presented Mrs. Brookfield with a copy of one of his books, receiving in return her first preserved letter to him and an invitation to dinner. While he lodged in Jermyn Street, Brookfield habitually called to carry him off for a walk, and loved to dine out with him at his Bohemian resorts, receiving notes of invitation such as Barham delighted to have from James Smith and Theodore Hook. Like Barham, he quoted them in his correspondence, one such note from 'Titmarsh' reading:

'If you like two or three
Of your cronies to see
There's a swarry
To-morry
At Mitre court B.'

It was in 1845, however, when the Brookfields were established in Great Pulteney Street, that Thackeray commenced familiar intimacy and almost daily communication with them. Hitherto he had been a pseudo-bachelor friend of Brookfield's, whom he encountered chiefly outside his home, but now the footing of familiar friendliness extended to the wife, and soon he addressed his letters and notes to her instead of her husband. Every Saturday he breakfasted at their house on a standing invitation, usually alone, though, according to Brookfield's diary, Tom Taylor was his fellow-guest on one occasion, and Spedding, Aubrey de Vere, and Stephen Spring-Rice were present on another. If he had been less busy and more methodical, Brookfield might have been another Pepys; for he had an ear for the right kind of gossip and he went everywhere and knew everybody, but his entries, unfortunately, are bare jottings of engagements and lists of names. From them, however, may be gleaned a glimpse of Thackeray's social life this year. On 15th March he was with them at breakfast, after which Charles Buller came in and the three men went to Baker Street Bazaar, Buller and Thackeray then returning to escort Mrs. Brookfield to 'Miss Linwood's exhibition.' On the 25th, Jane Brookfield's birthday, he dined with them, the other guests being Mrs. Brookfield's sister-in-law, her husband, and her cousin, Henry Fitzmaurice Hallam, and he gave her a Turkish shawl. Four evenings later the Brookfields dined with Henry Hallam, the guests including Bartle Frere, Tom Taylor, and Spedding, and 'in the evening Thackeray joined the smoking. Home about two.' On 19th April Thackeray and Tom Taylor, the latest recruit to *Punch*, breakfasted, and then went with Brookfield to call on Alfred Tennyson. In May, his mother and the children came over from Paris and, while Thackeray was staying with them at his Aunt Becher's little house at Fareham, he found time to run over to Southampton, where the Brookfields were visiting friends.

Through him the Brookfields became intimate with the Procters, though Mrs. Procter soon exhibited symptoms of jealousy for Mrs. Brookfield, whose brilliancy of wit in conversation equalled that of the elder woman, while her attractions were visibly enhanced by youth and beauty. Her feelings were probably inspired on Thackeray's account when observing his obvious admiration for the brilliant young beauty, in whom she saw a dangerous rival for the position of *confidante* and mentor, which she had gained by her womanly sympathy in the dark days following his wife's affliction. Thackeray perceived her feelings, and remarked on them to Brookfield, who already appreciated the antipathy between the two women. In his correspondence with his wife, who went into the country during July and August, Mrs. Procter figures as the 'Proctoress' and the 'Proctrix,' Brookfield writing on 9th August:

> 'At 7¼ yesterday to the Proctrix. Only Count Revel and Thackeray, and Procter and wife and daughter. Very pleasant. Procter is fearfully hospitable. I don't wonder at fellows being so fond of him. So modest, has not even the degree of impudence needful for expressing himself. Everything good and true about him. We left him fast asleep on the sofa. . . . Thence to Thackeray's rooms where we had a weed. . . . The Proctrix has not one smallest sparklet of humour. Witty, well-informed—or what you like . . . but not one jot of humour. It is a sad deficiency. They sail for Paris next Saturday. Thackeray and Procter propose going unbeknownst at the same time for a day or two. But I think they will not (unbeknownst I mean to Mrs. and Miss P.).'

Thackeray's affection for the Procters continued undimmed by time or new ties, though, as Mrs. Procter feared, he soon accorded to Mrs. Brookfield a completeness of intimate confidence such as she had never shared. To the kind and generous Procter he publicly expressed his grateful affection in the dedication of *Vanity Fair*, and recorded an interesting day passed in his company at this time.

'Had a very pleasant stroll on Monday on Wimbledon Common with Procter, Forster, and Leigh Hunt. Hunt as usual in great force; his good-humoured face encircled with a clean shirt-collar, and a sort of holiday dress put on to receive us. . . . I won't put down the bad puns the good fellow made at a most comfortable dinner at the Rose and Crown. . . . All was very good, too good, the champagne and claret just for all the world like London wine. The Common was noble, and the air and the green country delightfully fresh. The day quite a holiday.'[1]

Here again he is playing a part in Forster's busy life, and another clue to his friendly relations, so sedulously suppressed, with Forster and Dickens occurs in a letter from Mrs. Procter to Monckton Milnes of 9th August, when she tells him how the two friends intend to act in amateur theatricals, and 'Mr. Thackeray has offered to sing between the Acts, but they decline his services.'

Mrs. Brookfield at this time affected an attitude of sarcastic tolerance towards her husband's familiarity with Thackeray. She pretended displeasure on hearing that he discussed ' "matrimonial irritations" and "domestic matters" with *yourr frriend* Thackeray,' and, commenting on the frequency of his friend's name in his letters, she remarked, 'You seem very hand in glove with Thackeray; don't become a second Father Prout.' This remark refers to Mahony's firm belief in Thackeray's genius, an opinion which he expressed with such frequency and generous warmth that he came to be regarded as Titmarsh's retainer, sitting in dog-like admiration at his master's feet. He possessed, however, a considerable streak of genius, which he wasted in miscellaneous journalism and a disorderly manner of living. Harrison Ainsworth, with whom he had a lasting quarrel, described him, long after his death, as 'an admirable scholar, a wit, a charming poet, and gener-

[1] Biographical Introduction to *Contributions to Punch.*

ally—not always—a very genial companion.'[1] When drunk he could be definitely objectionable, though even then often amusing, as when he entertained the austere Macready, over wine or brandy and a cigar, with a detailed account of his favour with the Pope and his prospects of becoming a knight of the Holy Roman Empire. Macready called him 'a wild dissolute character, though certainly a clever man,' and Joseph Crowe, who tells how, when official correspondent of the *Daily News* at Rome, he usually wrote his Roman letter in disreputable lodgings in Whitefriars, described him as 'the most delightful unbeliever that I ever met.' A quaint, mysterious figure during the latter part of his life, dividing his time between Paris and Rome with occasional fleeting visits to London, he became the subject of picturesque rumours, Samuel Carter Hall, the original Pecksniff, suspecting him of being a Jesuit spy and indulging secret vices in his Paris attic.

This odd little man, an intellectual scholar of low habits, clad in shabby, often uncleanly clothes, with blue eyes twinkling innocently behind spectacles as he entertained his eager listeners with pungent epigram, ribald anecdote, or rollicking song, was one of Thackeray's closest companions. They frequented together a resort called the Deanery Club, in Dean Street, where not only George Augustus Sala, himself a prince of Bohemia in the next generation, but the respectable Mr. Frith, not then R.A., though a brand-new associate, was first introduced to the great Michael Angelo Titmarsh. Mrs. Brookfield, though too tactful to say so in as many words, hardly approved of 'Father Prout' as a suitable friend for an ambitious young preacher, and her husband felt it necessary to describe him defiantly as 'a very nice fellow—not what his name (a sobriquet of his own manufacture) would indicate or at least a good deal more. A clever scholar and pleasant companion and not indecorous.'

[1] *William Harrison Ainsworth and His Friends,* by S. M. Ellis. London, 2 vols., 1911.

Thackeray was almost daily in Brookfield's company in the late summer and autumn, their companions including Mahony, Milnes, and Kinglake. One night in August, having sat at Brookfield's till half-past one, he sprained his ankle on the way home, and being confined to his rooms in consequence, invited Brookfield to share a brace of grouse the following night, Mahony coming in afterwards 'for serious smoking.' In the first week of September Brookfield accompanied him to Brighton and describes him drawing on wood before breakfast, which is followed by a cigar and a walk along the beach, where he sketches some of the people they see passing by, before Brookfield takes a second walk alone, leaving Thackeray engaged in 'earning a little dinner for us by his fluent pen.' A month later, after dining with the Brookfields, all three intended going out for the evening, 'but Jane was ill and Thackeray kept on with me.' At this time, he went over to Paris and apparently learned the truth at last from his wife's doctors. All hopes of her recovering sufficiently to resume her normal life were finally dispelled, but the nature of her disorder permitted her being placed under judicious supervision without close confinement. On 30th October, noting that he sat a couple of hours with Thackeray on the previous evening, Brookfield wrote: 'He brought back his poor little wife yesterday—she is at Camberwell and he seems well pleased with the people.'

§ 2

Throughout these months he was contributing weekly to *Punch* and working steadily on *Cornhill to Cairo* and *Mrs. Perkins's Ball*, besides writing occasional periodical articles. His work for *Punch* had not only stabilised his income, but now began to augment his reputation. On 12th April, Macvey Napier, the editor of the *Edinburgh Review*, wrote to Abraham Hayward:

'Will you tell me—confidently, of course—whether you know anything of a Mr. Thackeray, about whom Longman has written me, thinking he would be a good hand for light articles? He says (Longman) that this Mr. Thackeray is one of the best writers in *Punch*. One requires to be very much on one's guard in engaging with mere strangers. In a Journal like the *Edinbro'*, it is always of importance to keep up in respect of names. Who is "Eothen"? I know he is a lawyer and highly respectable; but I should like to know a little more of his personal history.'[1]

The letter indicates the unenterprising, academically conventional type of mind upon which the mantle of Francis Jeffrey had fallen. His correspondent was born to be the chosen recipient of the confidence of men like Napier. 'A lawyer and highly respectable,' Hayward was also a political, social, and literary puppy, perpetually picking up crumbs from beneath the tables of his betters. A lesser Taper or Tadpole, he endeavoured always to be 'in the know,' thereby attaining a certain social *cachet*, especially in the estimation of literary ladies, with whom he enjoyed a pleasant popularity. Having weighed the matter carefully, he decided that Thackeray might be worthy of cultivation, and consequently, after some correspondence through the medium of the publisher Longman, Thackeray was invited to address the editor personally and to suggest subjects for an article. He proposed a study of Eugène Sue's novels for a long article or a review of Laman Blanchard's *Sketches from Life* and N. P. Willis's *Dashes at Life* for a shorter and lighter article, failing either of which he hoped to be able to treat Lady Hester Stanhope's *Memoirs* to Napier's satisfaction. The editor selected N. P. Willis, and Thackeray's article appeared in the October number, but in a form so mutilated by editorial pruning that the style

[1] *A Selection from the Correspondence of Abraham Hayward*, edited by Henry E. Carlisle. London, 2 vols., 1886.

is scarcely recognisable as that of Titmarsh. On 16th October Thackeray wrote to Napier:[1]

'My dear Sir,—I have just received and acknowledge with many thanks your banker's bill. From them or from you, I shall always be delighted to receive communications of this nature. From your liberal payment I can't but conclude that you reward me not only for labouring, but for being mutilated in your service. I assure you I suffered cruelly by the amputation which you were obliged to inflict upon my poor dear paper. I mourn still—as what father can help doing for his children?—for several lovely jokes and promising *facetiæ*, which were born and might have lived but for your scissors urged by ruthless necessity. I trust however there are many more which the future may bring forth, and which will meet with more favour in your eyes. I quite agree with your friends who say Willis was too leniently used. O, to think of my pet passages gone for ever!—Very faithfully yours,

W. M. THACKERAY.'

So closed his connection with the *Edinburgh*, for he no longer valued an occasional periodical commission to the extent that he needed to submit to the insult of cutting without advice or apology.

He contributed *A Legend of the Rhine*, a story in seven numbers, based on Dumas' *Othon L'Archer*, to *George Cruikshank's Table Book*, which was issued from the *Punch* office in twelve monthly parts. This fact and that of the work being edited by his *Punch* colleague, Gilbert à Beckett, induced him to contribute, for he had finally renounced any connection with Cruikshank's publications after he had received only a sovereign in full payment for his contributions to the *Omnibus* in 1841. He still wrote frequently for *Fraser* and supplied one or two short stories under the pseudonym of 'Lancelot Wagstaff' to the *New*

[1] *Selections from the Correspondence of the late Macvey Napier*, edited by his son. London, 1879.

Monthly, the publisher and proprietor of which, Henry Colburn, commissioned him to write a serial story or series of articles, making an advance payment. In June, however, Colburn sold the *New Monthly* to Harrison Ainsworth, and Thackeray found himself in the position of having received payment for work, a part of which was already submitted, though the rest remained to be written, from a publisher now possessing no magazine in which to print it. Properly, he should have demanded full payment from Colburn, whether the commissioned work was completed or not, but, whether under the impression that Ainsworth assumed responsibility for the liability or that Colburn had handed over his manuscript to the new proprietor, he wrote to Ainsworth demanding satisfaction. The latter, of course, knew nothing of the matter, and being busily preoccupied with the details of taking over the magazine, he delayed seeking an explanation from Colburn, with the result that he received three letters, each more indignant in tone, before writing a satisfactory reply. Colburn undoubtedly treated Thackeray badly, taking advantage of the absence of any written contract to demand the refund of the advance payment before returning the manuscript, which he could no longer utilise in the magazine and considered unworthy of volume publication. On discovering the facts of the matter, Ainsworth naturally sympathised with the author, and wrote a cordial letter, inviting his contributions and expressing his readiness to consider the manuscript rejected by Colburn. On 30th June Thackeray replied:

'I'm glad I wrote the 3rd letter. It's the only one which has produced a satisfactory reply. Of course I'll come to dinner on Sunday: and we are just as good friends as ever. Wasn't it much better to complain and explain? I think so—and the imperial house of Titmarsh is now satisfied. . . . Your terms are prodigiously good—and if I can see the material for a funny story you shall have it. . . . That for which Colburn paid in advance, and which he would not trust into the author's hands until he got his money back, will run to 30, possibly to 100 pages, and is too long for you.

There's one thing I regret very much, too, and must be told to you now in making a clean breast of it—is a certain paragraph in the next *Punch*, relating to a certain advertisement about contributors, "not only of talent *but of rank*." This moved my wrath; and has been hardly handled—this was before our meeting and explanation—I always must think it a very objectionable advertisement—but shouldn't have lifted my hand to smite my friend, had explanation come earlier, so that now *you* must be called upon to play the part of forgiver, in which I'm sure you will shine.'

The piece in *Punch* to which he refers appeared in the issue of 5th July under the heading, 'Immense Opportunity.' Ainsworth always had a weakness for high-sounding names, welcoming as contributors to the pages of all his magazines the titled scribblers of the annuals, and Thackeray seized upon the foible as a subject for savage sarcasm, while believing that Ainsworth was a party to Colburn's scurvy conduct. Two stories, signed 'Lancelot Wagstaff,' appeared in the first two numbers of the magazine issued by its new proprietor, and his friendly relations with Ainsworth continued, for the latter was with him at Brighton in the following February, of which meeting he wrote to Horace Smith on his return to town:

'Titmarsh was out of humour because he was reviewed and attacked, as he thinks, in the last *New Monthly*. The paper, on the contrary, was very friendly. . . . He went home with me to the Albion and kept me up till one o'clock, drinking brandy and soda, and abusing Byron in a ludicrously absurd, and Cockney fashion.'

The review of *Cornhill to Cairo*, entitled 'Michael Angelo Titmarsh in the East,' to which Ainsworth referred, may be characterised as 'friendly,' so far as the book is concerned, for it contains no adverse criticism, but the references to Titmarsh himself are delivered in a distinctly satirical tone, representing him as the traditional Cockney, impudently inquiring, knowing, confident, and democratically materialistic. It was the character generally ascribed to the early writers on *Punch*, as formerly to Hunt, Hazlitt, and the *London Magazine* coterie.

In December, *Notes of a Journey from Cornhill to Cairo* was published. It was generally well received, the critics regarding it with more respect than the average book of travel. As he told his mother about this time, his professional reputation was 'of the best sort after the great guns'—'the admirers of Mr. Titmarsh are a small clique, but a good and increasing one, if I may gather from the daily offers that are made me, and the increased sums bid for my writings.' The writer of an article in *Fraser*, called 'Titmarsh's Tour through Turkeydom,' through the veil of whose anonymity beamed the friendly enthusiasm of 'Father Prout,' prefaced a critical eulogy of the book with a detailed examination of his literary career, which, with sympathetic insight and sound judgment, summarises the extent of Thackeray's literary achievement prior to the epoch of *Vanity Fair*. On 16th February he wrote to his mother:

'I have just got my foot in the stirrup to be off to Brighton for two or three days' meditation, and have not a word to say even to fill this half-sheet. Haven't I gorged you with flummery from the newspapers? They are all mighty polite, except one fellow, a friend of mine, who calls me a heartless and self-sufficient Cockney. The book is not only praised, but also sells very well. They have already got rid of a thousand more than the Irish book sold altogether.'

Evidently he suspected Ainsworth himself of having written the *New Monthly* review, though Ainsworth apparently only admitted editorial responsibility when they met at Brighton a few days later.

It was on this visit to Brighton that he met Kate Perry, who wrote to her married sister, Mrs. Frederick (afterwards) Lady) Elliot:

'I have made a great friendship with one of the principal contributors of *Punch*—Mr. Thackeray; he is now writing a novel, but cannot hit upon a name for it. I may be wrong, but it seems to me the cleverest thing I ever read. The first time he dined with us I was fearfully alarmed at him. The next day we walked in Chichester Park, when he told all about his little girls, and of his great friendship with the Brookfields, and I told him about you and Chesham Place.'

Her wit, cheerful temperament, and sincerity of character appealed strongly to Thackeray, and, starving for the sympathy and understanding of a woman, he eagerly sought her society as a pleasant recreation from his work, soon arriving at a sufficient degree of friendship to read to her in the evening the result of his efforts during the day. When she expressed her high opinion of the novel, he laughed, saying: 'It is *not* small beer; but I do not know whether it will be palatable to the London folks.' He told her that the inimitable title of *Vanity Fair* occurred to him as an inspiration when he lay awake one night.

The rudimentary beginnings of *Vanity Fair* evidently comprised the manuscript rejected by Colburn on parting with the property of the *New Monthly Magazine*, for Thackeray himself told W. E. Aytoun in 1847 that 'Colburn refused the present "Novel without a Hero."'[1] It was hardly likely that he would approach Colburn again after his unjust treatment, and it is therefore probable that the genesis of *Vanity Fair*, passing under the title of *Pen and Pencil Sketches of English Society*, which figures as the sub-title in the first edition in monthly parts, was originally intended to feature in the *New Monthly* as a series

[1] *Memoir of William Edmondstone Aytoun*, by Theodore Martin. Edinburgh, 1867.

similar to the *Yellowplush* and *Fitz-Boodle Papers*. The myth of the manuscript being hawked about London before eventually finding a publisher owes its origin to sentimental journalism, which delighted to depict Thackeray as the traditional man of genius, impoverished, unrecognised, out at elbows, down at heel, vainly offering a masterpiece to potentates obese of body and obtuse of mind. Possessing a manuscript which, as he informed Ainsworth, seemed unsuitable for magazine use, Thackeray naturally offered it to Bradbury and Evans, as the proprietors of the periodical to which he was an important contributor and a firm specialising in cheap serial publication. As naturally, they on their side eagerly accepted the offer from one of their most successful contributors.

The evidence of Vizetelly, one of the most reliable and entertaining writers of Victorian literary memoirs, confirms this version. Since the end of their relations on the *Pictorial Times*, Vizetelly had printed *Cornhill to Cairo* and obliged Thackeray by recommending a young artist in his employ named Thwaites, to touch up the drawings on wood for *Mrs. Perkins's Ball*, which was in preparation while the earlier part of *Vanity Fair* was being written. Calling upon Vizetelly one day about his drawings, Thackeray showed him two sketches for the page plates of *Vanity Fair*, which he took from a brown paper parcel.

'Tied up with them,' says Vizetelly, 'was the manuscript of the earlier portion of the work, of which he had several times spoken to me. . . . His present intention, he told me, was to see Bradbury & Evans, and offer the work to them. . . . In little more than half an hour Mr. Thackeray again made his appearance, and with a beaming face gleefully informed me that he had settled the business. "B. & E.," said he, "accepted so readily, that I am deuced sorry I didn't ask them another tenner. I am certain they would have given it." He then explained to me that he had named fifty guineas per part, including the two sheets of letterpress, a couple of etchings, and the initials at the commencement of the chapters. He reckoned the text, I remember, at no more than five-and-twenty shillings a page, the two etchings at six guineas each, while, as for the few initials at the beginning of the chapters, he threw these in.'

Vizetelly proceeds to the positive declaration that, when the bargain with Bradbury and Evans was concluded, no more than the first number of the novel had been written. In that case the agreement may have been reached at any time between Ainsworth's purchase of the *New Monthly* in June 1845 and Thackeray's visit to Brighton in the following February, when he began to work steadily upon the development of the original draft. It seems likely, however, that the actual date of the arrangement was either immediately before or after the Brighton visit.

The success of *Jeames's Diary*, which ran through *Punch* between November and February, together with the favourable reception of *Cornhill to Cairo*, probably inspired the readiness of Bradbury and Evans to close with Thackeray's offer. Almost immediately they had cause to congratulate themselves upon their decision, for *The Snobs of England*, commencing on 28th February, created a sensation only equalled in *Punch* by *Mrs. Caudle's Curtain Lectures* of the previous year. Speaking of the profound sensation occasioned by the *Snob Papers*, Mr. Spielmann observes:

'It may be compared to that of Jerrold's *Caudle Lectures*, save that they appealed to a more cultivated and less demonstrative class, and were appreciated in proportion to their superior merits. The circulation of *Punch* rose surprisingly under their benign influence, and Thackeray did not leave the subject until he had handled it from every point of view and even carried it abroad.'

Although Caroline Norton told Jerrold that the article on 'Clerical Snobs' reminded her of the *Essays of Elia* and the papers are generally regarded as models of polished satire, Thackeray told J. L. Motley many years later that, of all his writings, he liked them least. As he regretted his juvenile attacks on Bulwer, his matured philosophy deprecated the scathing censoriousness of the *Snob Papers.* Yet he ought to have felt some sentimental regard for them, for they not only presented him with the first taste of popular success but undoubtedly paved the way for the reception of *Mrs. Perkins's Ball* and *Vanity Fair.*

Though the time came when the incessant necessity for writing something for *Punch* became irksome drudgery, the connection now provided him with the means to discontinue much of his miscellaneous journalism and afford leisure for application to his novel. After March, when he wrote a reflective article in the form of a letter to 'Father Prout' upon his former colleague on the *Constitutional,* Laman Blanchard, who had recently committed suicide, and a book review in the following month, his contributions to *Fraser* languished, and in spite of appeals for more articles from the publisher Nickisson, he supplied only one more article, a review of the Christmas books in the following January, before allowing the old connection finally to lapse. Apart from his work on *Punch,* he wrote for no other paper during 1846 except the *Morning Chronicle,* and he even considered the severance of this connection, writing to his mother in July: 'I am going to quit the *Chronicle* very likely, but if I do it will be something better.' A month later he adds: 'I have health, and much more work and leisure too.' The years of intense financial anxiety, of living from hand to mouth and searching his pockets for the price of the next day's dinner, were now over, and for the first time he found himself free to concentrate upon work productive of no immediately lucrative return.

§ 3

He now determined to make a new home. The hopes that his wife might soon return were now dissipated, thus removing any reason for further delay in establishing his household. He had his life to live, and with his career now advancing in accordance with ambition, he urgently needed a suitable home at which to return the hospitality received from his friends and acquaintance. Moreover, he desired the society of his children, not only to satisfy his craving for their affection, but from an urgent sense of duty. The elder, at least, had now attained an age when her mind was susceptible to lasting impressions and the fact of her being deprived of a mother's attention emphasised the extent of his obligation as a father. In this wish he met with obstinate opposition from his mother. She had become fondly devoted to her grandchildren and dreaded the prospect of her lonely exile being deprived of their cheering presence. Vainly did her son expostulate that she and his stepfather could share the house with them; she did not wish to leave Paris, where she had formed her own circle of friends and fallen into the settled routine of advancing age. From Brighton, in February, Thackeray wrote:

'I have been house-hunting like a maniac. What do you say to a beautiful house, field, farm of seven acres, at three miles from London, cocks, hens, paddocks, gardens, &c.? This can be had for £200 a year—a perfect country domain.'

But his mother answered evasively, presenting difficulties and offering objections. She had developed devout religious principles, which her son neither shared nor entertained with sufficient seriousness, and she anticipated qualms concerning the spiritual welfare of the children in the guardianship of their father. She objected that the presence of herself and the children in his house would prove an inconvenience for the entertainment of his friends. Thackeray argued and humoured her, until, taking the bull by the horns, he established himself at 13 Young Street, Kensington Square, in June.

Besides his old predilection that he must live in London to succeed in his ambition, his work for *Punch* now necessitated his presence in town. On settling in his new home he wrote on 1st July:

'MY DEAREST MAMMY,—G. P. [for grandpapa, the name by which he refers to his step-father] writes me a word that you are unwell and that a change of air wd. do you good; what such a good change as to come here with the little ones? and I hope & pray in God that we shall be able to live together and that I may not be deprived of my Mother & my children. There are 2 capital bed-rooms and a little sitting-room for you & G. P.—a famous bed-room for G. M. [grandmama, meaning his own grandmother, old Mrs. Butler] on the first floor—2 rooms for the children on the second very airy and comfortable; a couple of rooms big enough for servants, & 2 little ones quite large enough for me.—There's a good study down-stairs & a dining-room & drawing-room, and a little court yard & garden and a little green house; and Kensington Gardens at the gate, and omnibuses every 2 minutes. What can mortal want more? If I ask my friends I can ask them to my own quarters. We may all be independent and together. At all events I ask it as a favour that the experiment should be tried: and am sure that we shall all be the happier & better for it. I'm not ready for you yet: but hope in a fortnight's time to be prepared. I have been opening the trunks to-day full of the lumbering useless old books: and woeful relics of old days.'

With the resignation of a woman no longer young, his mother withdrew her resistance. Within a fortnight Major Carmichael-Smyth came over from Paris to look over his stepson's abode, for, on the 15th, Brookfield attended a masculine party at 'the hospitable mansion of Mr. Titmarsh,' where he met him and Thackeray's brother-in-law, Arthur Shawe, in company with Leech, Kinglake, and the Rev. William Harness, a well-known writer, who had been friendly with Byron. In August, he tells his mother that he is 'beginning to count the days now till you come,' and eventually, in the late autumn, she arrived with the children.

There ensued for his mother the final pain of parting with her grandchildren. Having remained a few weeks at her son's house, she returned to Paris, where she received a letter intended to soften the blow:

'Now the children are with me,' Thackeray wrote, 'I am getting so fond of them that I can understand the pang of the dear old Mother who loses them: and who by instinct is 100 times fonder of them than ever a man could be. But it is best that they should be away from you:—at least that they should be away either from you or me. There can't be two first principles in a house. We should secretly be jealous of one another: or I should resign the parental place altogether to you, and be a bachelor still. Whereas now God Almighty grant I may be a father to my children. . . . I write so far to give my dearest old Mother a consolation in her bereavement. Remember the children are in their natural place: with their nearest friend working their natural influence: getting and giving the good, let us hope, wh. the Divine Benevolence appointed to result from the union between parents & children. . . . How thankful this makes me to you & my dear old G. P. who have kept the children for me, and watched them so nobly and tenderly. . . .'

Evidently compiled with careful deliberation, the letter seeks to sympathise with his mother's loneliness and to assure her of his sense of responsibility, while asserting the conviction that he was acting rightly. The devout expressions were doubtless chosen to accord with her habitually religious mental attitude. A more spontaneous and characteristic letter followed about a fortnight later, where he sends 'a line just to wish you—though I know it's a humbug—a merry Xmas. Next year please God you shall have such a one really, and your old eyes will be gladdened by the sight of the children. They are meanwhile doing the greatest good to their father. That must be the poor dear old Mother's only consolation.' And he goes on to talk of his work, his prospects, and household affairs.

The manner in which Thackeray fulfilled his duty to his motherless children invoked the admiration of everybody. In his determination that they should not miss too much their mother's presence, his affection assumed a tenderness almost maternal. While they were little, he shared their amusements, their hobbies and their childish troubles, solving their problems and offering advice with patient sympathy and quiet humour. He walked with them, one on each side holding his forefinger, took them away with him to the country and the Continent, and fetched them home himself from their parties at other houses. As they grew up they acquired with him the closest intimacy and understanding, the elder acting as his amanuensis and interesting herself in his work. When he died, expressing his deep distress for the girls, John Blackwood remarked: 'Poor things, he completely made companions of them, and I cannot think how they are to recover from the blow.' No sooner had success at last befallen him, relieving the burden of debt and affording the means of ease and comfort, than he applied himself to his work with renewed ardour to amass a suitable provision for them in the event of his death. Both his lecture tours in America were undertaken expressly with this end in view. The latter part of his life was a pilgrimage dedicated to the welfare of his daughters.

The sanity of his philosophy was reflected in the religious upbringing of his children. He taught them the simple faith in which he himself had been brought up, encouraging them to read the Bible with intelligence and interpreting its messages in an interesting way, justly assuming that sectarian doctrines might be left to their own examination in adolescence. His mother, who had vainly attempted to inspire her son with enthusiasm for the fervent beliefs acquired with her declining years, a disappointment which created a breach in her former sympathetic understanding of her son, disapproved of this policy, desiring the children to be trained in the lore of her particular notions, which appear to have leaned towards spiritualism. Thackeray quietly persisted in his simple method, and when his mother lent the elder girl some books of her recommendation, he advised her to read all 'that Granny wishes,' and form her own ideas about their teachings. He confessed ignorance of the latest sectarian movements, but declared that he had studied the so-called Evangelical doctrine in his youth and developed a lasting distaste for such dogma. He regarded the Old Testament as imperfect history, denying its divine inspiration, and recommending an examination of the Gospels as sufficient preparation for the formation of a faith. In religion, as in politics, he contemptuously ignored the controversial, basing his beliefs upon the conception of right and wrong, derived from knowledge and experience.

§ 4

The dinner-party which Brookfield attended on 15th July was probably the first of many similar evenings while Thackeray lived at Young Street. His name occurs frequently in Macready's diary during the year, a sure sign of his metamorphosis into an important figure in literary society. It is significant that Macready records no meeting with him in the lean years following his wife's breakdown; during that period he had no money for more than an occasional tavern supper with those of his literary friends addicted to Bohemianism, and he refrained from the acceptance of invitations except from friends so intimate as the Procters, because he lacked the means to return their hospitality. Always convivial and fond of company, as soon as *Punch* restored the lining of his pockets, he eagerly entered the society for which he was fitted by breeding, education, and culture, and which he had frequented before the epoch of misfortune. His Bohemian associates naturally commented on his change of habit, and their scoffing jokes deepened into envious sneers, as he continued to frequent with familiarity the society to which they had no prospect of admittance. Hence the legend that Thackeray's head was turned and swollen by success, though he merely resumed social relations such as he had always been accustomed to enjoy, with the difference that he now appeared as a man distinguished by achievement instead of a young fellow of talent and promise.

During the spring he dined three times with Pollock, once with Spedding as his fellow-guest, again with Tennyson, and the third time with F. D. Maurice, the painter Laurence, and his host's father, the Chief Baron. Before going to Brighton in February he attended the reading of his friend the Rev. James White's play, *The King of the Commons*, at Macready's house, where he dined in company with White, Dickens, and Forster. Dickens and others privately expressed disappointment in White's play, but Thackeray performed a friend's office by writing his appreciation of it to Macready. In May he again appeared at Macready's as one of a big party, including Abraham Hayward, Mrs. Jameson, and the Rev. William Harness, and subsequently he was a frequent guest at the actor's literary evenings. Mrs. Brookfield was out of town during the summer, but her husband saw only less of him than in the previous year, meeting him at Pollock's, calling at Young Street, and dining with him at the Garrick to meet Procter, John Kenyon, and Robert Browning.

The idea of Thackeray consorting with 'high society' only after *Vanity Fair* had made him a lion arose from the legend of his swelled head. In November 1845 he was the guest of no less a person than a former Prime Minister, Lord Melbourne, along with Anthony Panizzi, the librarian of the British Museum, Albany Fonblanque, and Sir Alexander and Lady Duff-Gordon, who were intimate friends of the Brookfields, and, through them, of Thackeray. It was Caroline Norton who obtained for him this invitation. She herself issued the invitation to Panizzi, begging him, as Thackeray's friend, to make excuses for the informality of Lord Melbourne's invitation without a previous introduction, though she declared she could not convince Melbourne that he was not already acquainted with Thackeray, whom he remembered vaguely as a clergyman, evidently confusing him with his uncle, the biographer of Chatham. Mrs. Norton, thus early, was already cultivating Thackeray as a notable man of letters, whom she persuaded to contribute to *Fisher's Drawing Room Scrap-Book*, an annual under her editorship.

As Caroline Norton was the most beautiful ornament of literary society, Thackeray only followed the fashion in gratifying her wish, but he evinced equal good-nature when he met young Coventry Patmore at the Procters'. Patmore was then struggling for subsistence as a periodical writer, often working sixteen hours a day for twenty-five shillings a week, and on hearing of his circumstances from Mrs. Procter, Thackeray promptly asked the young man to give him something suitable for *Fraser*, of which he wrote to Nickisson on 3rd October 1846:

'Will you pay a special attention to the accompanying paper by young Patmore the poet—he is himself a most deserving and clever young fellow who will be a genius some day; and his paper is so odd, humorous and amusing that I hope you will secure it, and its author as a future contributor. . . . If you will use this for next month I promise you an article (D.V.). The fact is that young Mr. Patmore wants help at this present juncture.'[1]

To ensure the acceptance of the unknown youth's article Thackeray wrote, in spite of pressure upon his time, his 'Grumble about the Christmas Books' for the January *Fraser*, which was the last of Titmarsh's contributions to the periodical which introduced him to the public. Patmore's experience verifies Vizetelly's statement that 'Thackeray was especially good to young men,' when remarking that he himself 'always met with the greatest kindness from him.' Instances of his kindness to struggling young men frequently occurred during his latter years, but these earlier examples of his generosity disprove any suggestions that, as a celebrity, he indulged in conscious benevolence for the sake of obtaining a reputation for kindness. James Hannay, who described himself as 'one whom Thackeray had loaded with benefits,' first derived assistance from him in the days when he was himself wrestling with penury, and he conferred many such kindnesses of which he never expected anybody besides the recipients to hear.

As far as literary society was concerned, Mrs. Procter's drawing-room, to which Thackeray had long been a welcome visitor, was the Mecca of the intellectuals. Carlyle, Kinglake, Dickens, Forster, Leigh Hunt, Milnes, and many more went there regularly, while few of Thackeray's tavern friends ever received an invitation thither. When the change in his fortunes rendered it possible for him to return to his former mode of life, it was these Bohemians, conscious of inferiority and sneering at his fine friends, who sowed the seeds of mischievous rumour about his tendency to be spoiled by success. If they heard of him dining with a peer in the party, they called him a tuft-hunter, and some

[1] *Memoirs and Correspondence of Coventry Patmore*, by Basil Champneys. London, 2 vols., 1901.

malicious wit was quick to suggest that he wrote so well of snobs because he was one himself. Posterity has echoed their sneers, because the memoir-writers of the period were largely drawn from this class of lower literary journalism, and in their reminiscences recalled as facts the conjectures of malicious gossip, often repeating a tale told to themselves as a memory at first hand. It is an unfortunate fact that so much literary history has to be sifted from the ill-written, incoherent meanderings of broken-down journalists, who write their reminiscences of their betters as a last resource, when age and careless living had rendered them incapable of adequately performing their former duties.

CHAPTER 8

§ 1

WHEN *Mrs. Perkins's Ball* appeared in December 1846 and the first monthly part of *Vanity Fair* on New Year's Day, Thackeray was in his thirty-sixth year. He had finally left behind the bitter years of disappointment and penury. Already, by means of the *Snob Papers*, he possessed a little fame, but it was only the flicker of a match, which would quickly burn itself out. He fully realised the fact, and throughout the year 1846, in spite of his work for *Punch*, his domestic arrangements and his social engagements, he devoted the full force of his intellectual energies to manufacture the tinder which the match might light into a brilliant conflagration. At Christmas he told his mother:

'My prospects are very much improved and *Vanity Fair* may make me. . . . *Mrs. Perkins* is a great success—the greatest I have had—very nearly as great as Dickens, that is *Perkins* 500, Dickens 25,000, only that difference! but we are selling out our edition very fast, near 1500 are gonc out of 2000 already—and this is a great success for the likes of me.'

Obviously *Punch* had succeeded, where *Fraser* had failed, in winning for its contributor a small public. The early Titmarsh books had proved frankly failures, and the *Irish Sketch Book* only a modest success, despite the advantage of topical interest. The first book published after his accession to *Punch*, *Cornhill to Cairo*, had marked the turning of the tide.

He appreciated that upon *Vanity Fair* depended the future

of his career. Sending W. E. Aytoun a copy of *Mrs. Perkins's Ball*, he wrote on 2nd January:

'I think I have never had any ambition hitherto, or cared what the world thought of my work, good or bad; but now the truth forces itself upon me, if the world will once take to admiring Titmarsh, all his guineas will be multiplied by 10. Guineas are good. I have got children, only 10 years more to the fore, say, &c.; now is the time, my lad, to make your A when the sun at length has begun to shine.

Well, I think if I can make a push at the present minute —if my friends will shout, Titmarsh for ever!—hurrah for, &c., &c., I may go up with a run to a pretty fair place in my trade, and be allowed to appear before the public as among the first fiddles. But my tunes must be heard in the streets, and organs must grind them. Ha! Now do you read me?'

He goes on to ask Aytoun to use his influence with the conductors of *Blackwood's Magazine* to give him a review, but, within a fortnight, he regretted the impulse, realising that the success or failure of his novel must depend upon its own merits, unaffected by critical puffing in a magazine.

'I have been thinking of the other matter on which I un-busmd myself to you, and withdraw my former letter. Puffs are good, and the testimony of good men; but I don't think these will make a success for a man, and he ought to stand as the public chooses to put him. I will try, please God, to do my best, and the money will come perhaps some day! Meanwhile a man so lucky as myself has no reason to complain. So let all puffing alone, though as you know, I am glad if I can have and deserve your private good opinion. The women like *Vanity Fair*, I find, very much, and the publishers are quite in good spirits regarding that venture.'

Lady Ritchie declared that, at first, 'the sale of *Vanity Fair* was so small that it was a question at that time whether its publication should not be discontinued altogether,' but the statement was probably an exaggeration produced by picturesque tradition, like the story of the book being refused by numerous publishers, for Thackeray told his mother in July that 'the publishers are quite contented.' Its reception seems to have resulted as might have been reasonably expected. Thackeray's public was small and drawn from the more intellectual and cultured class, which preferred to read a novel in its entirety rather than in monthly instalments. Thus, Macready and Mrs. Browning record their impressions of the novel when it appeared in volume form, two years after the commencement of its serial publication. The monthly magazines rarely noticed a novel issued in monthly parts, for the obvious reason that they were, to some extent, competitive with their interests, and few of the dailies and weeklies troubled to insert more than a paragraph about such publications, except from the popular pen of Dickens. Apart from a friendly puff by Jerrold in *Punch* and a discerning article in the *Scotsman*, the early numbers appear to have passed unnoticed.

It was the wit of a woman that turned the scale. Mrs. Procter, loud in her praise of the novel, happened to be execrating the obtuseness of the critics when Abraham Hayward was present, and her eye lighting on his dapper figure, she asked him why he did not review it. Hayward was torn between fears of offending a fashionable hostess and committing an error of critical judgment likely to prejudice his reputation with his academic friends. His biographer, with a pomposity worthy of his subject, observes that 'he was very good-natured about it, but happened to be busied about other things, and fancied he could not undertake it.' Mrs. Procter knew her man, and was not so easily deterred. She took the trouble to mark passages in the published numbers suitable for quotation in a review, sending them to Hayward with a letter, describing her own impressions of the story's merits as suggestions for the points which should be selected for praise, knowing very well that he dare not offend her by evading her wish after such implicit directions. Apart from notes on the characters and incidents of the story, she declared the quality for which 'Mr. Thackeray deserves the highest praise is the total absence of affectation,' that 'he seems to me to excel in the pathetic parts,' and that 'the characters are neither devils nor angels, but living, breathing people,' who 'are neither above nor below one's sympathy.' Her letter was dated 23rd July, and poor Hayward shuffled and dallied for several months until, gathering the impression from his acquaintance that the tale was gaining ground and being acclaimed as a work of genius, he finally wrote an article for the *Edinburgh Review* of January 1848. Mrs. Procter literally dictated the article, Hayward apparently not even troubling to read the earlier numbers, but he was able to strut and preen his feathers for the rest of his days as the first to pronounce the genius of the greatest novelist since Fielding. Doubtless he invoked blessings upon the shrewd woman who compelled him to commit his academical indiscretion. On 8th November, in gleeful anticipation of his article, he offers Thackeray the avuncular advice that he must not 'get nervous or think about criticism, or trouble yourself about the opinions of friends; you have completely beaten Dickens out of the inner circle already.' Concluding with a flourish, as if to say, 'you are now one of *us*,' he remarks: 'I dine at Gore House to-day: look in if you can,' and signs himself familiarly, 'Ever yours, A. H.' Thackeray sent the note to Mrs. Brookfield, thinking that it would appeal to her sense of humour, and remarking, 'how great that phrase about the "inner circle" is.'

When an Olympian organ like the *Edinburgh* condescended to notice a novel in shilling monthly parts, which had not even attained the dignity of completion, widespread curiosity was created. People read it, and, before or after reading alike, they accepted the *Edinburgh's* estimate of its remarkable brilliance. The season of 1848 witnessed the advent of a new literary star. All sorts of fine ladies who had never heard of Titmarsh eagerly invited the author of *Vanity Fair* to dinner and begged him for autographs. Few would decline an invitation from a duchess, and Thackeray did not. He went everywhere, accepting everything that offered, realising that social success materially assisted to increase his reputation, and enjoying himself, as he always enjoyed good dinners and good company. Naturally the pressure of his engagements occasioned less opportunities for meeting his old friends, some of whom expressed resentment at his apparent neglect of them for the society flatterers of his success, forgetting that it was to these potentates that he must look for the stabilisation of his reputation. The dour Carlyle, who had thought Thackeray demeaned himself and his profession by accepting a free passage on a steamboat, now considered him degraded by the acceptance of adulation from the butterflies of high society. Gloomily he stated his opinion to FitzGerald, who reproached his friend on that account. Thackeray replied:

'It is not true what Gurlyle has written to you about my having become a tremenjous lion, etc. too grand to, etc. . . . All that about being a Lion is nonsense. I can't eat more dinners than I used last year, and dine at home with my dear little women three times a week: but two or three great people ask me to their houses: and *Vanity Fair* does everything but pay. I am glad if you like it. I don't care a dem if some other people do or don't: and always try to keep that damper against flattery. . . . This letter has been delayed and delayed, until I fancied it would never go; nevertheless I am always yours, and like you almost as much as I did twenty years ago.'

FitzGerald had never believed that he was spoiled by success, only repeating Carlyle's remark as a playfully suggested reason for not having heard lately from his friend. Before receiving the foregoing belated letter, he had written to Frederick Tennyson:

'Thackeray is progressing greatly in his line: he publishes a Novel in numbers—*Vanity Fair*—which began dull, I thought: but gets better every number, and has some very fine things indeed in it. He is become a great man I am told: goes to Holland House, and Devonshire House: and for some reason or other, will not write a word to me. But I am sure this is not because he is asked to Holland House.'

When he came up to town he found Thackeray 'just the same,' in spite of the change in his fortunes.

Except for dining out occasionally at Gore House, Holland House, and similar strongholds of the *beau monde*, his mode of life was little altered. His name continues to occur in the company of his old friends in familiar surroundings whenever it is mentioned in the diaries and letters of his contemporaries. In his diary for 1847 his dinner engagements include all the old names—Duff-Gordon, Pollock, Serjeant Murphy, Kenyon, Reeve, Buller, Talfourd, Macready, Procter, Molesworth—only Lord Holland intervenes to mark his accession to fashionable celebrity. He is more than ever intimate with the Procters and the Brookfields. He asks himself to dinner with Brookfield, Lord Lyttelton asks himself also, and Brookfield asks Kinglake to complete the party—'a learned, pious peer—the chief writer in *Punch*—and Eothen.' A little later, he calls in one evening with James Spedding to talk and smoke with Brookfield till midnight. He attends the Sterling Club dinner with Pollock, Spring Rice, Anthony Sterling, Venables, Merivale, and Spedding. He dines with Macready, meeting Tom Taylor, William Jerdan, the composer Berlioz, and all the usual set. In the same month that Hayward asks him to look in at Gore House, he entertains to dinner no more exalted folk than Leech, Brookfield, one of the Merivales, and Alfred Montgomery.

When *Vanity Fair* began to earn money as well as praise, his sole ostentatious extravagance consisted of the purchase of a cob: 'I have bought a hoss, and ride in the Park with great elegance,' he tells his brother-in-law. 'Strange to say, not knowing a horse from a cow, everybody says I have got a most wonderful bargain.' And he promises FitzGerald a ride behind him when he comes to town.

A swelled head from the intoxication of success would have been inconsistent with his character. He loved praise just as much as when he found his vanity tickled by the parody of 'Timbuctoo' at Cambridge. But much water had flowed beneath his bridge since then. His sense of humour and bitter experience of life enabled him to recognise flattery, as in Hayward's case. But his philosophy and love of life, which had preserved him from misanthropic bitterness in the years of sorrow and disappointment, now prevented him from assuming an attitude of haughty disdain, such as Carlyle might have approved, towards the littleness of success. With both hands he grasped the cup of life, draining its contents with an eager thirst, swallowing the dregs along with the sweet flavour of the wine.

§ 2

While breathlessly watching the progress of *Vanity Fair*, he did not neglect his interests with *Punch*. The success of the *Snob Papers* was followed by *Punch's Prize Novelists*, in which the leading novelists of the day were parodied. The unfortunate Bulwer inevitably led the way, 'George De Barnwell, by Sir E.L. B.L. BB. LL. BBB. LLL.,' appearing in three numbers during April 1847. He had commenced work upon the series three months before, for on 27th January he wrote to Albany Fonblanque:

'A great qualm has just come over me about our conversation this morning. I am going to do a series of novels by the most popular authors for *Punch*, and Bulwer is actually done, the blocks designed, and the story in progress. It is George de Barnwell. He will quote Plato, speak in Big Phrases, and let out his Nunky's old, etc. . . . Numbers of others are to follow—Cooper, James, Dickens, Lever, &c. —but they will all be good-natured, and I can't afford to give up my plan. It is my bread, indeed, for next year.

I am bound to tell you this (how the deuce did I forget it in our talk this morning?), lest you should be putting your hospitable intentions into execution, and after having had my legs *sub iisdem trabibus* with Bulwer, should seem to betray him. I can't leave him out of the caricature; all that I promise is to be friendly and meek in spirit.'

The former editor of the *Examiner*, a friend of both Bulwer and Thackeray, had evidently intended to bring them together at his table, but was prevented by Thackeray's delicacy. In view of his attitude towards Deady Keane over the latter's offensive article in *Fraser* four years before and towards Edmund Yates in the *cause célèbre* of eleven years later, this letter to Fonblanque supplies a significant commentary upon the fastidiousness for which he was condemned by the partisans of Yates.

Disraeli succeeded Bulwer in the pillory, and never forgave the author of 'Codlingsby, by B. de Shrewsbury, Esq.' On the appearance of 'Phil Fogarty, by Harry Rollicker,' Lever's former exasperation against Thackeray revived, and his biographer, Fitzpatrick, declares that he wrote 'to know what he meant by it,' adding that 'the satirist did not heal the wound by his reply.' Unfortunately, Fitzpatrick omitted to quote these letters, which he saw in the hands of Frederick Chapman, the publisher, and valuable light upon the details of Lever's indignation is therefore lost. Subsequently, Lever frankly expressed his admiration of Thackeray's remarkably faithful imitation of his style, which impressed him from the first to such an extent that he altered the style of his novels. Nevertheless, the bitterness of his resentment found expression in the same novel which marked his change of manner, *Roland Cashel*, which contained a caricature of Thackeray as 'Elias Howle,' the English tourist—'a publisher's man of all work, ready for everything, from statistics to satire, and equally prepared to expound prophecy, or write squibs for *Punch*'—a likeness readily recognisable by Irishmen who knew Thackeray's cousin, the Rev. Elias Thackeray. On reading *Roland Cashel*, Thackeray wrote to Mrs. Brookfield:

'Should you like to see me lampooned in a novel? I found one on my return home last night with a notice from a dimgoodnatured friend—in which Harry Lorrequer has paid me off for jokes upon him. He is very savage and evidently hurt. This is rather good coming 2 days after the announcement in the *Chronicle* that I was "a Satirist without an enemy." I'll send that to Lever, I think.'

Of how they became reconciled, there is no evidence, but when Lever came to London in 1852 with a rash notion of editing a political paper, it was Thackeray who persuaded him to continue his career as a novelist rather than damage his reputation with ephemeral journalism. From that time onwards they maintained cordial relations, frequently meeting in Italy when Lever was living there.

The novelist who suffered most severely from Thackeray's parodies offered neither retaliation nor resentment. The opening of 'Barbazure, by G. P. R. Jeames, Esq.' so deftly reproduced the style of G. P. R. James that it might actually have been the beginning of one of his perennially popular romances. James is now remembered as a minor historical novelist whose tales of chivalry invariably commence with 'a solitary horseman' or 'two cavaliers' riding along through a prelude to romantic adventure. He owes that memory to Thackeray, who lighted upon the horsemen as his principal characteristic and branded them on James with the indelible mark of ridicule. As his biographer has demonstrated,[1] James, like Lever, took a lesson from the caricature of his style, for, of the many novels in which the cavaliers figure, not one was written after the appearance of 'Barbazure.'

Thackeray was embroiled in another quarrel in some way connected with *Punch* while the *Prize Novelists* were appearing, in which Tom Taylor was associated with him against John Forster. There was no extraordinary distinction in quarrelling with Forster; few of his most intimate friends failed to fall foul of his impetuous violence, and Macready, with whom he was usually on confidential and even affectionate terms, frequently decided that he was 'impossible,' 'insincere,' or 'grossly impertinent,' only to be delighted with his 'dear Forster' a few days later. In this case Forster was apparently guilty of some hasty action, like his publication in *Punch* of Tennyson's retort to Bulwer's *New Timon* in the previous year. On the evening of 12th June he confided to Macready the details of his 'imbroglio with Thackeray and Tom Taylor,' on which the actor comments with a gesture of condescension: 'Words, words, words!' Apparently he confided with more tangible effect in Dickens, who consented to play the peacemaker. On the 21st Thackeray intended to give a dinner at Greenwich, but he wrote to Brookfield a few days before: 'There will be no dinner at Greenwich on Monday. Dickens has chosen that day for a reconciliation banquet between Forster and me.' To Mrs. Macready he wrote more formally:

'I am sure, considering the circumstances, you and Mr. Macready will give me some other day but the 21st for Greenwich. Dickens has just written begging me to dine with him and meet Foster [*sic*] and make up quarrels and be friends.'

[1] *The Solitary Horseman: or, The Life and Adventures of G. P. R. James*, by S. M. Ellis. London, 1927.

The Macreadys were invited by Dickens to be of the party, which consisted, besides Thackeray, Taylor, and Forster, of the Duff-Gordons and Sir William Allan, the painter.

With both Dickens and Forster his friendly relations continued until, some three or four years later, they languished into a formal courtesy concealing a certain constraint, which only developed into enmity on the occasion of the Yates *fracas* in 1858. From time to time he is found dining with Dickens, and he felt a grateful regard for Dickens's wife and sister-in-law, who regularly invited his daughters to their children's parties. In the spring of 1848 he tells FitzGerald of a party he intends to give: 'Mrs. Dickens and Miss Hogarth made me give it.' About the same time, when Forster had generously reviewed *Vanity Fair*, he informed Mrs. Brookfield that 'his article in the *Examiner* did not please me so much as his genuine good nature in insisting upon walking with Annie at night, and holding an umbrella over her through the pouring rain.' Lady Ritchie herself related that 'the Dickens children's parties were shining facts in our early London days,'[1] and recollected one Christmas party when Dickens organised a pleasant compliment to her father, his eldest son marshalling all the boys on Thackeray's arrival to fetch his children home, and greeting his entry with rousing cheers.

§ 3

Hayward left it rather late to claim the credit for ensuring the success of *Vanity Fair*. If he had acted immediately upon Mrs. Procter's suggestion, the case might have been altered, but in January 1848, the month of his article's appearance, there was issued a publication calculated to occasion more curious interest in *Vanity Fair* than any critical review. This was the second edition of *Jane Eyre*,

[1] *Chapters from Some Memoirs*, by Anne Thackeray Ritchie. London, 1894.

dedicated by the pseudonymous author to Thackeray as 'the first social regenerator of the day.' This novel, since its appearance some two months before, had rapidly developed a popularity largely due to its description as 'a tale of passion.' According to current standards, it possessed a spicy flavour, and since the critics unanimously acclaimed it as a powerfully written work of curious genius, it carried the ingredients of popular success. The identity of the author afforded a topic for speculative gossip, the full force of which was directed upon Thackeray by the dedication of the second edition.

Having read *Vanity Fair* as the monthly parts appeared, Charlotte Brontë developed an enthusiastic admiration for Thackeray. The range of her reading being narrow, and feeling this a handicap in a blue-stocking, she affected an aggressive attitude of originality in taste, which is reflected in a letter to her publishers of 22nd January:

> 'I do not know if the part which relates to Mr. Thackeray is likely to be as well received; but whether generally approved of and understood or not, I shall not regret having written it, for I am convinced of its truth.'

Even to her publishers she was known at this time only as 'Currer Bell.' Evidently they had recognised and pointed out to her that the dedication was likely to create a fund of curious gossip, though they can scarcely have realised the full extent of that which was in effect created. The information speedily circulated that Thackeray's wife, like the wife of Rochester, the hero of *Jane Eyre*, was of unsound mind, and scandalmongers suggested rumours creditable neither to Thackeray nor 'Currer Bell.' He himself felt mystification and amazement at the coincidence, something of which he confessed when writing to her through her publishers to thank her for the compliment of the dedication. On 28th January she wrote:

'I need not tell you that when I saw Mr. Thackeray's letter inclosed under your cover, the sight made me very happy. It was some time before I dared open it, lest my pleasure in receiving it should be mixed with pain on learning its contents—lest, in short, the dedication should have been, in some way inacceptable to him.

And, to tell you the truth, I fear this must have been the case; he does not say so, his letter is most friendly in its noble simplicity, but he apprises me, at the commencement, of a circumstance which both surprised and dismayed me.

I suppose it is no indiscretion to tell you this circumstance, for you doubtless know it already. It appears that his private position is in some points similar to that I have ascribed to Mr. Rochester; that thence arose a report that *Jane Eyre* had been written by a governess in his family, and that the dedication coming now has confirmed everybody in the surmise.

Well may it be said that fact is often stranger than fiction! The coincidence struck me as equally unfortunate and extraordinary. Of course, I know nothing whatever of Mr. Thackeray's domestic concerns, he existed for me only as an author. Of all regarding his personality, station, connections, private history, I was, and am still in a great measure, totally in the dark; but I am *very very* sorry that my inadvertent blunder should have made his name and affairs a subject for common gossip.

The very fact of his not complaining at all and addressing me with such kindness, notwithstanding the pain and annoyance I must have caused him, increases my chagrin. I could not half express my regret to him in my answer, for I was restrained by the consciousness that the regret was just worth nothing at all—quite valueless for healing the mischief I had done.'

In mentioning the report of *Jane Eyre* being ascribed to a former governess in his employ, Thackeray observed the bounds of delicacy; he might have added that common scandal did not hesitate to suggest that the governess had also been his mistress. A man of genius, still under forty, living alone with two young children about whose absent mother there was some mystery, afforded an intriguing subject for discussion in the days when Queen Victoria was sharing domestic bliss with her 'poor dear gentlewoman,' as Thackeray once called the Prince Consort.

Gathering picturesqueness from repetition, the rumours received careful consideration from Elizabeth Rigby, subsequently the wife of Sir Charles Eastlake, who secured for herself a mean little niche in the memory of posterity by a venomous review in the *Quarterly* for December 1848 of *Vanity Fair*, *Jane Eyre*, and the annual report of the Governesses' Benevolent Institution. Lockhart, the editor of the *Quarterly*, famous as the 'Scorpion' in the early days of *Blackwood*, was popularly supposed to have lent the sting to the article, but he is exonerated by his correspondence with his contributor. Having repeated the legend of the governess, she dismisses it as of 'no great interest,' proceeding to express her amusingly ingenious belief that 'Currer Bell' could not be a woman or she would never have committed so many errors in description of fashionable feminine attire, but, finally reverting to the scandalous, decides that, if indeed a woman, she must be one 'who has, for some sufficient reason, long forfeited the society of her own sex.'

Commenting upon Miss Rigby's lucubrations, Charlotte Brontë expressed indignation only on Thackeray's account, as well she might, being herself secure from scandal in the sanctuary of her pseudonym. Thackeray, on the other hand, though deriving valuable publicity from the gossip, must have suffered considerable discomfort, feeling, whenever he entered a fashionable drawing-room, that the ladies in the background were laying their heads together and describing him in breathless whispers, not only as the author of *Vanity Fair*, but the prototype of Mr. Rochester. Of the nature of Mr. Abraham Hayward's replies to the eager questions he must have received on the subject from his many female friends, there is no record, but there were doubtless many malicious tongues to paint the rumours in colours of reality. Thackeray must have thought that 'Currer Bell' might have declared herself without prejudice to her reputation, especially as her book was an established success, but he was still ignorant of her identity on 8th May 1849, when she informed her publishers: 'Should Mr. Thackeray again ask after Currer Bell, say the secret is and will be well kept because it is not worth disclosure.' He bore her somewhat selfish reticence with good-humour, sending her soon afterwards, with his 'grateful regards,' a presentation copy of *Vanity Fair*.

His complete ignorance of her identity and consequent mystification are witnessed in a letter to Brookfield of October 1848, after the final number of *Vanity Fair* had appeared in the previous July with a dedication to Procter, the old friend whose wife had comforted him in the first shock of his wife's illness and lent her influence to assist the success of the novel.

'Old Dilke of the *Athenæum*,' he writes, 'vows that Procter and his wife, between them, wrote *Jane Eyre*, and when I protest ignorance, says "Pooh! you know who wrote it, you are the deepest rogue in England, &c." I wonder whether it can be true? It is just possible, and then what a singular circumstance is the + fire of the two dedications.'

In spite of the assurance received from her publishers that 'Currer Bell' had no acquaintance with him, he obviously entertained doubts of their statement under the influence of the universal scepticism he encountered among his friends. He had to run the gauntlet of gossip until it subsided in course of time under the weight of a new sensation, for it was only in November 1849, a month before he met her personally, that the information of 'Currer Bell's' identity leaked out through G. H. Lewes.

§ 4

The success of *Mrs. Perkins's Ball* was exceeded by that of his second Christmas book, *Our Street*, published in December 1847. Both are obviously branded with the mark of *Punch*, relying for much of their humour upon the illustrations, which represent Thackeray's most carefully finished efforts as an artist. Displaying only too plainly the poverty of his draughtsmanship, these illustrations at the same time reveal his aptitude for catching and conveying the precise conception of a character, a faculty which imparts to his roughest sketches a reality and personality frequently lacking in the more accomplished work of superior illustrations. It was this characteristic which aroused the admiration of Charlotte Brontë, who appreciated the novelist's difficulty of discovering an artist possessing the perception necessary to an accurate portrayal of the effects produced by the creator's imagination. Thackeray himself, with his usual self-criticism, realised his defects and advantages as an illustrator. Aware of his technical deficiency, he secured from Vizetelly the services of a young artist named Thwaites to touch up his drawings for *Mrs. Perkins's Ball*, but the results were unsatisfactory, and, writing to Vizetelly to instruct the artist to 'confine his improvements to the Mulligans' and Mrs. Perkins's others guests' extremities,' he remarked:

> 'In your young gentleman's otherwise praiseworthy corrections of my vile drawing, a certain *je ne sais quoi*, which I flatter myself exists in the original sketches, seems to have given him the slip, and I have tried in vain to recapture it. Somehow I prefer my own Nuremburg dolls to Mr. Thwaites's superfine wax models.'

According to Vizetelly, Thwaites put on the wood many of the sketches for *Mrs. Perkins's Ball*, and presumably Thackeray regularly employed young artists to save him the time and trouble of the task, for it was in this capacity that Frederick Walker was first employed before illustrating *Philip*.

Both *Mrs. Perkins's Ball* and *Our Street* achieved success because they exactly conformed with public expectations from the humorous satirist of the *Snob Papers* and *Vanity Fair*. As satirical sketches of contemporary society they scarcely entered the same category of 'Christmas books' as Dickens's seasonable stories. But literary society—especially Hayward's 'inner circle'—considered Thackeray not only as equalling Dickens, but surpassing him, for his style was always preferred, as in succeeding generations, by the cultured classes, though he never appealed, either then or since, to the great circulating library public drawn from the commercial middle-class of the big provincial cities. Writing to his mother on the publication of *Our Street*, he remarked:

'There's no use denying the matter or blinking it, now I am become a sort of great man in my way—all but at the top of the tree, indeed there, if the truth were known, and having a great fight up there with Dickens. I get such a deal of praise wherever I go, that it is rather wearisome to hear. I don't think my head is a bit turned, please God, for I have always got my own opinion, and when men and newspapers say "*Our Street* is the finest," &c., I know a devilish deal better, and don't disguise the truth either. This London world is full of good-natured Tom Fools, and directly one begins to cry O, all the rest say Prodigious. . . .'

There are obvious foundations for J. C. Jeaffreson's theory that Thackeray was first inspired with an ambition to emulate and surpass the success of Dickens by Hayward's remark that the latter was beaten 'out of the inner circle' by the early numbers of *Vanity Fair*. For ten years Dickens had held an unassailed position in the English-speaking world; not only was he the criterion of critics, but many of those in Mayfair welcomed the appearance of a new star whose brilliance might dim his solitary lustre. Thackeray's jealousy of Dickens provided the memoir-writers with a subject for discussion over half a century, though Procter told FitzGerald at the time of Dickens's death that he had never witnessed any signs of such jealousy. Few could judge better than Procter, for, though a man so abundantly generous and guileless might be suspected of suppressing any knowledge of petty ill-feeling for the sake of preventing gossip, he was equally the friend of both parties and expressing a private opinion to a friend whom he knew to possess discretion and a kindliness of heart comparable with his own. He was right; all the posthumous gossipers supply not a tittle of evidence to convict Thackeray of jealousy.

His feeling towards Dickens was envy. He had always envied him from the commencement of their acquaintance, when he saw Dickens leap suddenly from the obscurity of a reporter's table to a celebrity surpassing that of writers like Bulwer, who had several years' start of him. He realised that he was almost the same age as Dickens and had begun life with immeasurably superior advantages; yet, at the epoch of the other's rise to fame, he was condemned to the monotonous toil of a working journalist. In his Fraserian days, his envy was detached, for he never contemplated the achievement of success so dazzling. But when everybody he met flavoured their praise of *Vanity Fair* with remarks like Hayward's regarding Dickens, envy was magnified by ambition into emulation. *Vanity Fair* received enthusiastic plaudits of praise long before its success was reflected in its sales, and though the majority of reviewers always lavished more unstinted praise upon his works than upon those of Dickens, the latter's books continued to outdistance his in sales. He could never understand that his appeal was directed to a smaller public than Dickens's, and cherished hopes of one day exceeding the sales of his rival. He is reported once to have entered the office of Chapman and Hall with the request to be told the average monthly sale of Dickens's current novel, and, on being shown the accounts, exclaimed in 'mingled surprise and mortification,' 'What!—so far ahead of me as all that!' A similar story is told of his visit to Harpers' in New York, where he learned that G. P. R. James outstripped even Dickens in popularity, and he told Maunsell B. Field, as an item of information likely to occasion surprise, that five of Dickens's books were sold to every one of his own.

From the frankness with which he freely expressed his feelings and numerous acquaintances who reported them, it is evident that he felt towards Dickens nothing of which he need have been ashamed. Passionately desirous of earning money in order to make suitable provision for his daughters, he envied Dickens his greater popularity solely on account of its financial aspect. The suggestion that his ambition to surpass his rival in popularity arose from an 'appetite for social distinction' supposes a non-existent motive; his measure of success had already secured for him a reputation in society second to none. Moreover, he estimated adulation at its proper value, and would gladly, as he once remarked, have sacrificed his praise for Dickens's sales.

Partisans of Dickens have sought to exonerate him from blame for any coolness in their relations by demonstrating that he never evinced jealousy of Thackeray. Obviously he had cause for no such feeling, for he had enjoyed ten years of unparalleled success before his rival rose to fame, and the supremacy of his popularity was never threatened. The fact that he invited rivals like Bulwer and Wilkie Collins to contribute to his magazine implies no superiority of generosity over Thackeray, who personally applied to almost every reputable writer to contribute to the *Cornhill* under his editorship. It cannot be contended that Dickens ever felt the admiration for Thackeray's work that Thackeray felt for his; George Augustus Sala, who knew them both and worked at one time under Dickens, definitely stated as much.[1] In a story about two popular novelists similarly installed as rivals for public favour by the gossip of literary 'fans,' Mr. Max Beerbohm has described one of them invariably interrupting praise of his own work by launching into expressions of admiration for his rival. Thackeray may be suspected of the same affectation, for his self-consciousness would suggest such a resort to escape the embarrassment of hearing his own praises. But his admiration was sincere. He praised *A Christmas Carol* without reserve in *Fraser* before he entered into competition with Dickens, and while *Vanity Fair* was appearing, he walked one day into the *Punch* office, flinging down the current number of *Dombey and Son* containing the death of Paul Dombey, and exclaiming, with unconscious confession of his ambition to surpass Dickens: 'There's no writing against this; one hasn't an atom of chance. It's stupendous!'

So far from developing a swelled head from the sudden splendour of success, the old mistrust of his abilities afflicting him as an undergraduate now recurred with increased anxiety. While writing *Vanity Fair* number by number in time for publication, he told his mother: 'Towards the end of the month I get so nervous, that I don't speak to anybody scarcely, and once actually got up in the middle of the night and came down and wrote in my night chimee.' The thought of his success, he confessed, 'makes me very humble and frightened—not elated.' And, actually, while busily engaged upon the rackingly anxious task of sustaining the quality of *Vanity Fair* month by month, he was eating dinners at the Middle Temple with a view to obtaining

[1] *Things I have Seen and People I have Known*, by George Augustus Sala. London, 2 vols., 1894.

his call to the Bar. He was eventually called on 26th May 1848, five weeks before he wrote the last lines of *Vanity Fair* on 2nd July. He had no intention of practising, but hoped to secure a metropolitan magistracy, like Fielding, or some similar post. He confided his plan to Milnes, asking him to use his interest on his behalf, and his friend suggested a post to him the following year, in reply to which he wrote:

'You are a good and lovable adviser and M.P., but I cannot get the Magistrate's place, not being eligible. I was only called to the Bar last year, and they require barristers of seven years' standing. Time will qualify me, however, and I hope to be able to last six years in the literary world; for though I shall write I dare say, very badly, yet the public won't find it out for some time, and I shall live upon my past reputation. It is a pity, to be sure. If I could get a place and rest, I think I could do something better than I have done, and leave a good and lasting book behind me; but Fate is overruling. I have written to thank L. for his kind letter, and to beg him to remember me if any opportunity occurs of serving me. I wonder whether Lord Palmerston could? But I would rather be in London. Thank you for thinking of me, and believe that I am grateful.'

Speaking of living upon his 'past reputation' at a time when only the early numbers of *Pendennis* had been issued, he reveals alike genuine humility with respect to his powers and a cynical view of the fickleness of popular favour. No man, intoxicated by success and satisfied of his celebrity, could have expressed such pessimistic resignation. Milnes himself must have wondered at the man of whom he had written to a friend only a month or two before, on 19th May 1849:

'Thackeray is winning great social success, dining at the Academy, Sir R. Peel's, &c. I doubt whether he will be much the happier for it, though I think people generally are the better for satisfied vanity.'

He was certainly happier for recognition, which he had craved so long. He was happier still for possessing money sufficient for his immediate needs and the means to gratify his taste for good company and good-fellowship in the society for which he was intellectually and morally fitted.

CHAPTER 9

§ 1

To the years between his rise to fame as the author of *Vanity Fair* and his first visit to America belongs his intimate correspondence with Mrs. Brookfield. For five years she was the dominant influence on his life, a sweet, sympathetic, essentially feminine personality, alluring and elusive. Nearly ten years his junior, she was twenty-six in the year of *Vanity Fair*, thus newly arrived at the full bloom of her beauty and charm. George Richmond's portrait of her, painted four years later, depicts an exquisite face, with a forehead expressive of intellect, a straight nose widening at the nostrils, and a pointed chin, framed in a delicate oval by the hair, parted in the middle and drawn down tightly over the ears according to current fashion, presenting the appearance of a girlish 'bob.' Her large blue eyes, set beneath well-defined brows, are serene and steadfast, gentle and rather sad; the mouth is a Cupid's bow, mobile, sensuous, sensitive, and tender. Save for the wistful depth of her eyes, it is the face of an entrancingly lovely girl.

From the time of the 'two-penny tart' dinner till 1845, he regarded her merely as the very attractive young wife of an intimate friend. Then, during the time he was lodging in St. James's Street and habitually taking his Saturday breakfasts with the Brookfields, his friendship for the husband extended to the wife and he adopted the attitude of an elder brother to her. Brookfield delighted in the pleasant relations between his young wife and his gifted friend, feeling no jealousy when Thackeray addressed his letters to his wife instead of himself or inscribed presentation copies of his books to her alone. Nor was there any cause. Accustomed to confide his thoughts and doings in long letters to his mother throughout his life, he always found it easier to address a woman, because his essentially masculine temperament, which rendered him a convivial companion and a great clubman, shrank self-consciously from intimate confidence and revelation of feeling in correspondence with one of his own sex. Asking Lucy Baxter to apologise for him to her father for not writing to him, he remarks: 'I don't to any man except on business.'[1] With the single exception of FitzGerald, this statement was true. As to the presentation of autographed copies of his books, he invariably inscribed them to the wives of his friends, because he rightly judged that women value such compliments from an author more than men. Only a man of Macready's peevish susceptibility could resent such a harmless compliment and declare himself, as did Macready on receiving a copy of *Vanity Fair* inscribed by Thackeray 'to Mrs. Macready,' 'not satisfied of his sincerity towards *me*.' Brookfield welcomed such attentions from Thackeray to his wife, and encouraged him to talk about her in her absence, sometimes telling her afterwards of his friend's enthusiastic expressions of admiration for her, sometimes playfully declining to repeat such flattering encomiums.

At the end of January 1847 Thackeray ran down for a week-end to Southampton, where Brookfield and his wife were staying with her close friend, Mrs. Fanshawe, the wife of a clergyman. There apparently he expressed his admiration with such fervour in the presence of others that Brookfield demanded to know what he meant by it. Thackeray replied 'under the confessional seal in the railway,' when returning to London:

'Her innocence, looks, angelical sweetness and kindness charm and ravish me to the highest degree; and every now

[1] *Thackeray's Letters to An American Family*, edited by Lucy W. Baxter. London, 1904.

ANE OCTAVIA BROOKFIELD AT THE AGE OF THIRTY

From a painting by George Richmond, R.A.

and then in contemplating them I burst out into uncouth raptures. They are not in the least dangerous—it is a sort of artistical delight (a spiritual sensuality so to speak)—other beautiful objects in Nature so affect me, children, landscapes, harmonies of colour, music, etc. . . . My dear old fellow, you and God Almighty may know all my thoughts about your wife; I'm not ashamed of one of them, since the days of the dear old two-penny tart dinner till now. . . . Well, I have opened my bowels to you. Indeed, there has not been much secret before; and I've always admired the generous spirit in which you have witnessed my queer raptures. If I had envy, or what you call passion, or a wicked thought . . . I should have cut you long ago.'

Brookfield could not deny the justice of the latter remarks; moreover, if his wife knew of his reprimand to Thackeray, she probably expressed, being entirely innocent of any inclination to infidelity, considerable displeasure at his conduct. In any case, he accepted Thackeray's explanation and received him at his house a fortnight later.

Thackeray's sentiments were entirely sincere. He harboured no other feelings than those of admiration and affection for Jane Brookfield, who, on her side, was flattered by the devotion of a man whose name was on everybody's lips and whose genius was generally acknowledged. In the early days of their acquaintance she had assumed an attitude almost of coolness towards him, scarcely approving the Bohemian Titmarsh, with his boon companions like 'Father Prout,' as a suitable associate for a young clergyman ambitious of advancement. Her husband, however, persisted in his intimacy with Thackeray, whom he repeatedly praised enthusiastically to her, and did his utmost to facilitate a friendship between them. Fond of literary society and vain of his intimacy with the wits, he encouraged her in similar tastes, to which she was naturally inclined by her culture and intellectual attainments. Thus she gradually melted into friendship with Thackeray, eagerly welcoming his confidence about his work and its difficulties, probably not without an additional satisfaction derived from the thought, natural in a young woman towards an older rival of recognised brilliance, that she was superseding Mrs. Procter as his mentor.

Her letters to him were couched in the formal phrasing consistent with current convention, their tone sounding a note of humorous raillery and demure wit. Besides their literary flavour they differ in their style of banter little from those to her husband; she never forgot that she was a beautiful and clever woman addressing a man. But for Thackeray she manifested an intellectual respect which she did not accord to her husband. In this lay the secret of her attraction, fostered by her husband's passion for literature and the literary. Her husband's career and ambitions assumed a humble appearance beside the great work of a brilliant genius, an impression intensified by his acquired habit of imitating Thackeray's mannerisms, notable in the style and the 'Jeames' spelling of his correspondence. Though innocently unsuspecting that she might be playing with fire, she resigned herself to the gratification of her vanity by accepting a measure of confidence usually only given with so much spontaneity and intimacy by a man to his wife or mother. 'A very woman,' with her youth, her beauty, her wit and ambition, how could her vanity not be tickled by the knowledge that her personality had suggested the conception of the heroine in the novel of which the whole world was talking! In October 1847 she wrote to her young cousin, Harry Hallam:

'There is a New *Vanity* not good—except the wicked ones—Mr. Thackeray has now got a 2nd Amelia, Lady Jane Sheepshanks. I wish he had made Amelia more exciting especially as the remark is he has thought of me in her character. And on the plan of 2 negatives making one affirmative, I suppose I may take the 2 dull ones of the book to make one Mrs. B. You know he told William that though Amelia was not a copy of me he should not have conceived the character if he had not known me—and though she has the right amount of antiphlegm and affectionateness she is really an uncommonly dull and a selfish character, and very apathetic to the only person who cares for her, the quaint Capt. Dobbin.'

Three months before she had expressed the wish that 'he would give Amelia a few more brains,' when informing her husband that her eldest sister had read the current number 'and rates it (even on such a mere scrap of it) much above Dickens.' From which it appears that Jeaffreson imputed to Abraham Hayward an undeserved credit for originality, for it was only in November that Hayward informed Thackeray of his beating Dickens 'out of the inner circle.'

The Brookfields at this time were so poor that they found it necessary to give up their home in Great Pulteney Street. Evidence of Thackeray's generous friendship and the innocence of his affection for Mrs. Brookfield appear in an invitation that 'you and Mrs. Brookfield will come and take these three nice little rooms here, and stop with me until you have found other lodgment.' The three rooms were the '2 capital bed-rooms' and the 'little sitting-room' always reserved for his parents' visits since his instalment at Young Street. The 'famous bed-room for G. M. on the first floor' had been lately vacated by the death of old Mrs. Butler, who had spent the last years of her life with her grandson. Brookfield declined the invitation for obvious reasons; apart from reluctance to accept hospitality suggestive almost of charity, gossip injurious to his wife's reputation must have resulted from their residence in a pseudo-bachelor's house, especially in view of their impecuniosity and Thackeray's avowed admiration for her. Mrs. Brookfield, too, probably expressed objections, for when, a few months later, the Duff-Gordons made a similar offer, which her husband enthusiastically entertained, she decisively rejected the proposal on various grounds, particularly because two separate families, however friendly in casual intercourse, were unlikely long to live in amity and comfort under the same roof. She suffered from delicate health and went into the country for the greater part of the year, staying with her father and married sisters, while her husband, then minister at St. Luke's, Berwick Street, a parish incorporated with St. James's, Piccadilly, took up his lodgings in the vestry of his church. He continued as intimate as ever with Thackeray, visiting him daily, and if not meeting him at the Macreadys', the Procters', or the Duff-Gordons', dining out with him either at Young Street, the Garrick Club, or at No. 10 Crown Office Row, the chambers in the Temple which Thackeray rented at this time, while preparing for his call to the Bar. On 3rd November he wrote to his wife:

'After Litany I behoved to push on to Kensington and found Thack. droring for his new Annual which is to be called *Our Street*. He has engaged a Governess—a young person from Richmond. He invited us to go there for two or three weeks. What think you? *i.e.*, after Governidge and babes are arrived.'

Mrs. Brookfield did not return to town, however, her husband joining her in the country for the Christmas season. She was thus absent from London almost continuously for nine or ten months, from the early summer of 1847 to the following spring, during which time she saw nothing of Thackeray and corresponded with him but rarely.

In conjunction with Jane Brookfield's uncle, the historian Hallam, Thackeray used his interest to obtain for Brookfield the post of Inspector of Schools, affording an income sufficient for him to resume the maintenance of a home. Consequently, in April the Brookfields established themselves at 15 Portman Street, where young Harry Hallam, just down from Cambridge, lived with them. Always fond of the company of young men, Thackeray formed a friendly affection for young Hallam, whose dead elder brother, the subject of Tennyson's *In Memoriam*, he had known at Cambridge. Hallam's relations with his beautiful cousin were those of a younger brother, and Thackeray came to be regarded in the light of an elder brother. Mrs. Brookfield was still an invalid, lying all day on a sofa in her drawing-room, where she received her visitors. It was now that she came to know Thackeray intimately, to realise that, beneath the mask of high spirits and quizzical humour, lay a reflective melancholy, impassioned earnestness, and a heart hungry for feminine sympathy. Her invalid condition enabled her to see him at his best, for he had learned in the most painful circumstances the art of anticipating an invalid's unspoken whims and fancies, while he possessed the gentle tenderness peculiar to physically big men. He demanded of her a comforting understanding which her heart and intellect alike gloried in giving and which her husband had never exacted. A comparison between the letters of Thackeray and her husband displays the different function which each asked of her; Brookfield's are busy accounts of his comings, goings, and the people he met, flippantly joking and poking fun at her, while Thackeray's are contemplative and reflective, the spontaneous unloading of heart and brain. One asked only the play of her lively wit and tolerant humour; the other invoked the utmost resources of her womanly feeling, sympathy, understanding, encouragement—the inimitable solace of a wife or a mother.

Thackeray surrendered to her charm like a sufferer from insomnia succumbing to an opiate. He was pitiably lonely and alone. He had married for love and enjoyed domestic happiness long enough to learn its irreplaceable value. His young wife's devotion and interest in his work only emphasised the magnitude of his loss. From childhood his mother had encouraged in him a reliance upon feminine counsel, consolation, and confidence; he still loved and confided in her, but he no longer felt complete accord of sympathy with her, for she was growing old, full of fads, and obsessed with devotional doctrines. He craved communion with a woman of his own generation, of his own habit of life, who could appreciate his problems and realise his point of view. He wanted that which a wife only can give with complete satisfaction, for he represented the intrinsically masculine type of man to whom a woman is the natural complement.

He became an almost daily visitor at her house, amusing the tedious hours of her invalid inactivity and gradually increasing their intimacy until he confided everything to her. He began to bring her the work he had just written, upon which she would pass an opinion on his next visit; he showed her any of his correspondence likely to interest her, and discussed his domestic affairs. The visits became rays of sunlight in his life, beside which the remainder was dull and clouded. With light, eager step he approached the door of the Portman Street house, and went away again invigorated, determined each time to do a better day's work, with which to excite her praise and admiration. The summer which saw the finish of *Vanity Fair* in some respects resembled a fool's paradise; pursuing his usual policy of taking gladly the pleasures life offered, he took no heed of the future. The time quickly came when he realised that his life without that daily communion presented an aspect intolerably drear and lonely.

§ 2

Having finished *Vanity Fair* on 2nd July, he wrote in a panic lest Mrs. Brookfield might be offended because, in the last chapter, he used her own maid's name for the lady's maid of his heroine. 'You know,' he added, 'you are only a piece of Amelia, my mother is another half, my poor little wife—*y est pour beaucoup.*' He immediately made plans for a trip down the Rhine, with the idea of collecting local colour for his next Christmas book, already in commission from Chapman and Hall. On Tuesday, 18th July, he wrote to Chapman:

'I think of making my move at the beginning of next week and passing some time at Spa or Aix la Chapelle but as usual want some money before I go. If you could give me 50 pounds in advance now of the Kickelburys abroad you would very much oblige me.'

The letter proceeds to explain that he wants the money to liquidate the last remaining claim against his stepfather as a birthday present, thus revealing that the cloud of the *Constitutional* disaster only finally lifted before the risen sun of *Vanity Fair*. *The Kickleburys on the Rhine* did not appear till two years later; apparently he found that he could not afford the time for it, as he began *Pendennis* within the next three weeks. In its place he followed the plan of his previous Christmas books in *Doctor Birch and His Young Friends*, issued by Chapman and Hall in December.

Leaving the children in his mother's charge, 'after a day in the rain at Hampton Court,' where Forster was dining with the publisher Chapman, he spent 'Monday night and part of Tuesday' at Canterbury, where his brother-in-law, Arthur Shawe, was stationed with his military unit, before going on to Dover on Wednesday, the 26th, and arriving at Brussels the next day. From there he wrote a long letter to Brookfield, describing his itinerary and remarking that he is going to the 'Hotel de la Terrasse, where Becky used to live, and shall pass by Captain Osborn's lodgings.' 'How curious it is,' he adds. 'I believe perfectly in all those people, and feel quite an interest in the Inn in which they lived.' He concludes with 'Good-bye, my dear gentleman and lady, and let me hear the latter is getting well,' and, though the letter is addressed to Brookfield, its message is directed to the *confidante* of his inner self.

From Spa he wrote a long letter to his mother and two to the Brookfields, the first, on the 5th August, addressed to both conjointly, the other, on the 11th, to the wife alone. In the last he speaks of having 'finished writing page seven of PENDENNIS,' of receiving 'a beautiful thick 2/4 letter, in a fine large hand,' and, having described at length with entertaining humour all he has seen and done, he refers playfully to a bargain between them that they would exchange correspondence regularly during his absence, and wonders 'whether anybody will write to me *poste restante* at Homburg, near Frankfort-on-the-Maine?' These letters represent an almost pathetic effort to provide the invalid lady with some amusement in her enforced idleness. His tender consideration for her comfort must have captivated the gratitude of any woman. Once, thinking to alleviate her boredom, he begged Mrs. Sartoris—*née* Adelaide Kemble, with whom, unlike her sister Fanny, he had retained a friendly acquaintance since the days of his youthful intimacy with their brother—to go one afternoon and sing to her, an honour which much embarrassed its recipient.

Back in London on 21st August, he wrote immediately to Brookfield, who had taken his wife down to her father's Somerset home, that he had heard during his travels of a German spa exactly suited to Mrs. Brookfield's complaint: 'Y not take Madame there, go, drink, bathe, and be cured?' Almost immediately he received an invitation to spend a few days at Clevedon Court, the seat of Mrs. Brookfield's father, Sir Charles Elton, and went down there in September, probably delaying a few weeks to make up his arrears of work for *Punch* and his Christmas book. Mrs. Brookfield, writing to Harry Hallam in town to inform him of her husband's return the next day, says: 'Mr. Thackeray arrived here Thursday and is busy sketching out and inside the house.' He did no work at Clevedon, but evinced great interest in the historic old house, part of which dated back to the fourteenth century and had been the seat of the Earls of Bristol before the first Elton baronet acquired it at the beginning of the previous century. His impressions gathered on his visit furnished the model for the Castlewood of *Esmond* and *The Virginians*.

Returning from the pleasant society of the Elton family and more particularly of the baronet's youngest daughter, he faced his work despondently. He went down to Brighton to engage rooms for the reception of his parents and children, whom he intended to take down there for the month of October, and on his return wrote a letter descriptive of his movements to 'my dear Lady Brookfield.' He was aggravating his melancholy by reading *The Great Hoggarty Diamond*, reviving painful memories of the time of its composition.

'Why shouldn't I start off this instant for the G.W. Station and come and shake hands, and ask your family for some dinner; I should like it very much. Well, I am looking out of the window to see if the rain will stop, or give me an excuse for not going to Hatton to the Chief Baron's. I won't go—that's a comfort.'

A day or two later, on 4th October, he adds wistfully:

'As I passed by Portman Street, after you were gone, just to take a look up at the windows, the usual boy started forward to take the horse. I laughed a sad laugh. I didn't want nobody to take the horse. It's a long time since you were away. The cab is at the door to take me to the railroad. Mrs. Procter was very kind and Adelaide sympathised with me. I have just opened my desk, there are all the papers I had at Spa—*Pendennis*, unread since, and your letter.'

In a postscript, mentioning his approaching visit to Brighton, he makes a wistful joke that he thought of choosing Weston-super-Mare instead of Brighton, 'only it seemed such a hint.' To Brookfield, who had gone down to join his wife at Clevedon, he wrote from the Garrick Club:

'I have passed the day writing and trying to alter *Pendennis*, which is without any manner of doubt, awfully stupid; the very best passages, which pleased the author only last week, looking hideously dull by the dull fog of this day. I pray, I pray, that it may be the weather. . . . My old parents arrived last night, it was quite a sight to see the poor old mother with the children: and Bradbury the printer, coming to dun me for *Pendennis* this morning. I slunk away from home, where writing is an utter impossibility, and have been operating on it here.'

Again he hints at a visit to Clevedon 'as soon as my work is done.' He tells of having been to the Cyder Cellars 'to hear the man sing about going to be hanged'; this was a tavern singer named Ross, who sang a ditty called 'Sam Hall,' celebrated by Vizetelly, Edmund Yates, Sala, Burnand, and other memoir-writers. Ross and his song duly appeared in *Pendennis* as Hodgen and the 'Body-snatcher.' Evidently he had carried out his intention, hinted to his mother more than two years before, of quitting his work on the *Morning Chronicle*, for he tells Brookfield: 'As if I had not enough to do, I have begun to blaze away in the *Chronicle* again; it's an awful bribe—that five guineas an article.'

Bradbury and Evans issued the first monthly part of *Pendennis* in November, early in which month Thackeray visited Oxford, meeting for the first time Arthur Hugh Clough. On meeting Clough the following year, Mrs. Brookfield found him 'ununderstandable,' and his manner of staring—'his eyes cut one through and through'—very embarrassing, to which impression Thackeray replied by recording his own:

'I took a very great liking and admiration for Clough. He is a real poet and a simple affectionate creature. Last year we went to Blenheim from Oxford (it was after a stay at Cl-ved-n C-rt the seat of Sir C- E-n B-t) and I liked him for sitting down in the Inn yard and beginning to teach a child to read off a bit of *Punch* wh. was lying on the ground. Subsequently he sent me his pomes wh. were rough but contain the real genuine sacred flame I think. He is very learned: he has evidently been crossed in love: he gave up his fellowship and university prospects on religious scruples. He is one of those thinking men, who I daresay will begin to speak out before many years are over, and protest against Gothic Xtianity.'

The visit to Blenheim 'in an Oxford cart' is described in a letter of 1st November. Mrs. Brookfield had just returned from Clevedon to town, and, expressing his sorrow on hearing that she was unwell, Thackeray says: 'I was afraid the journey would agitate you, that was what I was thinking of as I was lying in the Oxford man's bed awake.' She was always in his thoughts. Telling her of a dinner he had attended, he says: 'it was all over by nine o'clock, half an hour before Payne [her maid] comes to fetch you to bed,' and he describes himself arriving at Oxford 'by the time your dinner was over.'

On his return from Oxford he called on her in town before going down to Brighton to join his family. At Brighton he applied himself diligently to the writing of *Pendennis*. He had few distractions beyond occasionally dining out with James Morier and Horace Smith, whose daughters evinced great interest in his work, one of them supplying the name of the heroine, Laura, in the book. More than ever he craved the society of 'his lady,' and his mother, soon discovering the cause of his melancholy abstraction, lavished upon him the treasures of maternal tenderness in her efforts to soothe his affliction. She grew nearer to him than at any time since his youth, and, witnessing her unstinted love for himself and his children he exclaimed to Mrs. Brookfield:

'I look at her character, and go down on my knees as it were with wonder and pity. It is Mater Dolorosa, with a heart bleeding with love. Is not that a pretty phrase? I wrote it yesterday in a book, whilst I was thinking about her—and have no shame somehow now in writing thus sentimentally to all the public; though there are very few people in the world to whom I would have the face to talk in this way *tête-à-tête.*'

There are modern critics, by no means indisposed to make allowance for the sentimental tendencies prevalent in the early Victorian novelists, who find the sentimentality of *Pendennis* intolerably sickly and mawkish. This sentimentality obviously resulted from the satisfaction he confessedly derived from unburdening his heart in his writing. The very nature of his subject encouraged the tendency. As he ransacked his memory for the material of the youthful Pen's active and mental experiences, his life passed in panorama before the vision of his mind, reviewing not only the careless happiness of boyhood, the reckless gaiety of adolescence, and the joyous rapture of courtship, but the grim succession of the wasted opportunities, exploded hopes, sorrows, troubles, trials, and anxieties. Remembering his present pitiable state of mind, the reader of *Pendennis* can only marvel at the fidelity and sympathy with which he rehabilitated departed emotions and half-forgotten experiences; having read the novel and realised the mental strain under which it was written, the writer is revealed as a figure of tragedy and pathos.

The untimely death of his old friend, Charles Buller, at the age of forty-two, awakened morbid reflections. He wrote to his 'dear lady' on 29th November:

'I am very much pained and shocked at the news brought at dinner to-day that poor dear Charles Buller is gone. Good God! think about the poor mother surviving, and what an anguish that must be! If I were to die I cannot bear to think of my mother living beyond me, as I daresay she will. But isn't it an awful, awful, sudden summons? There go wit, fame, friendship, ambition, high repute! Ah! *aimons nous bien.* It seems to me that is the only thing we can carry away. When we go, let us have some who love us wherever we are. I send you this little line as I tell you and William most things. Good-night.'

Buller had enjoyed an intimate and affectionate friendship with Lady Ashburton, the first wife of the second baron, and Thackeray adopted the somewhat unconventional course of writing her a letter of condolence, 'ending with some pretty phrases about poor old C. B. whose fate affects me very much, so much that I feel as if I were making my will and getting ready to march too.' Mrs. Brookfield wrote her approval of his action:

'I think she must have felt your letter very much, as so few would really understand her grief, and it is one of the most painful and absurd ways of the world to assume that one is in affliction for anyone who happens to have been related to us, while intimacies which must have a much deeper root from having been sought out for ourselves and made where real sympathy exists,—these are so soon to be forgotten, "only a friend, no relation," you hear said many times when the words should be reversed into "only a relation!" Not but that I am very fond of my relations, but there must be exceptions.'

She was staying at Southampton with an ecclesiastical family named Bullar, and her correspondence with Thackeray dwelt much upon questions of religious belief. In a long letter written over four days in the form of a diary, from 28th November to 1st December, he argues his simple faith in a manner similar to that in which he wrote to his daughter when she asked his advice about her grandmother's doctrinal tracts:

'The light upon all the saints in Heaven is just as much and no more God's work, as the sun which shall shine to-morrow upon this infinitesimal speck of creation, and under which I shall read, please God, a letter from my kindest Lady and friend. About my future state I don't know; I leave it in the disposal of the awful Father,—but for to-day I thank God that I can love you, and that you yonder and others besides are thinking of me with a tender regard. Hallelujah may be greater in degree than this, but not in kind, and countless ages of stars may be blazing infinitely, but you and I have a right to rejoice and believe in our little part and to trust in to-day as in to-morrow. God bless my dear lady and her husband. I hope you are asleep now, and I must go too, for the candles are just winking out.'

It was in answer to some such letter as this, expressive of philosophical fortitude and serene resolution, that Mrs. Brookfield wrote:

'You must sometimes feel happy when you think of the good you are able to do,—I should wonder if you did not feel a very vivid confidence and hope for the future. You quite give it to me when you write as you did to-day,—and this power of influencing others which you have is so evidently an inspiration. You have only to recall your talents and to remember that you have not misused them, but increasingly used them for good, and you have at once an evidence of God's favour towards you, which the stupid untalented class must seek for in a few benevolent impulses carried out, or a little endurance more or less humble,—don't you see what a little handful of grain most can lay hold on for self comfort, while you may look on a whole barn full of corn, always before you.'

Her letters meant only less to him than her inspiring presence. They were the sunshine of his life, for which he looked with the eagerness of a boy coming out of school.

'It is near upon three o'clock,' he writes, 'and I am getting rather anxious about the post from Southampton via London. Why, if it doesn't come in, you won't get any letter to-morrow, no, nothing—and I made so sure. Well, I will try and go to work. . . . God bless you, dear lady.' "

And the next day:

'I have had a good morning's work, and at two o'clock comes your letter; dear friend, thank you. What a coward I was, I will go and walk and be happy for an hour, it is a grand frosty sunshine.'

He no longer deceived himself concerning the nature of his regard for her. He admitted his love for her, and realised that she returned his feeling, in spite of her determination to restrain its expression within the bounds of decorum. The situation was impossible of solution. A married man, who was morally a widower, and had been so for eight years, yet indissolubly united for the duration of his life to a woman who would never again be his wife, in love with the wife of his most intimate friend! Early Victorian convention may have added to its hopelessness and horror, but the predicament would have appeared equally inextricable three generations later to a man of Thackeray's morality. A man of stoical fortitude might have made a clean break, renouncing all correspondence with the object of his hopeless attachment, but Thackeray could not bear the thought of life thus bereft of its beauty:

'We will love each other while we may here and afterwards,' he wrote: 'if you go first you will kneel for me in Heaven and bring me there; if I, I swear the best thought I have is to remember that I shall have your love surviving me and with a constant tenderness blessing my memory. I can't all perish living in your heart. That in itself is a sort of seal and assurance of Heaven. . . . Say that I die and live yet in the love of my survivors? Isn't that a warrant of immortality almost? Say that my two dearest friends precede me and enter into God's futurity spotless and angelical, I feel that I have two advocates in Heaven and that my love penetrates there as it were. It seems to me that love proves God. By love I believe and am saved.'

With this letter he enclosed a presentation copy of *The Haunted Man*, received from Dickens, which his mother had read and recommended Mrs. Brookfield to read because 'there's something in it will affect you personally,' together with the doggerel ballad commencing, ' 'Tis one o'clock, the boy from *Punch* is sitting in the passage here.' In her reply of the 21st December Mrs. Brookfield contrived gently to rebuke him for the exuberance of his transports while yet acknowledging his devotion.

'MY DEAR MR. THACKERAY,

It is so very cold and dismal to-day I don't feel as if I could write though I wish to thank you for your letter and the notes of the Ballad—which I shall keep as a curiosity and perhaps leave it, with all your letters as a legacy to Annie for her to work into your memoir according to her discretion 50 years hence. Do you know that if you do not write in more commonplace style to me I shall be quite unable to answer you at all—I have just read your letter over again and thought how flat and dull all that I could say would be and how presumptuous I am to be writing anything by way of an answer, except to say I am grateful.

I saw that Dickens's was a presentation copy to you and will take care of it—there is a bit at the end about a little dead child which is very touching and perhaps was what your mother thought I should feel. . . . If I had time I would write all this over again as an entirely new letter—for my awe of you with which I began writing has quite disappeared and I don't mind a bit whether I have written idiotcy or sense—which is a great proof of my confidence in you.

Ever your friend,

JANE BROOKFIELD.'

She, too, though neither contemplating any consummation of their love nor ever faltering in conjugal fidelity, could not eradicate from the garden of her life this wild, exotic flower, disseminating a fragrance intoxicating her secret senses. Building her faith upon his affection for her husband, his respect for herself, and her own skill in controlling the expression of his passion, she devoted her heart and brain to the function of a platonic Egeria.

Since receiving and accepting his friend's candid explanation of his attitude towards his wife, Brookfield recognised the nature of their relations. He must have felt regret and some apprehension concerning the tenderness of their intimacy, but he reposed implicit confidence in his wife's purity of mind and the honourable sincerity of his friend. He had known Thackeray for nearly twenty years and his opinion of him, expressed to his brother soon after Cambridge days, that he was 'a man utterly incapable of entertaining a moment's feeling towards any being on earth, which should give pain,' had been fortified by the familiar friendship of recent years, enabling him to appreciate the qualities of heart and mind which had sustained the assaults of extraordinary tribulation. Moreover, he cannot have been unconscious of the fact that there were recesses of his wife's character to which he had never penetrated and which must sooner or later receive development for the fulfilment of her being. Others, however, without the means to acquire such philosophy, regarded the attachment in another light, and Harry Hallam, with the impetuosity and single-mindedness of youth, construed Thackeray's undisguised devotion as impertinent and unseemly. Having been daily in Mrs. Brookfield's company after Christmas, Thackeray wrote on 3rd January 1849:

'My dear Lady,—I like to write you a line to-night to show you how I was right about a point wh. has been long clear to me, who can understand very well how any man who has been near you and lived or travelled with you must end by what I arrived at years ago, and cannot do otherwise than regard you. When H. Hallam spoke as he did to-night I'm sure he said what has been upon his mind for many months: that he was angry at my constant visits to you. But thank God I have never concealed the affection I have for you—your husband knows it as well as you or I do, and I think I have such a claim to the love of both of you as no relationship, however close, ought to question or supersede. If ever he asks the question I hope it will frankly be told him that I claim to be as one of your brothers, or the closest and dearest of your friends. As for William, I am bound to him by benefits, by the most generous confidence, and repeated proofs of friendship; and to you, dear lady, by an affection wh. I hope won't finish with my life of wh. you have formed for a long time past one of the greatest and I hope the purest pleasures. If I had a bad thought towards you I think I could not look my friend or you in the face and I see no shame in owning that I love you. I have Wm.'s permission, yours, that of my own heart and conscience for constantly, daily, if I can, seeing you. Who has a right to forbid me my great happiness? If neither of those three, who else? God bless you and us all, dear Sister and Friend. I like to say so and declare how much and how entirely I regard you.

W. M. T.'

The letter represents the catechism of his attitude towards her. So long as he was permitted to enjoy her society and correspondence, he was content to play the role of a *preux chevalier*. Equally intent upon deriving such happiness as was possible in the circumstances, her situation was even more difficult, for she had to reconcile her conduct with her duty to her husband, to defy the disapproval of her young cousin, and to preserve herself warily from the contamination of gossip. Consequently, she continually deprecated too ardent expressions of feeling, to which he once retorted by asking with bitter mockery if he should begin to call her Mrs. Brookfield again. Repenting at once of a remark likely to wound her, he added: 'Ah, no, I have not got to that, dear lady. You shall be my dear lady always to me.' With thoughts of her ever in his mind, her personality naturally impressed its influence upon his work, and in *Esmond*, which, with *Pendennis*, was written during the period of their deepest intimacy, he sought to idealise his attitude towards her in the attitude of his hero towards Lady Castlewood.

§ 3

At the end of January he went over to Paris, where he spent much of his time with his Aunt Ritchie and Aunt Halliday, the latter of whom had joined the Paris colony since her husband's retirement from India. He renewed an old acquaintance with Jules Janin, the dramatic critic of the *Journal des Débats*, whom he had first known when acting as correspondent for the *Constitutional* and had playfully satirised in his *Fraser* article on *Dickens in France*. He described this old friend to Mrs. Brookfield, as he always described anything of importance so that she might share his impressions and appreciate his actions and their motives.

'He has the most wonderful verve, humour, oddity, honesty, bonhomie. He was ill with the gout, or recovering perhaps; but bounced about the room, gesticulating, joking, gasconading, quoting Latin, pulling out his books which are very handsome, and tossing about his curling brown hair;—a magnificent jolly intelligent face such as would suit Pan I should think, a flood of humorous, rich, jovial talk.'

He went to see John Bowes, the friend whom he had helped in the South Durham election of 1841, 'who has forty thousand a year and places in the country, and here he is a manager of a Theatre of Varieties, and his talk was about actors and coulisses all the time of our interview.' He is pained at his dear lady having been unwell:—'I thought you must have been, when Saturday came without any letter.'

Back in London in March, he visited Cambridge with Brookfield, breakfasting with Henry Maine, the regius professor of civil law, calling on old Dr. Thackeray, his father's cousin, dining in hall with W. H. Thompson, and receiving complimentary tickets to hear a concert of Jenny Lind's.

'I think William is a little disappointed that I have not been made enough a lion of, whereas my timid nature trembles before such honours, and my vanity would be to go through life as a gentleman—as a Major Pendennis—you have hit it. I believe I never do think about my public character, and certainly didn't see the gyps, waiters and undergraduates whispering in hall, as your William did, or thought he did.'

Soon after his return to town Mrs. Brookfield went down to Clevedon, where she wrote to him on 23rd April, commencing 'Dear William Thackeray,' and ending, 'yours, J. O. B.,' a letter containing little of interest, merely composed to gratify his wish to hear from her. She was looking forward to the new number of *Pendennis* and expecting to see in it 'a great deal of the Major.' Thackeray replied on finishing the seventh number:

'I am so beat that I ought to go to bed, and not inflict my yawns upon anyone; but I can't begin snoring yet. I am waiting at the Club, till the printer's boy brings the proofs of No. 7, which is all done; there are two new women in it, not like anybody that you know or I know; your favourite Major appears rather in an amiable light. I don't know whether it is good or bad. The latter probably. Well, it is done, that's a comfort.'

He tells her of his mother's plan to spend the summer in Switzerland, taking the children with her, of Adelaide Procter's reproaches for not having called for three weeks, of being invited to dinner at the Academy, and of a sculptor wanting to model his bust, of the old Miss Berrys—all the details of his busy life which she delighted to read. She answered on the 28th:

'What a shame that you should read my letter to your mother. I thought it remarkably freely written and neatly expressed, and I congratulated myself on your being away at the time and that I could therefore be so easy—not that I care at all for being stupid to you but I expect you to feel ashamed of me if I show my dulness to people who already wonder (as you do yourself), "what there is in me." . . . We walked to the sea yesterday, and I boldly went into the library and ordered No. seven to be sent to me immediately on its appearance down here. "We get it either the 1st or 2nd of the month," they said, which seems very behindhand when we get it in London on the 30th. I am glad you are to dine at the Royal Academy, and is the Bust to be made? . . . What an odd girl Adelaide Procter is, I should give her a little quiet set down some day if I were you. I think it would be friendly and do her good. Do you think me very spiteful to-day? I am afraid I have abused everybody I have mentioned, which seems ill-natured. . . . I am glad William was to dine with you last night. I have heard from him every day though he was so busy as hardly to have time for it, and Harry penned me a note which came with yours this morning, and another letter from Mrs. F. very kind as usual, but giving but a bad account of herself, and a prim, well-worded A. Bullar. Five letters, all so different. I read them while I was dressing, William's and yours first,—and they made me so late I was obliged to breakfast upstairs. I sang for two hours yesterday by myself in the schoolroom, fully believing that no one could hear me, when I came down and found they were all listening in the Hall which was unpleasant. Give my love to Anny and Minny, and thank you for being so kind as to write to me, but please do not feel *gênéd* any more. Good-bye.

He told Vizetelly that the Academy banquet was 'a very cold and formal affair,' comparing it to a dinner to which he had been invited by Lord Carlisle along with several of his *Punch* colleagues:

'We all know each others' pet stories, and all the dear old jokes, and this acted as a wet blanket upon us. No one would have thought of trotting out a good new story simply for one of his *confrères* to crib for his next magazine article. If Lord Carlisle had asked half a dozen literary men and half a dozen lords, we should in this case have fit audience found, and been able to amuse the quality at the trifling inconvenience of boring ourselves.'

On 5th May, when the erstwhile Miss Rigby made her social *début* as the wife of Charles Eastlake at Lady Davy's, she met the author of *Vanity Fair*, who 'pleased me much.'[1] Kinglake, Hallam, Lady Lovelace, Byron's daughter, and a number of titled nonentities made up the party. On the 14th she met him again at the same house, where he was 'very diverting,' the company including Kinglake, Hallam, Milnes, and John Murray. Pollock, meeting him at the Eastlakes' on the 7th with Venables and Herman Merivale, remarked that he had 'grown a little *blasé*, and is not quite such good company as he used to be.' At the dinner given by Dickens to celebrate the first number of *David Copperfield* on the 12th, besides the inevitable Forster, there were present the Carlyles, Thackeray and old Samuel Rogers, Mrs. Gaskell, Kenyon, Jerrold, and Hablot Browne, and Thackeray relieved the tension of a metaphysical disquisition by a story about 'Megreedy,' told with 'a quaint whimsicality.' He always shone on occasions like

[1] *Journals and Correspondence of Lady Eastlake,* edited by her nephew, C. E. Smith. London, 2 vols., 1895.

this, with humorous anecdotes and witty comments; it was on more formal occasions that he showed to disadvantage. Attending the dinner of the Literary Fund this month, he made one of those disastrous speeches for which he became subsequently notorious. Writing to Mrs. Brookfield, who was visiting Cambridge with her husband, he said:

'I have made an awful smash at the Literary Fund and have tumbled into 'Evins knows where;—It was a tremendous exhibition of imbecility. Good night. I hope you 2 are sound asleep. Why isn't there somebody that I could go and smoke a pipe to?

Bon Soir

But O! what a smash I have made!

I am talking quite loud out to myself at the Garrick sentences I intended to have uttered: but they wouldn't come in time.'

His mother, who had been present without his knowledgc, insisted that he had made 'a beautiful speech,' and told the children so. He decided that his discomfiture would 'make a good chapter for Pen.'

At this time the effects at Gore House were sold by auction, Lady Blessington and Count D'Orsay having retired to Paris. In the first flush of celebrity he had consorted with the brilliant company there in the previous year and had known D'Orsay slightly in his youth. Of his visit to the sale he told Mrs. Brookfield:

'I have just come away from a dismal sight; Gore House full of snobs looking at the furniture. Foul Jews; odious bombazine women, who drove up in mysterious flys which they had hired, the wretches, to be fined, so as to come in state to a fashionable lounge; brutes keeping their hats on in the kind old drawing room,—I longed to knock some of them off, and say "Sir, be civil in a lady's room." . . .

There was one of the servants there, not a powdered one, but a butler, a *whatdoyoucallit.* My heart melted towards him and I gave him a pound. Ah! it was a strange, sad picture of *Vanity Fair*. My mind is all boiling up with it; indeed, it is in a queer state.'

Writing his impressions of the sale to his mistress, Lady Blessington's French valet (doubtless the 'whatdoyoucallit'!) remarked:

'M. Thackeray est venu aussi, et avait les larmes aux yeux en partant. *C'est peut-être la seule personne qui j'ai vu réellement affecté en votre départ.*'[1]

Thackeray had sent Lady Blessington a small contribution for the last issue of the *Keepsake* at the previous Christmas, and he good-naturedly supplied two more in 1851 and 1853, when the editorship of the annual had passed, at Lady Blessington's death, into the hands of her niece, Marguerite Power. To her he performed a further kindness when Charles Mackay, aware of his exceptional knowledge of Parisian affairs, asked him to suggest a suitable Paris correspondent for the *Illustrated London News*. Remarking that he would have liked such a post himself ten years earlier, he first suggested 'Father Prout' as 'a good man,' who 'lives in Paris, and loves it, and can write well.' Then he remembered Miss Power, 'who writes, if not so brilliantly as Mahony, quite brilliantly enough for any newspaper in the world, and to whom the salary would be a perfect god-send of good fortune.'[2] Representing to Mackay that he would consider himself personally obliged by her engagement, he obtained the post for her.

[1] *Literary Life and Correspondence of the Countess of Blessington*, by R. R. Madden. London, 3 vols., 1855.
[2] *Forty Years' Recollections of Life, Literature, and Public Affairs*, by Charles Mackay. London, 2 vols., 1877.

CHAPTER 10

§ 1

WHEN he told Milnes that 'if I could get a place and rest, I think I would do something better than I have done, and leave a good and lasting book behind me,' Thackeray was gradually realising that his incessant activity was at last beginning to affect his health. FitzGerald had foreseen such an eventuality, and others of his friends now noticed the effect. Mrs. Brookfield, who knew of his anxiety to amass a suitable provision for his children, wrote to him in September 1849:

'I wish you could be made independent of having to work so constantly. I sometimes imagine legacies from unknown individuals coming in to me, and I make the handsomest settlements in an anonymous manner upon Annie and Minny. I wish they would come true some day and that I could "hand you over your freedom." '

About the same time Thackeray told her that his friend, Matthew James Higgins, the celebrated 'Jacob Omnium' of *The Times*, had said to him: 'If you are tired and want to lie fallow for a year, come to me for the money, I have much more than I want.' 'Big' Higgins appears to have become his intimate friend some two years before, as his name then begins to occur frequently in company with Thackeray's in the diaries of their contemporaries. Vizetelly describes him as Thackeray's *fidus Achates*, and many memoir-writers remembered having seen people stop to stare in the street as the pair passed by together, for while Thackeray, who stood six feet three inches in height, towered above a crowd, Higgins was five inches taller than he. Dean Hole relates how they once visited a Brobdingnagian show, and the man in the pay-box at the door inquired 'whether they were in the business, because, if so, no charge would be made.'[1]

He was still harassed by financial worries. In May he told his brother-in-law that 'though I am at the top of the tree in my business and making a good income now, near upon £2000 a year let us say—yet it is only within the last few months that I have got to this point: and was abominably hit by an unfortunate railway speculation of which I have still not discharged the obligation—so that I am in debt.' The 'railway mania' of the middle 'forties brought ruin to many reckless gamblers, and though Thackeray himself had satirised 'those dismal beggars who spoke of nothing but railroad shares' in *Punch*, he had evidently, with his old optimism in speculation, fallen a victim to the latest lure of the money market. More than ever he craved the consolation of Mrs. Brookfield's conversation, but she was out of town for the greatest part of the summer. 'I have written such a stupid number of *Pendennis* in consequence of not seeing you,' he told her in May, 'that I shall be ruined if you are to stay away much longer.'[2]

She returned to Portman Street for a short time in June, on the first of which month Pollock met Thackeray there in company with Kinglake, Spedding, Higgins, Harry Hallam, and Doyle. On his daughter Annie's birthday, the ninth, he asked her to take his children to the Coliseum or the Zoo in the afternoon and 'to give them some dinner or tea in the evening,' while she and her husband, along with the Pollocks and the Carlyles, dined at Young Street on the 11th. The next day he went down to join his mother at Fareham, where she was tending the deathbed

[1] *The Memories of Dean Hole.* London, 1892.

[2] The 'stupid number' was the eighth (June), containing Chapters XXIV-XXVI, descriptive of the house-party at Clavering.

of his Great-aunt Becher, whom he found 'preparing to go out of the world, in which she has been living very virtuously for more than eighty years, as calmly and happily as may be.' Returning to town after performing his last duty to this old friend of his childhood, he saw Mrs. Brookfield before she went to stay with the Fanshawes at Southampton. On 13th July he wrote her an account of a party at the Procters', describing an amusing incident concerning Mrs. Sartoris and proposing to send his mother and the children to Clevedon.

'The old people are charming at home, with their kindness. They are going away at the end of the week, somewhere, they don't say where, with the children. The dear old step-father moves me rather the most, he is so gentle and good humoured. Last night Harry came to dinner, and being Sunday there was none, and none to be had, and we went to the tavern hard-by, where he didn't eat a bit. I did. . . .'

Mrs. Brookfield replied that her sisters would be glad to welcome his mother and the children, 'but it sounds melancholy their going there and you by yourself.' His mother, however, decided to spend her holiday in Wales, and Thackeray went down to Brighton for a few days, where he was joined by Brookfield. On the 16th he wrote:

'I've been many hours writing 2 pages, and thinking where I might be instead of being here. Yet I like this, like the solitude, like the early waking and rising; am determined that Mr. Pendinnis sha'nt dawdle any more, and that I'll do something to fetch up my languishing reputation—something uncommonly sarcastic, pathetic, humorous it must be. Can you give me a hint or two? A guinea for a hint or two. Wednesday 18th is my birthday. 38 if you please. What will you give me for a birthday present? What wouldn't I give to see this day as I wish it in 1850.'

Two days later he wrote to his mother in Wales:

'I must go up to town on Saturday to do my plates, and then to finish my number somehow or other, which isn't nearly done. I wonder, could I do two next month? If I could, I'd be off for September somewhere, but that is too great a piece of luck to hope for. . . . How do you like your Welsh retreat? I wish I knew how to hunt, shoot, course, or play at cards. . . . I have . . . spent most of the time reading novels. Alexandre Dumas is wonderful; he kept me on a stretch for nearly nine hours one day. What wouldn't I give to have his knack of putting a story together. And yet in degree the one is infinitely below the other, but the business habit is the thing I admire in him.'

No writer of genius was ever more conscious of his deficiencies. Throughout his life he adhered to the habit, acquired in early Grub Street days from the pattern of Maginn, of writing with the printer's boy waiting at the door for his copy. Aware of the anxiety and strain devolving upon himself and the deleterious effect upon his work from such imperative haste, he repeatedly resolved to adopt a more methodical habit, but if ever he succeeded in his plans for writing a little in front of the clock, he invariably conceived the achievement as an excuse for procrastination and longer leisure, so that eventually he found his last-minute labours the more exacting on account of the increased lapse of time since his last spell of energy. He had no more notion of Trollope's habit of working to a time-table than of his method of drawing up beforehand a synopsis of his plot, with an 'advance lay-out' of the characters and course of action. His procedure was to create one or two principal characters and follow up their adventures, introducing fresh ones as opportunity offered. 'I don't control my characters,' he told Jeaffreson, 'I am in their hands, and they take me where they please.' To Fields he remarked humorously that, when 'he had been dining late and did not feel in remarkably good-humour next morning, he was inclined to make his characters villainously wicked; but if he rose serene with an unclouded brain, there was no end to the lovely actions he was willing to make his men and women perform.' This haphazard absence of form received encouragement from the publication of his novels in magazine or monthly numbers; Dickens and others fell into the same laxity to a more or less mitigated degree, but he lacked Dickens's systematic application as he lacked Charles Reade's dogged enthusiasm, with the latter's determinate object of pointing a moral or illustrating propaganda from his organised abundance of extraneous references. It is significant that *Esmond*, by far the most compact and cohesive of his novels, was also the only one not originally issued in some serial form.

After a few days with Brookfield at Brighton, he joined his family in Wales, where he spent most of the next few weeks, though he appears to have paid a short visit in August to the Ashburtons at Alresford Grange, a house as famous for its hospitality to literary men in early Victorian times as in the days, a century and a half earlier, when Anthony Henley had loved to entertain there Congreve, Addison and Steele. At the end of the month he crossed hurriedly to Paris on hearing that his Aunt Halliday was dangerously ill.

'I got here at twelve last night,' he tells his mother, 'and am very glad to see my dear old Aunt [Ritchie] and the two girls, who were kind and cordial, as they always are. Then I went to see Dr. Halliday, who is not long for this world, I should think, and greatly depressed about Mrs. Halliday: she has been wandering in her mind for weeks past—very seldom recognises anybody. I am glad I set out to be here and pay the last duties to one of our race which is dropping away. Charlotte Ritchie says that two days ago Mrs. Halliday was wandering, and fancying she was in the boat with my father dying; it affected me. . . . I shall stay on until the end comes.'

He tells Mrs. Brookfield that he expects to stay ten days

more, and describes visits to another sick friend besides the Hallidays, and to an old servant. Having received from her the next day a letter descriptive of her doings and recounting encouraging praise of the new *Pendennis* number, he immediately wrote again on the 2nd September, telling of a merry evening with Jules Janin and a visit to the Tuileries which he expects to describe in 'an historical disquisition in the Titmarsh manner' for *Punch*. Almost daily he wrote to her and she replied only less regularly. The failing state of his health conspired with his close contact with death in the past three months to afflict his mind with a morbid depression. In July, in reply to her news that Mrs. Fanshawe's medical attendant gave her only two or three years to live, he had written:

'What you say about Mrs. Fanshawe being doomed does not affect me very much, I am afraid. I don't see that living is such a benefit, and could find it in my heart pretty readily to have an end of it,—After wasting a good deal of opportunities and time and desires in vanitarianism. What is it makes one so blasé and tired I wonder at 38? Is it pain or pleasure? Present solitude or too much company before? both very likely. You see I am here as yesterday, gloomy again, and thrumming on the old egotistical string.'

Now he reverted to this despondent strain on 3rd September:

'My poor Aunt is still in life, but that is all; she has quite lost her senses. I talked for some time with her old husband, who has been the most affectionate husband to her, and who is looking on, he being 72 years old himself, with a calm resolution and awaiting the moment which is to take away his life's companion. . . . As for *Pendennis*, I began upon No. 7 to-day and found a picture which was perfectly new and a passage which I had as utterly forgotten as if I had never read or written it. This shortness of memory frightens me, and makes me have gloomy anticipations. Will poor Annie have to nurse an old imbecile of a father some day, who will ramble incoherently about old days and people whom he used to love? What a shame it is to talk such gloomy stuff to my dear lady: well, you are accustomed to hear my chatter, gloomy or otherwise, as my thoughts go by. I fancy myself by the dear old sofa almost, as I sit here prating; and shut my eyes and see you quite clear. I am glad you have been doing works of art with your needle. . . . W. H. Ainsworth, Esquire, is here; we dined next each other at the 3 Frères yesterday and rather fraternized. He showed a friendly disposition I thought, and a desire to forgive me my success; but beyond a good-humoured acquiescence in his good will, I don't care. I suppose one doesn't care for people, only for a very, very few. A man came in just now who told me he had heard how I was dead. I began to laugh, and my laugh meant, "Well old fellow, you don't care, do you?" And why should he? How often I must have said and said these things over to you.'

Mrs. Brookfield sought to distract him by raillery, remarking that, if he ended 'in a fatuous old age without memory, &c.,' she would then be better suited for his friend by him being 'brought a little more to my level,' and narrating an amusing anecdote of Ainsworth's introduction to her Uncle Hallam. But her badinage concealed a tender anxiety which caused her to exclaim at the end of the letter: 'Forgive this nonsense, I wish I could make you laugh even if it were only at me.'

The next day he announced the death of his aunt. He describes his visit of condolence to the old widower with grim realism; the poor old man, himself at the verge of the grave, solacing himself with gin-and-water, confides the details of his financial affairs and family secrets to the dead woman's nephew, whom the valet believes to be the heir come to take possession, and while he rambles on and Thackeray bawls replies into his ear, 'they were rapping at a coffin in the bedroom, but he was too deaf to hear, and seems too old to care very much.' Such an atmosphere could only aggravate his feelings of depression, though the following day was spent in recreation, reading Dumas and the last number of *David Copperfield*, which he thought 'the very best thing the author has yet done,' before going to a theatre in the evening. 'The funeral takes place to-morrow,' he wrote on the 6th, 'and as I don't seem to do much work here, I shall be soon probably on the wing.' He hoped to hear from her once more before leaving, and apologising for assaulting 'my dear lady with my blue devils,' he added:

'Who could help looking to the day of failing powers, but if I last a few years, no doubt I can get a shelter somewhere against that certain adversity, and so I ought not to show you my glum face or my dismal feelings. . . . You are so kind to me that I like to tell you all, and to think that in good or ill fortune I have your sympathy.'

Though accentuated by his state of mind and health, this was not a mood of the moment. As at twenty years of age, he had mistrusted the quality of his intellectual gifts, now, at thirty-eight, he mistrusted the stability of his genius. Time and experience failed to inspire confidence, and, to the end of his life he was haunted by the spectral prospect of intellectual decay.

§ 2

He remained in Paris for a week after the funeral, the alteration of plan being evidently due to the craving of old Dr. Halliday and his Aunt Ritchie for his society, as he spent each evening with them. 'This isn't very amusing,' he remarked, 'but the sense of virtue and self-denial tickles one, as it were, and I come home rather pleased to my bed of a night.' 'To-morrow,' he added, 'I dine with Mr. T. B. Macaulay, who is staying in this hotel.' A day or two later he and Macaulay were the guests of honour at Sir George Napier's, and, on being told that an American lady, greatly desirous of meeting them both, was expected after dinner, he proposed that Macaulay should pose as the author of *Vanity Fair* while he was presented as the author of the *Lays of Ancient Rome*. Macaulay, however, 'said solemnly that he did not approve of practical jokes.' He went one morning to visit 'those two poor Miss Powers, and the poor old faded and unhappy D'Orsay.' His departure was again delayed by an invitation to dine with the French President, Louis Napoleon, though he had intended leaving that day for Boulogne, where he hoped to see Mrs. Procter on his way home.

His protracted stay proved disastrous, for an epidemic of cholera was harrowing Paris and his low state of health, together with his continual contact with sick and ailing friends, rendered him very liable to infection. On his return to London he was taken ill while dining out with his cousin, Lady Rodd.[1]

'I was in such hag'nies at dinner,' he wrote the next day to Mrs. Brookfield, 'that though they got me a slipper . . . I was obliged to go home and send for a doctor. He put me to bed, where I am to stop to-day and perhaps to-morrow working at *Pendennis*.'

As usual, he had deferred the writing of his monthly number to the latest possible moment. He had done nothing in Paris, and, with the third week of the month far advanced, he felt it necessary to work on his sick-bed. But he regarded his illness much too lightly when he told Mrs. Brookfield that he expected to be well and able to come and see her in a couple of days. Brookfield wrote to Harry Hallam on 24th September:

'You will be happy to know that our Thackeray seems to have quite turned the corner. Yesterday he seemed

[1] Jane, only daughter of Thackeray's great-aunt Jane, sister of the elephant-hunter, by her marriage with Major James Rennell, married Vice-Admiral Sir John Tremayne Rodd, K.C.B.

low and very uneasy, and thinks himself that his crisis did not come till yesterday evening. This morning, however, he seems quite fresh and like himself, and as I think the words of so eminent a party ought not to be garbled by a minister of truth, I must inform you that he sent word to you by me that "he is apparently recovering." He is very grateful for your kindness in looking after him. It does not seem that anybody is calling upon him, as his illness has not been bruited, which is all the better, as his servant is very efficient. If it has been Cholera, he has no idea of it himself, but calls it a liver attack. An advertisement will have to postpone *Pendennis* for some days.'

Pendennis had to be postponed for no less than three months, for Brookfield, going out of town for a few days satisfied of his friend's prospective recovery, was speedily disillusioned by a letter from his wife, who wrote on the 27th the result of her visit to the invalid that morning:

'John said he had been worse before the bleeding, but that he was now better, only exceedingly weak. I sent up word that I should be writing to his Mother if he had any message, and he begged I would come up and speak to him for a minute. John held the door of his room open so that I saw him, looking terribly pulled down and his voice very weak, he looked still feverish, and seemed low about himself, altho' he said he hoped he should not be in bed more than four or five days longer, but I am afraid he is still very seriously ill. He seemed very anxious to have you back again, and asked when you would be coming, and if you were well. I don't feel easy about him, especially after his so often speaking of presentiments lately, that he should be cut off early, like Charles Buller. Just now I had a note from Mr. Spring Rice to tell me he had been to see Mr. Thackeray this morning, and that he told him he did not expect to be really re-established in less than six weeks, but that he considered himself to be getting daily better, only so very weak as to feel very ill still. I enclose his Mother's letter. I am afraid I can be of no use at all, but she seems to imply by her gratitude that I am.'

His mother was still in Wales with the children, but, on hearing from Mrs. Brookfield of the seriousness of his illness, she travelled home with all speed. The children, following with Major Carmichael-Smyth, stayed with Mrs. Brookfield while their father's period of danger lasted.

Mrs. Brookfield visited him daily, either with her husband or Mrs. Elliot, Kate Perry's sister, with whom she established a friendship at this crisis of their friend's life. On 1st October she tells Harry Hallam that 'there is still fear of a continuance of fever' and that his nourishment is limited to tea and lemonade.

'I saw him with William yesterday. . . . I only wish Mr. Thackeray had anything to fall back upon when he recovers from this illness, instead of that constant writing which wears him so much, and which he can never have any rest from, unless he could get some settled employment, which would not be such a strain upon him as this fagging composition is.'

Two days later his condition reached its worst and Mrs. Brookfield wrote in an agony of anxiety to her husband:

'He has had a very bad night, his room is darkened, and he is ordered to be perfectly quiet, and not to talk at all. Henry[1] overheard the doctors say that what they are now anxious about is some former complaint of his which is more to be feared than his present attack of illness. Of course I could not ask what this complaint is; I can only fear that it is serious, because I remember Mr. Thackeray's

[1] A note by the authors of *Mrs. Brookfield and Her Circle*, wherein all her letters are to be found, states that 'Henry was an extra servant lent by the Hallams to Mr. Thackeray.' The servant, John, mentioned in a previous letter, was Thackeray's own man—the 'lackey out of livery,' whom Vizetelly mentions as having been engaged on the strength of the success of *Vanity Fair*.

once saying that he had something which prevented his being able to insure his life. Henry says the doctors are there three and four times a day and that they feared he was worse last night, but to-day he seemed a little better since the blister. I feel sorry that you are not able to be with him, as he can see no one to whom he can talk at all seriously, or who can really be of comfort. The day I was there he talked of the end as possibly near at hand, and said he could look forward without dread to it, that he felt a great love and charity to all mankind, and tho' there were many things he would wish undone in his life he yet felt a great trust and hope in God's love and mercy, and if it was His will, he would go to-morrow, and only feel about leaving the children unprotected. I did not think then that he was likely again to be in danger, and felt afraid of his exciting himself by talking in that strain, but I am now sorry I did not encourage him to say more, as it seemed a comfort to him to speak of it, and he said he felt quite happy and peaceful, that it had done him good to speak to me, and that you were the only other person he could do so to, and he spoke of you with much affection. Now I reproach myself for having rather turned off his thoughts from his own state, and tried to amuse him by talking of indifferent things, when perhaps it may have been the last opportunity he would have to talk to anyone of his feelings in dying, if that is really near at hand, which I cannot help fearing, and as you did not seem to be in any alarm about him when you left, dear William, I thought I ought to tell you all I had heard tho' I know you will very much grieve to hear it. I will write again to-morrow to Southampton, and hope it may be better news, but I cannot feel much confidence in reports of amendment which are always contradicted by fresh relapses.'

Apart from its illustration of Thackeray's fortitude in the face of prospective death, his inevitable concern for his children, and the gravity of his condition reflected in Mrs. Brookfield's grievous anxiety, this letter is of paramount importance for supplying the only evidence to dispel the generally accepted belief that this serious illness left him with the malady afflicting him during the rest of his life and eventually causing his death. Evidently he had some dormant disease which was aggravated by this illness and the constitutional strain created by his erratic habits. The precise nature of his complaint can only be a matter for speculation, for doctors in those days did not diagnose internal disorders which are now within the province of the general practitioner. It is probable, however, that the skill of modern surgery might have prolonged his life by many years, so enriching the world with an appreciable addition to his collected works.

§ 3

The rapidity of his recovery from an illness so dangerous bears witness to the great physical strength of his natural constitution. On 21st October he surprised Mrs. Brookfield by going down to Brighton, accompanied only by his servant. Sitting in a bath-chair on the pier he wrote notes on his progress to her and his mother, while Horace Smith's daughters, in mourning for their father, gladly danced attendance on him. Mrs. Brookfield wrote him bright, cheerful letters, recounting the news in town and begging him to take care of his health.

'I wish,' she wrote, 'you would make John tell people not to talk while you are *airing yourself* as it will do away with the good of the sea-breezes if you are tired with talking. . . . You will see Mrs. Elliot, I suppose, to-morrow, as she set off for Brighton to-day. . . . I called in Young St. to-day and brought Anny and Minny back with me, packed three in a Hansom. They are sitting here buried each in a book while I write, and they send their love to you. . . . Pray be very martyrising upon yourself about yourself.'

On the 25th he replied:

'I cannot write you long, dear lady; I have two notes to my mother daily, and a long one to Elliotson, &c.; but I am getting on *doucement*, like the change of air exceedingly, the salt water baths, and the bath-chair journeys to the pier when it is almost as fresh as being at sea. But do you go on writing, please, and as often as you can.'

John Elliotson, a notable London physician, was Macready's medical attendant and numbered many literary men among his patients; to him Thackeray ultimately dedicated *Pendennis* as a mark of gratitude for his services to him in his illness.

Harry Hallam joined him for company at the end of the month, when he assured the Brookfields that he was progressing 'by steps which grow every day more firm towards convalescence.' As he recovered, he made no effort as yet to resume work upon *Pendennis*, for his limited energies were entirely engrossed by *Rebecca and Rowena*, his Christmas book, due for publication the following month. As in the previous year, he postponed his plans for *The Kickleburys on the Rhine*, the occasion obviously calling for a subject exacting the minimum of labour. In August and September 1846 he had contributed to *Fraser* his *Proposals for a Continuation of 'Ivanhoe*,' and probably the rough draft of *Rebecca and Rowena* was drawn up at that time. Realising the hopelessness of attempting illustrations as well as the letterpress, he engaged the services of his young *Punch* colleague, 'Dicky' Doyle. The collaboration supplied an excuse for occasional excursions to town from his Brighton retreat, the first of which appears to have occurred late in November, for Macready found him dining at Forster's on the 27th, the company including Brookfield, Procter, Kinglake, Kenyon, Alfred Tennyson, and R. S. Rintoul of the *Spectator*. Seeing him about the same time, FitzGerald wrote on 7th December:

'I saw poor old Thackeray in London: getting very slowly better of a bilious fever that had almost killed him.

Some one told me that he was gone or going to the Water Doctor at Malvern. People in general thought *Pendennis* got dull as it got on; and I confess I thought so too: he would do well to take the opportunity of his illness to discontinue it altogether. He told me last June he himself was tired of it: must not his readers naturally tire too?'

FitzGerald had expressed his liking for the earlier numbers, which Tennyson thought 'quite delicious' because they 'seemed to him so *mature*,' and his strictures on the more recent numbers precisely coincided with Thackeray's own sentiments confided to Mrs. Brookfield at the time of writing—indeed, in a later letter, FitzGerald applies to them the same epithet of 'stupid.' On the 8th, the day after FitzGerald's lugubrious reflections, Thackeray, back again at Brighton, remarked as he wrote to Mrs. Brookfield that 'the paper looks so nice and white, I should like, I should like to write a page of *Pendennis*,' asking cheerfully if this did not 'prove I am getting stronger.'

But he had few opportunities to recommence work upon *Pendennis*, for his Christmas book, now overdue, occupied all his available time. In spite of his pressing work and convalescent state, he returned to town to meet Charlotte Brontë at the house of her publisher, George Smith. Both recorded their impressions of their first meeting. In the *Roundabout Papers* Thackeray wrote:

'I remember the trembling little frame, the little hand, the great honest eyes. An impetuous honesty seemed to me to characterise the woman. Twice I recollect she took me to task for what she held to be errors in doctrine. Once about Fielding we had a disputation. She spoke her mind out. She jumped too rapidly to conclusions. . . . I fancied an austere little Joan of Arc marching in upon us, and rebuking our easy lives, our easy morals. She gave me the impression of being a very pure, and lofty, and high-minded person.'

Charlotte Brontë had so idolised Thackeray's genius that she trembled in trepidation at the prospect of meeting him in the flesh:

'When Mr. Thackeray was announced,' she wrote, 'and I saw him enter, looked up at his tall figure, heard his voice, the whole incident was truly dream-like, I was only certain it was true because I became miserably destitute of self-possession. . . . Had I not been obliged to speak, I could have managed well, but it behoved me to answer when addressed, and the effort was torture—I spoke stupidly.'

Elsewhere, she observed that 'I felt sufficiently at my ease with all but Thackeray; with him I was fearfully stupid.'[1] Her discomfort was mainly due to her preconceived attitude of awe, but her literal earnestness contributed to the effect, for, as she confided to Mrs. Gaskell, she found it difficult 'to decide whether he was speaking in jest or in earnest.' She nevertheless admired his easy simplicity of manner, as, remarking that 'I by no means dislike Mr. Forster'—for Forster was present on this occasion, as he always was at any literary function of importance—'quite the contrary, but the distance from his loud swagger to Thackeray's simple port is as the distance from Shakespeare's writing to Macready's acting.' In a letter to her father, she recorded a more general impression:

'He is a very tall man—above six feet high, with a peculiar face—not handsome, very ugly indeed, generally somewhat stern and satirical in expression, but capable also of a kind look. He was not told who I was, he was not introduced to me, but I soon saw him looking at me through his spectacles; and when we all rose to go down to dinner he just stepped quietly up and said, "Shake hands"; so I shook hands. He spoke very few words to me, but when he went away he shook hands again in a very kind way. It is better, I should think, to have him for a friend than an

[1] *Life of Charlotte Brontë*, by Mrs. Gaskell. London, 1857.

enemy, for he is a most formidable-looking personage. I listened to him as he conversed with the other gentlemen. All he says is most simple, but often cynical, harsh, and contradictory.'[1]

It is curious to compare this awestruck impression with the strikingly dissimilar portrait of him she drew in her letters of eighteen months later, when greater familiarity had dispelled her attitude of dread idolatry.

He completed *Rebecca and Rowena* barely in time for Christmas, the preface being dated the 20th. 'I have been working now until seven o'clock,' he told Mrs. Brookfield, 'and am dead beat, having done a poor dawdling day's work, writing too much, hipped, hacked, and blue-devilled.' He went for Christmas to Brighton, where he could 'be alone, and think about my friend Mr. Pendennis, whom I have been forced to neglect.' In spite of this neglect on account of the Christmas book, he had already completed the next number—the twelfth—which duly appeared in January—and so far departed from his habit of procrastination that he was nearing the end of the February number at Christmas, when he paused 'in the middle of Costigan' (Ch. XLII) to write a letter to Mrs. Brookfield.

The new year opened with two incidents relating to *Pendennis*. The first consisted of an attack upon Thackeray by the *Examiner* and the *Morning Chronicle* for 'fostering a

[1] In *Charlotte Brontë and Her Circle*, Clement Shorter gives the date of this letter as 'May 28th, 1851.' Yet it is obvious that she is speaking of her first meeting with Thackeray. Moreover, in the same letter, she speaks of having seen Macready in *Macbeth*, and Macready retired from the stage in February 1851. Nor could the letter have been written during her London visit of the previous summer, as Macready was then out of town. But he was acting *Macbeth* during November and early December 1849, when the weather—'exceedingly changeful, and often damp and misty, so that it is necessary to guard against taking cold,' as she says in the same letter—was more likely to be as she described than at the end of May. Similarly, the letter to Miss Wooler of 'February 6th, 1852,' must have been written two years earlier, as it describes 'a fortnight in London last December,' and also mentions Macready in *Macbeth*. 'Mr. Thackeray, for instance,' she says here, 'is a man of quiet, simple demeanour; he is, however, looked upon with some awe and even distrust. His conversation is very peculiar, too perverse to be pleasant.'

baneful prejudice' against literary men, and 'condescending to caricature (as is too often his habit) his literary fellow-labourers in order to pay court to the non-literary class.'[1]

Thackeray replied with a skilful defence entitled 'The Dignity of Literature,' addressed to the *Chronicle* on 8th January, and published in that paper on the 12th. With regard to the charge of caricature, he declares:

'My attempt was to tell the truth, and I meant to tell it not unkindly. I have seen the bookseller whom Bludyer robbed of his books; I have carried money, and from a noble brother man-of-letters, to some one not unlike Shandon in prison, and have watched the beautiful devotion of his wife in that place. Why are these things not to be described, if they illustrate, as they appear to me to do, that strange and awful struggle of good and wrong which takes place in our hearts and in the world?'

In the course of his letter he sided with the *Examiner* against the *Chronicle* on a point at issue between them concerning 'the propriety of public rewards and honours to literary men,' believing that they could, without loss of dignity, accept 'all the honours, places, and prizes they can get,' and pointing out that their profession was as much entitled to public honours as lawyers or soldiers. Queen Victoria had not yet acquired the habit of rewarding the achieve-

[1] Those who sought to construe disingenuous motive from Thackeray's use of his Irish experiences in *Barry Lyndon* and his caricature of Lever's style in *Punch* must feel equal indignation against Forster, for his article in the *Examiner* appeared little more than a month after Thackeray had dinner at his house. Forster may be taken as the typical man of letters of his generation, of whom might be expected an expert knowledge of contemporary literary etiquette. If he could ignore personal friendship in pungent criticism, Thackeray committed no breach of formality by his caricature and parody. In his reply he contented himself with a shrewd knock at Forster's notorious impetuosity by remarking that 'the editor of the *Examiner* may perhaps occasionally write, like other authors, in a hurry, and not be aware of the conclusions to which some of his sentences may lead.' Thackeray wrote to Dr. John Brown on 24th May 1853: 'I have just come away from seeing poor Jack Forster laid up with rheumatism. . . . But, poor fellow, we shall fight when he is up again from his sick-bed. There's no mingling our two sorts comfortably together.'—*Letters of Dr. John Brown*, edited by his son and D. W. Forrest. London, 1907.

ments of writers with titles, and nearly twenty years later Charles Reade expressed his indignation that Dickens had not been offered a peerage.

The second incident, partly a pendant to the first, was the rejection of Thackeray by the Athenæum Club. The accusation of caricaturing fellow-members of his profession, together with the notorious fact that Foker was drawn from Andrew Arcedeckne, who himself openly boasted about it, inspired at least one member of the committee with the fear that he might be selected, on familiar acquaintance at the club, as a subject for satire. Dean Milman, his proposer, wrote to Abraham Hayward that he would never have subjected Thackeray to the hazard of rejection if he had not been confident of success. Hallam, Macaulay, Lord Mahon (afterwards Earl Stanhope, the historian), and even Croker, who had suffered more at Thackeray's hands than anybody except, perhaps, Bulwer, all voted for him. In a flippant letter to Hayward, consoling himself that Dr. Johnson would certainly have black-balled Fielding, he remarked:

'As a satirical writer, I rather wonder that I have not made more enemies than I have. . . . There must be thousands of men to whom the practice of ridicule must be very offensive; doesn't one see such in society, or in one's own family? persons whose nature was not gifted with a sense of humour?'

Though he did not tell Hayward, he had an additional reason for these reflections, as it was at this time that Lever caricatured him in *Roland Cashel*. The Athenæum made amends a year later by electing him to their membership on 25th February 1851.

§ 4

On 18th January 1850 FitzGerald remarked that 'Thackeray is well again except not quite strong yet.' It was marvellous that he had recovered so quickly, for there is little doubt that he had suffered from an attack of cholera. Though he was so soon resuming his normal activities, the illness left a lasting mark upon him, having apparently irritated the internal complaint which had long lain latent. Throughout the remainder of his life he was subject to periodical attacks of colic and vomiting, which grew gradually more frequent and exhausting. By an odd chance none of his numerous acquaintances noticed precisely when a change took place in his personal appearance. A drawing of himself in the middle 'forties shows him a burly young man, with a small moustache and imperial, his hair still dark, looking no more than his thirty odd years. Yet portraits immediately following the period of writing *Pendennis* reveal the popular conception of Thackeray, with a great leonine head of waving white hair and the face and figure of a man of sixty. It seems probable that most of his contemporaries so long outlived him that they recollected him only as he appeared in the last twelve years of his life. Serjeant Ballantine confessed that his memory was at fault on reading Planché's description of Thackeray as a young man, forgetting that he was ever 'tall and slight,' before his hair whitened and his weight increased. Nevertheless, though Ballantine and others, writing after an interval of years, may have been puzzled by their fickle memories, it is remarkable that none of the diarists and letter-writers, recording immediate impressions, ever remarked upon the alteration in his appearance, which was obviously surprisingly sudden. His illness, reacting on the stress of past troubles, erratic living, and his present restless state of mind, seems to have deprived him of middle age, plunging him directly from comparative youth into elderly decline.

Necessity compelled a resumption of work during convalescence, and he appears barely to have dispensed with his bath-chair as a means of conveyance before he was dining out as regularly as ever. In March he visited Paris, taking his children to stay with his parents in their apartment off the Champs Élysées. There his mother entertained her little social circle, 'a very noble-looking old lady, holding her head high,' with her diamond cap-pin flashing as she moved regally about her little drawing-room. Apart from occasional references in Thackeray's letters to Mrs. Brookfield, there is nothing beyond Lady Ritchie's reminiscences from which to reconstruct that quaint little society, which she described as *Cranford en voyage.* The gallant old major, who was always found alone in the twilight watching for his wife's return when she had taken the children for a walk, still retained his susceptibility to speculation, entertaining ideas of restoring his fallen fortunes with inventions for the manufacture of peat fuel and mechanical horses of a 'robot' pattern. Adored by his wife's female friends, 'he used to sign their pension papers, administer globules for their colds, give point and support to their political opinions.' It was all painfully *vieux jeu*, and describing affectionately how 'good old G. P. bears the bore of the children constantly in his room, with great good humour,' Thackeray was moved to melancholy reflection by this end to the careers of a celebrated beauty and a distinguished soldier.

Thackeray, however, was lionised in Paris as much as in London. In a series of letters to Mrs. Brookfield and one to Kate Perry, he tells of his adventures in fashionable society. The British ambassador, Lord Normanby, who had obtained his introduction to Louis Napoleon in the previous September, lost no opportunity of doing him honour. He gained him the *entrée* to the highest circles, Thackeray attending a ball given by Lady Sandwich, where he made a pleasant acquaintance with Lord and Lady Castlereagh, and escorted him to the President's *soirée.* On this occasion, Thackeray remarked in mock dismay that his shoe-lace was untied, flippantly asking if the President would notice it. Lord Normanby replied, with ambassadorial courtliness, that 'the President will look up at you—not down.' Meeting Victor Hugo, he found him 'a queer heathen.' He was delighted by one of his daughters having sat next to Guizot in church, and was tempted to attend a purely literary evening by the prospect of meeting Scribe and Dumas.

It was on his return to London that FitzGerald wrote, on 17th April, that 'Thackeray is in such a great world that I am afraid of him.' Living in the country with his books and his hobbies and rarely coming to town, the years had altered FitzGerald little, except that seclusion had in some respects narrowed his perspective. He regarded his old friend's erratic tendencies with less indulgence than formerly, and in his rueful regret of old Coram Street evenings spent in smoking and yarning, resented Thackeray's present manner of life for renouncing those simple pleasures. Their former intimate correspondence had flagged, and the feeling, fostered by the scornful Carlyle and others, grew upon him that success was causing Thackeray to forget his old friends. As Thackeray once remarked, those who so accused him failed to realise the endless obligations of a public man, inundated with invitations and correspondence. Moreover, FitzGerald knew little or nothing of Mrs. Brookfield's predominant influence upon his life. As Thackeray once remarked to her, speaking of the deep affection he had felt for FitzGerald for more than twenty years, 'when our friendship began, I had not yet learned to love a woman.'

In cultivating the high lights of society, Thackeray did not forget his friends. Apart from the Brookfields', his regular resorts were the Procters', the Elliots' in Chesham Place, where Kate Perry lived with her sister, and the house of his cousin and neighbour in Kensington, Mrs. Irvine, a sister of his boyhood playmate, Richmond Shakespear. He frequently visited the Crowes', the friends of his student days in Paris, and he dined during the summer season with Higgins, John Kenyon, and Forster, with whom apparently his relations remained unaffected by their exchanges concerning 'the dignity of literature.' In a letter to Mrs. Brookfield of Tuesday, 23rd April, he gives a fairly typical week's list of engagements.

'I have an awful week of festivities before me; to-day Shakespeare's birthday at the Garrick Club, dinner and speech. Lunch, Madame Lionel Rothschild's; ball, Lady Waldegrave's; she gives the finest balls in London, and I have never seen one yet. To-morrow, of five invitations to dinner, the first is Mr. Marshall, the Duke of Devonshire's evening party, Lady Emily Dundas' ditto. Thursday, Sir Anthony Rothschild. Friday, the domestic affections. Saturday, Sir Robert Peel; Sunday, Lord Lansdowne's.'

Even so, he found time to call at his old tavern haunts, for, after attending the Water-Colour Society's exhibition, 'which was choke-full of bishops and other big-wigs, among them Sir Robert Peel elaborately gracious,' he declares that the next person with whom he shook hands after Peel was 'Mrs. Rhodes of the Back Kitchen,' the landlady of the Cyder Cellars.

His letters reveal the constancy of his visits to the house of the old Misses Berry in Curzon Street. With his love of the eighteenth century, his delight in listening to the gossiping reminiscences of the two old ladies, both nearing ninety years of age, may well be imagined. Kate Perry related how they declared 'what a very remarkable man he was,' and whenever they were arranging one of their literary dinner-parties insisted that 'we *must* have Thackeray.' She declared that Thackeray always maintained the rather unusual view that Agnes Berry was more naturally gifted than her elder sister, possibly because, at the period that he knew them, she retained her faculties undimmed by advancing age. A year after the elder sister's death he told Kate Perry, in November 1853, of some talk with a publisher of 'editing Walpole and writing a life of him,' the idea doubtless arising from the knowledge that Miss Berry had been Horace Walpole's literary executor. But he never found time to approach the task, which was soon afterwards undertaken by Peter Cunningham.

CHAPTER 11

§ 1

Ever since his formal appointment to a seat at Mr. Punch's table at Christmas, 1843, a week had rarely passed without an article or sketch of his appearing in the periodical. *Punch* had not merely established his financial fortunes, but had paved the way for his success as a novelist. But it had now finally effected its purpose in Thackeray's career, and he found increasingly irksome the perpetual necessity of writing squibs and skits while struggling to concentrate upon a novel in numbers. When working on *Vanity Fair* he had felt impatience with his obligations to *Punch*, for William Archer Shee, meeting him with Horace Smith at Brighton, remembered him breaking up a pleasant conversation with the remark, 'Now I must go and be funny,' adding with a sigh, 'You little know what dreary work it is to be obliged to be funny under all the circumstances.'[1] In July 1850, when he felt some dissatisfaction with *Pendennis* and wished to avoid distractions in order to confine his energies to its composition, his exasperation found frequent expression. Early in the month he suddenly went over to Dieppe to seek the solitude necessary for the completion of the nineteenth number of the novel, writing on the 11th to Mrs. Brookfield: 'I was so sick and ill this morning that I determined on instant flight . . . and I've been working at *Punch* for dear life ever since I've been here.' On his return he wrote again:

'I have had a bad week and a most cruel time of it this month; my groans are heart-rending, my sufferings

[1] *My Contemporaries*, by William Archer Shee. London, 1893.

immense; I thought No. XIX would never be born alive;—It is but stupid, ricketty, and of feeble intellect, I fear. . . . It is but a hasty letter I send you, dear lady, but my hand's weary with writing *Pendennis*—and my head boiling up with some nonsense that I must do after dinner for *Punch*. Isn't it strange that, in the midst of all the selfishness, that one of doing one's business, is the strongest of all. What funny songs I've written when fit to hang myself!'

Mrs. Brookfield probably felt little surprise at the final bursting of the bomb of his exasperation:

'What do you think I have done to-day?' he wrote. 'I have sent in my resignation to *Punch*. There appears in next *Punch* an article, so wicked, I think, by poor [Jerrold] that upon my word I don't think I ought to pull any longer in the same boat with such a savage little Robespierre.'

Mrs. Brookfield replied:

'I cannot feel sorry for the resignation from *Punch*, which is really a grand thing to have done as testimony,—but they ought to cut out the Jerrold article and make you come back. . . . Pray don't make yourself ill again, I mean I hope you take proper care of yourself.'

The proprietors of *Punch* adopted precisely the course she suggested; they withdrew the offending article and declined to accept Thackeray's resignation. In response to such handsome consideration he could scarcely have done otherwise than continue his connection with the periodical, and he remained upon the staff for another eighteen months, though his subsequent contributions contain little of importance, bearing the obvious impress of having been executed to order, without enthusiasm or careful preparation.

Presumably the article was directed against Louis Napoleon, a favourite butt of *Punch*, of which policy Thackeray, an ardent republican, expressed open disapproval. But it is unlikely that Douglas Jerrold wrote it, as his active connection with *Punch* had almost entirely ceased by this time. Nevertheless, because the editor of the Brookfield correspondence carelessly ascribed Thackeray's undated letter to 1854, the year in which appeared his last contributions to *Punch*, Jerrold for many years suffered under the unjust charge of having caused Thackeray's rupture with the paper, a charge which acquired the weight of conviction from the reputed hostility persisting between the two colleagues. Jerrold's principal biographer[1] has demonstrated that many of the ill-natured remarks against Thackeray attributed to him have been distorted and misreported in the course of repetition. Herman Merivale sought to show that Thackeray liked to tell stories against himself by declaring that he repeated Jerrold's joke, 'when he had just stood godfather to some friend's boy—"Lord, Thackeray, I hope you didn't present the child with your own mug!" ' As it stands, the remark is rude without being witty, but the true version of the anecdote appears in the diary of Brookfield, who noted on 12th February 1853, that when John Forster apologised for being late for dinner because he had been standing godfather to one of Dickens's children, Jerrold remarked: 'I hope that if you gave the child a mug it wasn't your own.' Neat, if personal, the wit of the remark received point from application to Forster, pompously proclaiming in his loud voice proof of his familiarity

[1] In his *Douglas Jerrold and Punch*, Mr. Walter Jerrold accurately identified the precise date and cause of Thackeray's final resignation. He also commented on the discrepancy between the dates of Thackeray's letter to Mrs. Brookfield and her reply, as given by the editors of their correspondence. But he did not acknowledge the accuracy of the authors of *Mrs. Brookfield and Her Circle* in ignoring the error of J. R. Lowell (presumably responsible for the editorial of the Brookfield letters) and ascribing the correspondence to 'about July,' 1850. The date is conclusively proved by references in both letters, as they appear in the original, to Harry Hallam's departure to assume his duties on the Midland Circuit. The letters could not refer, as Mr. Jerrold suggested, to the article entitled *Napoleon's Book of Fate*, published in *Punch* at the end of 1851, because young Hallam died in October 1850.

with Dickens. The story of somebody saying: 'I hear that you say — is the worst book I ever wrote,' and Jerrold's reply, 'No, I said it was the worst book anyone ever wrote,' has been identified with Thackeray and *The Virginians*, though the first number of that novel appeared five months after Jerrold's death. Similarly, Jerrold never made the comment on Thackeray's lectures: 'Very good; but wants a piano though'; it was Arcedeckne, the original Foker, who, being present when Thackeray was discussing the reception of his first lecture with a circle of friends at the Garrick Club, said: 'Ah, Thack, my boy, you ought to ha' had a pianner.'

Obviously these stories were repeated with reference to Jerrold and Thackeray by journalists possessing more professional skill than conscience. A good joke at Smith's expense by plain Mr. Brown, or even by Douglas Jerrold, must be taken on its merits, but even a bad joke at Thackeray's expense by Mr. Brown is good 'copy,' which gains in flavour if Mr. Brown, like Jerrold, is known to have been on terms of antagonism with him. Consequently, the relations between Jerrold and Thackeray have been tainted with an acrimony which never existed in fact. Dr. John Brown aptly diagnosed the feeling between them as one of 'constitutional antipathy.' Loud, aggressive, excitable, and careless of offering offence in exercising the the play of his caustic wit, Jerrold jarred on Thackeray, who excelled in company by means of quiet humour and witty comment, never attempting to monopolise conversation in an effort to appear brilliant. The secret of his social success was his pleasant ability to sustain general conversation, contriving by his own provocative suggestions and apt repartee that every member of the company spoke his share and consequently derived a feeling of satisfaction from seeming to play a part in the entertainment. Jerrold's was the Johnsonian method of securing for himself general attention by arrogant bombast, a habit compatible with his reputation as a wit but scarcely conducive to conviviality. Hence, when the French caricaturist, 'Cham,' visited London and Thackeray gave a breakfast in his honour at Young Street, he invited Higgins and most of the *Punch* set, including Leech, Doyle, and Tom Taylor, but omitted Jerrold, because, as he explained to Vizetelly, 'young Douglas, if asked, would most likely not come, but if he did, he'd take especial care that his own effulgence should obscure all lesser lights, Cham's included.' The result was, as Vizetelly described, that 'Cham' delighted the company with his skill as a *raconteur*, his stories being capped by efforts from the rest of the party, except Thackeray, who 'contented himself by encouraging anyone who was disposed to contribute to the general entertainment.'

There is no doubt that, in his Grub Street days, when he hungered for success and saw so many of his contemporaries leaving him behind in the race for fame, he was afflicted with a feeling of envy towards Jerrold, his rival in his own *genre* on *Punch*, who, before the appearance of the *Snob Papers*, enjoyed superior popularity with the readers of the journal. Vizetelly relates how, when his copy of the week's *Punch* was delivered at Young Street, he would eagerly tear off the wrapper, exclaiming: 'Now let's see what young Douglas has to say this week.' Misquoting the exclamation, Mr. Spielmann interpreted 'a world of dislike and scorn' in the diminutive prefix to Jerrold's name, but it implies rather the attitude of derisive banter adopted by a physically big man to one of short and slight stature, who compensated for his lack of inches by loud self-assertion and vituperative sarcasm. The instinctive distaste for Jerrold's manner persisted throughout their long acquaintance, preventing Thackeray, in spite of their intimate professional association, from ever admitting him to such friendly intimacy as he shared with others of his colleagues like Leech and Doyle. All symptoms of envy towards him, however, were dissipated by the success of *Vanity Fair*, which elevated him to a sphere outside the scope of Jerrold, and inspired him with the same ambition of emulation towards Dickens as he had formerly felt towards Jerrold. His introspective habit rendered him uncomfortably conscious of these feelings, which he deprecated in defiance of instinct, and when he expressed pleasure upon hearing of the success of *Lloyd's Newspaper* under Jerrold's editorship, there was genuine sincerity in the superficially flippant remark: 'I am quite pleased with myself at finding myself pleased at men getting on in the world.' Writing to Mrs. Brookfield from America on 23rd January 1853 he expressed an exactly similar sentiment, when 'the other night some men were talking of Dickens and Bulwer as if they were equal to Shakespeare, and I was pleased to find myself pleased at hearing them praised.'

§ 2

In August 1850 Thackeray and his children joined the Brookfields at Southampton, the children staying in lodgings with Mrs. Brookfield while Thackeray had rooms at a neighbouring inn. Dining in the evenings with Mrs. Brookfield, he put in a spell of satisfactory work on *Pendennis*, remaining there till the third week of the month. Returning to town on the 20th he wrote the next day:

'I wonder whether ever again, I shall have such a happy peaceful fortnight as that last! How sunshiny the landscape remains in my mind, I hope for always; and the smiles of the dear children and the aspect of the kindest and tenderest face in the world to me. . . . How happy your dear regard makes me, how it takes off the solitude and eases it, may it continue, pray God, till your head is as white as mine, and our children have children of their own. O Love and Duty—I hope you'll never leave us quite. Instead of being unhappy because that delightful holiday is over or all but over, I intend that the thoughts of it should serve to make me only the more cheerful and help me, please God, to do my duty better. All such pleasures ought to brace and strengthen one against work days, and lo, here they are.'

In the same letter he describes having travelled up from Southampton on the train with 'Miss G[ore], who says she is Blanche Amory, and I think she is Blanche Amory; amiable at times, amusing, clever and depraved.' He proceeds to say that 'the idea of her will help me to a good chapter, in which I will make Pendennis and Blanche play at being in love, such a wicked false humbugging London love, as two *blasé* London people might act, and half deceive themselves that they were in earnest. That,' he adds, 'will complete the cycle of Mr. Pen's worldly experiences, and then we will make, or try and make, a good man of him.'[1]

He had talked of a visit to Scotland, but, being faced with the choice of a subject for his next Christmas book, he decided to tour the Rhine valley again with a view to proceeding with the long-postponed project of *The Kickleburys*. He announced his departure to Mrs. Brookfield in the first week of September, intending to leave for Antwerp on the Sunday morning, spend Monday night at Cologne or Bonn, and proceed thence to Frankfort. Having spent five days at Homburg, however, he was back in Brussels, on 15th September, when he wrote to his daughters that his journey had been 'but a dull one,' though 'I'm glad I came as it has given me what I wanted for my Xmas Book.' He stayed a few days in Brussels,

[1] On 7th January 1851 Jane Carlyle wrote to her uncle a vivacious account of a young lady whom she took as the original Blanche Amory, who had been staying with her at Chelsea to the great discomfort of Carlyle. 'Not that the poor little —,' she wrote, 'is quite such a little devil as Thackeray, who has detested her from a child, has here represented, but the looks, the manners, the wiles, the *larmes*, "and all that sort of thing," are a perfect likeness.' Cf. *Letters and Memorials of Jane Welsh Carlyle*, edited by James Anthony Froude. London, 3 vols., 1883.

working quietly during the day and going in the evening to the theatre, where he saw Déjazet, an old favourite of his early time in Paris. 'It is pleasant at the theatre,' he told his mother, 'to think there's no printer's devil waiting.'

At the beginning of October he went to stay with the Gores in Hampshire, having intended to go on from there to the Ashburtons at Alresford Grange. Before he left London, however, he received a letter from Lady Ashburton, begging him to defer his visit, as he had offended Henry Taylor and his wife, who were staying with her—'she could not say how, but she saw it wouldn't do for them to be at Grange together.' The cause of the offence was contained in the fourth paper by 'The Proser,' entitled 'On a Good-looking Young Lady,' in *Punch* of 8th June, celebrating the charms of a certain 'Erminia,' probably to be identified with Virginia Pattle, afterwards Lady Somers,[1] in one paragraph of which article he says:

'This almost peerless creature, on a visit to the country, met the great poet, Timotheus, whose habitation is not far from the country house of Erminia's friend, and who, upon seeing the young lady, felt for her that admiration which every man of taste experiences upon beholding her, and which, if Mrs. Timotheus had not been an exceedingly

[1] The Pattles were an Anglo-Indian family connected by friendship in successive generations with the Thackerays. Their ancestor, Thomas Pattle, went out to India with the elephant-hunter in 1766. Thackeray remarks that 'I knew Erminia's family long before the young lady was born, Victoria her mother, Boa her aunt, Chinchilla her grandmother—I have been intimate with every one of these ladies, and at the table of Sabilla, her married sister, with whom Erminia lives, have a cover laid for me whenever I choose to ask for it.' He had known 'Victoria' in Paris in his art-student days, for his cousin William Ritchie, writing from India to his sister on 12th February 1844 asked if she remembered 'Mrs. Pattle, in Paris, about ten years since,' remarking that her two youngest daughters were 'two of the prettiest and nicest girls here,' and that she had asked him 'to remember her very kindly to my mother, if she recollected her, and to give her love to William Thackeray.' On her return to England Virginia, the youngest daughter, lived with an elder sister, Mrs. Thoby Prinsep, close by Thackeray in Kensington until her marriage, on 2nd October 1850, to the third Earl Somers. Thackeray frequently mentions her in his letters to Mrs. Brookfield.

sensible person, would have caused a jealousy between her and the great bard her husband. But, charming and beautiful herself, Mrs. Timotheus can even pardon another woman for being so; nay, with perfect good sense, though possibly with a *little* factitious enthusiasm, she professes to share to its fullest the admiration of the illustrious Timotheus for the young lady.'

'Timotheus' was Henry Taylor, an eminently respectable gentleman, who had taken the precaution in early life of assiduously cultivating the right people, with the result that he was Southey's literary executor, reputed to be a considerable poet on the strength of his *Philip van Artevelde*, which Charles Lamb found 'nothing extraordinary,' though it was sent to him as 'equal to Shakespeare,' an implacable Tory, a respected permanent official, and the husband of Lord Monteagle's youngest daughter, sister of Stephen Spring Rice, a friend of Thackeray and the Brookfields. Taylor's magnificent respectability recoiled in horror from such flippancy, and he apparently informed Lady Ashburton that he and his lady could not fraternise under the same roof with its perpetrator, though on meeting Thackeray at Virginia Pattle's wedding a few days before and hearing that they were likely to meet at the Grange, he had 'seemed friendly enough.' His dignity prevented him from informing Lady Ashburton of the trivial cause of his attitude, and Thackeray told her of it in his reply to her letter, admitting that 'the article had been unintentionally vulgar and impertinent.' She thereupon advised him to be rid of such an absurd impediment to their plans by apologising to Taylor, and he wrote to Mrs. Brookfield from the Gores' house:

'Please to tell Spring Rice this with my best regards, tomorrow. I thought over the confounded Erminia matter in the railroad, and wrote instantly on arriving here, a letter of contrition and apology to Henry Taylor for having made, what I see now, was a flippant and offensive allusion to Mrs. Taylor.'

The comedy greatly amused Jane Carlyle, who was also a guest at the Grange, and she told her husband:

'Thackeray is here—arrived yesterday, greatly to the discomfort of [Taylor] evidently, who had "had the gang all to himself" so long. First he (Thackeray) wrote he was coming. Then Lady A. put him off on account of some *Punch*-offence to the [Taylor]s then Thackeray wrote an apology to [Taylor]! then Lady A. wrote he was to come after all, and went to Winchester to meet him, and [Taylor] sulked all yesterday evening, and to-day is solemn as death. In fact he has been making a sort of superior *agapemone* here, in which he was the Mr. Prince, the Spirit of Love; and no wonder he dislikes the turn that has been given to things by the arrival of the Spirit of Punch. Col. Rawlinson comes tomorrow, Kinglake and Brookfield on the 15th.'

Three days later, on 8th October, she wrote to Carlyle:

'Henry Taylor and Thackeray have fraternised finally, *not* "like the carriage horses and the railway steam-engine," as might have been supposed, but like men and brothers! I lie by, and observe them with a certain interest; it is as good as a play!'[1]

Even the cold and formal Taylor, determined to sustain his dignity, could not withstand Thackeray's genial *bonhomie* when he exerted himself to please and to amuse. Writing from the Grange to Mrs. Brookfield, Thackeray said, 'I like Taylor, whose grandeur wears off in ten minutes and in whom one perceives an extremely gentle and loving human creature I think—not a man to be intimate with ever, but to admire and like from a distance and to have a sort of artistical good will to.' Returning to town by 16th October,

[1] *New Letters and Memorials of Jane Welsh Carlyle*, edited by Alexander Carlyle. London, 2 vols., 1903.

he applied himself vigorously to the finishing off of *Pendennis*. He saw Mrs. Brookfield every evening, dining either at her house, at the Elliots', or inviting a small party to Young Street. He finally completed the novel in the middle of November, after a feverish spell of energetic concentration which left him utterly exhausted.

'Having completed my story this day,' he informed his mother, 'and wrote *Finis*, I am very tired, weary, and solemn-minded. So say, God bless my dearest mother and G. P. ere I try and get some sleep. . . . I've been in bed for the best part of two days since I wrote this, and asleep the greater part of the time. I was much done up, had a small fever, boiled myself in a warm bath, went without dinner, slept fifteen hours, and am now as brisk as a bee and as fresh as a daisy.'

On the same day he wrote to thank William Allingham for the gift of a copy of *The Music Master*. Speaking of Leigh Hunt, who had introduced Allingham to him, he hoped 'dear old Leigh Hunt won't take the loss of the laurels to heart after bidding for them so naïvely as he did in those pleasant memoirs,' referring to Hunt's *Autobiography* and his hopes of succeeding Wordsworth as Poet Laureate, to which post Tennyson had just been appointed. Of Thornton Hunt, Leigh Hunt's son, who had lately started the *Leader* in conjunction with G. H. Lewes, he said that 'Thornton seems a fine fellow to me; wrong very often, but looking after truth sacredly.' He assisted Allingham, as he had assisted Coventry Patmore, with an introduction to his own editor, for when Allingham, then living in Ireland, asked if there was any chance of his doing any work for *Punch*, Thackeray replied: 'I don't think it would answer—from your distance from London; but if you'll send me any first chop bits I will send them to Mr. Lemon and try.'[1]

He had hoped to run over to Paris for Christmas, taking

[1] *Letters to William Allingham*, edited by H. Allingham and E. Baumer Williams. London, 1911.

the children to stay with his parents, but the sudden death of the widow of his uncle, the Rev. Francis Thackeray, robbed her two sons of their home, and he generously invited them both to spend their holidays at Young Street. The elder boy, Francis St. John Thackeray, whom he described as 'a very clever, hard-reading lad,' was then nearing the end of his time at Eton; the younger, Edward, who subsequently entered the army and won the V.C. in the Indian Mutiny, was at Marlborough. Both frequently spent holidays and vacations with their cousin in the following years, and one of them eventually married his bride from Thackeray's house.

Christmas was marked by a melancholy event—the funeral of Harry Hallam, who had died of malarial fever in Italy on 24th October. His father, who had now lost nine of his eleven children, in addition to his wife, brought the body home to be buried at Clevedon beside that of his elder son, Arthur. The obsequies were attended only by the male members of the family, the bereaved father, Sir Charles Elton, his son Arthur, and the husbands of his daughters, including Brookfield and Tennyson's brother-in-law, Edmund Law Lushington. Thackeray, however, decided to pay a final tribute to the young friend who had so often shared happy evenings with him at the Brookfields', and went down to Bristol for the purpose. Mrs. Brookfield, who remained in town with her cousin, wrote to her husband on the day of the funeral:

'Mr. Thackeray said he intended to go straight to the Church and should very likely not see anybody to speak to; he said he thought it would be "most modest" in him to keep aloof in that way as my Uncle wished for privacy, but I begged him just to call and shake hands with Arthur and Rhoda if he could.'

Writing the same night, to comfort her in her affliction, for young Hallam had been more like a brother than a cousin to her, Thackeray described how he had waited in the village shop till the last carriage had driven to the church before taking his stand beside the grave to await the coming of the procession.

'Those ceremonies over a corpse,' he wrote, 'the immortal soul of a man being in the keeping of God, and beyond the reach of all undertakers,—always appear to me shocking rather than solemn,—and the horses and plumes give me pain.—The awful moment was when the dear old father—the coffin being lowered into the vault where so much of his affection and tenderest love lies buried, went down into the cave and gave the coffin a last kiss;—there was no standing that last affecting touch of Nature.'

After the ceremony, Brookfield, seeing him at the graveside, insisted on his going up to the house, but in spite of pressure from the bereaved father, touched by the tribute of friendship from his son's distinguished friend, that he should stay the night, he returned to Bristol, wrote an affectionate letter to cheer Mrs. Brookfield, and proceeded the next day to the house of Sir John Cam Hobhouse, Byron's friend, where apparently he spent Christmas. This was one of the characteristically graceful acts, inspired by a spontaneous impulse of affection, without premeditated motive or ostentatious formality and often occasioning considerable personal inconvenience, which endeared him to all those of his relatives and friends who suffered sorrow or trouble.

§ 3

On 16th December *The Kickleburys on the Rhine* was advertised for publication—not by Chapman and Hall, but by Smith, Elder and Co. In his *Memoir of George Smith*, compiled for the first supplement to the *Dictionary of National Biography*, Sir Sidney Lee remarked that 'Thackeray's regular publishers, Chapman and Hall, had not been successful with his recent Christmas books, *Doctor Birch and his Young Friends* and *Rebecca and Rowena*, and they deprecated the issue of another that year.'[1] This is scarcely accurate. Chapman and Hall were willing to publish *The Kickleburys* on the same terms as his previous Christmas books, but, on 22nd August, before leaving for the Continent to collect material for the book, Thackeray wrote to them:

'If I do a Xmas book with you this year, the price will be £150 for an edition of 3000. Of course I have spoken to no other publisher as yet on the subject but I think I have a right to a shilling per copy of a 5 and often 7 shilling book; and intend to stipulate for that sum with my publisher.'

Chapman replied that his firm could not undertake the publication on those terms, as they would lose money by it. Thackeray was therefore free to go elsewhere and he naturally approached George Smith, whom he had recently met with Charlotte Brontë. In his *Reminiscences* Smith declares that Thackeray frankly explained that 'his last Christmas book, *Rebecca and Rowena*, had not been successful, and, as a result, Chapman and Hall could not see their way to paying him his price for the next book.'[2] Afterwards celebrated for the munificence of his agreements with authors, Smith did not haggle; he had long wished to publish for Thackeray, having once approached him through his reader, W. S. Williams, long before *Vanity Fair* had appeared, and on Thackeray naming his price, he promptly asked if he might write a cheque for it.

Though Smith gracefully omitted to mention the fact, Thackeray occasioned trepidation by his usual lateness in delivering his manuscript. With the book advertised to

[1] *George Smith: A Memoir, with Some Pages of Autobiography*, printed for private circulation. London, 1902.

[2] *The House of Smith Elder*, printed for private circulation. London, 1923.

appear, he was still engaged upon its composition, scribbling away feverishly with the printer's boy waiting at the door. Williams, the firm's reader and adviser, told Charlotte Brontë that, 'if he had not been helped out with the vigour, energy, and method of Mr. Smith, he must have sunk under the day and night labour of the last few weeks,' while she informed a friend on 8th January that 'Thackeray has given dreadful trouble by his want of punctuality.'[1] As in the case of *Rebecca and Rowena*, the book seems to have been put on the market barely in time for Christmas, though it was the customary practice, then as now, for such publications to be issued about the beginning of December. The delay evidently produced an adverse effect upon the sales of *Rebecca and Rowena*, but *The Kickleburys on the Rhine* was in such demand that the first edition of three thousand copies sold out in a few days and a second edition was called for in the first week of the new year.

The second edition included, as a preface, 'An Essay on Thunder and Small Beer,' an effort in his early Fraserian vein ridiculing with the most bitter scorn and ironical invective an adverse review of *The Kickleburys* in *The Times*. The authorship of the review has been a subject of dispute. Thackeray believed it to have been written by Samuel Phillips, a minor novelist, who enjoyed some contemporary reputation as the principal exponent of the tortuous phraseology and inflated pomposity of style for which

[1] On 7th January 1851 Charlotte Brontë addressed a letter to George Smith, dilating in her heavy style of unnatural humour upon the anxiety Thackeray had caused the firm by his erratic habits, suggesting that, as a penance, he should be condemned to build a church with two shrines dedicated to St. Bungay and St. Bacon, and to lay on each shrine 'a neatly written MS., being a tale without any allusion to Belgravia in it.' She proceeded to thank Smith for having dissuaded Thackeray from sending her a presentation copy of *Pendennis* and so relieved her from the necessity of writing a note of acknowledgment, as 'to have spoken my mind would have been to displease, and I know, if I had written at all, my mind would have insisted on speaking itself.' Cf. *Thackeray and Charlotte Brontë, being some hitherto unpublished letters to her publisher by Charlotte Brontë*, privately printed by Clement Shorter. London, January 1919.

The Times became notorious.[1] According to Sutherland Edwards, Jeaffreson and others, Charles Lamb Kenney, who was on friendly terms with Thackeray and had posed as a model to him for the sketches of the somewhat effeminate-looking hero in the illustrations to *Pendennis*, was the author. Edwards declares that, on hearing of Thackeray's anger at the article, Kenney went to him, 'confessed his fault, and was at once forgiven.' Jeaffreson also believed that Thackeray knew the writer to be Kenney, who was then only commencing his connection with *The Times*, because he described 'the Thunderer's man, Jupiter Jeames, taking his master's place, adopting his manner, and trying to dazzle and roar like his awful employer.' Years afterwards Kenney confessed to Jeaffreson that he had written the article, in spite of his friendly feelings for Thackeray, because he wished to please his employers, who disliked Thackeray.

Here is the obvious reason for Thackeray's onslaught. He was not wasting powder and shot on Kenney or Phillips, but seized an opportunity to deride the supercilious pomposity of a paper, with which, for some reason, he was on terms of hostility. Before this open declaration of war, there appears no reason for Kenney's assumption that the governing powers of *The Times* nourished inimical feelings towards Thackeray, though, with the exception of three articles ascribed to his hand during 1848, he had ceased to write for the paper after the death of Barnes, but subsequently he received rough treatment at their hands. In the early 'fifties *The Times* possessed a circulation more

[1] John Camden Hotten, who, under the pseudonym of Theodore Taylor, compiled *Thackeray: the Humourist and the Man of Letters* (London 1864) said the article was 'generally attributed to the late Mr. Samuel Phillips,' and the reliable Vizetelly declared that he heard Thackeray frequently refer to Phillips as the author. In *Bentley's Miscellany* for August 1855, the reviewer of *Essays from The Times*, ascribing the anonymous volume to 'the late Samuel Phillips,' discerns 'a pomp of phrase, and a roll of sentences, befitting the high seat of the Jupiter Tonans of the press—the Thunderer with whose thunder Mr. Thackeray once made himself and the town merry, *à propos* of small beer.'

than seven times greater than its nearest rival and often wielded its wide influence in literary matters with scant justice and judgment, as in the cases of Reade and Swinburne. Its disparaging review of *Esmond* is said to have caused a temporary decline in the sales of the book.

The review appeared on 4th January, the same day that the publishers informed him of the demand for a second edition, and, having written his preface the following day, he departed for Paris with the children on the 8th. He had promised his mother, on finishing *Pendennis*, that he would visit her before beginning another book, though he assured her that 'I've got a better subject for a novel than any I've yet had.' Writing to Mrs. Brookfield soon after his arrival in Paris, he said: 'A story is biling up in my interior, in which there shall appear some very good, lofty and generous people.' This resolution was inspired by a remark of Arthur Helps in the Elliots' drawing-room. When speaking of Thackeray, he asked: 'Is he an amiable man?' adding, 'I want to know, for his books don't give me the impression that he is.'[1] Thackeray, entering the room at that moment, overheard the remark. Mrs. Brookfield therefore informed him that 'I should like you to write a novel to startle Helps and such like objectors who think your heart does not keep pace with your head.' As he tells her that he has 'got a very amusing book, the *Tatler* newspaper of 1709,' it is evident that he was already evolving the plan of *Esmond*. A week or two later he remarked that 'I want to begin to write again very much; my mighty mind is tired of idleness, and ill employs the intervals of rest.'

He spent some six weeks at Paris in social amusements. He again visits D'Orsay, now nearing his last years of life, and wrote to Mrs. Brookfield a description of the decayed

[1] Mrs. Brookfield thus related Helps's remark in a letter to her husband of 8th January, but Kate Perry, writing after an interval of thirty-six years in her appendix to the Brookfield Letters, represents him as having expressed himself more strongly.

beau, which supplies probably the best portrait of him in his decline. He expressed discomfort at the manner in which his mother's friends lionised him, treating him as 'a sort of foreign emperor with the princesses my daughters,' so eliciting from his correspondent the discerning reflection:

'I was thinking over your chafing against the petty homage and the small sets at Paris, and debating whether you ought not to chafe as *much* against the adulation on a grand scale, but I merely throw this out, I don't think you care about the sublimer flatteries in the least, but it does not irritate you in the same way.'

Less generous minds, debating the same point, discovered evidence of his snobbery, but Mrs. Brookfield appreciated the different effect upon him of flattery from different sources. In the presence of respectable middle-class poverty, pinching on their pensions to preserve a semblance of the dignity due to retired Indian Army colonels and the relicts of deceased military officers and civil servants, he felt at once shamefully conscious of his success as a flaunting insult to their disappointed, half-forgotten hopes, and uncomfortably aware that he was undoubtedly the only celebrity they had ever encountered at close quarters, appearing to them, indeed, as a 'foreign emperor' or the chieftain of a legendary barbaric tribe. The praise and admiration of the highest London social circles was a very different thing. To receive the compliments of Peel or Palmerston, accustomed to consort daily with men whose names were in the mouths of the nation, who enjoyed the acquaintance of every notable man of letters, must have tickled the vanity of anybody. The compliments of such men, moreover, carried an honourable value, savouring nothing of adulation or sycophantic flattery, but as a friendly tribute in the fraternity of achievement.

In London again before the end of February, he witnessed Macready's farewell performance at Drury Lane from a seat in Mrs. Procter's box. On 1st March he officiated as a steward at the farewell dinner to the actor and had to propose the toast of Mrs. Macready and her family. Following Bulwer, Dickens, Forster, and Charles Kemble, all accomplished speakers, his speech, as usual, was the worst of the evening. Remarking that it was the only speech 'out of tune,' Pollock said, 'he indulges in a humour to turn things the seamy side out, which is at least not appropriate to a festive occasion.' He confessed himself that he was 'all the while feeling in so terrible a panic that I scarcely knew at the time what I was uttering, and didn't know at all when I sat down.'

On this occasion he was particularly interested in his ability to face an audience, as he was devoting all his time to the preparation of his lectures on *The English Humourists of the Eighteenth Century*. Daily in Mrs. Brookfield's company during March and early April, she sometimes acted as his secretary, taking down parts of the lectures at his dictation. As the time approached for their delivery, he developed a fever of nervous anxiety. One day he went down to Willis's Rooms, which he had engaged for his *début*, and recited from the platform part of the multiplication table to a waiter stationed at the farther end of the room, 'so as to try the voice.' He was desperately eager to succeed, because he saw in his success as a lecturer the one great chance of speedily amassing a sum of money sufficient to provide a competence for his children. Always mistrustful of his powers, he feared to delay such an enterprise lest his popularity should wane. He had first determined upon something of the sort immediately after his illness, his idea being, in the event of his success in London, to follow the example of Dickens by making a tour of America. Evidently he had confided his intention to Mrs. Brookfield at that time, for lamenting the uneven quality of *Pendennis* in a letter of July 1850, and expressing the hope that he might write a completely good story, he wondered: 'Will he die before doing so? or come back from America and do it?' Again, two months later, from Brussels, he promises his daughters that he will take them on a Continental tour in 1852, 'when I'm back from America and you are grown even bigger stronger & fatter than at present.' Whatever his doctors had told him, he now considered himself a doomed man, who must make the best possible use of his few remaining years on earth. The knowledge that he had only a short space of life before him accounts for much of the fatalism and sentimentalism characterising his habit of thought. But, with unselfish courage, he devoted all his energies, in defiance of medical advice, to assure the security of his children after his death, contemptuously rejecting the possibility of purchasing an additional year or two of life by prudent care of his health at the expense of their subsequent comfort. No pilgrim ever procured the salvage of his soul by more selfless sacrifice than Thackeray in his last twelve years of life.

CHAPTER 12

§ 1

A FASIONABLE crowd assembled at Willis's Rooms on 21st May 1851. It was one of the social events of the season which saw the opening of the Great Exhibition by the Prince Consort. Mr. Thackeray, the great satirist, was going to lecture, and few of the fine ladies and gentlemen had, presumably, paid for their seats. He had issued invitations to all his friends and acquaintances. Mrs. Procter was there, with all the *intelligentsia* accustomed to frequent her drawing-room; Lady Ashburton, with her somewhat more exalted set, and, of course, the Elliots, Miss Perry, Mrs. Brookfield, and their circle. Henry Hallam went as a duty; Lord Carlisle, Macaulay, and Dean Milman as a compliment to a man they admired. Even Carlyle, though he disapproved of authors lecturing, brooded gloomily over the scene. The great folk condescended to honour the function: Lady Waldegrave, Lady Molesworth, the Lord Chief Baron, with, perhaps, only a selection from his twenty-four children, and Sir Robert Peel. At the other end of the scale was the *Punch* set, notably 'Dicky' Doyle, who, being invited to 'the tight rope exhibition' by his colleague, was instructed to bring with him 'a very noisy umbrella' for use at proper intervals, to exclaim 'God bless my soul, how beautiful!' when the lecturer touched his watch-chain, to applaud when he touched his neck-cloth, and to burst into tears when he used his handkerchief—or, 'if you can't cry at the pathetic parts, please blow your nose very hard.'

Behind the scenes Fanny Kemble found the lecturer

'sick at my stomach with fright.'[1] Fidgeting about he expressed a wish to have a last look at his manuscript, which was lying on the high desk, specially adapted to his great height, on the platform. She volunteered to fetch it for him, but, being a small woman, in reaching up, she upset the loose leaves of the book, which fluttered down about her. With profuse apologies she presented the disordered leaves to the lecturer, whose eyes brightened as he exclaimed that nothing better could have happened, as the task of arranging the manuscript in its proper pagination would serve as a distraction in the quarter of an hour he had still to wait.

As might be expected from his ineptitude for public speaking, Thackeray had none of Dickens's declamatory rhetoric and dramatic effect as a lecturer. Justin McCarthy said: 'his voice, though clear and penetrating and sometimes thrilling, had nothing like the variety and richness of intonation which the voice of Dickens could always command; he was simply an educated gentleman reading aloud to an educated assembly.' 'No accompaniment of gesture set off his quiet intonation,' adds McCarthy, 'and he seemed in fact to be talking rather at than to the crowd which hung upon his every word. . . . Even when his audience broke into irrepressible applause at some passage of especial beauty and power, the lecturer did not seem to gain any fresh impulse from the plaudits which broke forth, but went on to his next sentence with the same self-absorbed composure as though he were only thinking aloud and were unconscious of the presence of listeners. . . . I observed on many occasions, that the audience seemed to become possessed by a common dread lest anything, even an outburst of premature applause, should interrupt the discourse and cause a word to be lost.'[2] Sala was impressed by 'the perfection of his elocutionary manner,' and Long-

[1] *Records of Later Life*, by Frances Ann Kemble. London, 3 vols., 1882.

[2] Justin McCarthy's *Reminiscences*. London, 2 vols., 1899; and *Portraits of the 'Sixties*. London, 1903.

fellow, on hearing the lecture on Congreve and Addison, observed that it was 'a light graphic lecture; pleasant to hear from that soft, deep, sonorous voice of his.'[1]

He was bewildered by his success. After the dinner given to celebrate the occasion he scribbled a note to Mrs. Brookfield, saying 'that the night's proceedings are over, that the speech went off very well (I don't in the least know what occurred) and that Peel made a pointed and handsome compliment at the end of the address.' He was afraid of a flash in the pan, of the bubble of novelty being pricked by further experience, of his own power to sustain the success which he considered fortuitous. Writing on 23rd May to Abraham Hayward, who lost no opportunity of singing praise of the man whose genius he professed to have been the first to recognise, and thanking him for an article applauding the first lecture, he said dubiously:

'The truth is that lectures won't do. They were all friends, and a packed house; though to be sure, it goes to a man's heart to find amongst his friends such men as you and Kinglake and Venables, Higgins, Rawlinson, Carlyle, Ashburton and Hallam, Milman, Macaulay, Wilberforce looking on kindly.'

Speaking of his first lectures to old Dr. Thackeray of Cambridge, he said: 'What pleased me most and best, Mr. Macaulay and Mr. Hallam came almost every time. Macaulay noted a visit to one of the lectures on 12th June:

'He is full of humour and imagination, and I only wish that these lectures may answer both in the way of fame and money. He told me, as I was going out, that the scheme had done wonders for him; and I told him, and from my heart, that I wished he had made ten times as much.'[2]

[1] *Life of Henry Wadsworth Longfellow*, by Samuel Longfellow. London, 2 vols., 1886.

[2] *Life and Letters of Lord Macaulay*, by G. O. Trevelyan. London, 2 vols., 1876. (Enlarged and Complete Edition, London, 1908.)

He had impressed Macaulay more favourably than he thought when they met in Paris in the autumn of 1849, for Macaulay had bought *Rebecca and Rowena* the following Christmas, and, calling it 'a very pretty, clever piece of fooling,' observed, 'I wish him success heartily.'

The venerable Hallam attended at first purely as a duty to his dead son's friend, rather with the feeling that he was going as a grandmother to be taught how to suck eggs. He was greatly pleased by the second lecture and is said to have been won over by the personal emphasis with which Thackeray delivered the sentence relating to Addison: 'How can I ask my superior to say that I am a wonder when he knows better than I?' Throughout the body of the lectures are sprinkled such personal or topical references which tickled the contemporary palate and which afford food for the annotations of future editors. An instance occurs in the reference to Congreve's preferments: 'Doesn't it sound like a fable, that place in the Pipe Office? "Ah, l'heureux temps que celui de ces fables!" Men of letters there still be: but I doubt whether any Pipe Offices are left.' This pointed reflection must have revived memories of the dispute between the *Examiner* and the *Morning Chronicle*, in which Thackeray had joined, concerning the propriety of literary men accepting official preferment. Nor was it inspired by personal interest, though such a sinecure as Congreve had enjoyed would have supplied Thackeray with the desirable relief from incessant labour, for he is found, a few weeks later, to have been the principal means of securing a pension for Mrs. Jameson, the miscellaneous writer on art subjects, who was struggling in straitened circumstances. Writing to announce the granting of the pension, Lord Derby begged him to communicate the news to Mrs. Jameson, 'as it was through your representations to me of the circumstances and condition of that lady that I brought her case before Lord Russell.'

Thackeray acted as her trustee, conjointly with John Murray, till her death in 1860.

The success of the lectures was soon so obvious that even Thackeray's doubts were dispelled. They were the talk of town, and everybody flocked to Willis's Rooms. Charlotte Brontë attended on 29th May and described the scene to her father.

'The audience was composed of the *élite* of London society. Duchesses were there by the score, and amongst them the great and beautiful Duchess of Sutherland, the Queen's Mistress of the Robes. Amidst all this Thackeray just got up and spoke with as much simplicity and ease as if he had been speaking to a few friends by his own fireside. The lecture was truly good: he had taken pains with the composition. It was finished without being in the least studied; a quiet humour and graphic force enlivened it throughout. He saw me as I entered the room, and came straight up and spoke kindly. He then took me to his mother, a fine, handsome old lady, and introduced me to her.'

According to George Smith, with whom Charlotte was staying in London, Thackeray greatly disconcerted her on this occasion by saying to his mother: 'Mother, you must allow me to introduce you to Jane Eyre,' thereby causing everybody in their vicinity to turn round and stare. She showed to disadvantage in London society, which she affected to despise as 'this vast Vanity Fair,' though a ring of envy sounds in her contemptuous description of Thackeray's success. With the impertinent frankness upon which she prided herself, she told him he did wrong to postpone a lecture in the second week of June 'at the earnest petition of the duchesses and marchionesses, who, on the day it should have been delivered, were necessitated to go down with the Queen and Court to Ascot races,' inferring a motive of snobbery and quite ignoring the fact that, if Thackeray had insisted upon holding his lecture in defiance of 'the duchesses and marchionesses,' he would have addressed an audience consisting of few besides Miss Brontë herself. Speaking of the 'triumphant success' of the lectures and remarking that 'he says they will enable him to make a provision for his daughters,' while 'Mr. Smith believes he will not get less than four thousand pounds by them,' she added:

'Of course Mr. T. is a good deal spoiled by all this, and indeed it cannot be otherwise. He has offered two or three times to introduce me to some of his great friends, and says he knows many great ladies who would receive me with open arms if I would go to their houses; but, seriously, I cannot see that this sort of society produces so good an effect on him as to tempt me in the least to try the same experiment, so I remain obscure.'

Rather than the effect upon Thackeray, it was consciousness of her inability to shine in society which deterred her from accepting his offers of introductions.

With generous courtesy, Thackeray did his best to honour the authoress of *Jane Eyre*. When she had been in London the previous summer, he had made a morning call, and sat about two hours, 'while she was moved to speak to him of some of his short-comings (literary of course).' Remarking that he defended himself 'like a great Turk and heathen; that is to say, the excuses were often worse than the crime itself,' she failed to perceive either his humorous banter or his graceful tolerance of her conversation, which, to a third person, must have seemed impertinently presumptuous, especially in an early-Victorian maiden lady. She dined at his house the same evening—12th June—when Mrs. Brookfield found her 'the most difficult woman to talk to she had ever met.' In answer to her conversational opening, 'Do you like London, Miss Brontë?' she answered curtly, 'Yes and no,' or 'I do and

I don't,' and relapsed into resolute silence. According to a letter from Miss Perry to Mrs. Brookfield, it was not on this occasion, but a year later, during the course of Thackeray's lectures, that the disastrous party in Charlotte Brontë's honour, described by Lady Ritchie, took place at Young Street. Rather rashly, Thackeray convened a 'hen' party, asking Mrs. Procter and her daughter Adelaide, Mrs. Elliot and Miss Perry, Mrs. Crowe and Jane Carlyle. The effect was as flat as Lord Carlisle's dinner to the wits of *Punch*. As it happened, Carlyle turned up without an invitation, being the only male present besides the host, but as he spent his time 'railing at the appearance of Cockneys upon Scotch mountain sides,' he contributed little to alleviate the tension. The chief hen steadfastly declined to cluck. Turning her back upon the brilliant Mrs. Procter, she sat on a sofa and 'murmured a low word now and then' to Miss Trulock, the children's governess. The situation proved too much even for Thackeray, invariably a watchful and tactful host, who eventually slipped quietly out of the house and fled to the sanctuary of his club. None of this appears in the little provincial lady's brave letters to her friends, and one wonders what really happened when she breakfasted with Samuel Rogers and described the experience as 'a most calm, refined, and intellectual treat.'

Though she knew nothing of Thackeray when she drew the character of Rochester in *Jane Eyre*, she introduced at least a trait of his character, according to her conception, into that of Paul Emanuel in *Villette*. After the lecture which she attended Thackeray descended from the platform and went straight up to her to ask her opinion. Characteristically, she construed no compliment from his action, reflecting upon it in such terms to Mrs. Gaskell as appear in *Villette*.

'As our party left the Hall, he stood at the entrance; he saw and knew me, and lifted his hat; he offered his hand in passing, and uttered the words "Qu'en dites-vous?"—question eminently characteristic and reminding me, even in this his moment of triumph, of the inquisitive restlessness, that absence of what I considered desirable self-control, which were amongst his faults. He should not have cared just then to ask what I thought, or what anybody thought; but he did care, and he was too natural to conceal, too impulsive to repress his wish. Well! if I blamed his over-eagerness, I liked his naïveté. I would have praised him; I had plenty of praise in my heart; but alas! no words on my lips. Who has words at the right moment? I stammered some lame expressions; but was truly glad when other people, coming up with profuse compliments, covered my deficiency by their redundancy.'

This eagerness for criticism occasioned a variety of comment. Serjeant Ballantine, an acquaintance at the Garrick Club, condemned him as 'very egotistical, greedy of flattery, and sensitive of criticism to a ridiculous extent,' solely on the evidence of this habit and the unfortunate Yates affair. Yet, as Charlotte Brontë observed, while the habit detracted from his dignity, it evinced sincerity and spontaneity. His lack of confidence in his powers and his perpetual dread of their decay rendered him avidly eager for impartial opinions of his work in order to assuage his anxious doubt. Thus, when he confessed to feelings of dissatisfaction with the first two or three numbers of *The Newcomes* and asked Frederick Locker's opinion of them, he frankly displayed almost boyish disappointment when Locker remarked jokingly: 'Perhaps there may be some kind people who will say that *you* did the cuts and Doyle the letterpress.'[1] His genuine desire for disinterested criticism was void of vanity, for he did not court the criticism only of his friends or persons of importance. He once sent for a young reporter who had attended one of his lectures in a professional capacity, receiving him in a private room with perfunctory courtesy, and encouraged him to declare his honest opinion

[1] *My Confidences*, by Frederick Locker-Lampson. London, 1896.

of the lecture, asking his reasons for adverse comment.[1] Miss Brontë would have expressed horror at such utter disregard of dignity, but his anxious doubt of his ability sharpened his thirst for candid criticism to such a degree that he mistrusted even the opinion of his friends and sought enlightenment, as he cruelly explained to the reporter on dismissing him, *ex oribus parvulorum.*

§ 2

After the lectures had closed their first triumphant course, Thackeray's mother returned to Paris, and, on 9th July, Mrs. Brookfield dined *en famille* with the Procters to bid farewell to Thackeray before he left for the Rhine, whither he was taking his children on their promised tour. From Antwerp they proceeded to Cologne, Mayence, Wiesbaden, and Heidelberg, where they met Charles Kingsley touring with his parents.

'A fine honest go-ahead fellow,' wrote Thackeray, who had read *Alton Locke* at Alresford the previous autumn, to Mrs. Brookfield, 'who charges a subject heartily, impetuously, with the greatest courage and simplicity; but with narrow eyes (his are extraordinarily brave, blue and honest), and with little knowledge of the world, I think. But he is superior to us worldlings in many ways, and I wish I had some of his honest pluck.'

In the eighth of her *Chapters from Some Memoirs*, Lady Ritchie gave an account of this happy holiday, describing the meeting with the Kingsleys and Thackeray's renewal of acquaintance with old Dr. Weissenborn, his former tutor at Weimar. Touring these familiar scenes with his daughters revived sad memories of the trip taken with his wife in the hope of her recovery, and, reflecting on his present affluence, he told Mrs. Brookfield how 'I recollect ten years back, a

[1] *An Editor's Retrospect,* by Charles A. Cooper. London, 1896.

poor devil looking wistfully at the few napoleons in his *gousset*, and giving himself no airs at all. . . . I was a boy ten years ago, bleating out my simple cries in *The Great Hoggarty Diamond*.'

The letters written from the Rhine, though not the last he ever wrote to Mrs. Brookfield, were the last composed in the spirit of complete confidence. For four years she had been as near and as dear to him as the most devoted of wives, almost his second self. A barrier now reared between them, robbing him of all he had to love besides his mother and children. Brookfield was ill, suffering from the first signs of a disease of the lungs which threatened to abbreviate his life. Becoming irritable and exacting, he became impatient of his wife's devotion to their friend, demanding all her attention for himself. Thackeray soon became aware of his attitude, and, when Brookfield revealed in his presence harshness in his demeanour towards his wife, he upbraided him in terms which, even in the heat of the moment, he admitted to be 'quite unjustifiable.' 'The affair is at an end and the rupture complete,' he told Kate Perry, who knew the depth of his attachment; 'I am going out of town and I don't know where.'

He went down to Matlock, where he tried to forget his feelings in furious concentration on his new novel, but his work only reminded him the more painfully of the woman to whom he would formerly have confided the details of all he was writing. 'I write because I'm unhappy,' he apologised when unburdening his tortured feelings to Kate Perry. 'If I write my book in this frame of mind it will be diabolical.' He begged her, if she could, to 'do anything to soothe and ease that poor lady.' She must have suffered at the time, though little evidence of her feelings now remains and, even at the time, she restrained their expression in the knowledge that unreserved revelation would only increase his anguish. Seeking comfort from her old friend, Mrs. Fanshawe, she wrote a letter to her which she intended for Thackeray's eyes. On receiving it he honourably pointed out that even such a 'roundabout correspondence' must not proceed without her husband's authority. In reply he tried to write in his old vein, describing his hopes and plans, but quickly gave it up in despair, remarking on the hopelessness of attaining the old perfection of confidence when each knew the other was concealing misery and unhappiness.

Brookfield also suffered, a remorseful conscience reproaching him for inflicting unhappiness upon his wife and injustice upon his oldest and closest friend. On Thackeray's return to town he sought him out in an effort to heal the breach. 'The morning was spent in parleys,' Thackeray told Kate Perry, 'and the Inspector [Brookfield's familiar nickname derived from his position as an inspector of schools] and I shook hands at the end and I'm very thankful that her dear little heart is made tranquil on the score of our enmity at least.' But the storm, so quickly past, left clouds in the sky of perfect amity. Each preserved an attitude of careful constraint. Brookfield was 'full of queer ceremonies' and 'punctilios,' while his wife and Thackeray consistently curbed every spontaneous expression of feeling in their resolution to observe the bounds of honour and duty. Two years later, in November 1853, Thackeray wrote from Paris to Kate Perry: 'I think I am nearer her when away than when sitting by her, talking of things we don't feel,' adding, 'It's happier that we should love each other in the grave, as it were, than that we should meet by sham-chance, and that there should be secrets or deceit.'

The painful story of the pathetic tragedy, involving the happiness of three lives, lies graphically narrated by Thackeray himself, interspersed with outbursts of uncontrollable agony, outpourings of suppressed passion, and reflections of melancholy tenderness, in a little packet of letters addressed to Kate Perry, who remained the faithful friend of him and Mrs. Brookfield until both had gone to their graves. Publishing extracts from the letters, the editor of the *Lambert Catalogue* expressed surprise at their suppression, as 'every feature redounds to the credit of all parties concerned.' The essentially intimate nature of their contents afforded obvious reasons for reluctance to assume the responsibility of publication, while there might be some living likely to feel discomfort or distress by the letters becoming public property. With such reasons of delicacy invalidated by the passage of time, the letters will doubtless be included in the completely revised edition of Thackeray's letters which is so badly needed, and clearly reveal the remarkable fortitude and forbearance with which Thackeray negotiated the second supreme tragedy of his career.

§ 3

Lady Ritchie remarked that '*Esmond* did not seem to be a part of our lives, as *Pendennis* had been.' The obvious reason was that, unlike *Pendennis* and all the other long novels, *Esmond* was written for publication in three volumes, without previously appearing in monthly numbers or magazine instalments, and consequently there was no printer's boy waiting at the door. George Smith commissioned *Esmond* on hearing Thackeray mention its design, agreeing to pay twelve hundred pounds for a first edition of 2500 copies and subsequent half profits. He received half the sum on account, the remaining six hundred pounds to be paid when the manuscript was delivered on a certain fixed date. Owing to his mental anguish throughout the time of writing, his lecturing engagements, and his inevitable procrastination, he failed to finish the book till several months after the prescribed date. In a letter addressed to Kate Perry from Matlock in September, delineating his lecturing plans, he said: 'In October I shall go to Oxford and Cambridge; then in November to Liverpool and Edinburgh, then in January to America most likely.' On

9th October he told Dr. John Brown that he was 'under stringent engagements to write a novel which will come out as I sail for America.'[1] It may be assumed, therefore, that he arranged to complete *Esmond* for publication in the early spring of 1852; it was actually finished at the end of the following May[2] and published in the autumn. Remarking upon Thackeray's punctiliousness in money matters, his publisher relates that, when he found he could not finish the novel by the prescribed date, he returned the cheque for six hundred pounds, which he had received on signing the agreement and never paid into his bank, and was only persuaded with great difficulty to retain it. Always short of money, it was his custom, during his editorship of the *Cornhill*, to indicate the condition of his financial circumstances by entering the publisher's private office with his trouser-pockets turned inside out. Smith readily obliged him with advance payments on account of his contributions, but never realised Thackeray's punctilious sense of his obligations until, after his death, there was found in his desk a slip of paper bearing the note: 'I.O. S.E. & Co., 35 pp.'

Another reason for his daughter remembering little of the writing of *Esmond* was the breach in his relations with the Brookfields, causing him to seek solitude as an antidote to the first agonies of unhappiness. Writing to his mother on 15th March that he soon discarded the idea of issuing the novel in numbers, not only on account of insufficiency of incident, but because 'It's much too grave and sad,' he said, 'It was written at a period of grief and pain so severe that I don't like to think of it.' Moreover, he was frequently away from home at this time. As in the previous year, he visited the Ashburtons at the Grange in October, before proceeding to deliver the lectures at both Oxford

[1] *Recollections of Dr. John Brown*, by Alexander Peddie. Edinburgh, 1894.

[2] *With Thackeray in America*, by Eyre Crowe. London, 1893. Crowe says *Esmond* was finished on Saturday, 28th May, but the date is an error, 29th May falling on Saturday in 1852.

and Cambridge during the following month. At Oxford he was the guest of an old schoolfellow, at Cambridge of Dr. Thackeray. Both universities accorded the lectures a favourable reception, which did much to dispel the doubts of their continued success still present in his mind. Before going to Oxford he wrote:

'I am very well in health, I think, having staved off my old complaint; and the only thing that alarms me sometimes is the absurd fancy that, now the money-making is actually at hand, some disaster may drop down and topple me over.'

The friends who accused him of swollen-headed vanity in the sunshine of success bore testimony to the truth of Douglas Jerrold's remark, delivered with shrewdness and candour: 'I have known Thackeray eighteen years, and don't know him yet.' No man was less 'the captain of his soul' or more incapable of strident optimism. Success and maturity only enhanced the humility of his attitude towards his own ability; with the whole of London at his feet and a brilliant record of literary achievement, he contemplated his prospects with the dubious indecision and uncertainty of his law-student days, when he was hesitating over the choice of a career.

Duty and responsibility were always his salvation—in the disaster of the *Constitutional*, in the calamity of his wife's malady and the subsequent struggle with penury, in the crisis of his relations with the Brookfields. Repeatedly he revealed a fortitude and fearless resolution surprising in the man who had airily laughed at the loss of his patrimony and continually harassed brain and body by aimless procrastination. The lecturing was naturally distasteful to one constitutionally unfitted for addressing a public audience, besides being an occupation generally considered derogatory to the dignity of a man of letters. Carlyle never hesitated to deride it as a mountebank's manner of entertainment, and Forster deprecated Dickens's decision to give public readings from his works as likely to imperil his reputation as a writer and a gentleman. Many of his friends represented to Thackeray the same arguments enlisted by Forster, but he held steadfastly to the determination, in defiance of criticism, to make what money he could from his present popularity. Explaining to old Dr. Thackeray that he hoped 'to make a little fortune for my little people' out of the lectures in America, he said significantly, 'If I ever get *another* fortune, I will keep it.'

After Oxford and Cambridge he lectured early in December at Edinburgh, where he commenced a cordial friendship with Dr. John Brown, the author of *Rab and his Friends*. Brown had introduced himself to Thackeray in the spring of 1848, when he engineered a subscription from eighty Edinburgh residents, including Francis Jeffrey and Sir William Hamilton, to present a silver statuette of 'Mr. Punch' to the author of the *Snob Papers* and *Vanity Fair*. Though they had never met, Brown exerted himself to ensure a good reception for the lectures, and, on meeting in person the writer he had long admired, experienced no disappointment to his expectations. Describing him in one letter as 'big as well as great, six feet two and built largely, with a big, happy, shrewd head, and as natural in all his ways as you yourself,' he told another of his closest friends:

'I wish you had been here for the last fortnight to have seen, heard, and known Thackeray,—a fellow after your own heart,—a strong-headed, sound-hearted, judicious fellow. . . . I have seen a great deal of him and talked with him on all sorts of things, and next to yourself I know no man so much to my mind. He is much better and greater than his works. His lectures have been very well attended, and I hope he will carry off £300. I wish he could have taken as much from Glasgow, but this has not been found possible. . . . He is 6 feet 3 in height, with a broad kindly face and an immense skull. . . . He makes no figure in company, except as very good-humoured, and by saying now and then a quietly strong thing. I so much wish you had met him. He is as much bigger than Dickens as a three-decker of 120 guns is bigger than a small steamer with one long-range swivel gun.'

Brown declared Thackeray to be 'surprised and pleased at his success' in Edinburgh, and Franklin Lushington told Brookfield that the lectures were delivered 'with great success to enthusiastic audiences.'

At Christmas came the end of his regular connection with *Punch*. Continually seeking an excuse to be rid of work which had long been irksome and irritating, he repeatedly professed 'serious public differences with the Conduct of *Punch*—about the abuse of Prince Albert and the Chrystal [*sic*] Palace at wh. I very nearly resigned, about abuse of Lord Palmerston, about abuse finally of L. Napoleon—in all which *Punch* followed the "Times," wh. I think and thought was writing unjustly at that time, and dangerously for the welfare and peace of the Country.' Doubtless he had vainly protested against these points of policy at the weekly *Punch* dinners and felt annoyance at being over-ruled by the opinion of a majority, but the real reason of his resignation lay in the fact that he literally had time for nothing but *Esmond* in the leisure of intervals between his lecturing, which now discounted any reluctance on account of financial consideration he might formerly have felt before relinquishing a connection so long providing the principal source of his income.

'Coming from Edinburgh,' he wrote to one of the proprietors more than three years later in explanation of his conduct, 'I bought a *Punch* containing the picture of a Beggar on Horseback, in wh. the Emperor was represented galloping to hell with a sword reeking with blood. As soon as ever I could after my return (a day or 2 days after), I went to Bouverie St., saw you and gave in my resignation.'

'No engagement afterwards took place between us,' he added, but, though he wrote nothing for the paper during the following year, he contributed one or two occasional articles in 1854. His friendly relations with *Punch* and its proprietors continued till his death, and his seat at the dinners was always reserved for him, though latterly he rarely attended, while it was Bradbury and Evans who published the numbers of both *The Newcomes* and *The Virginians*, besides his collected miscellanies.

Following this drastic step he spent a few days in the new year with the Ashburtons at the Grange, taking his children with him and devoting much of his time to *Esmond*. Carlyle was among the guests, and wrote to his brother on 3rd January 1852:

'Thackeray and his two girls were with us. . . . I had never seen him so well before. There is a great deal of talent in him, a great deal of sensibility,—irritability, sensuality, vanity without limit,—and nothing, or little, but sentimentalism and play-actorism to guide it all with: not a good or well-found ship in such waters on such a voyage.'

In the throes of one of his dyspeptic attacks, Carlyle would have seen the worst side of his best friend, and Thackeray never attained to a close intimacy with him, though he never wavered in the admiration first publicly expressed when Carlyle sorely needed such appreciation. They were poles apart, Carlyle condemning in the more human, gregarious character all those weaknesses from which his gloomy austerity rendered him immune.

He lectured in London in January, having received 'an offer of £150 at the Portman Square Rooms—pretty well for six hours.' He then buried himself at Brighton to concentrate upon *Esmond*, before going to Glasgow to lecture at the end of the month. Franklin Lushington told Brookfield that Thackeray was 'in a fix about his novel—which has been advertised some time—and for which the public are naturally becoming impatient, while he wishes to re-write it altogether.' 'I wish I had six months more to put into the novel,' he told his mother. 'It's scarce more than a sketch, and it might have been made a durable history. . . . But at the end of six months it would want other six.' He was bitter with the lust for completeness commonly afflicting the historian and the biographer. 'It takes as much trouble as Macaulay's *History* almost,' he declared. But he chiefly feared that its solemnity of tone would detract from its popularity, especially the first volume, which had been written under the stress of the Brookfield trouble. 'I wish the new novel wasn't so grand and melancholy,' he remarked as it neared completion, though he was relieved of his 'lugubrious doubts' when Charlotte Brontë saw the first volume and pronounced it 'admirable and odious.'

In Glasgow, 'a hideous smoking Babel,' which he disliked for 'the number of Hirishmen and women,' and remembered being similarly repelled by Dublin ten years before, he celebrated another success with the lectures, before returning to London to finish his novel. Glimpses of him occur giving a dinner to Kate Perry, Higgins and his wife, and Abraham Hayward, and again at a party including the Ashburtons, the Carlyles, and Thiers. In March he engaged a secretary for the first time, employing Eyre Crowe, the eldest son of his old friend, to attend to his business correspondence concerning the lectures, to hunt up *minutiæ* of research at the British Museum, and to fill in his spare time by giving lessons in drawing to his daughters.

On finishing *Esmond* he went abroad for a holiday. FitzGerald, in town at the end of May, saw him 'but twice for a few minutes, as he was just in the agony of finishing a Novel,' and wrote on 2nd June that 'he finished his Novel last Saturday and is gone, I believe, to the

Continent.' His holiday began much the same as in the previous year, his parents joining him and the children on the Rhine. But, leaving them at Zurich he journeyed alone through 'Tyrol and Salzkammergut, Munich and the Franconian towns,' to Dresden by way of Prague, and on to Berlin. 'I am glad I have seen the places,' he said, 'but there's no book to be made about 'em.' 'It was a dreary lonely journey,' he told Dr. John Brown. 'My mother wanted the children so much that I gave them up, nor was it possible that we could travel together, and the girls have two powers over them. So I had a dismal holiday alone, in place of a pleasant one with them.' Late in July he returned to England alone to fulfil a series of lecturing engagements before embarking for America.

Though he had contemplated the trip several months before making his *début* as a lecturer, he had repeatedly deferred making definite arrangements for departure. A year before, on 25th August 1851, Carlyle had written to Emerson: 'Item Thackeray; who is coming over to lecture to you: a mad world, my Masters!'[1] Now, in July, he frankly expressed his reluctance to his elder daughter: 'Ah me, I wish I was back from America!' He made the correction of the proofs of *Esmond* an excuse for further delay. As Crowe related, the proofs came slowly from the printers, owing to the scant supply of the Queen Anne style of type in which the first edition was set. He finally decided almost desperately to depart as soon as the book was ready to appear, and when Smith proposed to publish at the end of October he began to make his preparations. FitzGerald, deceived by repeated delays into doubting whether the expedition would ever materialise, exclaimed in mild surprise on 10th August, 'Dear old Thackeray is really going to America!'—while Thackeray himself, resting at Brighton between his lecturing engagements, told his

[1] *Correspondence of Thomas Carlyle and Ralph Waldo Emerson.* London, 2 vols., 1883.

younger daughter, 'I believe I am going to Birmingham next week with the lectures and then to Manchester & Liverpool and then Steward: bring a basin.' In making the resolution, he said: 'I must and will go to America, not because I like it, but because it is right I should secure some money against my death for your poor mother and you two girls.' The reason served, not only as his excuse for going to America, but as the motive for all the remaining labours of his life.

He spent three weeks at Manchester and Liverpool, delivering the six lectures at both cities, on Tuesdays and Thursdays in Manchester, Wednesdays and Fridays at Liverpool, between 28th September and 15th October. He then set off for a few farewell visits, staying with Lord and Lady Stanley at Alderley and spending a day or two at Young Street before going to the Ashburtons at the Grange. Carlyle glowered there gloomily, telling his mother, on 23rd October:

> 'Thackeray is coming, for whom I care nothing, tho' he is a clever and friendly man; he comes to-day with a nobleman and a Portrait-Painter: comes but is soon to go.'[1]

His dyspepsia was apparently less troublesome than in the previous January, and still less so when, a year later, he wrote to Emerson of Thackeray on 9th September 1853:

> 'He is a big fellow, soul and body; of many gifts and qualities (particularly in the Hogarth line, with a dash of Sterne superadded), of enormous *appetite* withal, and very uncertain and chaotic in all points except his *outer breeding*, which is fixed enough, and *perfect* according to the modern English style. I rather dread explosions in his history. A big, fierce, weeping, hungry man; not a strong one.'

[1] Remembering Carlyle's attitude towards him in the first flush of *Vanity Fair's* success (p. 173 *ante*), it is not surprising that Thackeray remarked in 1858: 'Carlyle hates everybody that has arrived—if they are on the road, he may perhaps treat them civilly.'—*Correspondence of John Lothorp Motley*, ed. George William Curtis. London, 2 vols., 1889.

However much he knew of Thackeray's intimate affairs and whatever else he suspected, Carlyle here summarised his character with shrewd discernment, according to his own conception. Under the shock of the death of the man he had known for a quarter of a century, he remembered the best in him:

'He had many fine qualities, no guile or malice against any mortal; a big mass of a soul, but not strong in proportion; a beautiful vein of genius lay struggling about in him. Nobody in our day wrote, I should say, with such perfection of style.'

Such an epitaph from Carlyle conveys a truer message than the laudatory apostrophes of enthusiastic admirers wallowing in an excess of sentiment.

Having booked the passage of himself and Eyre Crowe on board the *Canada*, leaving Liverpool on 30th October, he passed his last night at Young Street on the 28th, having spent much of his time in writing letters of farewell to friends and arranging his affairs. Even to an ubiquitous traveller like Thackeray, a voyage to America was a momentous undertaking in those days. A letter dated the 27th testifies that he had never forgotten his friendship for FitzGerald and the faith he still placed in him beyond all others.

'MY DEAREST OLD FRIEND,

I mustn't go away without shaking your hand, and saying Farewell and God bless you. If anything happens to me, you by these presents must get ready the *Book of Ballads* which you like, and which I had not time to prepare before embarking on the voyage. And I should like my daughters to remember that you are the best and oldest friend their Father ever had, and that you would act as such; as my literary executor and so forth. My Books would yield a something as copyrights: and should anything occur, I have commissioned friends in good place to get a Pension for my poor little wife. . . . Does not this sound gloomily? Well: who knows what Fate is in store: and I feel not at all downcast, but very grave and solemn just at the brink of a great voyage.

I shall send you a copy of *Esmond* to-morrow or so which you shall yawn over when you are inclined. But the great comfort I have in thinking about my dear old boy is that recollection of our youth when we loved each other as I do now while I write Farewell.

Laurence has done a capital head of me ordered by Smith the Publisher: and I have ordered a copy and Lord Ashburton another. If Smith gives me this one, I shall send the copy to you. I care for you as you know, and always like to think that I am fondly and affectionately yours

W. M. T.

I sail from Liverpool on Saturday Morning by the *Canada* for Boston.'

CHAPTER 13

§ 1

FELLOW-PASSENGERS with Thackeray and Crowe on board the *Canada* were James Russell Lowell and Arthur Hugh Clough, the latter of whom kept a diary of the voyage.[1] 'Lowell, who is on board, is very friendly,' he wrote, 'Thackeray and I also get on.' Thackeray was seasick on 11th November, when Clough talked with him for half an hour while he 'was laid up in his berth.' He had liked Clough at their first meeting, and the Oxford poet now came to return the feeling of cordiality. After he had spent an evening in his company at Lowell's house two months later, he remarked:

'Thackeray doesn't sneer; he is really very sentimental; but he sees the silliness sentiment runs into, and so always tempers it by a little banter or ridicule. He is much farther into actual life than I am.'

'Half sick in bending with my head over the confounded quivering creaking table,' as the boat swayed and rocked 'within 70 miles of Cape Race,' making 'all the desks and glasses jingle and rattle,' Thackeray wrote to Kate Perry that 'there is an awful superior woman aboard, Mrs. Lowell, with a clever husband, very pleasant.'

The voyage lasted a fortnight, Thackeray landing at Boston on the frosty evening of Friday, 12th November, where he was met on the quay by James T. Fields, of Ticknor and Fields, the Boston publishers, who, acting as

[1] *Letters and Remains of Arthur Hugh Clough,* for private circulation only. London, 1865.

his agents, had made all arrangements for his reception and the course of his lecturing tour. Before leaving for Concord to see Emerson, Clough stayed a day to 'lionize with Thackeray and his friend Crowe through the streets.' It was characteristic of his kindly generosity that Thackeray introduced his paid secretary everywhere as his friend. After being lavishly entertained by Fields, he left Boston on the 16th for New York, where the first lecture was given on the 19th. His success was immediate and triumphant, the newspapers each striving to surpass the others in the fervour of their praise. W. C. Bryant recorded the popular impression in the New York *Evening Post*:

'Every one who saw Mr. Thackeray last evening for the first time seemed to have their impressions of his appearance and manner of speech corrected. Few expected to see so large a man: he is gigantic, six feet four at least; few expected to see so old a person; his hair appears to have kept silvery record over fifty years; and then there was a notion in the minds of many that there must be something dashing and "fast" in his appearance, whereas his costume was perfectly plain, the expressions of his face grave and earnest, his address perfectly unaffected and such as we might expect to meet with in a well-bred man somewhat advanced in years. His elocution also surprised those who had derived their impressions from the English journals. His voice is superb tenor, and possesses that pathetic tremble which is so effective in what is called emotive eloquence, while his delivery was as well suited to the communication he had to make as could well have been imagined.

His enunciation is perfect. Every word he uttered might have been heard in the remotest quarters of the room, yet he scarcely lifted his voice above a colloquial tone. The most striking feature in his whole manner was the utter absence of affectation of any kind. He did not permit himself to appear conscious that he was an object of peculiar interest in the audience, neither was he guilty of the greater error of not appearing to care whether they were interested or not. In other words, he inspired his audience with a respect for him, as a man proportioned to the admiration which his books have inspired for him as an author.'

Thackeray enclosed a cutting of this article in a letter of 23rd November to Mrs. Brookfield, thinking 'that you will be glad to know that I prosper and that I am well.'

> 'The passage is nothing, now it is over,' he wrote. 'I am rather ashamed of gloom and disquietude about such a trifling journey. I have made scores of new acquaintances and lighted on my legs as usual.'

His genial manner and unceremonious sociability gained him friends everywhere, friends, moreover, whom he retained, with that peculiar faculty for preserving friendship in spite of long separation by passage of time and divergence of interests. Among these was a New York family named Baxter, the daughters of which he much admired, declaring one of them to be the image of Beatrix Esmond.

While he was in New York the firm of Harper issued the American edition of *Esmond*. Showing Fields a copy of the book, he said: 'Here is the *very* best I can do. . . . I stand by this book, and am willing to leave it, when I go, as my card.' Though he considered *Esmond* to be his best work, he had repeatedly expressed doubt of its popular appeal, and he wrote from Boston to Mrs. Procter on 22nd December: 'The success of *Esmond* has quite surprised me, for I only looked for a few to like it.' The novel and the lectures each vied in reflecting the popularity of the other, and Appletons' hurriedly issued a cheap reprint of his collected works, for which he wrote the preface, included in the volume containing *Mr. Brown's Letters to a Young Man about Town*, in which he asked pardon of 'the author of *The Caxtons*' for two lampoons included in the *Yellowplush Papers*. Harpers also gave him a thousand dollars for the right to publish the *Lectures on the English Humourists* from the sheets of the English edition, which was being prepared in his absence by Smith, Elder, James Hannay having undertaken to supply the copious notes included in the book. Both the English and American editions appeared the following summer, but Harpers included in their publication the additional lecture on 'Charity and Humour,' which was written in America and delivered for the first time in New York on the 31st January, the proceeds being devoted to the funds of the Ladies' Society for the Employment and Relief of the Poor. Thackeray kept this lecture, which was first published in *Harper's Magazine* for June 1853, specially for charitable occasions and delivered it on 22nd July 1857 for the benefit of the family of Douglas Jerrold, whose death left his widow and children in straitened circumstances.[1]

Thackeray liked New York. 'The rush and restlessness pleases me,' he told Mrs. Brookfield, 'and I like, for a little, the dash of the stream.'

'Broadway is miles upon miles long, a rush of life such as I never have seen; not so full as the Strand, but so rapid. The houses are always being torn down and built up again, the railroad cars drive slap into the midst of the city. There are barricades and scaffoldings banging everywhere.'

[1] This lecture concludes with a long complimentary appreciation of Dickens, from whom it inspired a letter of thanks on being delivered for the first time.

'TAVISTOCK HOUSE,
Friday Evening, Twenty-third March 1855.

MY DEAR THACKERAY,

I have read in *The Times* to-day an account of your last night's lecture, and cannot refrain from assuring you in all truth and earnestness that I am profoundly touched by your generous reference to me. I do not know how to tell you what a glow it spread over my heart. Out of its fulness I do entreat you to believe that I shall never forget your words of commendation. If you could wholly know at once how you have moved me, and how you have animated me, you would be the happier I am very certain.

Faithfully yours ever,
CHARLES DICKENS.'

Cf. *Letters of Charles Dickens*, edited by his sister-in-law and his eldest daughter.

'It's nothing here but dollars and flattery,' he wrote to Kate Perry on 7th December; 'I am not half such a swell in my own country as they make of me out here.'

'It's the most curious varnish of Civilization. The girls are all dressed like the most stunning French actresses, the houses furnished like the most splendid gambling houses. It's all gold and yellow brocade and the little dandies are like little French shop boys, and the houses are all so new that the walls are not even papered, and on the walls in the midst of the hangings of brocade and the enormous gold frames and mirrors you see little twopenny pictures and colored prints. . . . The jolly manner answers here very well, which I have from Nature or Art possibly, and the Press and I, with the exception of the *Herald*, which abuses me like anythink, are the best of friends.'

The Court of St. James's could not have chosen a better unofficial ambassador, for the Americans, lavishly hospitable and eager to impress their distinguished guest, were delighted with his unaffected interest in all he saw and his ingenuous pleasure in everything they devised for his entertainment.

They were the more anxious to create a favourable impression on Thackeray, owing to Dickens having excoriated them in his *American Notes* after his visit. With his reputation as a social satirist, who had, moreover, already functioned as a picturesque reporter in the *Irish Sketch Book* and *Cornhill to Cairo*, he descended upon them like a notorious marauder, armed to the teeth for pillage and plunder. Many of them never for a moment doubted that he intended to capitalise his experiences and observations in such a volume as *American Notes*, and his old acquaintance, N. P. Willis, asked him, when they were fellow-guests at the house of Washington Irving, why he was taking no notes of the visit. Thackeray was 'about to answer what I thought of such a liberty, when I remembered that he had done such things himself, and was silent.' He himself had done 'such things' in Ireland, and punctilious delicacy was not a sufficient reason to deter him, if he had been minded to write such a book. But if he had ever contemplated such a project he discarded it very soon after his departure for America. One reason was given in a letter to his mother during the voyage.

'Shall I make a good bit of money in America, and write a book about it? I think not. It seems impudent to write a book, and mere sketches are somehow below my rank in the world—I mean, a grave old gentleman, father of young ladies, mustn't be comic and grinning too much.'

He meant that such a volume as the *Irish Sketch Book* or *Cornhill to Cairo*, though excellent journalism and worthy work for Titmarsh of *Fraser*, was scarcely calculated to enhance the reputation of an eminent novelist whose appeal was mainly directed to the cultured class. Moreover, his work on *Esmond* and the lectures had inspired him with the honest thoroughness of the serious scholar, rendering him impatient of superficial essays on subjects of importance. 'What could Dickens mean by writing that book of *American Notes*?' he exclaimed in a letter to Albany Fonblanque towards the end of his tour. 'No man should write about the country under 5 years of experience, and as many of previous reading.' Prudence supplied a second reason, for already his success had suggested a second visit—which would have been prevented or sterilised by a second *American Notes*—when he wrote to Kate Perry on 7th December:

'I don't intend to make a book. No. No. The goose is much too good a goosey to be killed. In fact, I'm looking ahead, and my dear friends must help me.'

Consequently Clough, returning to England some time after Thackeray, was able to write to Charles Eliot Norton in July 1853: 'Thackeray, they tell me, is full of the kindheartedness and generousness of the Americans, and is faithful to his purpose of writing no book.'

He liked Boston only less than New York, finding there 'very good literate company' and likening it to Edinburgh on that account—'a vast amount of toryism and donnishness everywhere.' New York was more simple and less pretentious, as 'it suffices that a man should keep a fine house, give parties, and have a daughter, to get all the world to him.' The Boston of George Ticknor, W. H. Prescott, and James T. Fields, was truly comparable with the Edinburgh of 'Christopher North,' Jeffrey, Aytoun, Cockburn, and the Blackwoods—literary and academic, blue-stocking and high-brow. Thackeray gave his first lecture there on 21st December, writing the next day to Mrs. Procter: 'Last night was the first lecture here—twelve hundred people, I should think—and I left behind me near a thousand pounds at New York, which Baring's house will invest for me, so that my girls will be very considerably the better for the journey.' Longfellow attended the second lecture on Christmas Eve, Thackeray having dined with Prescott, whom he thought 'delightful,' on the previous evening.[1] Writing to the Baxters in New York, he said: 'I am now engaged every day to dinner and supper at Boston (pronounced Bawsn). It is quieter, but I think we drink more than in New York.' When Oliver Wendell Holmes called on him he described him 'as a dear little fellow, a true poet.' On 5th January Longfellow noted in his diary:

'Lowell gave a supper to Thackeray. The other guests were Felton, Clough, Dana, Dr. Parsons (Dante's translator), Fields, Edmund Quincy, Estes Howe, and myself. We sat down at ten and did not leave the table till one. Very gay, with stories and jokes.'

R. H. Dana, the author of *Two Years before the Mast*, bore witness to Thackeray's habit of contributing pleasantly to

[1] *Life of William Hickling Prescott*, by George Ticknor. London, 1863.

general conversation without attempting to monopolise attention by personal brilliance.

'Thackeray is not a great talker,' he noted. 'He was interested in all that was said, and put in a pleasant word occasionally. Felton, Lowell, and I did nearly all the talking.'[1]

He gave his last lecture at Boston on the 7th, leaving the next day for New York, where he spent a few days before proceeding to Philadelphia, whither Crowe had already gone to make arrangements for his arrival. Prescott wrote on the 11th:

'Thackeray has left us. His campaign was a successful one, and he said, "It rained dollars." He dined with me thrice, and was in good flow of spirits till a late hour generally. He went much to the Ticknors' also. I do not think he made much impression as a critic. But the Thackeray vein is rich in what is better than cold criticism.'

On the 17th he travelled from New York to Philadelphia in company with Washington Irving, who wrote:

'In the gentlemen's cabin on the ferry-boat whom should I see but Thackeray? We greeted each other cordially. He was on his way to Philadelphia, to deliver a course of lectures. We took seats beside each other in the cars, and the morning passed off delightfully. He seems still to enjoy his visit to the United States exceedingly, and enters into our social life with great relish. He has made a pleasant visit to Boston; seen much of Prescott (whom he speaks highly of), Ticknor, Longfellow, &c. Said the Bostonians had published a smashing criticism on him; which, however, does not seem to have ruffled his temper, as I understand he cut it out of the newspaper, and enclosed it in a letter to a female friend in New York.'[2]

[1] *Richard Henry Dana: A Biography*, by C. F. Adams. Boston, 2 vols., 1890.
[2] *Life and Letters of Washington Irving*, by P. E. Irving. London, 2 vols., 1877.

Three weeks later Irving wrote from Washington on 10th February:

'Thackeray has delivered one of his lectures here, and delivers another to-morrow evening. I attended the first, and shall attend the next. He is well received here, both in public and private, and is going the round of dinner parties, &c. I find him a very pleasant companion.'

In Philadelphia he achieved a degree of popularity almost exceeding that at New York and Boston, the leading citizens liking him so well that they asked him to apply for the post of British Consul in that city. In a letter to W. B. Reed, one of the most distinguished Philadelphians, to whom he had been introduced by a letter from Lord Mahon, he expressed his pleasure at the suggestion, but gave his reasons for preferring to live in England—'home among my parents there, and some few friends I have made in the last twenty-five years, and a tolerably fair prospect of an honest livelihood on the familiar London flagstones, and the library at the Athenæum, and the ride in the Park, and the pleasant society afterwards; and a trip to Paris now and again, and to Switzerland and Italy in the summer—these are little temptations which make me not discontented with my lot, about which I grumble only for pastime, and because it is an Englishman's privilege.'[1]

Though he never for a moment contemplated a diplomatic post entailing a protracted period of exile, the Philadelphian suggestions revived his former notion of a civic appointment, which would relieve him of the ceaseless labour of literary work, at the same time offering an opportunity for useful public service. The spirit of service, so strong in his proconsular and pioneering ancestors,

[1] *Haud Immemor: A few Personal Recollections of Mr. Thackeray in Philadelphia*, by W. B. Reed, privately printed. Philadelphia, 1864. Reprinted in *Blackwood's Magazine* for June 1872.

lingered in his blood, occasionally seeking expression, as when, realising his responsibility as an unofficial ambassador, he exclaimed: 'If I can say anything to show that my name is really Makepeace, and increase the source of love between the two countries, then please God I will.' In view of his increased reputation, he no longer hoped for a municipal magistracy, but aspired to a seat in Parliament and a public career. In a letter written from Philadelphia between 21st and 23rd January he described his plans to Mrs. Brookfield, for he still preserved for her his most intimate confidences, though the former daily correspondence was discontinued.

'At present, I incline to come to England in June or July and get ready a new set of lectures, and bring them back with me. That second course will enable me to provide for the children and their mother finally and satisfactorily, and my mind will be easier after that, and I can sing *Nunc Dimittis* without faltering: There is money-making to try at, to be sure, and ambition,—I mean public life; perhaps that might interest a man, but not novels, nor lectures, nor fun, any more. I don't seem to care about these any more, or for praise, or for abuse, or for reputation of that kind. That literary play is played out, and the puppets going to be locked up for good and all.'

At the topmost pinnacle of success, he was as blind to his destiny as in the most hesitant days of his nonage, appreciating his abilities and limitations no more aptly than the self-conscious undergraduate hovering on the threshold of life.

From Philadelphia he proceeded to Baltimore and Washington, before moving southwards through Virginia to Richmond and Charleston. 'The Baltimoreans flock to the stale old lectures as numerously as you of Philadelphia,' he told W. B. Reed, while from Washington he wrote to Kate Perry that he was 'doing a good business at Baltimore and a small select one here.' He arrived at Richmond on

1st March, where the negro slaves, 'instead of horrifying me I am sorry to say amuse me with their never ending grotesqueness and please me with their air of happiness,' having travelled thither 'down the Potomac on which Mrs. Esmond-Warrington used to sail with her 2 sons when they went to visit their friend Mr. Washington. I wonder will anything ever come out of that preface, and will that story ever be born?' He was to pass that way again before *The Virginians* was written.

He told his publisher that he had 'a very pleasant and not unprofitable tour in the South, though the town of Providence furnished an audience of no more than five hundred,' and he insisted upon reimbursing the promoters with half his fee, because 'nobody must lose by me in America, where I have had such a welcome and hospitality.' By the time he arrived in Virginia he had become bored with the monotonous repetition of the lectures, for he told Fonblanque, on 14th March: 'I am doing very well with the lectures—the 2 Presidents came at Washington—I've saved some money, £2,000, in this country and shall probably make half as much more: but O how sick I am of the business!' To Kate Perry he had written on the previous day:

'I am getting so sick and ashamed of the confounded old lectures that I wonder I have the courage to go on delivering them. What a pluck Albert Smith must have not to loathe himself and hang himself after repeating that rubbish of his so many times. . . . I should like to give myself a week's holiday without my demd lecture box.'

He decided not to go to New Orleans on account of the distance, but persevered with his Virginian engagements, at the end of which he wrote to Dr. John Brown from Charleston on 25th March:

'I have no time to write letters scarcely, much more a book. I eat as usual 7 dinners a week, at other folk's charges, the lectures do pretty well, and I have laid by, but at 8 per cent. (that is the common interest here), £200 a year; 6 weeks more will give me £50 a year more, and next year—I come home of course *inter ea*—will help me to £150 more. This will make me easy against the day when work will be over, and then, and then who knows what Fate will bring. The idleness of the life is dreary and demoralising though; and the bore and humiliation of delivering these stale old lectures is growing intolerable. Why, what a superior heroism is Albert Smith's, who has ascended Mont Blanc 400 times!'

'To-morrow,' he added, 'I go to Richmond on my way to New York and thence to Canada; and in July or before, I hope to see that old country again which is after all the only country for us to live in.' Advertisements of his projected visit actually appeared in Montreal when he arrived in New York early in April, and on the 5th he wrote to his children's governess, Miss Trulock: 'When the coming back is to be I don't know; but I am so weary of reading those lectures . . . that I may revolt any day: and shall probably ere a couple more months are over.' On the 12th he gave a lecture at Albany, returning to New York for a short rest before proceeding to Canada. On the morning of the 20th Crowe entered his room to find him reading a newspaper. 'I see there's a Cunarder going this morning,' he said, and instructing Crowe to superintend the packing of their traps, he went off at once to book their berths.

§ 2

Reaching Liverpool on May Day he dashed up to town on the following day, so eager to find touch with his familiar way of life that, learning of a ball to be given by Lady Stanley of Alderley that night, he unceremoniously presented himself. Then he went the round of his clubs, with the result that he wrote to the Baxters, on the third day following his arrival, that 'I have seen almost all my old friends.' The house in Young Street was let to the Fanshawes till July, and he remained only a few days in London before joining his family in Paris. Here he spent two or three weeks of happy idleness, listening to his daughters playing his favourite Haydn and Mozart on the piano, and moving in the 'funny little world my old folks live in,' feeling 'a strange and heavy old Swell annoyed at the airs I can't help fancying I give myself.' He was unwell during his stay, so giving 'the kind old stepfather an opportunity to administer globules. He is 72 and the brave old soldier who mounted breaches and led storming parties is quite a quiet old man lean & slippered. My mother is as handsome and as good as ever.' About this time he made the acquaintance, either through his mother, Fanny Kemble, or Adelaide Sartoris, of Mrs. Lynn Linton, then Eliza Lynn, a struggling journalist, who was charmed by his good humour in mounting to her *atelier* on a fourth floor and seating himself on a flat trunk because the second chair in the room was heaped with papers.[1]

Back in London at the beginning of June, he met a more noted authoress, then in the fullest glare of notoriety from the recent appearance of *Uncle Tom's Cabin*—Harriet Beecher Stowe. 'I was very agreeably disappointed,' he wrote. 'In place of the woman I had imagined to myself after the hideous daguerrotype I found a gentle almost pretty person with a very great sweetness in her eyes and smile. I am sure she must be good and truth-telling from her face and behaviour.' He stayed only a few days in London, just long enough to conclude the business for which he came, and he wrote the news of it to the Baxters, on his way back to Paris, from Sterne's room in Dessein's Hotel at Calais, afterwards the subject of a *Roundabout Paper*:

[1] Cf. *Mrs. Lynn Linton: Her Life, Letters, and Opinions*, by G. S. Layard. London, 1901.

'I have signed and sealed with Bradbury and Evans for a new book in 24 numbers like *Pendennis*. Price 3600£+ 500£ from Harper and Tauchnitz. It's coining money isn't it? and if I can make another expedition to a certain country as remunerative as the last, why, 2 years hence will see my girls snugly provided for.'

His elder daughter, who was now old enough to act as an amanuensis and wrote much of the novel at his dictation, declared that the preface of *The Newcomes* was begun at Baden on 7th July. On the 13th he wrote from there to Kate Perry that 'three days ago I broke ground with the new book and have done 2 days' work ever since upon it.' He was well, full of enthusiasm, and eager to write—a very different state of mind from that in which *Esmond* was begun and most of *Pendennis* written. Happy and contented in the society of his daughters, he enjoyed all the recreative pleasures of a holiday between intervals of satisfactory work. By the time he moved from Baden, on the 18th, he had already begun the second number, which he hoped to finish 'before the month is over, but I can't but see it is a repetition of past performances, and think that vein is pretty nigh worked out in me.' 'Never mind,' he consoled himself, 'this is not written for glory but for quite as good an object, namely money, which will profit the children more than reputation when there's an end of me.'

The similarity of the early part of *The Newcomes* to the opening chapters of both *Vanity Fair* and *Pendennis* is obvious, the atmosphere of each being derived from different environments of his own youth. As in *Pendennis* he drew upon his reminiscences of Ottery St. Mary and South Devon, and in *Vanity Fair* he described the Sedley *ménage* from early London recollections, he now depicted on a large canvas the entire Anglo-Indian society of the various aunts and uncles into which he had entered, like Clive Newcome, as a lonely derelict boy. As he afterwards revealed in the *Roundabout Papers*, he preserved vivid recollections of his boyhood, and the narrative consequently proceeded with fluent ease. At Vevey, on 26th July, the story still advanced 'very pleasantly,' as he dictated to his daughter.

'I am not to be the author of it,' he wrote. 'Mr. Pendennis is to be the writer of his friend's memoirs and by the help of this little mask (wh. I borrowed from Pisistratus Bulwer I suppose) I shall be able to talk more at ease than in my own person. I only thought of the plan last night and am immensely relieved by adopting it.'

When he realised expectations by completing the second number at the end of the month, he told Kate Perry that he had spent 'as pleasant a fortnight as ever I have had in my life, plenty of work, play, health, money, good children. What could man ask for more? Only one thing that he can't have.' The third number was finished in another fortnight, though all the time he was flitting, with his children and one servant—not old John, the original 'Jeames,' who, after serving him so well for several years and faithfully tending his convalescence in 1849, had decided to retire when his master went to America, but Charles Pearman, whom he had engaged on his return to London in June and who proved an attendant as devoted as his predecessor—from place to place in Switzerland, from Vevey to Geneva, Lausanne, and back again, then to Berne and Zurich, where he began the fourth number, and so to Frankfort by Basle and Heidelberg. Arriving in London at the beginning of September he wrote to Bradbury and Evans:

'I am back with 4 numbers and want very much to see you about illustrations. . . . An American letter too has missed me in my absence offering me 10 pounds a number from Harpers. . . . Shall I have Doyle to illustrate?'

Although, in his plan to pursue the pattern of *Pendennis*, he had intended to illustrate the book himself and had actually begun the work, he now decided to hand over the task to Doyle.

This decision was probably prompted by another breakdown of health. He had fallen ill at Frankfort and was warned in time against risking a repetition of the *Pendennis* disaster by the exhausting labour of combining the functions of author and illustrator. To Brookfield, on 24th September, he said: 'When I was ill the other day I made a sort of will in which I begged you and FitzGerald to act as a sort of guardians to the children, and that you'd have them every year to stay with you and your dear wife.' To the last he valued Brookfield and FitzGerald beyond all other friends, though he now saw little of the latter, and thenceforth no more than was necessary of the Brookfields. He found that meeting continually on terms of restraint compatible with duty and honour only occasioned pain, not only to himself, but to Mrs. Brookfield. 'We have seen the poor Brookfields and the moral I have come to is "Thou shalt not pity thy neighbour's wife," ' he informed his mother. 'Keep out of his Harem; and it is better for you and him.' Though he sought honestly to banish any bitterness of spirit, a feeling of resentment towards the jealous husband's attitude caused him to launch a gibe against his friend, who was now a fashionable preacher at Berkeley Chapel, in the satirical picture of Charles Honeyman as the rhetorical prophet of Lady Whittlesea's Chapel.

He decided not to settle down again in Young Street, and bought, in October, 'a pretty house, 36, Onslow Square, Brompton, next door to Marochetti,' for which he paid in three annual instalments of about seven hundred pounds. Having spent the latter part of September at Brighton, he went to Young Street for the last time, intending to winter at Rome while the new house was got ready. This project was threatened with frustration by a publisher's proposal that he should edit Horace Walpole's letters, which 'is just the sort of work I should like—such as would keep me pleasantly employed some evenings and pottering over old volumes . . . of old biographies and histories.' Though he remarked that 'when the imaginative work is over, that is the kind of occupation I often propose to myself for my old age,' he soon realised that there was no immediate prospect of undertaking such a task with *The Newcomes* on hand and the preparation of a new course of lectures before him, and after the first number of the novel had appeared in October he went over to Paris, where he stayed a few weeks before leaving for Rome with the children on 27th November.

Since the inspired spell of the Swiss holiday he had written only one number of *The Newcomes*—the fifth, completed in Paris late in November. Repeated attacks of illness in England were followed by another immediately after his arrival at Rome, and he wrote to the Baxters on 17th December:

'We are here a fortnight—and the man who travels without a governess[1] and with 2 daughters finds himself pretty much the tall confidential old family servant of the young ladies. Not one word of writing have I done as yet, and to be sure have been ill for the last 4 days; with an attack of—well of leeches, blisters, calomel. I have been ill once a month for the last 5 months.'

[1] Miss Trulock, who had acted as governess to his children since 1848, was 'a superior person,' the daughter of some Parisian acquaintance of his mother. In a letter to the Baxters Thackeray explained that, 'her daily lessons over, she goes into the world with her mother and is everybody's equal,' but was 'too proud to bear the subordinate position these ladies must take in London.' In search of a successor, he called in the aid of Jane Carlyle, who approached an agency for German governesses, with the result that Thackeray wrote: 'My dear Mrs. Carlyle,—For God's sake stop Mme. Bolte. I have governidges calling at all hours with High Dutch accents and reams of testimonials. One to-day, one yesterday, and a letter the day before, and on going to dine at *Punch*, by Heavens! there was a letter from a German lady on my plate.' To oblige the Carlyles, he interviewed 'a Ger-woman,' but found he could not live with her—'there are some people . . . who shut me up or drive me to my own room and this would be one.' Such insignificant details witness an instance of the daily domestic trials and tribulations which he suffered as a wifeless father.

Worse was to come, for the elder daughter was taken ill with scarlatina, and the younger, having acted as nurse to her sister, caught the infection a week later. Fortunately, he secured the services of an Irish nurse, for he himself fell ill of 'Roman Fever,' so that all three were 'stretched on our backs looking out at the Mediterranean yonder.' No wonder that he wrote to his mother from Naples, whither they migrated in February, that 'I might have stayed at home for any good to *The Newcomes* which this journey has done.'

At Rome he encountered the Brownings, who arrived there about the same time. 'We have had various visits from Mr. Thackeray and his daughters,'[1] wrote Mrs. Browning to Mrs. Jameson, and describing the delights of Roman society to her sister on 30th December, she added:

> 'Mr. Thackeray . . . complains of dulness—he is disabled from work by the dulness. He "can't write in the morning without his good dinner and two parties over-night." From such a soil spring the *Vanity Fairs*! He is an amusing man-mountain enough and very courteous to us—but I never should get on with him much, I think—he is not sympathetic to me.'[2]

Later she speaks of him bringing 'small-talk by handfuls of glittering dust swept out of saloons,' and by the end of his stay, he 'won my heart rather' by his good nature to her little son, while 'as to the Thackeray girls I am inclined quite to love them!'

Thackeray, though never censorious, was not unduly impressed by the Sappho of Wimpole Street. Explaining that he had 'no head above my eyes' he agreed with Washington Irving that 'we do not read Robert Browning because we cannot altogether comprehend him,' and he

[1] *Elizabeth Barrett Browning in Her Letters*, by Percy Lubbock. London, 1906.

[2] *Elizabeth Barrett Browning: Letters to Her Sister, 1846-1859*, edited by Leonard Huxley. London, 1929.

had probably never attempted either to read or comprehend the poetry of Browning's wife. He told Kate Perry that 'I had nobody at Rome that I care for except Adelaide Sartoris, who is one of the best of creatures, but you know there must always be a little comedy in any intimacy in that quarter,' adding that 'I learned to admire but not to endure Fanny Kemble.' The reason for his inspiration in Mrs. Browning of a feeling 'not sympathetic' was reflected in their impressions of the gifted Kemble sisters. Mrs. Browning was impressed by Fanny's 'magnificence' and 'liked her much,' while she spoke more condescendingly of the 'genial and generous' Adelaide. Thackeray, on the other hand, was repelled by the elder sister's hard and unresilient brilliance, feeling that absence of artistic sympathy which enabled her to despise her own art. For Adelaide Sartoris he always felt a warm affection, describing her once to Mrs. Brookfield as 'the most artless, affected, good-natured, absurd, clever creature possible.' He liked her for her love of life, her generous sympathies and impulsive fancies. He admired Fanny's cold brilliance, sharp and shining as burnished steel, but he delighted in that of Adelaide, because it radiated the mellow splendour of purest gold. Possibly the difference derived from the dissimilarity of their matrimonial experiences. As Mrs. Browning observed, Adelaide's 'milk has had time to stand to cream, in her happy family relations,' while Fanny was separated from husband and children. In America, Thackeray had visited her husband, thinking 'she would like me to see the children if I could, and I asked about them particularly but they were not shown.' His impression of the sisters was shared by Mrs. Lynn Linton, who, with less tolerance and philosophy, found Adelaide as 'sweet and generous and sympathetic' as Fanny was 'arbitrary, insolent, and inhuman.'

Lockhart, too, in his last year of life, was at Rome, and Manning, not yet a cardinal. Thackeray met both, but recorded no opinion of either. He was as slow to register an estimate of those he met as he was to dislike any of them; he never contracted the habit of delivering judgments hastily formed from first impressions. It was characteristic both of his intellectual humility and his genial generosity that he was always prepared to like everybody until he had reason for doing otherwise.

§ 3

While his daughters were ill, he found it impossible to concentrate upon *The Newcomes*, and inspired by continual association with the children, he began to amuse himself with a 'nonsensical fairy tale with pictures.' The idea fired his imagination, and *The Rose and the Ring* grew so rapidly under pen and pencil that, at Naples in the middle of February, he informed Kate Perry that he had done the 'best part of a Child's Fairy Tale for next Xmas.' He also made progress with *The Newcomes* at intervals, writing five numbers, in spite of his illness, between his arrival at Rome and his departure from Naples at the end of March.

Reaching Paris on 7th April, he moved into 36 Onslow Square at the end of May. 'A pleasant bowery home with green curtains and carpets,' it seems to have meant even less to him than Young Street, and he used it during the seven years of his occupancy more than ever as a mere port of call. Ubiquitous and cosmopolitan, the little house in Great Coram Street was the only real home he ever knew after his parents left Larkbeare. Besides the sculptor, Baron Marochetti, who lived next door, his neighbours in Onslow Square included Theodore Martin and his wife, Helen Faucit, the Sybil Thorndike of her day.

'All our recollections of Thackeray were delightful. He used to pay us long visits at breakfast, and then he talked with frankness and unreserve more like those of a large-hearted boy than of a man who had seen life in so many phases, many of them of a kind to induce the *pensieri stretti*, for which strangers thought he was peculiar. His nature was obviously one that yearned for sympathy. It was full of tenderness, and showed it, where he was sure that it would be understood. In fact, of all men I have known he was the most tender-hearted; in this respect, indeed, almost womanly. He always showed a marked respect for my wife's opinion in all matters of literature and art.'[1]

His old friend Mrs. Crowe having died in the previous October, Thackeray performed a further act of generosity to her family by receiving into his household her daughter Amy as a companion for his girls.

'With the racket of moving and the hammering and ringing of bells incessantly going on,' he made little headway with *The Newcomes*, and the first work written in the new abode was *Important from the Seat of War*, almost his last 'piece of buffoonery for *Punch*,' which he undertook to pay the rent of a *château* he had taken at Boulogne for the summer. He went over there in the last week of June, taking his daughters and being joined there by his parents. Dickens also was at Boulogne for the summer with his family, and Thackeray speaks of dining with him and afterwards playing 'at forfeits and the game of "buzz" ' with his boys. It was probably at this time that his younger daughter Minnie formed a close friendship with Kate Dickens, afterwards successively Mrs. Charles Allston Collins and Mrs. Perugini.

Constantly ill at this time, Thackeray decided that the air of Boulogne did not suit him and consequently spent much of his time in going to and fro between there and London. He nevertheless wrote four numbers of *The Newcomes* during July and August and, having been to

[1] *Helena Faucit, Lady Martin*, by Sir Theodore Martin. Edinburgh, 1900.

Spa in the early autumn in search of health, he completed *The Rose and the Ring* on 1st November in time for Christmas publication by Smith, Elder. A week later he informed W. B. Reed that 'I am to-day just out of bed after another, about the dozenth, severe fit of spasms which I have this year,' and instead of joining his family in Paris for Christmas he went down to Brighton alone. A 'little trip to Brighton always braces and benefits me,' he once told his mother, 'it's wonderful how it seems to answer with me.'

He still cherished the plan for the future which he had confided to Mrs. Brookfield from America, having written from Naples in the previous February that 'I must take to politics when I have done *Newcomes* and the next set of lectures for America; and then in 1855, give up rambling.' Broken health delayed the fruition of his plans, however, and his determination to keep four numbers of his novel ahead of publication arose from fear of such a breakdown as had interrupted the appearance of *Pendennis*. The same fear prompted him to serious consideration of seeking a diplomatic post as his Philadelphian friends had proposed less than two years before, and he actually applied for a vacant secretaryship to the British Legation at Washington, only to be told that 'it would not be fair to appoint out of the service.' He was then advised by friends to apply for a magistracy, but the resignation of the Aberdeen ministry intervened to rob his application of any chance of success. His sarcastic reference to the legendary nature of 'those places in the Pipe Office' as rewards to men of letters conveyed no injustice, for the rise of the commercial bureaucracy under Victoria was already creating the baleful system of humdrum officialdom and professional monopoly, which sounded the death-knell of disinterested endeavour and ultimately sealed the doom of private enterprise. When John Forster received his appointment to the Lunacy Commission, Thackeray wrote: 'Forster's classification delights me. It's right that men of such ability and merit should get government recognition and honourable public employ. It is a compliment to all of us when one receives such promotion.'

With characteristic inconsistency, though seeking a permanent appointment likely to relieve him of continual literary labour, he projected the idea of a new newspaper, to be entitled *Fair Play*. Possibly he thought that the editorship of such a periodical would prove a valuable asset to his career in parliamentary life. He discussed the plan with George Smith, but eventually abandoned it, partly on account of the change of government, partly because of the unhappy sequel to his article on John Leech's *Pictures of Life and Character* in the *Quarterly Review* for December 1854. In this article he praised the art of his *Punch* colleague as he had praised that of Cruikshank in the *London and Westminster* fourteen years before. It was a generous 'puff' to an old friend. But unfortunately he wounded the *amour propre* of his other colleagues by exclaiming: 'Fancy a number of *Punch* without Leech's pictures! What would you give for it?' Jerrold in particular was bitterly incensed, calling him 'snob and flunkey,' but Thackeray conceived no resentment against him, feeling only horror at offending so many friends in a sentence intended to compliment another.[1] He wrote a frank apology to the editor and proprietors and similar explanations to his former colleagues, among them one to Percival Leigh.

[1] To Whitwell Elwin, the editor of the *Quarterly*, he wrote on 1st February 1855: 'Why did I say it? I slipped it over totally in the proof. It isn't quite true. Though partly so, certainly it oughtn't to have been said by me. But we get to write as fast as we talk, and an idle word does awful mischief. My dear, kind old comrades, how I wish I could swallow that one!' Having made his acquaintance on the acceptance of this article, Elwin became a sincere friend and admirer of Thackeray, earning his gratitude by a warmly appreciative review of *The Newcomes* in the *Quarterly*, counteracting an attack in *The Times* upon the 'morality and religion.' Cf. *Some XVIII Century Men of Letters*, by Rev. Whitwell Elwin, edited, with a Memoir, by his son, Warwick Elwin. London, 2 vols., 1902.

'Of all the slips of my fatal pen, there's none I regret more than the unlucky half line which has given pain to such a kind and valued old friend as you have been, and I trust will be still to me. I ought never to have said that *Punch* might as well be left unwritten but for Leech—it was more than my meaning, which is certainly that the drawing is a hundred times more popular than the writing, but I had no business to write any such thing; and forgot it so much that I was quite surprised when I first heard that I had been accused of sneering at *Punch*. I knew when I came back from Paris and read the line in the *Q.R.*, which I had forgotten as utterly as many another speech which I had made and didn't ought. Jerrold has had his fire into me, and do you know, I feel rather comforted.'

Mark Lemon also complained that the assertion in the article that 'the biographer of Jeames, the author of the *Snob Papers*, resigned his functions on account of Mr. Punch's assaults upon the present Emperor of the French nation,' was incorrect, in reply to which Thackeray wrote, on 24th March 1855, that important letter recounting the circumstances of his resignation in the last week of the year 1851. Having apologised for unwittingly wounding his old colleagues though he declared his firm belief in Leech's paramount value to the paper, 'wh. I have often said—but ought not to have written,' he thought it 'now about time that my old friends and publishers should set me right,' especially the latter, since he had preferred to allow 'old friends, who had acted honourably and kindly by me,' to publish *The Newcomes*, in spite of having received the offer of a larger sum from another publisher, probably George Smith. The proprietors and staff of *Punch* were appeased, but the little tea-cup tempest inspired him to write to George Smith: 'If in writing once in five years or so a literary criticism, intended to be good-natured, I managed to anger a body of old friends, to cause myself pain and regret . . . to lose rest and quiet, hadn't I better give up that game of

"Fair Play" which I thought of, stick to my old pursuits, and keep my health and temper?'

He spent the summer season in London, for the first time taking his daughters about with him. The elder, who was now eighteen, kept a desultory diary, revealing glimpses of their social life. In her 'right of out young lady,' she presided at a Sunday dinner-party, at which the guests included Millais, 'a tall, good-looking, Pre-Raphaelitish young man with a quantity of wavy hair,' Leech and his wife, Peter Cunningham, and Charles Taylor. FitzGerald, 'more melancholy than ever,' dined there with Thackeray's brother- and sister-in-law, and 'told Papa he wouldn't come again—"that everyone had had enough of Fitz." ' He came again, however, in the company of James Spedding, both 'kind and queer and melancholy,' and 'these kind old friends did my father more good than a dozen bottles of black dose alias poison.' With a flash of inspiration, she exclaimed: 'Surely Mr. Carlyle is our Dr. Johnson and I don't think my father is unlike Goldsmith, I am sure that he has as tender a heart though perhaps a better head.' At Mrs. Frederick Elliot's they found 'those kind Miss Barings and Henry Philip van Artevelde Taylor, a grand looking man with a high forehead, whom I felt very proud of talking to.' Morgan John O'Connell comes to dinner, and the Marochettis, Charles Kingsley's sermons are heard on Sundays, Mrs. Norton, Mrs. Procter, Mrs. Fanshawe, each gives teas or dinners or writes letters. She visits Mrs. Brookfield, goes out with her buying flowers to wear at a ball, and once, having been home and had a long talk with her, hopes 'I didn't say anything I ought not.' Thackeray and his daughters were among the audiences of the amateur theatricals at Tavistock House, seeing both *The Lighthouse* and Fielding's *Tom Thumb*, at the latter of which, Forster relates, 'Thackeray rolled off his seat in a burst of laughter that became absurdly contagious.' At Paris, toward the end of June, he met Prosper Mérimée at

Lady Ashburton's and remarked that it was 'very odd, admiring his writing as I do, what an antipathy I have to him.' He spends an evening with Maclise and breakfasts with 'honest Jules Janin, who lives up in his cinquième quite poor and honest and merry.'

He finished *The Newcomes* at Paris on 28th June 'with a very sad heart.' He had no cause for worry concerning its success, as in the cases of both *Vanity Fair* and *Pendennis*, for his readers now lived in the company of his characters from month to month, as did those of Dickens. 'So Clive Newcome has actually married that pretty simpleton, Rosy Mackenzie—isn't it abominable?' wrote Mrs. Stirling, the celebrated actress, to a friend. 'Really, it is very provoking of Thackeray that he will make his heroes and heroines marry the wrong people just as they do in real life.'[1] The lectures, supported by *Esmond*, had widened his circle of readers, promoting him from a position behind Bulwer and Lever to a popularity with the public only exceeded by Dickens. As for the reviewers, he was now beyond the cautious ambit of their criticism; they only argued about the aspects of comparison between him and Fielding.

Travelling to Baden and Homburg and home by the Rhine in July, he was ill again, but determined to lose no further time in carrying out his second visit to America. 'I am going to try in the next six weeks to write four lectures for the great North American Republic,' he wrote, 'and deliver them after they are tired of the stale old Humourists.'[2]

The idea of *The Four Georges* had first occurred to him during his Continental holiday of 1852, but even in July, at Homburg, he had not yet definitely decided on the subject, considering a plan 'to repeople Holland House, to revivify the old *Edinburgh Review* clique, to light up again

[1] *The Stage Life of Mrs. Stirling*, by Percy Allen. London, 1922.
[2] Biographical Introduction to *The Virginians*.

the poor dear old dead lights in Curzon Street and set the kind old souls talking round the hissing silver cauldron.' These lectures, however, were written, unlike the *Humourists*, primarily for America, without consideration of their reception by an English audience, and he chose the *Georges* for their transatlantic appeal.

Requiring a secretary to 'devil' for him in the British Museum, as Eyre Crowe had done for *Esmond*, he again combined charity with necessity by engaging George Hodder on 6th September. Hodder was a hanger-on of Jerrold's and the *Punch* set, who had grovelled in the mud of Grub Street for a decade, during which time he had frequently met Thackeray in such haunts as the Cyder Cellars. In the previous May, having lost his employment upon a newspaper, he had applied to Thackeray for a loan, promptly receiving the following reply:

'I am sincerely sorry to hear of your position and send the little contribution which came so opportunely from another friend whom I was enabled once to help. When you are well to do again I know you will pay it back, and I dare say somebody else will want the money, which is meanwhile most heartily at your service.'[1]

Hodder's task consisted of writing to Thackeray's dictation and making extracts, according to instructions, from books at the British Museum. He offered to accompany Thackeray to America in the same capacity as Eyre Crowe on the former visit, but Thackeray replied that he intended to take his servant instead of a secretary on this occasion, because 'I can ask a servant to hold a basin to me, but I doubt if I could so treat a secretary.'

Seeing him early in September Mrs. Brookfield 'did not think that he looked well,' but, keeping much to the house and shunning society, he progressed so well that three of the four lectures were completed before he sailed. All

[1] *Memories of My Time*, by George Hodder. London, 1870.

arrangements had been made two months before, his passage having been booked at the beginning of August. The Baxters invited him to bring his daughters with him and leave them at New York for the duration of his tour, but they 'agreed with very heavy hearts that it is best that they stay behind and take care of Granny and Colonel Newcome.' On 11th October, sixty people sat down to dinner at the London Tavern in honour of his departure, with Dickens in the chair. Peter Cunningham acted as secretary, and the company included Spedding, Leech, Lemon, Jerrold, Clarkson Stanfield, à Beckett, Bradbury and Evans, Rev. James White, Serjeant Murphy, and Charles Knight. Macready, Forster, Yates and Pollock, all recorded their impressions of the function. Dickens's speech was 'very good, but not his very best,' 'telling Thackeray not alone how much his friendship was prized by those present, and how proud they were of his genius, but offering him in the name of tens of thousands absent who had never touched his hand nor seen his face, lifelong thanks for the treasures of mirth, wit, and wisdom within the yellow-covered numbers of *Pendennis* and *Vanity Fair*.' Thackeray had dictated a fluent reply to Hodder in the morning, though in 'a state of great nervous anxiety, saying it was very kind of his friends to give him a dinner, but that he wished it was over,' and he appears to have negotiated his speech with less disastrous results than usual. Nevertheless, he was conscious of a compliment to Macready having gone astray, and wrote a long letter of explanation from America. 'The dinner was superb,' the menu including turtle soup *à la* 'Hobson-Newcome' and *à la* 'bon voyage,' omelettes *à la* 'Beck Sharpy,' and a salmi *à la* 'Fotheringay.' Macready said 'the dinner lasted about two hours' and was 'a great success—am glad to meet and pay a tribute to a man of genius.' None of the chroniclers remained after Dickens left the chair, and Thackeray was also preparing for departure, when Jerrold, on an impulse, took the chair, and all the old fraternity of *Punch* prolonged the festivities into the small hours, reviving memories of their ancient revels of a dozen years earlier.

Two days later, on 13th October 1855, he left Liverpool on board the *Africa*.

CHAPTER 14

§ 1

CHARLES PEARMAN, the valet, kept a diary of the second American tour which has yet to be published. 'People are mad to see the author of *The Newcomes*,' he wrote, 'hundreds of letters come for his autograph—the papers announced him with two colors.' The Lecture on George I was given for the first time in New York on 1st November. 'It was crowded,' said Pearman, 'persons were refused admission—little nervous going off—he was welcomed heartily the lecture was too smutty for the fair sex—1 hour ¾.' To 'Papa' Frank Fladgate, the *doyen* of the Garrick Club, Thackeray wrote on 14th November:

'At first there was a doubt—almost a defeat. The people did not know what to make of George I and his strumpets. Morality was staggered. But they liked better and better with each lecture, and now they're done and the success of the affair beyond a question. Last night at Brooklyn there were twenty-five hundred persons at the lecture.'

Later he found 'George the Third is the lecture they have liked best, on account of the pathetic business. George the First the least. . . .'

On his arrival his *Ballads and Poems*, collected principally from *Punch*, were published simultaneously in England and America. For the first fortnight he steadily declined all invitations while engaged upon completing the lecture on George IV. 'Now for the next six months I shall have hardly any writing to do,' he told his mother on 13th November,' and the rest will be the best of all doctors.'

The atmosphere affected him oddly. 'There is some electric influence in the air and sun here which we don't experience on our side of the globe,' he declared; 'people can't sit still, people can't ruminate over their dinners, dawdle in their studies; they must keep moving.' While feeling physically invigorated, his brain seemed numbed; when 'some rain began to fall I felt a leaden cap taken off my brain-pan.' On his former visit he had enjoyed uniformly excellent health, so that he had often regretted, on returning to Europe and being so frequently ill, the beneficial effects of the American climate. But the merciless advance of his nameless disease in the interval of three years was now manifested in attacks of illness little less persistent than he had been suffering at home. At a press dinner in his honour at Astor House, attended by Washington Irving, 'he was too ill to seat himself,' merely entering the room and shaking hands with his friends before retiring to bed. At Boston, whither he went from Brooklyn and New York in early December, he had 'a chill and fever' on him, and on the 14th, 'a fine attack of spasms (part of which I was obliged to bear grinning through the compliments of a Quaker family)' kept him in bed all day, compelling the postponement of a lecture at Providence.

Yet he persevered grimly with his engagements, maintaining his usual genial demeanour in company and leaving a long tale of triumphs behind him as he moved from place to place.

'It is day after day skurry and turmoil,' he wrote to Macready from New York on 20th November, 'friends calling, strangers calling, newspaper articles bawling out abuse or telling absurd personalities—you know the life well enough. . . . The dollars hardly compensate for it: nor the kindliness of the real friends on whom one lights. . . . As far as the money goes I am doing great things here and the dollars are rolling in. I shall make all but £1000 in five weeks—though not of course to continue at this rate.'

At Boston he was even more successful than at New York. Longfellow 'found a crowded audience' on the 7th, 'and had to take a back seat, where I could hear only about half of a very agreeable lecture on the times of the first George.' Thackeray had supper with him at Cambridge the following evening, finding him 'a kindly, pleasant gentleman,' and being charmed by 'a mad-cap fiddler . . . who played most wonderfully on his instrument.' Prescott gave him a copy of his recently published volume of *Philip II*, and at his house Thackeray saw the two crossed swords which he describes in the opening paragraph of *The Virginians*. He renewed his acquaintance, too, with George Ticknor, whom he considered 'a cleverer man than Prescott,' though nobody read his *History of Spanish Literature*. Both he and Prescott, he said, 'have comfortable old houses, handsome large libraries and famous Burgundy and Claret in their cellars.' Ticknor wrote on 23rd December:

'I have heard Thackeray's four lectures on the four Georges, truculent enough in their general satire,—though not much beyond the last half-volume of *Harry Esmond* about Queen Anne,—but full of generous passages about individuals. The sketches of the German princes of the seventeenth century, and down to the middle of the eighteenth, with which he opened, amused me more than anything else. They were capital. The passage most applauded was a beautiful tribute of loyalty to Queen Victoria, and the tone and manners of her Court. It was given, on his part, with much feeling, and brought down the house—always crowded—very fervently. . . . His audience was the best the city could give, and above twelve hundred strong, besides which, he repeated the lecture about George III to an audience of two thousand, two or three evenings ago.'[1]

Ticknor's remark about the 'tribute of loyalty to Queen Victoria' carries important significance, for the high Tories

[1] *Life, Letters, and Journals of George Ticknor*. London, 2 vols., 2nd ed., 1876.

at home soon charged Thackeray with disloyalty in the new series of lectures which he dare not deliver among his own countrymen. Two months later an attack in the newly established *Saturday Review* caused Thackeray to write half-humorously to Kate Perry that, 'after giving Vernon Harcourt 2/6 to send me the first five numbers, and only getting No. 1, it is too bad they should assault me—and for what?' As he pointed out, probably having foreseen some such grounds of attack, he had deliberately inserted in the lecture on George II a tasty confection of butter and sugar, apostrophising 'the mistress of Saint James's' as 'wise, moderate, exemplary of life, the good mother; the good wife; the accomplished lady; the enlightened friend of art; the tender sympathiser in her people's glories and sorrows.'

Before going to Boston he visited 'good old Washington Irving' at Yonkers, where he lived 'a very pleasant patriarchal life' in 'a funny little in-and-out cottage surrounded by a little domain of lawns not so smooth as ours, and woods rather small and scrubby—in little bits of small parlours, where we were served with cakes and wine,—with a little study not much bigger than my back room, with old dogs trotting about the premises, with flocks of ducks sailing on the ponds.' He was impressed by 'the general respect and affection' everywhere accorded to 'this good old man.'[1] In New York he met Bayard Taylor, who liked him 'very much,' and invited him to a Sunday breakfast at Delmonico's. They had 'a glorious time,' the breakfast lasting five hours.[2] Thackeray returned Taylor's liking, describing him as 'one of the most interesting men I have ever seen in my life,' and promising to introduce him to English literary society when he visited London in the following summer. To Taylor as a token of their cordial

[1] Cf. '*Nil Nisi Bonum*' in the *Roundabout Papers*.

[2] *Life and Letters of Bayard Taylor*, edited by Marie Hansen-Taylor and Horace E. Scudder. London, 2 vols., 1884.

friendship he subsequently presented Schiller's sword, a cherished possession purchased at Weimar in his student days.

In the new year he did very well at Philadelphia in spite of the severe wintry weather, but the rival attraction of an opera company caused his room at Baltimore to be only half-full. Again he was ill, 'and in these fits becoming exceedingly glum and the thoughts of rushing home at such times overpoweringly strong.' Heavy falls of snow and intense cold decided him to tour southwards, instead of following his original plan of penetrating the west. He lectured at Richmond and Charleston, at 'jolly, little, friendly Savannah,' at Macon, Columbus, Montgomery, before passing down the Alabama River to Mobile and New Orleans, which he reached early in March. He had thought of visiting Havannah, but decided that the Southern States offered prospects of greater profits. 'The wearisome lecturing business goes on,' he wrote from Savannah on 17th February, 'the little heaps of dollars roll in gently, and every week makes the girls about 500$ richer.' In the *Roundabout Papers*, he afterwards described his impressions of New Orleans in *A Mississippi Bubble*. At Mobile he found 'kind folks and pleasant company,' though he did not 'make a mint of money there.' New Orleans, with its quaint old houses, the pictures on the quays, the 'sweet kind French tongue' spoken in its shops, and 'streets which look for all the world like Havre,' he liked 'perhaps better than any other town in the Union.' Returning northward on 26th and 27th March, he gave two lectures at St. Louis, where his audience included Abraham Lincoln, then a name unknown outside his own State. On 24th March he wrote to Mrs. Elliot from 'the place they say that was Martin Chuzzlewit's Eden, Cairo, at the confluence of the Ohio and Miss.—such a dreary Heaven abandoned place!'

'Why need I go on making a quack of myself any more? But if when I come home—after speaking of Queen Vic. in the very handsomest manner, after making thousands of folks that hated him feel kindly about George, I am attacked for speaking my mind about George IV (mind I left out the Q. Caroline scandal entirely)—by Jupiter!— It will do me good. I want a fight, I have always told you I can hit harder than any man alive, and I never do— but O! I think a little exercise would do me good! . . . In fine I want to get home more and more every day. To do what? to dawdle about Europe again and write another novel? Who can say for to-morrow? But I want to kiss my dear children and see my bonnes sœurs and speak to people whom I can speak to.'

Having given two lectures at Cincinnatti on the 29th and 31st he set out for New York by way of Buffalo, declining to pause, in his eager haste to see familiar faces, to visit the falls of Niagara.

He arrived at New York on 5th April and stayed there as a guest of William Duer Robinson, who lived with two other bachelors, J. C. B. Davis and Samuel E. Lyons, at a house dubbed by Thackeray 'The Bower of Virtue.' Bayard Taylor wrote to James T. Fields on the 7th:

'Thackeray came here on Saturday. I breakfasted with him yesterday. He looks jolly and rosy, although he had a few chills on the Mississippi. He is staying with Robinson, 604 Houston Street. It is refreshing to see his good face and big body among us once more. He says he will stay until June 1st, but I expect he will disappear suddenly some Wednesday morning.'

Taylor accurately gauged the state of his friend's mind, for Thackeray wrote home the next day: 'Oh, how weary, weary I am of this lecturing. I shall do no more of it, I think.' And, commenting on his many dreary journeys, he spoke of the beauty of the snow-clad country and of

Lake Erie sparkling in the sun as he passed on his way to New York, 'but Europe is a prettier country still for me, and I long for it.'

Going to Philadelphia he was persuaded by W. B. Reed to revive the *Humourist* lectures, but they failed to attract on account of the lateness of the season and the fact that they were now obtainable in book form. In New York he entertained thirty-two guests to dinner at Delmonico's, stipulating that there should be no speeches, but that everybody should either sing a song or tell a story. G. W. Curtis and Lester Wallack sang several duets, James Wallack, now a veteran actor, whom Thackeray had known years before in Paris, declaimed his successful scene from Jerrold's play, *The Rent Day*, and Thackeray himself sang 'Little Billee,' which he had sung in Rome with Bevan and Emerson Tennent after the journey *From Cornhill to Cairo*. On Monday, 28th April, Bayard Taylor wrote:

'Thackeray went off in the *Baltic* on Saturday, running away from his friends, for fear of having to say good-by. I saw him off; he seemed sorry to leave.'

Three years before he had felt no regret on leaving, but now he knew that he was never likely to return.

§ 2

'Thackeray is back, not very well,' wrote FitzGerald in May. Having been miserably ill on the voyage, he placed himself in the doctor's hands immediately on his return. His doctor told him frankly that he had 'trembled for me and the risk I ran in going to America,' and renouncing all immediate thought of either work or pleasure, he confined his attention to his health and the directions of medical advice.

'I have had plenty of chill and fever since I returned,' he wrote on 19th June, 'but have had no attack for 3 weeks now; and believe they will diminish as I get cured of my other afflictions. What a bore for my poor Nanny! I have been able to take her to very few parties, and came away at one o'clock from the one or two balls we have been at just when the fun is at its best.'

His Boston friend, George Ticknor, who was spending the summer in England, wrote home to Prescott that 'Thackeray has been to see us a good deal, but he is very poorly.' The same week, lying ill in bed, Thackeray was lamenting that he could not entertain the Ticknors, because his doctor had strictly prohibited dinners and social engagements. 'I have been 2½ months in London now without doing the littlest bit of work except doctoring myself,' he told the Baxters on 12th July. He had taken his elder daughter to only two 'fine parties,' and as he had an ague attack after each, she was reconciled to remaining at home.

Eager to test the effect of *The Four Georges* on English audiences, but realising the impossibility of undertaking any lecturing engagements in his present state of health, he invited a select circle of friends to one or two private readings at his house. He eagerly awaited the verdict of his old schoolfellow, Venables, who was associated with the *Saturday Review*, the paper which had launched the charge of disloyalty, and was delighted when he highly praised the first lecture. Towards the end of July he was sufficiently recovered to dine out occasionally, attending, in company with the Procters, the Brownings, Venables, and Spedding, a literary party given by Milnes on the 18th. Bayard Taylor, on his arrival in London, found him 'as jovial and as tender-hearted as ever,' and very ready to keep his promise of introducing him to literary society. Besides giving him a letter of introduction to Tennyson, he invited almost the entire staff of *Punch*, including Mark Lemon, Leech, Tom Taylor, Shirley Brooks,

Horace Mayhew, and the two proprietors, to meet Taylor and three other Americans at dinner on 1st August. He lost no opportunity of repaying the hospitality he had received in America. Having dinner with Ticknor, who had taken a house in London, he carried off his host and Longfellow's brother-in-law, Thomas Appleton, for a night at Evans's, and Lowell was one of three Americans whom he invited to dine at the Garrick Club before proceeding to the Cyder Cellars, where he read to them the death of Colonel Newcome, over a glass of gin-and-water.

All these festivities, following so soon upon his rising from a sick-bed, must have been undertaken in defiance of his doctor's orders. After so many years of incessant work, accompanied by perpetual indulgence in social pleasures, he found the force of habit too strong to permit the restrictions of activity and diet ordered by the doctors. Having witnessed one of his 'attacks of spasms' and being shocked by the agonies he endured, George Hodder inquired if he had not called in sound medical advice. 'What is the use of advice, if you don't follow it?' demanded Thackeray. 'They tell me not to drink, and I *do* drink. They tell me not to smoke, and I *do* smoke. They tell me not to eat, and I *do* eat. In short, I do everything that I am desired *not* to do, and therefore, what am I to expect?' His philosophy was fatalism. Ever since his illness in 1849 he had realised that he carried a disease which, sooner or later, would develop fatal symptoms. Already he suffered agonies of pain under attacks becoming rapidly more frequent, so why seek to prolong his life by renunciation of all that made it worth living, when its prolongation only entailed the endurance of protracted suffering? His aim now, as formerly, was merely to make the most of his time on earth.

To prepare himself for a lecturing campaign in the winter months, he accompanied his daughters to the Continent in August, having first signed a contract with

Bradbury and Evans for another novel in numbers. Having spent a pleasant time at Spa, they went on to Dusseldorf and, 'in an evil hour,' to Aix-la-Chapelle, 'which disagreed with me as it always does.' Throughout the holiday he never felt sufficiently well to commence work upon the new novel, and when he was called suddenly to Paris by the death of his stepfather's sister-in-law, he was 'haunted by No. 1 of Mr. Thackeray's new serial which won't leave me alone, which follows me about in all my walks, wakes me up at night, prevents me from hearing what is said at the play, and yet seems farther off than ever.' Although he had conceived the idea of a sequel to *Esmond*, dealing with the emigrant branch of the family, during his first visit to America, he did not now immediately contemplate the plan of *The Virginians*. In the conclusion of *The Newcomes* he had hinted his intention of making 'J. J.' the central figure of his next book, and it was on this that he was working in Paris. 'I began a story, was dissatisfied with it, and burnt it,' he told Whitwell Elwin on his return to London in October.

'I intended to show J. J. married, and exhibit him with the trials of a wife and children. I meant to make him in love with another man's wife and recover him through his attachment for the little ones.'

He would thus have continued the autobiographical strain of *Pendennis* and *The Newcomes*, and on that account he rejected the plan. 'It ran in the old track,' he informed Elwin. 'I have exhausted all the types of character with which I am familiar, and it is very difficult to strike out anything new.' To Kate Perry and her sister he wrote:

'It seems to me as if I had said my say, as if anything I write must be repetition, and that people will say with justice "he has worn himself out, I always told you he would, etc., etc." . . . Suppose I do wear myself out, and that posterity say so, why shouldn't she? and what care I to appear to future ages (who will be deeply interested in discussing the subject) as other than I really am?'

Illness, as he confessed to the Baxters, always induced a feeling of depression, which was now aggravated by news of the death of his old *Punch* colleague, Gilbert Abbott à Beckett, a man no more than six months his senior.

'My poor friend A'Beckett's death has shocked me. He has left no money and hasn't insured his life—Down from competence and comfort goes a whole family into absolute penury. One boy $\frac{1}{2}$ through the University, and likely to have done well there I believe—another at a public school, daughters with masters, and Mamma with tastes for music and millinery. What is to happen to these people? Had I dropped 3 years ago my poor wife and young ones would have been no better off. Yes, we must do the forthcoming serial work, and never mind if it should turn out a failure.'

He did not add that, on hearing of his friend's death and knowing his financial circumstances, he had promptly written to *Punch* asking if 'we, his old comrades,' could not 'do something to show his poor widow and family our sense of his worth,' and offering to subscribe a hundred pounds towards a fund for the son's maintenance during the remainder of his course at Oxford.

Early in October he commenced arrangements for a lecturing tour. On the 19th he wrote to Dr. John Brown, advising him of his intention to initiate the campaign at Edinburgh. He had hoped to take his daughters with him, but his mother fell ill at Paris and he sent them over to nurse her. He himself was seized with 'one of my old attacks of spasms' on the eve of departure. 'Not a word of that book is written though I have spent hours & weeks of pains on it,' he wrote on 2nd November. The next day he left for Edinburgh, where the lectures were received with an enthusiasm equalling that excited by the *Humourists*, though a patriotic section of the audience hissed his unceremonious reference to Mary Queen of Scots, and Aytoun, angry for the same reason, told him to 'stick to his Jeames,' as more in his line than the *Georges*. Dr. John Brown, with whom Thackeray had formed a friendship so intimate on his previous visit, which had occurred after the shock of his trouble with the Brookfields, that he had confided to him an inkling of his tragedy, wrote to a friend:

'We have just come home from the third George. We liked it better than the first time. What power and gentleness and restraint! I wonder at and love him more and more. To-night he took the whole house by the heart, and held them; they were still, and serious, and broke out wildly at the end. We have seen a great deal of him; he comes and sits for hours, and lays that great nature out before us, with its depths and bitterness, its tenderness and desperate truth. It is so sad to see him so shut out from all cheer and hope.'

Brown, with his love of good wine and good literature, his honest sincerity, and broad-minded sympathy and understanding, was one of the few men permitted to glimpse the wistful melancholy beneath the veneer of genial good-humour and cheerful conviviality in these latter years.

Besides the Browns, whose house offered the same familiar hospitality as the Baxters' in New York, he renewed his friendly relations with Aytoun, the Blackwoods, and Colonel E. B. Hamley. John Ritchie and his nephew, J. R. Findlay, the proprietors of the *Scotsman*, which had staunchly praised all his work since it had been almost the first notable newspaper to recognise the genius of *Vanity Fair*, gave a dinner in his honour on 22nd November, to which De Quincey was invited, but did not attend, ostensibly on account of 'a most distressing affliction of the chest.'[1] This

[1] Cf. *De Quincey and His Friends*, by James Hogg. London, 1895.

dinner necessitated a dash back across country from Glasgow, where he delivered his first lecture to an audience of two thousand on 19th November. Returning to Glasgow the following week, he was hailed as 'the greatest satirist of the age,' and formed the opinion that the lectures were 'a much greater success here than in America—as great even pecuniarily.' Proceeding thence to Inverness, he returned through Edinburgh, Paisley, and Glasgow, giving one lecture to packed audiences at each place. At Edinburgh he stayed the night with John Blackwood, 'the most hospitable and magnificent inn I ever put up in . . . the 4 Blackwood brothers liking each other hugely and sitting jovially together night after night over bottle after bottle of the most prodigious good claret.'

All the time he was in 'a dreadful fright lest my attacks should come on,' and after spending a satisfactory week at Hull, he was confined to his bed and prevented from lecturing at Bradford on the 9th and 10th December. 'My spirits are very much better,' he wrote to the Baxters from Manchester on the 12th:

'Think that at the end of next year if I work I shall be worth 20,000£! It's as much as I want—10,000 apiece for the girls is enough for any author's daughters—and then when I am independent what shall we do? Hush—perhaps have a try at politics for which I don't care now—but one must do something and when you begin to play you get interested in the game—I have taken share in the *Transatlantic Telegraph*—I felt glad somehow to contribute to a thread that shall tie our two countries together—for though I don't love America I love Americans with all my heart.'

Returning to London and being joined by his daughters, they attended Dickens's Twelfth Night performance of *The Frozen Deep* at Tavistock House. FitzGerald was paying one of his rare visits to town, and Thackeray 'came in looking gray, grand, and good-humoured.'

'He goes lecturing all over England; has fifty pounds for each Lecture: and says he is ashamed of the Fortune he is making. But he deserves it.'

While in London he rid himself of the anxious and irksome business of arranging his own lecturing engagements, by contracting with Cramer, Beale and Co., pianoforte makers and entertainment caterers, to deliver such lectures as they should arrange at a fee of fifty guineas a lecture. George Hodder, now employed by this firm, accompanied him in the capacity of manager, and he was advertised everywhere with all the blatant publicity methods of a circus, greatly to the indignation of those who sanctified 'the dignity of literature' and the grandeur of gentility.

'Endless letters, constant moving from place to place, not particklar good health, but it can't be helped,' he wrote to his mother on 23rd January. 'To-morrow I lecture in Brighton at two, in London at eight. The town is at present placarded with my name in enormous type, announcing my lectures at the Surrey Zoological. The bigwigs and great folks are furious. The halls of splendour are shut to me. . . . Shall I ever write a book again? Some day, please God, when these astonishing Georges have put a few thousands more into my pocket. And now comes Charles! Pack up the bag, and let's be off to London-super-Mare.'

He invited Harrison Ainsworth, now living in retirement at Brighton, to come up with him to hear the lecture on George III, promising 'it won't offend your loyalty,' and to stay over the week-end at Onslow Square. Where was the snob, with head swollen by success, forsaking old friends for the grand parasites who batten upon every celebrity? Was he not now good-humouredly ignoring the sneers of the snobs, as he had ignored them when he accepted a free passage from the P. and O. Company to journey to

Cairo? And he could offer a courteous welcome to Ainsworth, never a close friend, now shorn of his brilliant plumage and feverishly writing a mediocre romance every year in the wake of a waning reputation.

'Thackeray we see very little of as he is always on the move, one day at Bath and another at Brighton,' wrote Kate Perry to Brookfield on 26th January. 'He has made a much better bargain for himself now, having found a Barnum, and in 3 or 4 months he says he will be able to rest on his oars, having then made enough to endow his daughters.' On his first journey under the new management—to the west, Exeter, Plymouth, Bristol, and Bath—he was accompanied by his daughters, who saw for the first time the Clavering country of *Pendennis*, whither their father had clattered down by coach from Charterhouse and Cambridge some thirty years before. After a fortnight he returned to town before setting off for the north, writing to an American friend on 8th February:

'The Georges are so astoundingly popular here that I go on month after month hauling in fresh bags of soverings, wondering that the people are not tired and that the lecturer is not found out. Tomorrow I am away for 2 months to the North—have found a Barnum who pays me an awful sum for April and May, and let us hope June—shall make £10,000 by my beloved monarchs one way or the other.'

At the outset of his northern tour, he was taken ill at Halifax, but, choosing his diet with unusual care, he hoped to be 'able to get through the rest of the campaign without trouble.' While in Yorkshire he spent a day with Milnes at Fryston, recalling memories of his last visit nearly sixteen years before, when he was returning from the South Durham election of 1841. He lectured at Leeds, York, and Sheffield, before proceeding to Scotland in March. The Scottish tour was 'a failure as regards money, but pleasant enough otherwise.' A general election, following Palmerston's resignation, militated against the attraction of the lectures for two or three weeks. He travelled widely in Scotland—visiting Dundee, Aberdeen, Inverness, Perth, and Stirling, besides Glasgow, Edinburgh, and several Lowland towns. At Edinburgh he was ill again, causing the postponement of a dinner in his honour from 28th to 31st March. On this occasion, Lord Neaves, who presided, mentioned satire and sympathy as the cardinal characteristics of his work, speaking of the one quality equalling the other—a tribute which touched Thackeray, so accustomed to the imputation of heartlessness—Brown observed his 'pathetic, dumb face, like a great child going to cry, when he stood up to return thanks.' He made a graceful response, referring to the silver statuette of *Punch* presented by the Edinburgh admirers of *Vanity Fair* as the first testimonial he had ever received, but 'he thought he had made an immense fool of himself in his speech till he saw it next morning.'

In the third week in April he lectured at Cambridge, where he saw Pollock, who wrote to Macready on the 24th:

'Thackeray was there. The four Georges have been good friends to him, and many parts of the country remain to be perambulated with them. When he gives only two of the lectures in the same town he receives fifty guineas for each, when all four, thirty or forty guineas.'

Early in May, he went to Oxford, a young don named Dodgson noting in his journal on the 9th:

'I breakfasted this morning with Fowler of Lincoln to meet Thackeray (the author), who delivered his lecture on George III in Oxford last night. I was much pleased with what I saw of him; his manner is simple and unaffected; he shows no anxiety to shine in conversation, though full of fun and anecdote when drawn out. He seemed delighted with the reception he had met with last night; the undergraduates seem to have behaved with most unusual moderation.'[1]

Hodder reports that the Oxonians proved a singularly appreciative audience, regarding the lecture with the reverence due to a modern classic and almost anticipating each opportunity for applause, and that Thackeray, on descending from the platform, exclaimed: 'There's an audience for you! Gad, I would lecture to those young fellows for nothing!'

§ 3

On 12th May, he was present at the funeral of Lady Ashburton, who had been for ten years a sincere and sympathetic friend. He stood over her grave beside Carlyle, Brookfield, Henry Taylor, Venables, and many others who had enjoyed her hospitality at the Grange. A similarly melancholy duty awaited him a month later, when, on 15th June, he walked alongside Dickens as a pall-bearer at the passing of Douglas Jerrold. Only three years before he had written to Percival Leigh, expressing pleasure at Jerrold's success as editor of *Lloyd's Newspaper* and hoping that 'D. J. will lay by a little money. What's the business of us fathers of families but that?' The feelings inspired by the death of à Beckett were revived by that of Jerrold, more than ever confirming his determination to make the most of his life and strength to provide for the future of his daughters.

An opportunity to open his ambition of entering politics had offered at the general election in the spring, when 'the Whig whipper-in' had sent him a seat in Parliament. He had then declined the offer, since a contest at that time would have necessitated the abandonment of his lecturing engagements. But he had now reaped the harvest of his lectures, and when the member for Oxford was unseated

[1] *Life and Letters of Lewis Carroll*, by S. D. Collingwood. London, 1898.

for some technical breach of the electoral regulations, he consented to stand in the Liberal interest. In his election address, dated from the Mitre on 9th July, he promised to use his 'utmost endeavour to increase and advance the social happiness, the knowledge, and the power of the people.' Suffrage reform, vote by ballot, and the features of the current Liberal policy were included in his programme. Lord Monck first appeared in the field as champion of the Tory interest, but retired at the last moment in favour of Edward Cardwell, a Peelite, subsequently Minister of War under Gladstone. Against Monck, Thackeray stood an excellent chance of being returned, but Cardwell was a much more formidable antagonist, whom he candidly confessed that he would not have faced if he had known of his candidature. He conducted his campaign with pluck and punctilious courtesy, referring always to his opponent in friendly and respectful terms and deprecating the slightest demonstration of hissing or hooting. He humorously invited Dickens to come down and speak on his behalf to tell them who he was, 'for he doubted whether more than two of the electors had ever heard of him, and he thought there might be as many as six or eight who had heard of Dickens.' He was narrowly defeated, the result of the poll, declared on 21st July, declaring Cardwell the victor by 1085 votes to 1018. He concluded a graceful acknowledgment of his defeat with the remark, 'I will retire and take my place with my pen and ink at my desk, and leave to Mr. Cardwell a business which I am sure he understands better than I do.'

Comforting himself that he was quite 'as well out of Parliament as in,' he can have felt little real regret for the frustration of a plan which he had cherished for nearly five years. His health was in no state to sustain the undertaking of increased work and added anxieties. In fact, he was seized with illness immediately upon his return from Oxford and confined to his bed until he went down to

Brighton, his favourite resort for recuperation, on 4th August. After a month of pleasant idleness, while his daughters bathed and took riding lessons, he spent some time at Homburg and Paris in September. All this time, though now more than a year since he had received the commission from Bradbury and Evans and begun to worry about the beginning of the novel, he had written nothing of *The Virginians*. Fighting against broken health, he had husbanded all his energies to carry out his lecturing campaign. Now, 'rather better in health, I think, but becoming more silent and selfish every day,' he applied himself to the task, not only of writing, but of illustrating, the new novel. He had felt some dissatisfaction with Doyle's drawings for *The Newcomes*, besides experiencing annoyance at his friend's frequent delays in supplying the designs, and he decided, being now relieved of any concern with lectures or an impending visit to America, to risk another breakdown in health by uniting the labours of author and illustrator. The habit of hurried toil was so strong upon him that, even now, when necessity no longer demanded it and his health required ease and leisure, he invited almost eagerly the prospect of the printer's boy waiting at his door.

The first number of *The Virginians* appeared in November 1857, yet, on 10th October, he sent Dr. John Brown a tracing of the design for its wrapper with the remark, 'this is the best part of *The Virginians* which is done as yet. I have been working hard and don't like what I've done.' On the appearance of the first number, he wrote to the Baxters:

'I don't think *The Virginians* is good yct, though it has taken me immense deal of trouble, but I know it will be good at the end. I tremble for the poor publishers who gave me 300£ a number—I don't think they can afford it and shall have the melancholy duty of disgorging.'

His honesty and generosity in dealing with publishers approximated to altruism. Having spent so many years writing magazine articles, which often occupied two or three weeks of hard work, for no more than twenty pounds a time, he regarded with incredulity the idea that a novel of his could be worth six or seven thousand pounds to a publisher. He doubtless believed that the firm of Harpers behaved handsomely in paying him £480 for the right to print from his proof-sheets, so enabling them to run *The Virginians* as a serial in their magazine concurrently with the English issue in numbers. When the *New York Tribune* shamelessly pirated the novel, issuing the instalments in their weekly edition in competition with *Harper's Magazine*, Thackeray wrote on 11th December, in response to a protest lodged by the Harpers' London agent:

'I am sorry to hear from you that the New York *Tribune* is reprinting *The Virginians*, and no doubt hurting the Messrs. Harper's issue of the story, who pay me $100 per month for early impressions. But I do not see what good any remonstrances of mine can effect. If American houses choose to reprint our books we can't prevent them, and the *Tribune* will doubtless take its own course, in spite of any objections of mine or Messrs. Harper. Could English writers have remonstrated with any effect we should have done so years ago: but I am sure that an outcry at present would neither be useful nor dignified; and can only express my regret that I don't see how, in the present instance, I can be of service to a House which shows itself inclined to act in a kind and friendly manner to English literary men.'[1]

He expressed the attitude common to English novelists in the 'fifties. It was left to Charles Reade—who, in this same year, was going to law against such a publishing potentate as Richard Bentley to expose what he termed 'the half-profit swindle,' and manfully waging war single-handed

[1] *The House of Harper*, by J. Henry Harper. London, 1912.

against the despotism of Mudie's library—to agitate persistently during the next twenty years, with all his dogged tenacity, ruthless violence, and sound commercial shrewdness, for a rational system of international copyright.

§ 4

He worked well during November and December, completing the first three numbers of *The Virginians*. His mother, having recovered from her illness, and his stepfather, who 'grows to be more and more like Colonel Newcome every day,' returned to Paris after spending three months with him, and he took his daughters to stay with Russell Sturgis, the American partner in the banking firm of Barings, for Christmas. 'I read no new books,' he told Dr. John Brown in the new year, 'only Newspapers and Magazines of 1756, get out my numbers with extraordinary throes and difficulty.' His old habit of procrastination soon brought the printer's boy to the door, and he wrote each number for the waiting press. Writing to W. D. Robinson on 23rd January, to ask 'where the deuce was George Warrington carried after he was knocked down at Braddock's defeat,' remarking that he wanted that character out of the way for a year and a half, he declared:

'I only got my number done last night, and am getting more disgustingly lazy every day. I *can't* do the work until it's wanted. And yet with all these attacks of illness wch. I have, I ought, you know I ought.'

During the five weeks following he wrote two more numbers and suffered '3 confounded attacks of spasms.' 'Claret drunk not wisely, but too well,' he wrote to Robinson, 'an immoderate use of the fleshpots are beginning to tell upon the friend of W. D. R.' He idly considered the idea of visiting America again in the autumn to finish the novel '*sur les lieux*,' and thought of trying again for Parliament in the event of another election. Occasionally he gave a lecture, but never for profit. Receiving a cheque for twenty-five pounds for a lecture to a suburban society, he handed it to his doctor, who had declined to accept a fee for his attentions. When Macready offered him fifty pounds to lecture in two little towns near his Dorset retreat, he consented to the request, but refused the money, 'because I am sick of letting myself out for hire.'

Though he made his money by the exertion of brain and body, he remained as careless of expenditure as in the days when he had airily scattered his patrimony to the winds. Discussing with his mother the plan of taking a cheap house at Brighton while writing *Pendennis*, he scoffed at the indignity of living in an unpretentious abode.

'Tom Carlyle lives in perfect dignity in a little £40 house at Chelsea, with a snuffy Scotch maid to open the door, and the best company in England ringing at it. It is only the second or third chop great folks who care about show. "And why don't you live with a maid yourself?" I think I hear somebody saying. Well, I can't; I want a man to be going my own messages, which occupy him pretty well. There must be a cook, and a woman about the children, and that horse is the best doctor I get in London; in fine, there are a hundred good reasons for a lazy, liberal, not extravagant, but costly way of life.'

He humorously observed that Charles Pearman omitted to resume his livery on returning from America, deciding that plain black best suited his dignity as confidential servant, after which concession, 'Mr. Chawls is such a great man now that he can't do without a young man in livery to help him.' Thus:

'When the girls dine off 2 mutton chops they have the pleasure of being waited on by 2 menials who walk round and round them. We give very good dinners, our house is full of pretty little things, our cellar is not badly off. . . . I am going in a few days to pay 100£ for 18 dozen of '48 claret that is not be drunk for 4 years.'

He kept 'a very pretty open carriage and a brougham if you please,' and refused nothing to his daughters—music-masters, drawing-masters, lessons in dancing and riding. Though the lectures on *The Four Georges* had produced the sum required to provide dowries for his daughters, his manner of life still demanded unremitted application to profitable work.

The sluggish movement and digressive garrulity of *The Virginians* was inspired by the manner in which it was written—fits of contemplative hesitancy, attacks of illness, then feverish bursts of pot-boiling to supply the waiting printer.[1] On 10th April, having suffered '2 attacks within the last fortnight of my enemy,' he had written only three pages of his next number. He was well aware of the defects in the story, for he wrote on the 23rd to the Baxters:

'On Friday night after awful trouble, I only got my number done just in time to send it by post to Liverpool and America. The book's clever but stupid, thats the fact. I hate story-making incidents, surprises, love-making, &c. more and more every day; and here is a third of a great story done equal to two thirds of an ordinary novel—and nothing has actually happened, except that a young gentleman has come from America to England.'

[1] Nearly nine years after Mrs. Brookfield had expressed the wish that Thackeray 'could be made independent of having to work so constantly,' the historian Motley wrote on 27th June 1858:

'I can conceive nothing more harassing in the literary way than his way of living from hand to mouth. I mean in regard to the way in which he furnishes food for the printer's devil. Here he is just finishing the number which must appear in a few days. Of course, whether ill or well, stupid or fertile, he must produce the same amount of fun, pathos, or sentiment. His gun must be regularly loaded and discharged at command. I should think it would wear his life out.'

A month later, on 23rd May, John Blackwood wrote to G. H. Lewes:

'Thackeray's daughters had a soirée last night, and to be out of the way of the preparations the venerable man dined with us. He says he cannot get ahead with *The Virginians*, and was desperately pushed with the last No., having written the last 16 pages in one day, the last he had to spare. The last two Nos. are, I think, better than their predecessors, but he must improve much or the book will not keep up his reputation.'

The action of *The Virginians* appreciably quickens as Harry Warrington approaches the climax of his 'rake's progress' and the scene is set for George Warrington's reappearance. The most monotonous part of the book concerns Harry's initiation into English society. Thackeray realised this when, telling Dr. John Brown that he did not like the story 'half as much as you do,' he wrote on 4th November:

'Very good writing, but it ought to have been at its present stage of the story at No. x. I dawdled fatally between v. and x. . . . I am old, or I am tired, or some other reason.'

The reason lay in his ill-health and the consequently hurried composition. The story gathers momentum from the time when, having written the eleventh number during a Swiss holiday in July, he took a house at Brighton for the month of August, and continually travelling up and down from there to town, deriving benefit from the sea air and doing most of his writing in London among his books of history and reference, he began to write ahead of publication. Even so, illness still hindered concentration, and he fell frequently into fits of despondence.

'I am constantly unwell now,' he wrote to the Baxters on 23rd August, 'a fit of spasms—then get well in about

5 days; then 5 days grumbling and thinking of my work; then 14 days work and spasms da capo—and what a horribly stupid story I am writing! . . . No incident, no character, no go left in this dreary old expiring carcass.'

He was only forty-seven, but he felt, as he looked, an old man. Whimsically telling Dr. John Brown that he now knew no greater pleasure than a beefsteak and a bottle of claret, and could part even from them without a severe pang, he declared, 'At 47 Venus may rise from the sea, and I for one should hardly put on my spectacles to have a look.' He had five years to live, but they were years of continual physical suffering under the inexorable encroachment of incurable disease.

CHAPTER 15

§ 1

An unpleasant interlude, occurring during the summer of 1858, bore no significance in regard to Thackeray's life, but was distorted by the malignant into a libel upon his character. On 12th June, there appeared in a cheap weekly paper of the most vulgar sort, called *Town Talk*, an article on Thackeray under the heading of 'Literary Talk.' Divided into three parts, dealing with his appearance, his career, and his success, it was obviously the work of one of those enterprising scavenging scribblers, who have festered in every age since Edmund Curll fostered his own breed, mistaking impertinence for wit and slander for criticism. Describing his appearance, the article said:

'His face is bloodless, and not particularly expressive, but remarkable for the fracture of the bridge of the nose, the result of an accident in youth. He wears a small grey whisker, but otherwise is clean shaven. No one meeting him could fail to recognise in him a gentleman; his bearing is cold and uninviting, his style of conversation either openly cynical, or affectedly good-natured and benevolent; his *bonhomie* is forced, his wit biting, his pride easily touched —but his appearance is invariably that of the cool, *suave*, well-bred gentleman, who, whatever may be rankling within, suffers no surface display of his emotion.'

In the 'sketch' of his career, having referred in terms of the cheapest irony to *Mr. Brown's Letters*, it said: 'Here, too, were published his buffooneries, his *Ballads of Policeman X*, his *Jeames's Diary*, and some other scraps, the mere form of which consisted in outrages on orthography, and of which he is now deservedly ashamed.' Praising *Vanity Fair*, it declared that the book was 'offered to and rejected by several of the first publishers in London,' a legend which, though utterly unfounded, was believed by several serious chroniclers in defiance of Vizetelly's evidence and Thackeray's own published letter to Aytoun. Praising *The Newcomes* as 'perhaps the best of all' his books, it lied again by describing *Esmond* as falling 'almost still-born from the press.' Finally, commenting on the success of the *Humourist* lectures, it concluded:

'The prices were extravagant, the lecturer's adulation of birth and position was extravagant, the success was extravagant. No one succeeds better than Mr. Thackeray in cutting his coat according to his cloth. Here he flattered the aristocracy; but when he crossed the Atlantic, George Washington became the idol of his worship, the "Four Georges" the objects of his bitterest attacks. These last named lectures have been dead failures in England, though as literary compositions they are most excellent. Our own opinion is that his success is on the wane. His writings never were understood or appreciated even by the middle classes; the aristocracy have been alienated by his American onslaught on their body; and the educated and refined are not sufficiently numerous to constitute an audience. Moreover, there is a want of heart in all he writes, which is not to be balanced by the most brilliant sarcasm and the most perfect knowledge of the workings of the human heart.'

The distorted versions of Thackeray's subsequent conduct may be judged from Jeaffreson's fatuous suggestion that he was principally annoyed by the reference to his broken nose, perhaps the least offensive remark in the article, and from Burnand's assertion, written forty years after Thackeray's death,[1] that he was described in the article as 'a broken-nosed satirist.'

[1] *Records and Reminscences,* by Sir Francis C. Burnand. London, 2 vols., 1903.

THACKERAY IN 1863

From a crayon drawing by E. Goodwyn Lewis, Kensington Library

He was annoyed, as he had been with Deady Keane fifteen years before, for the personal remarks upon his private conversation and manners, which he considered a breach of common decency. Finding that the author was Edmund Yates, a young man associated with a variety of cheap journalism, whom he had occasionally met at the Garrick Club and greeted with the kindly courtesy he always maintained towards his juniors, he promptly wrote, on 14th June, a dignified but crushing letter of expostulation to him. Ignoring his comments on his work, 'which of course you are at liberty to praise or condemn as a literary critic,' he objected to the publication of 'an incorrect account of my private dealings with my publishers,' the imputation of insincerity in private conversation, of 'dishonourable motives . . . for sentiments which I have delivered in public,' and of 'advancing statements which I have never delivered at all.' He pointed out that, if the article had proceeded from a stranger, he would have noticed it 'no more than other calumnies,' but, coming from a fellow clubman, he felt obliged to refute remarks which he considered 'to be not offensive and unfriendly merely, but slanderous and untrue.' He concluded by informing Yates that club conversation was not intended for newspaper remark, and asking 'that you will refrain from printing comments upon my private conversation: that you will forego discussions, however blundering, upon my private affairs; and that you will henceforth please to consider any question of my personal truth and sincerity as quite out of the province of your criticism.'[1]

If Yates had written ingenuously, as he professed, he would now have approached Thackeray, offering either

[1] The whole of this tedious and voluminous correspondence was printed for private circulation by Yates, with intent to annoy Thackeray as much as possible, in *Mr. Thackeray, Mr. Yates, and the Garrick Club. The Correspondence and Facts. Stated by Edmund Yates.* London, 1859. It was reprinted, with an additional private letter from Dickens and even more impudent comments by Yates, in *Edmund Yates: His Recollections and Experiences.* London, 2 vols., 1884.

an apology or a manly explanation of his conduct. But the insect delighted to find that its bite was felt. He first indited a *tu quoque* letter, referring to Thackeray's own lampooning of Bulwer. But, before sending it, he showed it to Dickens, who deprecated its impudence and doubtless perceived the difference in the suggested parallel, knowing that Thackeray had never been acquainted with Bulwer, had on at least one occasion deliberately declined the opportunity of meeting him socially to avoid the chance of being charged with unfriendliness, and had since publicly expressed regret for his juvenile personalities. He counselled a more dignified reply and there is little doubt that he never saw beforehand the letter which Yates actually sent. Declining in insolent terms to 'accept your angry "understanding" of my "phrases," ' he proceeded:

'I cannot characterise your letter in any other terms than those in which you characterise the article which has given you so much offence. If your letter to me were not both "slanderous and untrue," I should readily have discussed its subject with you, and avowed my earnest and frank desire to set right anything I may have left wrong.'

Obviously Thackeray had over-estimated his man. Charles Reade would have entered into no private correspondence with such a 'criticaster' and 'anonymuncule'; he would have sued the author of the article for lies and libel, and mulcted him cheerfully of damages. Reade would have recognised the insect; Thackeray fell into the error of conceiving a member of his own club as a gentleman.

He placed the correspondence before the club committee, asking it to 'decide whether the complaints I have against Mr. Yates are not well founded, and whether the practice of publishing such articles as that which I enclose will not be fatal to the comfort of the Club, and is not intolerable in a society of gentlemen.' Yates at once began to shuffle, asking for time to consult his friends and 'prepare my own version of the matter.' Having consulted his friends and finding that he had no legs to stand upon in his attitude towards Thackeray, he objected to the authority of the committee to arbitrate, though he tentatively admitted that the article was 'in exceedingly bad taste' and 'most unintentionally, incorrect in details.'

The deliberations of the committee resulted in Yates being given the choice between a satisfactory apology to Thackeray and resignation from the club. Yates refused to apologise or to resign, but, badly frightened, ludicrously attempted to hedge by apologising to the club for having written the article, though declining to apologise personally to Thackeray. A general meeting of the club was then called, and the only members favouring Yates were the friends of Dickens, many of them, like Wilkie Collins, W. H. Wills, and Arthur Smith, his employees on *All the Year Round.* On the committee, Dickens stood alone. The result was Yates's expulsion from the club. His subsequent antics, including a law-suit against the club secretary, call for no comment, except that he derived no satisfaction except notoriety and that he had the effrontery, after personally soliciting Dickens's intervention, to pose as the unfortunate scapegoat of a personal quarrel between Dickens and Thackeray.

Jeaffreson, who reported a wildly improbable conversation with Thackeray on the subject, lent colour to Yates's posture thirty-five years after the event, by asserting that Thackeray told him he was not quarrelling with Yates, but 'hitting the man behind him.' Yet, when Thackeray addressed himself to Yates, Dickens had not appeared in the affair. Subsequently, he doubtless wished that he had never noticed the article on account of the unforeseen developments, but he had obviously no ulterior motive. As he told the Baxters on 25th August:

'I went away having got into trouble with a young fellow who told lies of me in a newspaper, which I was obliged to notice as we are acquaintances, and meet together at a little club. . . . The little papers are still going on abusing me about it, I hear—and don't care as I never read one.'

Naturally, he was wounded and offended by Dickens openly appearing against him on behalf of one who was, in plain words, a scurrilous slanderer, but the initiative was taken by Dickens.

One of Thackeray's principal biographers (General J. G. Wilson) declared, without any authority, that 'there had been some estrangement between Thackeray and Dickens since the autumn of 1853.' Yet, in the summer of the following year, they fraternised together at Boulogne, and Dickens had invited him to Tavistock House on Twelfth Night, 1857. Only four months before the Yates affair, early in February, they had corresponded about a literary charity which Thackeray desired to secure for an indigent friend. Without doubt Dickens's animosity was inspired by the knowledge that Thackeray still continued an informal member of the governing body of *Punch* and was on friendly terms with its proprietors, who were also his publishers and partners with Dickens in the publication of *Household Words*. On 12th June, the same day upon which Yates's offensive article appeared, Dickens, who had recently separated from his wife, published in *Household Words* a statement concerning his own conjugal differences which was condemned as a miracle of bad taste by even the devoted Forster. Having committed this indiscretion in a moment of exasperation with scandalous gossip and in defiance of his friends' advice, he took the bit of reason between his teeth and persisted in his reckless course of conduct. When the next number of *Punch* appeared without reprinting the statement from *Household Words*, he construed the omission as an unfriendly action on the part of the proprietors and the editor, Mark Lemon, his intimate friend, and forthwith declared his intention of severing his connection with Bradbury and Evans as partners in his paper. A brain so clear as Dickens's must have been bitterly conscious of the false position in which his temper had placed himself. He had set the whole town sniggering and sneering about his most intimate affairs, and close friends like Lemon and Forster did not hesitate to let him understand that they considered him guilty, not only of bad taste, but of unchivalrous conduct towards his wife. He was in this frame of mind when Yates came to him, charged with a breach of decency only less distasteful than his own. He defended Yates, because, in doing so, he defended his own conduct. He would have done the same, whoever Yates's adversary might have been: chance only ordained that it was Thackeray.

The estrangement between Dickens and Thackeray, therefore, arose from no feeling of rivalry or any act of hostility inspired by personally inimical motives. The insect Yates was the scapegoat—not of a quarrel between the two novelists—but of Dickens's struggle to sustain his self-respect. Neither Dickens nor Thackeray attempted any further hostilities, they merely ceased their former cordial, though never intimate, intercourse, and avoided meeting. Vizetelly relates that the breach was eventually healed by Thackeray, who, having passed Dickens in the hall of the Athenæum Club, suddenly turned back, and grasping his hand, declared that 'he could no longer bear their being ill friends.' James Payn, who walked away from Thackeray's grave in Dickens's company, bears witness to the fact that the latter's *In Memoriam* notice, for which payment was refused when it was written for the *Cornhill*, was inspired by genuinely friendly feeling. The friendship of Dickens's younger daughter for Thackeray's continued unabated, and her first husband, Charles Allston Collins, was one of Thackeray's closest friends in his latter years and a frequent visitor at his house.

Yates, however, besides appropriating to himself for the rest of his days the glory of having been the bone of contention between the two greatest novelists of their age, continued to snap at Thackeray's heels in the cheap press. In his book of memoirs, he discreetly omitted to mention the result of his final effort in 'society journalism' at Thackeray's expense. For the *New York Herald*, the only important American paper which had adversely criticised Thackeray's first series of lectures, he wrote an article against the *Cornhill Magazine* of the same mendacious and libellous pattern as that upon Thackeray. He declared that the magazine 'shows symptoms of being on the wane,' that its publisher, George Smith, was 'a very good man, but totally unread,' and that the monthly editorial dinners were 'tremendously heavy,' adding sundry sneers about the guests and conversation at the dinners. He had, of course, never been present at one of the dinners, but derived his information from some unguarded remarks by Anthony Trollope. Thackeray annihilated him in a paper. 'On Screens in Dining Rooms,' appearing in the *Cornhill* for August 1860, and writing of Yates to W. D. Robinson on 26th September, he remarked: 'In consequence of this last business even Dickens has cut him.'

§ 2

George Smith venerated Thackeray as the greatest genius of his generation. To secure the honour of publishing *Esmond* and even such a trifle as *The Kickleburys on the Rhine*, he deprecated the discussion of money, giving the author what he asked without attempting to bargain. Thackeray's loyalty to Bradbury and Evans denied Smith the privilege of publishing either *The Newcomes* or *The Virginians*, and he foresaw that the novelist's quixotic sense of fairness would prevent him from ever placing elsewhere a novel for publication in numbers, while his old publishers were willing to offer reasonable terms. Smith therefore projected a magazine, the primary object of which was to serve as a medium for the publication of Thackeray's work. In a proposal dated 19th February 1859, when *The Virginians* was still appearing in monthly numbers, he offered Thackeray a salary of £350 a month to work exclusively for his firm, which retained the right to publish his novels serially in its magazine and subsequently in volume form, to receive all moneys accruing from American and translation rights, and to share equally with the author the profits of any cheap reprints. The proposition was eminently suited to Thackeray's inclinations, since it relieved him of the tiresome responsibility of business negotiations and offered at the same time a stabilised income, and he readily accepted it.

Smith then hesitated over the choice of a suitable editor. Unable to make up his mind, the idea occurred to him of asking Thackeray to accept the post. He had no illusions about the novelist's capacity to perform the function successfully, but he appreciated the glamour of his name, realising that he possessed 'a great reputation with men of letters as well as with the public, and any writer would be proud to contribute to a periodical under his editorship.' Deciding himself 'to supplement any want of business qualifications' on the part of his editor, he proposed to assume a secret control similar to that contrived by old William Blackwood when founding his magazine. Thackeray, for whom the launching of a periodical possessed the same fascination which had lured him to ruin in his youth, welcomed the proposal, for he had cherished some notion, which he confided to George Hodder, of founding a magazine bearing his own name, after the fashion of *Ainsworth's Magazine*, *Hood's Own*, and *Douglas Jerrold's Shilling Magazine*, on his return from his second visit to America. He accepted the editorship at a salary of a thousand a year, and it was he who christened the periodical as the *Cornhill Magazine*, deriving the name from the street in which the publishers' office was situated and setting a fashion followed by *Temple Bar*, *Belgravia*, *St. Paul's Magazine*, the *Pall Mall*, the *Strand*, and others.

The first nine months of 1859, like the whole of the preceding year, were monopolised by *The Virginians*. His 'attacks of spasms' recurred frequently, often at the rate of two a month, and his elder daughter, in a letter to Dr. John Brown, spoke of him having been well for nearly six weeks as a phenomenal period of freedom from suffering. The last number of the novel appeared in October; it was only completed in early September. Thus, to the end, he wrote it month by month for the waiting press, the extent to which he was hindered by illness being reflected in the postponement of his usual summer holiday on the Continent. He departed for the Mediterranean as soon as the task was completed, travelling from Tours to Genoa, Milan, Como, and finally to Chur, where his elder daughter fell ill. Here he wrote the first of the *Roundabout Papers*—'On a Lazy Idle Boy.' His attention was absorbed by the new magazine and the dazzling financial prospect it presented. To his mother he wrote on 1st October:

'If I can work for 3 years now, I shall have put back my patrimony and a little over—after 30 years of ups and downs. I made a calculation the other day of receipts in the last 20 years and can only sum up about 32000£ of moneys actually received, for which I have values and disbursement of 13000£ so that I haven't spent at the rate of more than 1000£ a year for 20 years. The profits of the lectures figure as the greatest of the receipts 9500£ —*Virginians* 6—*Vanity Fair* only 2. 3 years more, please the Fates, and the girls will then have the 8 or 10000 a piece that I want for them: and we mustn't say a word against filthy lucre, for I see the use and comfort of it every day more and more. What a blessing not to mind about bills!'

'If I can work for 3 years now!' He had four years yet to live, and he died in the midst of a second *Esmond.* What an Odyssey of penance for a modest crop of wild oats wasted on Mr. Deuceace and a brace of newspapers!

On his return to England he gave all his time to the magazine, his prospectus appearing in November, the month in which the first number of *Macmillan's Magazine* made its bow. He announced that the aim of the magazine was 'to amuse and interest,' and while fiction was to be a prominent feature, they wanted 'as much reality as possible —discussion and narrative of events interesting to the public, personal adventures and observations, familiar reports of scientific discovery, description of Social Institutions . . . there is hardly any subject we *don't* want to hear about, from lettered and instructed men who are competent to speak on it.' There was to be no party label or sectarian bias, and the moral tone was to render the magazine fit entertainment for family consumption.

In promising 'competent fellow-labourers a welcome and a good wage,' he made no flamboyant gesture. The magazine became celebrated for the munificence of its payment, George Eliot receiving seven thousand pounds for *Romola,* while Thackeray himself was paid twelve guineas a page for the *Roundabout Papers.* He wrote personally to invite contributions from numerous friends, including Longfellow, Tennyson, Carlyle, and George Augustus Sala, for whose work in *Household Words* he once expressed admiration to Hodder. Tennyson, declining because he had sent *Macmillan's* his only suitable poem, expressed pleasure at hearing from 'my good old friend' and regret that 'you have engaged for any quantity of money to let your brains be sucked periodically by Smith, Elder & Co.' Carlyle, working on his *Frederick the Great,* confessed that he was 'so crushed to death amid Prussian rubbish these long years past, I have nearly lost the power of thinking in any form,' and wondering 'how am I to get out of this cursed thing alive,' promised to write an article when he could think of a subject. Dr. John Brown offered a similar excuse, but Milnes, Landseer, Sala, and others responded readily to the invitation, while 'Father Prout,' devoted henchman and almost the first man of letters Thackeray had ever met, came forward with his 'Inauguration Ode,' dedicated to the author of *Vanity Fair*.

Thackeray himself, besides the *Roundabout Papers*, arranged, in accordance with his contract, to serialise a new novel, *Lovel the Widower*, based upon a play, originally entitled *The Shorn Lamb*, but afterwards altered to *The Wolves and the Lamb*, which had been actually offered to and rejected by Alfred Wigan at the Olympic Theatre in 1855. A second serial was deemed advisable, however, and Anthony Trollope was commissioned to write *Framley Parsonage*. Hearing of the new magazine, Trollope had written personally to Thackeray, offering to write some short stories. Within a week he received two replies, the first from the publishers offering terms for a serial story, the second from Thackeray himself. This letter, dated 28th October, was printed at length by Trollope in his *Autobiography*, and supplies an example of Thackeray's graceful courtesy as an editor. He had never met Trollope, yet he went out of his way to express pleasure at securing his collaboration in a letter which, as Trollope's biographer observes, 'with its neat phrasing and its pleasant compliment to *The Three Clerks* . . . is an answer such as Thackeray alone—the prince of letter-courtesy—would have had the intuition or have taken the trouble to write.'[1]

Reluctantly Trollope afterwards admitted that 'Thackeray was not a good editor.'[2] His publisher had never expected him to be otherwise when he employed him, and he quietly pursued the policy of allowing Thackeray to perform his

[1] *Trollope: A Commentary*, by Michael Sadleir. London, 1927.

[2] *Thackeray*, by Anthony Trollope. (English Men of Letters Series.) London, 1879.

function as he pleased, while the humdrum duties of routine devolved upon lesser men. Thackeray rarely read a manuscript; he would hand them to his daughters, to his secretary, or to Smith's readers, and abide by their verdict. Once he returned a story of Trollope's which had been commissioned, unknown to him, by the publisher, writing a long letter of apology for such treatment of a valued contributor, but—*virginibus puerisque*—Trollope being considered an only less salacious writer than Charles Reade in those days! Trollope bore no resentment, justly suspecting that the editor had never read the manuscript himself but relied upon the verdict of 'some moral deputy,' but Thackeray was so afraid of having given offence that he delayed opening Trollope's letter in reply. For similar reasons of propriety he was compelled to reject a poem of Mrs. Browning's, and his daughter printed, in the biographical introduction to *Philip*, a letter of graceful charm and conciliatory compliment which must have taken him an hour to write, exclaiming: 'Who am I to refuse the poems of Elizabeth Browning?' and 'to have to say no to my betters is one of the hardest duties I have.'

He maintained equal courtesy to obscure contributors, who not only sent in shoals of worthless manuscripts but pestered him for advice about the possibilities of their writings and future career, many even addressing their appeals to his private house. To one of these he once compiled a laboriously courteous epistle, explaining in the tenderest terms that, since his advice was asked, he recommended his correspondent to seek some other field of industry, since his contribution plainly revealed him unsuited to the profession of letters. To his astonishment he received a most offensive and abusive reply. In a *Roundabout Paper* entitled 'Thorns in the Cushion,' he related his editorial woes with a finely tempered humour verging upon pathos, quoting examples of the letters he received, with the remark, 'Before I was an editor I did not like the postman much;—but now!' Referring to one letter, from a contributor pleading poverty, sickness, an ailing and widowed mother, hungry children, he described the sinking heart with which he realised the impossibility of accepting the worthless contribution. 'No day passes,' he declared, 'but that argument *ad misericordiam* is used.' And as often as it was used, though unable to publish their pitiful stories and poems, as often he responded by enclosing a banknote with the rejected manuscript! His publisher observed with truth that 'Thackeray was far too tender-hearted to be happy as an editor.'

He made a further graceful gesture to Trollope by according pride of place in the first number to *Framley Parsonage*, which appeared at the front of the magazine, while *Lovel the Widower* took a back seat. Naturally, Trollope eagerly anticipated an introduction to the great novelist who had behaved towards him with such courtesy and cordiality. Their meeting, however, was almost a tragedy. Every month the publisher gave a dinner at his house to his editor and contributors. Inviting Trollope to one of these, he presented him to Thackeray, who, to Smith's surprise and Trollope's anger, said curtly: 'How do?' and turned away. Furiously indignant, Trollope swore that he would never speak to Thackeray again, and only Smith's tact averted a misunderstanding which might have marred the friendly relations between the two novelists. As Smith explained, Thackeray was afflicted by sudden spasms of internal pain, the severity of which rendered him incapable of thought or speech. Nearly three years before, Dr. John Brown had to perform Smith's office of intermediary with Lady Trevelyan, whom Thackeray had similarly offended by apparent discourtesy in a moment of physical agony. Sala, too, relates how he was one day walking with him in Piccadilly, chatting cheerfully, when he suddenly stopped outside a shop with an excuse that he wanted to buy something, and making a stately bow as he extended an icy-cold hand, stalked off, leaving the astonished Sala with the impression that he had suddenly forgotten his existence. Those ignorant of his physical infirmity not unnaturally ascribed such conduct to an affected eccentricity of manner, but the effect of the attacks was not confined to social irregularities. He confessed to Bayard Taylor that he wrote the *Roundabout Paper*, 'On Half a Loaf,' in a fit of spleen occasioned by reading, during an attack of illness, a suggestion by his old enemy, the *New York Herald*, that England would necessarily refrain from hostilities against America rather than risk the confiscation of American securities in the hands of English stockholders. Some years after his death, when reading the *Roundabout Papers*, FitzGerald wondered 'at his getting so fretted by what was said of him as some of these Papers show that he was; very unlike his old self, surely,' and reflected that his ill-health 'had something to do with this.' Probably his irritation against Yates was aggravated by illness, and likewise an affair which promised to assume similarly unpleasant notoriety when wagging tongues were silenced by the news of his death.

In the *Athenæum* of 25th April 1863 there appeared a scathing review, in the slashing style of Mr. Bludyer, of a novel called *The Story of Elizabeth.* The authoress of the novel was Anne Thackeray; the anonymous reviewer, on the authority of John Cordy Jeaffreson, was Geraldine Jewsbury, the friend of Jane Carlyle. Thackeray, however, was ignorant of the reviewer's identity; bitterly resenting the ferocity of the attack upon his daughter's first novel, he fastened the responsibility for the article upon Hepworth Dixon, the editor of the *Athenæum*, and his right-hand man, Jeaffreson, both of whom were members, like himself, of an institution called 'Our Club,' founded by Douglas Jerrold for journalists and literary men and holding its convivial meetings at Clunn's Hotel, next door to Evans's in Covent Garden. Two months later Dixon appeared as the principal promoter of a scheme to celebrate the tercentenary of Shakespeare. A committee having been formed, various notabilities were asked to become vice-presidents, the names selected to represent literature being Bulwer Lytton, Tennyson, Dickens, and Thackeray. The invitations were signed by Dixon as general secretary, and no reply was received from Thackeray. A second invitation, signed by Jeaffreson as Dixon's deputy, met with a similar fate. At a subsequent meeting of the committee, when Henry Vizetelly proposed that a further invitation should be extended, Dixon and Jeaffreson objected on the grounds that another application, after two refusals, would derogate from the dignity of the committee, and having a considerable following, 'composed of contributors to the *Athenæum* and timid literary men who trembled for their next book,' succeeded in defeating the motion.

Vizetelly wreaked vengenace by publishing an account of the proceedings in his paper, the *Illustrated Times*, which aroused vigorous comment from its contemporaries, Laurence Oliphant indignantly denouncing the disingenuousness of the committee in entrusting such an invitation to 'the David and Jonathan of a literary organ whose columns had been disfigured by a virulent and indecent criticism, needlessly cruel, offensive and unjust—on Miss Thackeray's charming novel,' when it was known that the father of the authoress resented the criticism and attributed its authorship, 'rightly or wrongly,' to one or both of them. At this juncture Thackeray's death was announced, and in an hysterical fervour of sentimental sympathy, the committee collapsed under the weight of a protest, headed by Theodore Martin and Shirley Brooks, against their proceedings. To all this stupid and trifling bickering Thackeray contributed nothing in word or deed, beyond declining to enter upon any correspondence or intercourse with Dixon and Jeaffreson. In pursuance of this policy he resolutely declined to enter the premises of 'Our Club' after presiding at its Shakespeare dinner on 25th April, the day on which the offending *Athenæum* article appeared. The secretary of the club, Frederick William Hamstede, a poor little hunchback who owed his position and countless kindnesses to Jerrold and Thackeray, secured a majority of the members to assure him that, if he would return to the club, they would take steps to compel the withdrawal of Hepworth Dixon, but he replied that he had already driven one man out of a club and had no desire to incur the odium of a repetition. It was of this affair that Shirley Brooks, who figures as one of his most prominent supporters, wrote to E. S. Dallas, another member of 'Our Club':

'I wish . . . that Thackeray would leave off caring about the snarls of these little Bohemian curs. They know he writhes, and therefore snap whenever they can. . . . Shakespeare be blowed. It's all cackle, but one daren't say so, except to the elect.'

§ 3

The phenomenal success of the *Cornhill Magazine* marked an epoch in the history of periodical literature. Having calculated upon a circulation little exceeding ten thousand copies, everybody was astounded by the sales of the first number mounting to the stupendous figure of 120,000. Thackeray was delirious with delight, declaring joyously that he could scarcely sleep 'for counting up his subscribers,' and Smith, jubilant at the public vindication of his judgment and appreciating his debt to the magic of Thackeray's name, promptly insisted upon doubling his editor's salary. Thackeray was much touched by his publisher's munificence, and repaid him by never once demurring to any proposal propounded by him, though Smith always consulted him on any point of policy, such consultations taking place, at Thackeray's request, over a pleasant dinner-table at Greenwich, where the third party was usually Sir Charles Taylor, the boon companion of his latter years, a member of the Garrick Club and a noted *bon viveur*. He was overwhelmed by his sudden access to wealth, exclaiming to James T. Fields, 'How can I spend the princely income which Smith allows me . . . unless I begin instantly somewhere?' In this mood he wrote on 4th May 1860:

'We've got two horses in our carriage now. The magazine goes on increasing and how much do you think my next twelve months' earnings and receipts will be if I work? £10,000! Cockadoodleoddloodle. We are going to spend four thousand in building a new house on Palace Green, Kensington. We have our health. We have brought Granny and G. P. to live at Brompton Crescent, close to us.'

After more than twenty years of exile in Paris, his parents were persuaded to return to London. But they did not live long at Brompton Crescent, for the gallant old gentleman, who had filled more than a father's place in his stepson's affection, died on 9th September 1861, aged eighty-one. Thackeray buried him at Ayr, and beneath a simple inscription on the memorial tablet appears the word *Adsum*, followed by the quotation from the end of *The Newcomes*: 'And lo, he, whose heart was as that of a little child, had answered to his name, and stood in the presence of The Master.' After his death the widow went to live with her son, whom she survived by a year, dying on 17th December 1864.

Writing of the *Cornhill* to Pollock on 23rd February 1860, FitzGerald said:

'Thackeray's first number was famous, I thought: his own little *Roundabout Paper* so pleasant: but the Second Number, I say, lets the Cockney in already: about Hogarth: Lewes is vulgar: and I don't think one can care much for Thackeray's Novel. He is always talking so of himself, too.'

No writer was more autobiographical than Thackeray. His journalistic apprenticeship, when the necessity of writing articles and stories with the utmost rapidity rendered him eager to seize upon any personal incident or observation for a subject, had encouraged the habit of introspective self-examination, which owed its origin to his mother's fond delight in receiving letters from him concerning his own thoughts and actions. The personal element in his published work became more and more pronounced, as FitzGerald observed, in later years, when illness deepened his melancholy, when the knowledge that his years were numbered aggravated his propensity for reminiscence, and when, moreover, his rupture with the Brookfields deprived him of a private outlet for the overflow of his overwrought feelings. The period of inspired parturition as a novelist closed with *The Newcomes*; the *Cornhill* opened a new field for his genius by offering an opportunity for the *Roundabout Papers*, which comprise his claim to consideration as the greatest exponent of the *causerie* essay since Elia.

Little can be said for *Lovel the Widower*. Plotless, discursive, void of incident, Thackeray himself must have realised its ineffectiveness, and, in exasperation, he summarily cut it short after six instalments, with the determination to start afresh upon a more resilient subject. The habit of harking back sentimentally to old scenes and sorrows suggested the subject of *Philip*, which was not merely a sequel to *A Shabby Genteel Story*, written under the torment of his wife's illness and frigidly received in *Fraser*, but sought also to revivify in the history of its hero the stress and struggle of those distant days. But the disillusioned indifference of age denied realistic rehabilitation of those remote emotions, for, as he told Mrs. Brookfield in 1851: 'I was a boy ten years ago, bleating out my simple cries in *The Great Hoggarty Diamond*.' 'Yesterday is gone, yes,' he wrote at Christmas, 1860, 'but very well remembered. And we think of it the more now we know that To-morrow is not going to bring us much.' And *Philip* possesses the mellow philosophy and reflective melancholy of grey hairs living among memories; striking a note of detachment, it lacks the virility and verve of spontaneous inspiration. With characteristic perception he early recognised the deficiency, for having written the lines in Chapter VI: 'There's Mr. Pendennis, who comes to see Mr. Ridley. I wonder how a married man can go on writing about love, and all that stuff!'—he added in the text of his story the comment which he actually addressed at the same time to the Baxters: 'And, indeed, it is rather absurd for elderly fingers to be still twanging Dan Cupid's toy bow and arrows.' Lever quoted him as once remarking: 'No old man must prate about love,' and he horrified the sedate Ticknor, who was discoursing upon the tender passion to a crowded dinner-table while he was in America, by suddenly exclaiming: 'What has the world come to, when two broken-nosed old fogies like you and me sit talking about love to each other?'

Writing on 'a bitter cold Christmas day' that he was 'unwell' and 'hard at work trying to get the new story on ahead,' he had lost the exhilarating, exultant mood, excited by the success of *Cornhill* in the previous spring. Speaking of his daughters, he remarked:

'I have not made their fortunes as yet, but am getting towards it and have saved a little since I wrote last; but I am free-handed, have to keep my wife, to help my parents, and to give to poor literary folks—in fine my expenses are very large. I am supposed to make 10,000£ a year. Write 5 and it is about the mark. Health very soso. Repeated attacks of illness. Great thankfulness to God Almighty for good means, for good children. And thats all.'

However much money he had, he would never have been free from financial anxiety. In his accession to affluence by means of the *Cornhill* he had begun to build a new house in Queen Anne style on Kensington Palace Green, which was to cost '6000£ and 100£ a year ground rent.' He had invested largely in American railway stock, and feared the loss of his dividends on account of the Civil War. He even considered letting his new house—'the reddest house in all the town'—on its completion, as he might then have been able to live 'almost without writing but then you know wife and parents are expensive.' After Macaulay's death at the end of 1859—with the first number of *Cornhill*, open at the first page of *Lovel the Widower*, on his reading stand—he was approached with a proposition to continue his *History of England*. Eagerly entertaining the idea, which was just the type of work he had promised himself when the creative vein began to thin, he proposed to write his *History of Queen Anne* in his new Queen Anne house. The time had come for the undertaking of such a task, for which he was eminently suited by his research for *Esmond* and *The Virginians*. But he still needed more money before he could resign himself to a comparatively unremunerative class of work. If he had lived another thirty years, he would have been writing fiction at the end, for he would still have needed money—it was out of his nature to save.

He delighted in the new house. When John Blackwood came up to town early in June 1861, he said: 'It was pleasant to see old Thack., as delighted as a child, showing me all over it.' The next day he went with Thackeray to the Blue Posts, 'where he seemed a sort of king, and we got a dinner and wines such as I never saw in the house before.' Whitwell Elwin, too, was invited up from his Norfolk rectory to look over it, and exclaimed in amazement when he declared that he would 'go to Greenwich and write a bit of *Philip*.'

'I cannot write comfortably in my own room,' he explained, 'I do most of my composition at hotels or at a club. There is an excitement at public places which sets my brain working.'

This habit was acquired in the course of his ubiquitous life, and, in consequence, his manuscripts usually consisted of all sorts of odds and ends, sheets of club and hotel notepaper, the backs of letters, and fly-leaves torn out of books. But, in his latter years, when he was frequently ill and yet compelled to work on his monthly numbers, he frequently dictated from his bed of sickness to his daughter or a secretary. After his second visit to America, he removed from his little back room in the Onslow Square house to a large apartment upstairs, which consisted of two rooms, bedroom and sitting-room, thrown into one, and divided only by a curtain. Lying in bed, often in agony, he would dictate through the dividing curtain to George Hodder, who described the apartment, as did John Hollingshead, who visited Thackeray there and found him resting on 'an iron truckle bedstead,' while his secretary wrote at a table by the window. This secretary was Hodder's successor, one Samuel Langley, who appears to have been the same S. Langley who, some ten or twelve years later, was employed by Charles Reade to ransack the newspaper-files of the British Museum for *materia novæ fabulæ*.

He moved into the new house in March 1862, the same month in which he resigned the editorship of *Cornhill*. In his farewell address, published in the April number and dated 18th March, he hoped 'long to remain a contributor to my friend's magazine' and 'stipulated for the liberty of continuing the little essays which have amused the public and the writer.' He also announced the preparation of another novel, 'on which I have worked at intervals for many years past, and which I hope to introduce in the ensuing year.' His idea was to resurrect the rudiments of that forgotten mediæval romance in 'the Queen-Hoo style,' recommended to him by Barham in 1841, for, discussing his plans with his mother after finishing *Philip*, he said: 'I think the story which I began 20 years ago and then, and then—' But the mediæval story was never written after all, as he decided to make further use of his intimate knowledge of the eighteenth century in *Denis Duval*.

He had never expected to retain the editorship for a long period. On undertaking the office, he had written to Longfellow on 16th November 1859:

'I am pressed into the service of this magazine, and engaged to write ever so much more for the next three years. Then, if I last so long, I shall be free of books and publishers.'

He was not free, and never would have been free. He was doomed to die in harness to his pen, dragging at the bridle which had driven him since his marriage on the strength of a salary paid by an insecurely established newspaper. Increased illness demanded his resignation; the task of writing a serial novel in time for monthly printing now taxed his strength to its limit, precluding the distracting responsibility of editorial duties. He was repeatedly pressed for time in delivering his copy, writing on 18th April, the month following his resignation: 'The May number not finished until to-day, after repeated derangements.' Suffering acutely from recent attacks, he went over to Paris to consult a specialist. The verdict was given with devastating frankness. He had a fatal disease and could not live beyond a prescribed date. Contemplating the possibility of the diagnosis being correct, he remarked to his publisher, '. . . in which case good-bye Queen Anne, or rather I shall see her sooner than I expected.' He suffered such excruciating agony from his ever more frequent attacks that death assumed to him the aspect of a benevolent release. A London doctor denied the accuracy of the Parisian's opinion, but Thackeray felt no pleasurable relief.

'I am constantly ill,' he wrote, on 9th May. 'A Doctor told me at Paris t'other day that I had a fatal complaint and I wasn't very sorry. It turns out not to be true—but, but, but . . .'

Some months before he had reason to suspect such a doom as the Parisian predicted, and characteristically sketched his emotions in the *Roundabout Paper*, 'On Letts's Diary,' appearing in the *Cornhill* for January 1862.

He finished *Philip*, to which he justly applied much the same criticism he had delivered on *The Virginians*—that it 'had not enough story'—on 3rd July. Two days later he wrote to his mother:

> 'On Thursday at 6.15 p.m. after working all day I wrote Finis to *Philip*: rather a lame ending. Yesterday I spent all day in great delectation and rest of mind making a very bad drawing. Young Walker who is 20 does twice as well: and at 20 you know we all thought I was a genius at drawing.'

Frederick Walker owed his recognition as an illustrator to Thackeray. Since the days when Vizetelly had supplied young artists to touch up his drawings, Eyre Crowe had for some time fulfilled that function, but when Thackeray began to illustrate *Philip*, he sent his sketches to the engraver, Joseph Swain, who, like Vizetelly, employed other artists to transfer them to the wood and add such improvements as his principal allowed. Walker did some of this work, succeeding so well that George Smith suggested to Thackeray that he was a likely artist to execute drawings from the novelist's designs. When Thackeray sent for him to make a test of his abilities, the young artist was in an agony of trembling nervousness. Perceiving his agitation, Thackeray said kindly: 'I'm going to shave; would you mind drawing my back?' thus considerately relieving the artist of the self-conscious feeling that he was being watched. The result was so satisfactory that Walker was commissioned to repeat the drawing as a frontispiece to the *Roundabout Paper*, 'Round About the Christmas Tree,' and to copy Thackeray's designs for the illustrations. Very soon he became dissatisfied with the menial nature of his task, and declined to continue on the ground that he wished to do original work. So far from resenting the young man's rebellion, Thackeray agreed that he should supply the remainder of the illustrations, providing that he accepted the author's suggestions of suitable subjects, and from May 1861 onwards, the drawings for *Philip* were by the hand of Walker.[1] On 21st July 1862 *Philip* was published in three volumes by Smith, Elder, with a dedication to 'Jacob Omnium,' 'in grateful remembrance of old friendship and kindness.'

Frederick Walker was one of a coterie of young artists who found a warm welcome at Palace Green. Millais, who had cherished a warm friendship for Thackeray for several years, was another. Many years afterwards he wrote to W. P. Frith: 'I found Thackeray always kind, and got on better with him than I did with Dickens but then I knew him & saw more of him.' He walked beside Walker and Theodore Martin to 'poor Thackeray's funeral' on 29th December 1863 at Kensal Green Cemetery. His close friend, Charles Collins, the brother of Wilkie, was even more intimate with Thackeray, and it was for him and his wife, Dickens's younger daughter, that the daughters sent, on making the dread discovery of that tragic Christmas Eve.

§ 4

Of late years, he had repeatedly expressed dread of the day when either of his daughters should marry. In their society and that of their young friends he now sought the little pleasure permitted by his health. When his adopted daughter, Amy Crowe, married his young cousin, Edward Thackeray, V.C., on 2nd December 1862, he spent the afternoon at Millais' studio in a state of abject misery at the thought of losing her.[2] He took more delight in his

[1] Cf. *Life and Letters of Frederick Walker*, by J. G. Marks. London, 1896.

[2] *Life and Letters of Sir John Everett Millais*, by his son, J. G. Millais. London, 2 vols., 1899.

elder daughter's success as a novelist than in any work of his own, though he confessed that he never read the only novel written by her during his lifetime, *The Story of Elizabeth*. 'I tried to, but I broke down,' he told George Smith, and when Fanny Kemble remonstrated with him, pointing out that it would give him pleasure, he declared that he couldn't: 'It would tear my guts out!' All the great capacity for tenderness, which he had formerly lavished upon the two women he had loved, was now concentrated on his children, for whose welfare he had devoted the latter half of his broken life.

In his state of health, with the knell of doom sounding in his ears, memories of old times pursued each other through his teeming brain, thus accounting for the autobiographical element and surprisingly vivid reminiscences of distant youth in his last writings. In December 1862 he attended Founder's Day at Charterhouse, reviving his old antagonism against Dr. Russell and his scribbling sketches clandestinely drawn under cover of his Latin grammar. At the following Easter he visited Milnes at Fryston, along with James Spedding. Carlyle was to be there, but cried off on account of his *Frederick the Great*, so leaving the three old Cantabs to cast back to Trinity days, to the *Snob* and *Gownsman*, to Tennyson's prize poem and Thackeray's parody. On 15th May he reviewed *Cruikshank's Gallery* in *The Times*, recalling that essay in the *London and Westminster* of long ago, the hack work for Cruikshank's almanacks, and their merry tavern meetings. He was the celebrity now, performing a kindness to the lesser man, for Cruikshank was old and broken, an object of derision by means of his fanatical advocacy of teetotalism—he, the former rollicking *bon viveur*. On 16th June he dined at the Garrick with E. S. Dallas, John Blackwood, Shirley Brooks, and Charles Reade—they had 'capital fun.'

He had commenced *Denis Duval* early in the year, but now his attacks were so frequent and devastating in their consequences that he did not dare to commence publication as he wrote the numbers. Doubtless, too, aware of the decay visible in his recent novels, he wished to write at leisure in the hope of achieving that book, completely satisfying in its perfection, which he had been yearning to write since the time of *Pendennis*. He took an infinity of pains over its composition, writing in May to the widow of his cousin, William Ritchie:

'For the last ten days I have been almost *non compos mentis*. When I am in labour with a book I don't quite know what happens. I sit for hours before my paper, not doing my book, but incapable of doing anything else, and thinking upon that subject always, waking with it, walking about with it, and going to bed with it. Oh, the struggles and bothers—oh, the throbs and pains about this trumpery!'

A daughter of his dead cousin, who stayed with him during the autumn, described his absorption 'in the full vein of historical romance,' of the long discussions with young Walker about proposed illustrations, of the fastidious detail of his research, which is witnessed in the published notes, edited by his *Cornhill* colleague, Frederick Greenwood.[1] On its completion he had considered *Esmond* the most perfect of his books, and he intended *Denis Duval* to surpass it in its own kind—to stand as his *magnum opus*. Yet his physical agonies often banished all mundane interest and pleasure. 'Did you read about poor Buckle when he got the fever at Damascus crying out, "O my book, my book!" ' he asked his mother. 'I don't care enough about mine to be disquieted, when that day comes.'

He wondered if he would live even to begin his *History of Queen Anne*. The prospect appeared remote, for he still worried over money matters, feeling much misgiving about his reckless expenditure in building the new house.

[1] Cf. *Some Family Letters of W. M. Thackeray, together with Recollections by his Kinswoman, Blanche Warre Cornish.* New York, 1911.

'If I don't mistake there was a man who lived at Abbotsford overhoused himself,' he wrote to Dr. John Brown, on 23rd September. 'I am not in debt, thank my stars, but instead of writing to you why am I not writing the history of Denis Duval, Esq., Admiral of the White Squadron?'

The parallel between himself and Scott, as that with Charles Lamb in earlier times, had occurred to him seven years before, when lecturing at Edinburgh, suffering from illness, yet persevering with his distasteful task in that ever-present determination to provide adequately for his daughters. Then he had remarked: 'I have been reading Walter Scott's Life all day and how at 60 odd he sat down to pay off a debt of 130,000£ with his pen. What a courage!' He himself had girded up his loins to replace his patrimony more than twenty-five years before, and he, like Scott, was at work to the last.

Early in December Charles Mackay saw him sitting with Leech in Evans's. Both were complaining of illness, yet both looked well, though one had a few weeks to live and the other only months. Thackeray himself, wistfully surveying his face in a mirror, asked his daughter: 'I am sure I look well enough, don't I?' Yet pain tortured him with unendurable agony. 'If I could get a month's ease,' he told George Smith on 17th December, 'I could finish the eight numbers handsomely with the marriage of Denis and Agnes, after the capture of Toulon by the English.' He rallied well, only to be seized as suddenly again by torment. Carlyle, 'riding in the dusk, heavy of heart, along by the Serpentine and Hyde Park,' was roused from his reverie by 'some human brother from a chariot, with a young lady in it,' throwing him 'a shower of salutations . . . it was Thackeray with his daughter: the last time I was to see him in this world.' On Monday, 21st December, he was at Charles Collins's house, as his host told his brother Wilkie, 'in famous spirits and full of fun.'

The next day he kept to his bed—another 'attack of

spasms.' His daughters were not unduly alarmed, as 'he had so often been ill and rallied,' but his widowed mother, who had lost both her husbands, perceived, with instinctive insight, that the time had come for a last parting, before a journey whence her only son would write no more of the letters which used to give her such delight. On the morning of Christmas Eve they found him, stretched upon his bed, his arms above his head, grasping the bed-rail in a last paroxysm of pain, which had stayed for ever the beating of his heart. They found his body, but the great soul had passed—unobtrusively, solitary, winging its way in the grey light of dawn, wondering wistfully, not of what lay beyond, but of the joys and sorrows left behind. But it left yet more behind—an indelible mark upon the scroll of fame, a great legacy bequeathed by genius, a memory perennially green. As FitzGerald wrote a few days later, 'A great Figure has sunk under Earth.'

APPENDIX I

THACKERAY'S LIFE AT A GLANCE: SUMMARY OF EVENTS

1811	18th July	Born at Calcutta.
1815	13th September	Death of his father.
1817	November	Arrival in England from India.
1818		At school in Hampshire and at Chiswick.
		Marriage of his mother to Major Henry Carmichael-Smyth.
1822	January	At school at Charterhouse.
1825		His parents move to Larkbeare, South Devon.
1828	April	Leaves Charterhouse.
1829	February	Goes up to Trinity College, Cambridge.
1830	July	Goes to Germany.
1831	Spring	Returns from Germany.
	Autumn	With Mr. Taprell at 1 Hare Court, Temple.
1832	June	Electioneering in Cornwall.
	18th July	Comes of age and abandons the law.
1833	May-December	Elected member of the Garrick Club.
		Paris correspondent of the *National Standard*.
1834	1st February	Last number of the *National Standard*.
1834-35		Studying art in Paris.
1836	1st March	*Flore et Zéphyr* published.
	20th August	Marries Isabella G. C. Shawe at Paris.
1836-37	September-July	Paris correspondent of the *Constitutional*.
1837	9th June	Birth of his daughter Anne.
	August	Appointed literary reviewer on *The Times*.

1837	August	Writing for *Fraser's Magazine*, *Bentley's Miscellany*, and *London and Westminster Review*.
		Living at 13 Great Coram Street.
1838	January-August	*Yellowplush Papers* in *Fraser*.
		Major Gahagan in the *New Monthly*.
		Member of the Sterling Club.
1839		Writing *Catherine* and articles by Titmarsh for *Fraser*, articles for *British and Foreign* and *London and Westminster* Reviews, *Anti-Corn Law Circular*, etc., and *The Great Hoggarty Diamond* (published *Fraser*, September-December, 1841).
	August	Appointed European correspondent of the New York *Corsair*.
1840	April	Writing essay on Cruikshank for *London and Westminster* (published June) and *Dionysius Diddler*.
	28th May	His daughter, Harriet Marian (Minny) born.
	July	The *Paris Sketch Book* published.
	Summer	Illness of his wife—writing *A Shabby Genteel Story* (published *Fraser*, June, August, October).
	August-September	At Margate.
	December	Writing *The Second Funeral of Napoleon* at Paris.
1841	February-December	Employed on the *Britannia* newspaper.
	March	Working on mediæval novel at Paris.
	May	*Comic Tales and Sketches* published.
	Autumn	In Paris.
1842		Writing *Fitz-Boodle Papers* for *Fraser*, articles for *Ainsworth's Magazine* and *Foreign Quarterly Review*.
		Probably appointed literary reviewer to the *Morning Chronicle* and on the staff of the *Examiner*.
	June	First contributions to *Punch*.
	July-October	In Ireland.
	Winter	Writing the *Irish Sketch Book* (published April 1843).
1843		In lodgings in Jermyn Street—continuing *Fitz-Boodle Papers*.

1843	18th March	Appointed art critic and literary reviewer to the *Pictorial Times*.
	Christmas	Appointed to the staff of *Punch*.
1844	January-November	Writing *Barry Lyndon* for *Fraser* and articles for *New Monthly Magazine* and *Punch*.
	April	At Brighton.
	Summer	In Belgium.
	22nd August	Sails from Southampton for Cairo.
	3rd November	*Barry Lyndon* finished at Malta.
	December	Writing his travels at Chelsea and Brighton.
1845		Lodging at 88 St. James's Street.
		Intimacy with the Brookfields begins.
		Writing *Cornhill to Cairo* (published December), *Mrs. Perkins's Ball*, and for *Punch*, *Fraser*, the *New Monthly*, *Edinburgh Review*, *George Cruikshank's Table Book*, etc.
1846		Writing *The Snobs of England* (*Punch*, 28th February to 27th February 1847).
	February	Begins *Vanity Fair* at Brighton.
	June	Goes to live at 13 Young Street.
	Autumn	Resigns from the *Morning Chronicle*, his last regular journalistic connection except *Punch*.
	December	*Mrs. Perkins's Ball*, his first Christmas book, published.
1847	January	First number of *Vanity Fair* issued.
		End of his regular connection with *Fraser's Magazine*.
		Writing *Vanity Fair* and the *Prize Novelists*, etc.
	December	*Our Street*, his second Christmas book, published.
1848	January	Second edition of *Jane Eyre* dedicated to Thackeray.
		Vanity Fair reviewed in the *Edinburgh*.
	26th May	Called to the Bar.
	2nd July	*Vanity Fair* finished.
	July-August	Holiday on the Rhine—begins *Pendennis*.
	September	At Clevedon Court, Somerset.
	November	First number of *Pendennis* issued.

1848	December	At Brighton. *Doctor Birch and His Young Friends* published.
1849	February	At Paris.
		Writing *Pendennis* and for *Punch*.
	June-July	At Fareham and Brighton.
	Early September	At Paris.
	Late September	Seriously ill.
	October-December	Convalescence at Brighton—publication of *Pendennis* suspended—writing *Rebecca and Rowena* (published December).
	9th or 10th December	Meets Charlotte Brontë.
1850	January	Twelfth number of *Pendennis* issued—controversy concerning *The Dignity of Literature*—rejected by the Athenæum—lampooned by Lever in *Roland Cashel*.
	March	At Paris.
	July	Threatened resignation from *Punch*.
	August	At Southampton.
	September	On the Rhine—writing *The Kicklebury*s (published December).
	About 6th-16th October	At The Grange, Alresford, Hants.
	November	*Pendennis* finished.
	23rd December	Funeral of Harry Hallam.
1851	January	At Paris.
	February-April	Writing the lectures on *The English Humourists*.
	21st May	First Lecture at Willis's Rooms.
	July	On the Rhine.
	September	Rupture of his friendship with the Brookfields—begins *Esmond*.
	Late October	At The Grange, Alresford.
	December	Lecturing in Scotland.
	Christmas	Final resignation from *Punch*.
1852	February	Lecturing in Scotland.
	March	Engages Eyre Crowe as secretary.
	c. April	Founds the Fielding Club.
	29th May	*Esmond* finished (published November).
	June-August	On the Continent.
	30th October	Sails for America.
1853	20th April	Returns from America.
	May	At Paris.
	7th July	*The Newcomes* begun at Baden.
	July-August	In Germany and Switzerland.

1853	October	First number of *The Newcomes* issued.
	November	At Paris.
	December to	
1854	March	Wintering at Rome and Naples—working on *The Newcomes* and *The Rose and the Ring*.
	May	Moves into 36 Onslow Square.
	June-September	Staying at Boulogne.
	1st November	*The Rose and the Ring* finished (published December).
1855	28th June	*The Newcomes* finished at Paris.
	July	On the Rhine.
	August-September	Writing *The Four Georges*.
	13th October	Leaves for America.
1856	26th April	Returns from America.
	August-September	On the Rhine.
	November-December	Lecturing in Scotland and the north of England.
1857	January-May	Lecturing in England and Scotland on *The Four Georges*.
	July	Parliamentary candidate for Oxford.
	August	At Brighton.
	September	At Homburg and Paris.
	October	*The Virginians* begun.
	November	First number of *The Virginians* issued.
1858	June	The Yates affair.
	July	In Switzerland.
	August	At Brighton.
1859	19th February	Contracts for future fiction with George Smith.
		Appointed editor of the *Cornhill Magazine*.
	Early September	*The Virginians* finished.
	September	In northern Italy.
		Writing *Lovel the Widower* and *Roundabout Papers*.
1860	January	First number of *Cornhill*.
	November	*Philip* begun.
1861	9th September	Death of his stepfather.
1862	March	Moves to Palace Green, Kensington.
	18th March	Resigns editorship of *Cornhill*.
	3rd July	*Philip* finished.

1863		Writing *Denis Duval*.
	Easter	At Fryston.
	25th April	The *Athenæum* review of Anne Thackeray's *Story of Elizabeth*.
	21st December	'In famous spirits and full of fun.'
	22nd December	Another 'attack of spasms.'
	24th December	Death.

APPENDIX II

BIBLIOGRAPHY[1]

(i) *Published Books: Novels, Stories, Sketches*

FLORE ET ZEPHYR: BALLET MYTHOLOGIQUE . . . PAR THEOPHILE WAGSTAFF. London, published March 1st 1836 by J. Mitchell, etc.

THE LOVING BALLAD OF LORD BATEMAN. London, Charles Tilt, Fleet Street, and Mustapha Syried, Constantinople, MDCCCXXXIX.

AN ESSAY ON THE GENIUS OF GEORGE CRUIKSHANK . . . (From the *Westminster Review*) No. LXVI). . . . Henry Hooper, 13 Pall Mall East, MDCCCXL.

THE PARIS SKETCH BOOK: BY MR. TITMARSH. With numerous designs by the author. . . . London: John Macrone . . . 1840. 2 vols., 8vo.

THE SECOND FUNERAL OF NAPOLEON: IN THREE LETTERS TO MISS SMITH, OF LONDON. AND THE CHRONICLE OF THE DRUM. By Mr. M. A. Titmarsh. London: Hugh Cunningham, St. Martin's Place, Trafalgar Square, 1841.

[1]*Note for the General Reader.*—Cheap editions and reprints of Thackeray's novels are innumerable. The most handsome and useful complete sets of the Works are:

The Biographical Edition, 13 vols., large crown 8vo, red cloth gilt. Edited by Lady Ritchie. First issued by Smith, Elder & Co., 1898-99. Subsequently issued by John Murray at 10s. 6d. per volume.

The Centenary Biographical Edition, 26 vols., 8vo, blue cloth gilt. Edited by Lady Ritchie. Smith, Elder & Co., 1910-11.

The Oxford Thackeray, 17 vols., 8vo, various bindings as required. Edited by George Saintsbury. Oxford University Press.

Odd volumes of the above editions are obtainable. Cheaper editions of the principal novels, at prices ranging from 2s., are issued in the World's Classics, Collins's Illustrated Pocket Classics, Everyman's Library (Dent), etc.

Note for the Bibliographer and Collector.—There is no complete bibliography of Thackeray. The most authentic and reliable is *A Thackeray Library. Collected by Henry Sayre van Duzer*, New York, privately printed, 1919. Of this work, which must form the basis of all subsequent bibliographical investigations, only 175 copies were printed.

COMIC TALES AND SKETCHES. Edited and Illustrated by Mr. Michael Angelo Titmarsh. . . . London: Hugh Cunningham, St. Martin's Place, Trafalgar Square, 1841. 2 vols., 8vo.

THE IRISH SKETCH BOOK. By Mr. M. A. Titmarsh. . . . London: Chapman and Hall, 186 Strand, MDCCCXLIII. 2 vols., 8vo. (Second Edition same year.)

NOTES OF A JOURNEY FROM CORNHILL TO GRAND CAIRO, BY WAY OF LISBON, ATHENS, CONSTANTINOPLE, AND JERUSALEM: PERFORMED IN THE STEAMERS OF THE PENINSULAR AND ORIENTAL COMPANY. By Mr. M. A. Titmarsh. . . . London: Chapman and Hall, 186 Strand, MDCCCXLVI.

MRS. PERKINS'S BALL. By M. A. Titmarsh. Chapman and Hall, 186 Strand.

(Sq. 8vo. Pink glazed boards, dated 1847. Three editions were issued, but the first has no letterpress under the plate facing title and no list of illustrations or advertisement on p. 47.)

OUR STREET. By Mr. M. A. Titmarsh. London: Chapman and Hall, 186 Strand, MDCCCXLVIII.

(Sq. 8vo. Pink glazed boards. The first 'issue' has coloured plates.)

THE BOOK OF SNOBS. By W. M. Thackeray. . . . London: *Punch* Office, 85 Fleet Street., MDCCCXLVIII.

(8vo. Green pictorial wrappers. Second edition issued in yellow wrappers by Bradbury and Evans, 11 Bouverie Street, 1855. Both editions are reprinted from *Punch*, omitting Chapters XVII to XXIII inclusive. The omitted chapters were included in the first American edition by D. Appleton & Co., New York, 1852.)

THE HISTORY OF SAMUEL TITMARSH AND THE GREAT HOGGARTY DIAMOND. By W. M. Thackeray. . . . London: Bradbury and Evans, 11 Bouverie Street, MDCCCXLIX.

(Sq. 8vo. Pictorial glazed boards. First American edition by Harpers', New York, n.d., but contemporary with the first English edition. Reprinted 1857.)

DOCTOR BIRCH AND HIS YOUNG FRIENDS. By Mr. M. A. Titmarsh. London: Chapman and Hall, 186 Strand, 1849.

(8vo. Pink pictorial boards. Like *Our Street*, the first is distinguished from the second 'issue' by the coloured plates. An edition in paper covers was published at Paris by Galignanis', 1849.)

AN INTERESTING EVENT. London, David Bogue, 1849.

(8vo. Paper sheets. Reprinted from the *Keepsake*, 1849.)

THE LANDSCAPE PAINTERS OF ENGLAND. Sketches after English Landscape Painters. By L. Marvy. With Short Notices by W. M. Thackeray. London: David Bogue, 86 Fleet Street. 4to. Blue cloth.

REBECCA AND ROWENA. A Romance upon Romance. By Mr. M. A. Titmarsh. With illustrations by Richard Doyle. London: Chapman and Hall, 186 Strand, 1850.

(Sq. 8vo. Pink glazed boards. The first distinguished from subsequent 'issues' by coloured plates.)

THE KICKLEBURYS ON THE RHINE. By Mr. M. A. Titmarsh. London: Smith, Elder & Co., 65 Cornhill, MDCCCL.

(Sq. 8vo. Pink boards. The first distinguished from subsequent 'issues' by coloured plates. A second edition, bearing date MDCCCLI, contains 'An Essay on Thunder and Small Beer,' as does the first American edition, New York, Stringer & Townsend, 1851. Unlike Thackeray's former Christmas books, the first edition bears on its title the actual year of issue, *e.g. Rebecca and Rowena*, published in December 1849, bears the year 1850).

THE CONFESSIONS OF FITZ-BOODLE AND SOME PASSAGES IN THE LIFE OF MAJOR GAHAGAN. By W. M. Thackeray. . . . New York: D. Appleton & Co., 200 Broadway, MDCCCLII.

(12mo. Red cloth. *The Fitz-Boodle Papers*, here reprinted for the first time from *Fraser's Magazine*, including the 'Third Profession' from the number of June 1842, subsequently omitted in the *Collected Works*, etc.)

THE HISTORY OF HENRY ESMOND. A COLONEL IN THE SERVICE OF HER MAJESTY Q. ANNE. WRITTEN BY HIMSELF. . . . London: Printed for Smith, Elder & Company. Over against St. Peter's Church in Cornhill. 1852.

(3 vols., 8vo. Green cloth, paper labels. A second edition followed in 1853.)

A SHABBY GENTEEL STORY AND OTHER TALES. D. Appleton & Co., New York, 1852.

(12mo. Cloth. Contains, besides 'A Shabby Genteel Story,' 'The Professor,' pp. 153-175, 'The Bedford Row Conspiracy,' pp. 177-242, and 'A Little Dinner at Timmins's,' pp. 243-267. A second edition, dated 1853, contains 283 pages, including the first numbers of 'A Little Dinner at Timmins's' omitted in the previous editions. The first English edition of the latter story, with 'The Bedford Row Conspiracy,' was published by Bradbury and Evans, 8vo, yellow wrappers, 1856. The first English edition of 'A Shabby Genteel Story' was issued likewise by Bradbury and Evans, 1857, with a note by Thackeray, dated 10th April 1857.)

MEN'S WIVES. New York, D. Appleton & Co., 1852.

(12mo. Cloth. Reprinted from *Fraser*. The first English edition, published by Bradbury and Evans, 1857, does not contain 'The [Executioner]'s Wife,' first reprinted in England in *Stray Papers*, edited by Lewis Melville. London, 1901.)

THE ENGLISH HUMOURISTS OF THE EIGHTEENTH CENTURY. A Series of Lectures. By W. M. Thackeray. . . . London: Smith, Elder, & Co., 65 Cornhill. Bombay: Smith, Taylor & Co., 1853.

(8vo. Blue marbled cloth. The first American edition, New York, Harper & Brothers, 1853, contains the additional lecture on 'Charity and Humour,' first published in England in the *Cornhill Magazine* for August 1910.)

PUNCH'S PRIZE NOVELISTS, THE FAT CONTRIBUTOR, AND TRAVELS IN LONDON. New York: D. Appleton & Co., 1853.

(12mo. Cloth. Reprinted from *Punch*.)

MR. BROWN'S LETTERS TO A YOUNG MAN ABOUT TOWN, WIT (*sic*) THE PROSER AND OTHER PAPERS. New York: Appleton, 1853.

(12mo. Reddish brown cloth. Contains the special preface by Thackeray, dated New York, December 1852.)

THE LUCK OF BARRY LYNDON: A ROMANCE OF THE LAST CENTURY. New York: D. Appleton & Co., 1853.

(2 vols., 12mo. Red cloth. First English edition, by Bradbury and Evans, 1856, as *The Memoirs of Barry Lyndon, Esq.*)

THE ROSE AND THE RING: OR, THE HISTORY OF PRINCE GIGLIO AND PRINCE BULBO. A Fire-Side Pantomime for Great and Small Children. By Mr. M. A. Titmarsh. . . . London: Smith, Elder & Co., 65 Cornhill, 1855.

(Sq. 8vo. Pink glazed boards. The sixth and last of the Christmas books, no copies were issued with coloured plates.)

MISCELLANIES. By W. M. Thackeray. London: Bradbury and Evans, 11 Bouverie Street, 1855-57. 13 vols., small crown 8vo, yellow wrappers, as follows:

(1) *The Book of Snobs*, 1855. (Second English edition.)

(2) *The Fatal Boots and Cox's Diary*, 1855. (First English edition reprinted from Cruikshank's *Comic Almanack* of 1839 and 1840.)

(3) *Ballads*, 1855. (Here first collected. An American edition was issued simultaneously by Ticknor and Fields, Boston, 1856, the preface by Thackeray being dated 'Boston, 27 October 1855.')

(4) *Novels by Eminent Hands, and Character Sketches*, 1856. (First English edition. The 'Character Sketches,' here reprinted for the first time from *Heads of the People*, 1840-41.)

(5) *Burlesques. A Legend of the Rhine: Rebecca and Rowena*, 1856. (The former here first reprinted from *George Cruikshank's Table Book*, 1845.)

(6) *A Little Dinner at Timmins's, and The Bedford Row Conspiracy*, 1856. (First English edition of the former; the latter reprinted from *Comic Tales and Sketches*.)

(7) *The Tremendous Adventures of Major Gahagan*, 1855. (Reprinted from *Comic Tales and Sketches*.)

(8) *The Memoirs of Mr. Charles J. Yellowplush, and the Diary of C. Jeames de la Pluche, Esq.*, 1856. (The former appeared as *The Yellowplush Papers*, in the first volume of *Comic Tales and Sketches*. A pirated edition was published in America as *The Yellowplush Correspondence*. Philadelphia: E. L. Carey & A. Hart, 1838. This volume contained only the first eight papers, and the first complete American edition was that by Appleton, New York, 1852. *Jeames's*

Diary, here reprinted from *Punch* for the first time in England, was pirated as *Jeames's Diary; or, Sudden Riches*. By Michael Angelo Titmarsh, Esq. . . . New York, Philadelphia, and Baltimore: William Taylor and Company. 1846. Appleton issued an edition in one volume with *A Legend of the Rhine* and *Rebecca and Rowena*. New York, 1853.)

(9) *Sketches and Travels in London*, 1856. (First English edition of *Mr. Brown's Letters*, *The Proser*, and *Travels in London*, reprinted from *Punch*, and *Going to See a Man Hanged*, from *Fraser*. All of these appeared in the two volumes issued by Appleton, New York, 1853, as *Mr. Brown's Letters to a Young Man About Town, with The Proser and Other Papers*, and *Punch's Prize Novelists, The Fat Contributor, and Travels in London*.)

(10) *The Memoirs of Barry Lyndon, Esq., of the Kingdom of Ireland*. . . . 1856. (First English edition.)

(11) *A Shabby Genteel Story*, 1857. (First English edition.)

(12) *The History of Samuel Titmarsh and the Great Hoggarty Diamond*, 1857.

(13) *The Fitz-Boodle Papers: and Men's Wives*, 1857. (Reprinted from *Fraser*. First English edition.)

LOVEL THE WIDOWER. By W. M. Thackeray. With Illustrations. London: Smith, Elder and Co., 65 Cornhill, M.DCCC.LXI.

(8vo. Purple cloth. First English edition, published November 1861. The first American edition, 8vo, grey wrappers, New York, Harper & Brothers, 1860, preceded the English edition by nearly eighteen months, being issued on 30th June 1860.)

THE FOUR GEORGES: SKETCHES OF MANNERS, MORALS, COURT, AND TOWN LIFE. By W. M. Thackeray. . . . With illustrations. London: Smith, Elder, and Co., 65 Cornhill, M.D.CCC.LXI.

(Post 8vo. Green cloth. Only the first issue has the words 'Sketches of Manners,' etc., on the title page. This volume was published at the same time as *Lovel the Widower*, and the American edition, like that of the novel, preceded the English edition by about a year, being published by Harpers', New York, 1860, after a serial appearance in *Harper's Magazine*, Aug.-Nov. 1860. A pirated edition, bearing the same date, 12mo, boards, was published at New York by James O. Noyes.)

THE ADVENTURES OF PHILIP ON HIS WAY THROUGH THE WORLD; SHEWING WHO ROBBED HIM, WHO HELPED HIM, AND WHO PASSED HIM BY. By W. M. Thackeray. . . . London: Smith, Elder and Co., 65 Cornhill, M.DCCC.LXII.

(3 vols., 8vo. Dark red cloth. The first American edition was published by Harpers, New York, 1862.)

ROUNDABOUT PAPERS. Reprinted from the *Cornhill Magazine*. With illustrations. By W. M. Thackeray. . . . London: Smith, Elder and Co., 65 Cornhill, MDCCCLXIII.

(Cr. 8vo. Cloth. The first American edition was published by Harper & Brothers, New York, 1863.)

DENIS DUVAL. By W. M. Thackeray. . . . London: Smith, Elder and Co., 65 Cornhill. 1867.

(Cr. 8vo. Maroon cloth. The first American edition was published by Harper & Brothers, New York, 1864, roy. 8vo, wrappers.)

Note.—It is impossible here to enumerate the posthumously published volumes possessing some first edition value by virtue often of only a hitherto unpublished letter, ballad, or fragment. The most important of such volumes are:

THE ORPHAN OF PIMLICO AND OTHER SKETCHES, FRAGMENTS, AND DRAWINGS. By William Makepeace Thackeray. With some notes by Anne Isabella Thackeray. London: Smith, Elder, & Co., 15 Waterloo Place, 1876.

SULTAN STORK AND OTHER STORIES AND SKETCHES. By William Makepeace Thackeray (1829-1844). Now First Collected, to which is added The Bibliography of Thackeray. . . . London: George Redway, York Street, Covent Garden, 1887.

THE EARLY WRITINGS OF WILLIAM MAKEPEACE THACKERAY. By Charles Plumptre Johnson. With Illustrations. . . . London: Elliot Stock, 62 Paternoster Row, E.C., 1888.

THE HITHERTO UNIDENTIFIED CONTRIBUTIONS OF W. M. THACKERAY TO 'PUNCH,' with a Complete and Authoritative Bibliography from 1843 to 1848 by M. H. Spielmann, Author of 'The History of "Punch,"' etc. With Numerous Illustrations and Explanatory Notes. London and New York: Harper & Brothers. . . . 1899.

STRAY PAPERS BY WILLIAM MAKEPEACE THACKERAY BEING, STORIES, REVIEWS, VERSES, AND SKETCHES (1821-1847). Edited, with an Introduction and Notes, by Lewis Melville. . . . With Illustrations. . . . London: Hutchinson and Co. . . . 1901.

THE NEW SKETCH BOOK, BEING ESSAYS NOW FIRST COLLECTED FROM THE FOREIGN QUARTERLY REVIEW. Edited, with an introduction, by Robert S. Garnett. . . . London: Alston Rivers, Ltd. . . . 1906.

(ii) *Novels in Numbers*

VANITY FAIR

Twenty monthly parts in nineteen, Nos. XIX and XX issued in a double number, price 2s., July 1848. The other numbers issued, price 1s. each, from January 1847 to June 1848 inclusive, in yellow wrappers. The cover of the first number reads:

No. 1.] January. [Price 1s. / (*Woodcut design*) / VANITY FAIR: / Pen and Pencil Sketches of English Society. / (*short rule*) / By W. M. THACKERAY. / Author of 'The Irish Sketch Book': 'Journey from Cornhill to Grand Cairo': of 'Jeames's

Diary' / and the 'Snob Papers' in Punch: &c. &c. / London: / Published at the Punch Office, 85, Fleet Street. / J. Menzies, Edinburgh; J. M'Leod, Glasgow; J. M'Glashan, Dublin. / 1847. / [Bradbury & Evans, Printers, Whitefriars.] /

The title-page of the first edition in one volume, 8vo, cloth, xvi+624 pp., with 40 full-page plates and 150 woodcuts, reads:

VANITY FAIR. / A Novel without a Hero. / By / William Makepeace Thackeray / With Illustrations on Steel and Wood by the Author. / London: Bradbury and Evans, 11, Bouverie Street. / 1848.

The main points to be noted are the subsequently suppressed woodcut of the Marquis of Steyne on p. 336, the heading on p. 1 in rustic, the misprint 'Mr. Pitt' for 'Sir Pitt' on p. 453, and the advertisement announcing 'Preparing for Publication, with Illustrations by the Author, / The / Great Hoggarty Diamond.'

PENDENNIS

Twenty-four monthly parts in twenty-three, Nos. XXIII and XXIV being issued in a double number, price 2s., December 1850. The first eleven numbers appeared from November 1848 to September 1849, but publication was then suspended for three months, the twelfth number being published in January 1850. In yellow wrappers, the cover of the first number reads:

[November.] / No. 1.—Price 1s. / THE HISTORY / of / PENDENNIS. / (*Woodcut design*) / His Fortunes and Misfortunes, / His Friends and His Greatest Enemy. / By / W. M. THACKERAY, / Author of 'Vanity Fair,' the 'Snob Papers' in Punch, &c. &c. / London. Bradbury & Evans, 11, Bouverie Street. / J. Menzies, Edinburgh; T. Murray, Glasgow; and J. M'Glashan, Dublin. / Bradbury & Evans.] 1848 [Printers, Whitefriars.

On completion of the serial issue, Thackeray deleted portions of Chapters XVI and XVIII, compressing the remainder into one chapter and at the same time sacrificing two plates. Thus, the first volume of the first edition in 2 vols., 8vo, cloth, contains thirty-eight instead of thirty-nine chapters, and twenty-two plates instead of twenty-four. The title-page reads:

The / History / of / Pendennis / His Fortunes and Misfortunes, His Friends and His / Greatest Enemy / By / William Makepeace Thackeray. / With illustrations on steel and wood by the author / Vol. I / London / Bradbury and Evans, 11, Bouverie St. / 1849.

The title of the second volume the same, except 'Vol. II' and '1850.' Harpers issued the novel serially in America in eight parts during 1849 and 1850, but without the plates. The first American edition in 2 vols., 8vo, half cloth and boards, New York,

Harper & Brothers, 1850, contains the original thirty-nine chapters in Vol. I, and also the two cancelled plates, making forty-eight plates in all, as compared with forty-six in the English edition.

THE NEWCOMES

Twenty-four monthly parts in twenty-three, yellow wrappers, Nos. XXIII and XXIV being issued in a double number, price 2s., August 1855, to which date the previous numbers were published in consecutive months from October 1853. The cover of the first number reads:

Mr. Thackeray's New Monthly Work. / (*rule*) / THE / NEWCOMES / (*eight circular drawings surrounding the legend* / Memoirs / of / a most / Respectable / Family /) / Edited by / ARTHUR PENDENNIS ESQ^RE / ILLUSTRATED by RICHARD DOYLE. / London: Bradbury and Evans, 11, Bouverie Street. / 1853 / No. I.—October.—Price 1s./

The title-page of the first volume of the first edition in 2 vols., 8vo, cloth, reads:

The / Newcomes / Memoirs of a Most Respectable Family / Edited by / Arthur Pendennis, Esq. / With illustrations on steel and wood by Richard Doyle / Vol. I. / London / Bradbury and Evans, 11, Bouverie Street. / 1854.

The title of the second volume the same, except 'Vol. II.' and '1855.' The woodcut of the Charterhouse boys playing at marbles in Vol. I appeared in both the first and second editions, but was afterwards suppressed. In America the novel ran serially in *Harper's Magazine*, from November 1853 to October 1855, omitting March 1854. It was then published in 2 vols., 8vo, half cloth and boards, New York, Harper & Brothers, 1855.

THE VIRGINIANS

Twenty-four separate monthly parts in yellow wrappers, published from November 1857 to October 1859 inclusive. The cover of the first number reads:

No. 1] [November] [Price 1s. / THE VIRGINIANS / A Tale of the Last Century / (*short rule*) / By W. M. Thackeray. / (*Woodcut enclosing* / Author of 'Esmond,' / 'Vanity Fair,' / 'The Newcomes,' / &c. &c. /) / London: / Bradbury and Evans, 11, Bouverie Street. / 1857.

The title-page of the first volume of the first edition, 2 vols., 8vo., cloth, reads:

THE VIRGINIANS. / A Tale of the Last Century. / By / W. M. Thackeray, / Author of 'Esmond,' 'Vanity Fair,' 'The Newcomes,' &c., &c. / With Illustrations on steel and wood by the author. / Vol. I / London: / Bradbury & Evans, 11, Bouverie Street. / 1858

The title of the second volume the same, except 'Vol. II' and '1859.' Both volumes possess two title-pages, one engraved, the other in letterpress, the engraved title in each case being faced by a full-page plate. The first 'issue' has a misprint, 'actresses' for 'ancestresses' on p. 207 of Vol. I, and Chapters XLVII and XLVIII wrongly numbered XLVIII and XLIX. In America the novel was issued serially in *Harper's Magazine*, from December 1857 to November 1859, and pirated in the *New York Semi-Weekly Tribune*, 20th November 1857 to 18th October 1859, and in the *New York Weekly Tribune*, 21st November 1857 to 22nd October 1859. In book form it was first published by Harper & Brothers, New York, 1859, in one vol., 8vo, cloth, with 136 woodcuts.

(iii) *Contributions to Newspapers and Periodicals.*

Note.—An asterisk * indicates doubtful authorship.

THE SNOB: A Literary and Scientific Journal. *Not* 'Conducted by Members of the University.' Cambridge: W. H. Smith, Rose Crescent, 1829.

Eleven numbers of this undergraduate paper, edited by W. G. Lettsom, appeared weekly between 9th April and 18th June. Thackeray's contributions were:

No. 3. *Our 'Snob's' Birth, Parentage, and Education*, and *Extract from a Letter, from one in Cambridge, to one in Town*, signed 'T. T.'
No. 4. *Timbuctoo.*
No. 6. *To Genevieve.*
Nos. 7 to 11, omitting 8. *The Ramsbottom Papers.*

Timbuctoo was reprinted in the *Works*, the remainder in Lewis Melville's *Stray Papers.*

THE GOWNSMAN: (formerly called) 'The Snob,' A Literary and Scientific Journal, Now Conducted by Members of the University. Cambridge: W. H. Smith, Rose Crescent, 1830.

Seventeen numbers appeared weekly from 5th November 1829 to 25th February 1830. It is believed that Thackeray's contributions were those signed '*Θ*,' as he used that signature some ten years later for his article on Cruikshank in the *London and Westminster Review.* These were the verses, 'I'd be a Butterfly' in No. 2, and 'From Anacreon' in No. 5. These, with the dedication of No. 1 and the 'Letter from Mrs. Ramsbottom' in No. 2, were reprinted in *Stray Papers*, while it is suggested that he also wrote 'An Extract from the Diary of the late Thomas Timmins' in No. 6.

FRASER'S MAGAZINE:

1832	August-September	**Elizabeth Brownrigge.*
	December	**The Annuals.*
1834	April	**A Dozen of Novels.*

1834	June	*Il était un Roi d'vetot (King of Brentford).*
		**Highways and Low Ways, or Ainsworth's Dictionary, with Notes by Turpin.*
1837	November	*Fashionable Fax and Polite Annygoats,* by Charles Yellowplush, Esq.
	December	*A Word on the Annuals.*
1838	January-August	*The Yellowplush Correspondence.*
	January	**One Batch of Novels for Christmas.*
	March	**Half-a-crown's worth of Cheap Knowledge.*
	June	*Strictures on Pictures, a Letter from Michael Angelo Titmarsh, Esq.*
	October-November	*Passages from the Diary of the late Dolly Duster.*
	December	*The Painter's Bargain.*
1839	January	*Our Annual Execution.*
	May-August	*Catherine.*
	June	*A Second Lecture on the Fine Arts by Michael Angelo Titmarsh, Esq.*
	September	*The Fêtes of July.*
	October	*The French Plutarch. I. Cartouche. II. Poinsinet.*
	November	*Catherine,* contd.
	December	*On the French School of Painting.*
1840	January-February	*Catherine,* concluded.
	January	*Epistles to the Literati, No. XIII. Ch-s Y-ll-wpl-sh, Esq., to Sir Edward Lytton Bulwer, Bart., etc.*
	February	**William Ainsworth and Jack Sheppard.*
	June-August	*A Shabby Genteel Story.*
	June-July	*A Pictorial Rhapsody by Michael Angelo Titmarsh.*
	August	*Epistles to the Literati, No. XV, On Old Fashioned Oaths.*
		Going to See a Man Hanged.
	October	*A Shabby Genteel Story* concluded.
1841	February	*Ainsworth's *Tower of London.*
	June	*Memorials of Gormandising.*
	July	*On Men and Pictures.*
	August	*Men and Coats.*
	September-December	*The History of Samuel Titmarsh and the Great Hoggarty Diamond, edited and illustrated by Sam's Cousin, Michael Angelo.*

1841	September-October	*Notes on the North What-d'ye-Callem Election. Being the Personal Narrative of Napoleon Putnam Wiggins, of Passimaquoddy.*
1842	March	*Dickens in France.*
	June	*Fitz-Boodle's Confessions.*
	July	*Professions by George Fitz-Boodle.*
	October	*Fitz-Boodle's Confessions: Miss Lowe.*
1843	January-June	*Confessions of George Fitz-Boodle. (Dorothea. Ottilia,* and *Men's Wives.)*
	August-November	*Men's Wives. By George Fitz-Boodle,* continued.
	September	*Jerome Paturot.*
	October	*Bluebeard's Ghost. By M. A. Titmarsh.*
	December	*Grant in Paris. By Fitz-Boodle.*
1844	January-December (omitting October)	*The Luck of Barry Lyndon, a Romance of the Last Century. By Fitz-Boodle.*
	February	*A Box of Novels.* (Includes notice of Dickens's *A Christmas Carol.*)
	March	Titmarsh's *Carmen Lilliense.*
	May	*Little Travels and Roadside Sketches by Titmarsh.*
	June	*May Gambols, or Titmarsh in the Picture Galleries.*
	October	*Little Travels and Roadside Sketches by Titmarsh.* No. II.
1845	January	*Little Travels and Roadside Sketches by Titmarsh.* No. III.
	June	*Picture Gossip.* (Titmarsh.)
	November	*Barmecide Banquets.* (Fitz-Boodle.)
	December	*About a 'Christmas Book.'* (Titmarsh.)
1846	January	*Ronsard to his Mistress.* (Titmarsh.)
	March	*A Brother of the Press on the History of a Literary Man, Laman Blanchard, and the Chances of the Literary Profession.*
	April	*On Some Illustrated Children's Books.* (Titmarsh.)
	August-September	*Proposals for a Continuation of 'Ivanhoe.' In a letter to Monsieur Alexandre Dumas by Monsieur Michael Angelo Titmarsh.*
1847	January	*A Grumble about the 'Christmas Books.'* (Includes notice of Dickens's *Battle of Life.*)
1853	January	*Mr. Thackeray in the United States.*

THE NATIONAL STANDARD of Literature, Science, Music, Theatricals, and the Fine Arts.

With the issue of the nineteenth number, 4th March 1833, Thackeray acquired control of this weekly paper, which became known as the *National Standard and Literary Representative* in the new year of 1834. The last number appeared on 1st February 1834. The contributions ascribed to Thackeray, who wrote something nearly every week and probably almost everything in the later numbers, are enumerated by Mr. van Duzer; some of them were reprinted in *Stray Papers*.

THE CONSTITUTIONAL: AND PUBLIC LEDGER.

A daily newspaper, Radical in politics, owned by the Metropolitan Newspaper Company, of which Thackeray's stepfather, Major Carmichael-Smyth, was chairman. The first number appeared on Thursday, 15th September 1836; the last on 1st July 1837. Thackeray was appointed Paris correspondent, and his letters, signed 'T. T.,' appeared two or three times a week from 19th September to 18th February. From March onwards he was attached to the editorial staff in London and contributed extensively to the paper.

GALIGNANI'S MESSENGER.

On 30th November 1848 Thackeray spoke of having 'worked in Galignani's newspaper for ten francs a day, very cheerfully ten years ago' (cf. *Brookfield Letters*, p. 36). Probably he was so engaged throughout the year 1836, when he was living in Paris, and possibly for some time in the previous year.

BRITISH AND FOREIGN REVIEW: or, European Quarterly Journal.

No. XVI, April 1839, contains a review of the 'Speeches of Henry, Lord Brougham,' the only article generally ascribed to Thackeray, but he probably contributed other articles between the autumn of 1836 and 1842. Founded in 1835 and changed to the *British Quarterly Review* ten years later, the review was edited by Thackeray's friend, John Mitchell Kemble.

LONDON AND WESTMINSTER REVIEW.

1837	July	Review of Dickens's *Sketches by Boz*, etc.
1839	April	*Parisian Caricatures*.
1840	June	*Essay on the Genius of George Cruikshank*.

THE TIMES.

Thackeray was employed as literary reviewer from August 1837 till early in 1841. His identified contributions are:

1837	3rd August	Carlyle's *French Revolution*.
1838	? January	*Old England*.
	6th January	Duchess of Marlborough's *Private Correspondence*.

1838	11th January	Lady Charlotte Bury's *Diary.*
	31st January	*Memoirs of Holt, the Irish Rebel.*
	11th April	Macready in *Macbeth.*
	17th April	*Poetical Works of Dr. Southey.*
	? April	Carlyle as a lecturer.
1840	2nd September	Fielding's *Works.*
1848	15th March	**The Tuileries.*
	17th March	**The Louvre.*
1851	30th April	*May Day Ode.*
1863	15th May	*The Cruikshank Gallery.*

BENTLEY'S MISCELLANY.

1837	September	*The Professor. By Goliah Gahagan.*

THE NEW MONTHLY MAGAZINE.

1838	October	*The Story of Mary Ancel.*
1838	February, March, November, December, and	*Some Passages in the Life of Major Gahagan.*
1839	February	
1840	January, March, April	*The Bedford Row Conspiracy.*
1844	May	*The Partie Fine. By Lancelot Wagstaff, Esq.*
	June	*Arabella; or, The Moral of 'The Partie Fine.'* (Titmarsh.)
	July	*Greenwich-Whitebait. By Mr. Wagstaff.*
1845	July	*The Chest of Cigars. By Lancelot Wagstaff, Esq.*
	August	*Bob Robinson's First Love. By Lancelot Wagstaff, Esq.*

ANTI-CORN LAW CIRCULAR.

1839	23rd July	*Illustrations of the Rent Laws: No. 1.*
	10th December	*Illustrations of the Rent Laws: No. 2.*

These two woodcuts, designed by Thackeray, were reproduced in Sir Henry Cole's *Fifty Years of Public Work* (London, 2 vols., 1884), Vol. II, p. 145. Others ascribed to Thackeray are mentioned by Mr. van Duzer.

THE CORSAIR: A Gazette of Literature, Art, Dramatic Criticism, Fashion and Novelty. (New York.)

1839		*Letters from London, Paris, Pekin, Petersburgh, &c. By the Author of 'The Yellowplush Correspondence,' 'The Memoirs of Major Gahagan.' &c.* Signed 'T. T.' letters appeared on 24th August, 14th September, 21st September, 5th, 19th, and 26th October

1839	28th September	*Capt Rook and Mr Pigeon. By William Thackeray, Author of 'The Yellowplush Correspondence,' &c., &c.*
	28th December	*A Ramble in the Picture Galleries.* ('T T')
1840	18th January	*A Ramble in the Picture Galleries.* ('M. A. T.')
	7th March	*Epistles to the Literati, Ch-s Y-ll-sh, Esq., to Sir Edward Lytton Bulwer, Bart.*, etc.

BRITANNIA: A Weekly Journal of News, Politics, and Literature.

1841	*Loose Sketches. By Mr. Michael Angelo Titmarsh.* (*Reading a Poem*, 2 nos., *St. Philip's Day at Paris*, 2 nos., *Shrove Tuesday in Paris*, and *Rolandseck.*)

Numerous reviews and other articles are attributed to Thackeray.

THE MORNING CHRONICLE.

1844	2nd April	Review of Horne's *New Spirit of the Age.*
1846	? July	Review of Horace Smith's *Poetical Works.*
1850	12th January	*The Dignity of Literature.*
	12th April	*Capers and Anchovies.*

Probably on the conclusion of his connection with *Britannia*, early in 1842, Thackeray obtained the post of literary reviewer, which he had formerly held on *The Times*. He resigned in the late summer of 1846 (cf. *Letters of Anne Thackeray Ritchie*, 1924, p. 20), but resumed the connection for a time in October 1848 (cf. *Brookfield Letters*, pp. 29-30).

THE EXAMINER: A Sunday Paper, on Politics, Literature, and the Fine Arts.

Thackeray was on the staff, possibly as sub-editor, for about two years, resigning in March 1844 (cf. Biographical Introduction to *Contributions to Punch*, pp. xviii-xix). Albany Fonblanque was owner, editor, and contributed the political articles; John Forster, as literary editor, wrote the leading literary reviews. All articles were anonymous, but Thackeray probably wrote some of the dramatic criticism and an occasional review. On 13th May 1843, the leading literary article 'puffed' the *Irish Sketch Book*, and refuted the charge of Cockneyism levelled by the reviewer in *Ainsworth's Magazine*. On 8th July following, the Fine Arts article on the *Cartoons* is probably by Titmarsh.

THE PICTORIAL TIMES: A Weekly Journal of News, Literature, Fine Arts, and the Drama.

Thackeray was art critic and literary reviewer from the first number, 18th March 1843 till August 1844. The following contributions, identified by Vizetelly, were reprinted in *Stray Papers*.

1843 — *Letters on the Fine Arts. By Michael Angelo Titmarsh.* (Three papers on *Art Unions*, 18th March, 1st and 8th April; *The Water-Colour Exhibition*, 6th May; two papers on *The Royal Academy*, 13th and 27th May).
1st April — *Mr. Macaulay's Essays.*
1844 25th May — *Coningsby: or The New Generation.*

THE FOREIGN QUARTERLY REVIEW.

1842 April — *Le Rhin: lettres à un ami. Par Victor Hugo.*
July — *The German in England.*
October — *Crimes Célèbres. Par Alexandre Dumas.*
1843 January — *Letters from Paris. By Karl von Gutzkow.*
April — Georg Herwegh's *Poems.*
July — *English History and Character on the French Stage.*
Balzac on the Newspapers of Paris.
Les Mystères de Paris. Par Eugène Sue.
October — *French Romancers on England.*
1844 January — *New Accounts of Paris.*
July — *Angleterre. Par Alfred Michiels.*

THE NATION. (Dublin.)

1843 13th May — *Daddy, I'm Hungry,* with an illustration.

PUNCH: or, The London Charivari.

Thackeray contributed nearly every week for seven years, from the beginning of 1844 to 1851, and there is here space for reference only to his principal contributions. Detailed bibliographies are given by Mr. Spielmann in his *Hitherto Unidentified Contributions of W. M. Thackeray to 'Punch,'* and by Mr. van Duzer.

1842 — *Miss Tickletoby's Lectures on English History* (2nd July to 1st October, omitting 23rd and 30th July, and 3rd September).
1844 — *History of the Next French Revolution* (24th February to 20th April).
3rd August — *Wanderings of Our Fat Contributor.*
Travelling Notes by Our Fat Contributor (10th and 17th August, 30th November, 7th and 14th December).
1845 — *Punch in the East* (11th January to 8th February).
1st May — *Railroad Speculators.*
2nd August — *A Lucky Speculator.*
9th August — *The Pimlico Pavilion.*

1845	16th August	*Letter from Jeames of Buckley Square.*
	18th October	*A Brighton Night Entertainment.*
	25th October	*Meditations over Brighton.*
	1st November	*Jeames on Time Bargings.*
		Jeames's Diary (8th November to 7th February, omitting 20th December and 24th January).
1846		*The Snobs of England* (28th February to 27th February 1847, being fifty-three consecutive numbers).
	14th March	*Titmarsh v. Tait.*
	9th May	*The Royal Academy.*
	16th May	*Jeames on the Gauge Question.*
	13th June	*Mr. Jeames Again.*
1847	9th January	*The Mahogany Tree.*
	6th March	*Love Songs Made Easy.*
		Mr. Jeames's Sentiments on the Cambridge Election.
		Love Songs by the Fat Contributor (27th March and 5th June).
		Punch's Prize Novelists (*George de Barnwell*, *Codlingsby*, *Lords and Liveries*, *Barbazure*, *Phil Fogarty*, *Crinoline*, and *The Stars and Stripes*, from 3rd April to 9th October, omitting 1st and 8th May, 5th June, 3rd and 31st July, 18th September and 2nd October).
		Brighton in 1847 (23rd and 30th October).
		Travels in London (from 20th November to 25th March, omitting 18th December, 5th and 26th February, 4th and 18th March).
1848		*Persecution of British Footmen. By Mr. Jeames* (1st and 8th April).
	27th May	*Mr. Snob's Remonstrance with Mr. Smith.*
		A Little Dinner at Timmins's (27th May, 17th and 24th June, 1st, 8th, 22nd and 29th July).
		Authors' Miseries (2nd, 9th, 23rd, and 30th September, 7th October, 4th November, and 2nd December).
		Bow-Street Ballads (25th November and 9th December).
1849		*Child's Parties* (13th and 27th January).
	10th February	*Paris Revisited.*
	17th February	*The Ballad of Bouillabaisse.*

Year	Date	Title
1849	24th February	*Two or Three Theatres at Paris.*
	3rd March	*On Some Dinners at Paris.*
		Mr. Brown's Letters to a Young Man About Town (24th March to 18th August, omitting 21st April, 2nd and 30th June, 28th July).
1850		*Hobson's Choice* (12th, 19th, 26th January).
	2nd February	*Thoughts on a New Comedy.*
	9th February	*Ballad of Eliza Davis.*
	23rd March	*Mr. Finigan's Lament (Molony's Lament).*
		The Proser (20th April, 4th and 18th May, 8th, 15th, and 29th June, and 3rd August).
	11th May	*Lines on a Late Hospicious Ewent.*
	25th May	*Jane Roney and Mary Brown.*
	3rd August	*Mr. Molony's Account of the Ball given to the Nepaulese Ambassador.*
	24th August	*Damages, Two Hundred Pounds.*
		The Lion Huntress of Belgravia (24th and 31st August and 21st September).
1851	22nd February	*A Plan for a Prize Novel.*
	26th April	*Mr. Molony's Account of the Crystal Palace.*
	10th May	*What I remarked at the Exhibition.*
	10th May	*Monsieur Gobemouche's Authentic Account of the Grand Exhibition.*
	1st November	*Portraits from the Late Exhibition.*
1853	1st October	*The Organ Boy's Appeal.*
1854		*Important from the Seat of War!* (24th June to 5th August).
	16th September	*Mr. Punch to an Eminent Personage.*
	23rd September	*Second Letter to an Eminent Personage.*

AINSWORTH'S MAGAZINE.

Year	Date	Title
1842	February	*Sultan Stork . . . By Major G. O'G. Gahagan, H.E.I.C.S. Part I, The Magic Powder.*
	May	*Part II, The Enchanted Princess.*
	June	*An Exhibition Gossip. By Michael Angelo Titmarsh.*

EDINBURGH REVIEW.

Year	Date	Title
1845	October	*Dashes at Life with a Free Pencil. By N. P. Willis.*

QUARTERLY REVIEW.

Year	Date	Title
1854	December	*Pictures of Life and Character. By John Leech.*

THE LEADER.

Founded in 1850 by Edward Pigott and G. H. Lewes, this paper was edited jointly by Lewes and Thornton Hunt, both of whom were friends of Thackeray's and among the earliest contributors to *Cornhill*. Thackeray is said to have contributed to this paper (cf. *Fifty Years of Fleet Street, being the Life and Recollections of Sir John R. Robinson*, edited by F. Moy Thomas. London, 1904).

CORNHILL MAGAZINE.

Prospectus. *A Letter from the Editor to a friend and contributor.* Signed 'W. M. Thackeray, November 1, 1859.'

1860		*Lovel the Widower* (January to June).
		Roundabout Papers:
	January	(1) *On a Lazy Idle Boy.*
	March	(2) *On Two Children in Black.*
	May	(3) *On Ribbons.*
	June	(4) *On Some Late Great Victories.*
	July	(5) *Thorns in the Cushion.*
	August	(6) *On Screens in Dining-Rooms.*
	September	(7) *Tunbridge Toys.*
	October	(8) *De Juventute.*
	December	(9) *On a Joke I once heard from the late Thomas Hood.*
	February	*Nil Nisi Bonum.*
	April	*The Last Sketch.*
	July	*Vanitas Vanitatum.*
		The Four Georges (July, August, September, October).
1861		*The Adventures of Philip on his way through the World; shewing who robbed him, who helped him, and who passed him by* (January to December).
		Roundabout Papers:
	February	(10) *Round About the Christmas Tree.*
	April	(11) *On a Chalk Mark on the Door.*
	May	(12) *On Being Found Out.*
	June	(13) *On a Hundred Years Hence.*
	July	(14) *Small-Beer Chronicle.*
	August	(15) *Ogres.*
	September	(16) *On Two Roundabout Papers which I intended to Write.*
	December	(17) *A Mississippi Bubble.*
1862		*The Adventures of Philip*, etc., continued (January to August).
		Roundabout Papers:
	January	(18) *On Letts's Diary.*
	February	(19) *On Half a Loaf.*
	April	(20) *The Notch on the Axe*, Part I.
	May	(21) *The Notch on the Axe*, Part II.
	June	(22) *The Notch on the Axe*, Part III.
	August	(23) *De Finibus.*
	September	(24) *On a Peal of Bells.*

1862	November	(25) *On a Pear-Tree.*
	December	(26) *Dessein's.*
	April	*Valedictory Address of the Editor to Contributors and Correspondents* (dated 18th March).
1863		*Roundabout Papers:*
	January	(27) *On some Carp at Sans Souci.*
	February	(28) *Autour de mon Chapeau.*
	April	*On Alexandrines.*
	August	*On a Medal of George the Fourth.*
	November	*Strange to say, on Club Paper.*
1864		*Denis Duval* (March to June).

THE AUTOGRAPHIC MIRROR.

The first volume of this publication, issued by Cassell, Petter, and Galpin, London and New York, folio, 1864, contains, with other Thackerayana, the *Whitey-Brown Paper Magazine: Dionysius Diddler*, which was here first reprinted from the proof-sheets of the original magazine, projected by Thackeray in the spring of 1840, but apparently never published. The only known copy of the proof-sheets is listed in the Catalogue of Major Lambert's library, p. 124.

(iv) *Contributions to Almanacks, Annuals, Miscellanies, &c.*

KING GLUMPUS: An Interlude in One Act. For private circulation only. London: 1837.

The author was John Barrow, who was at Charterhouse with Thackeray. Contains three illustrations by Thackeray.

MEN OF CHARACTER. By Douglas Jerrold. London, H. Colburn, 1838.

3 vols., 8vo, boards, paper labels. Contains twelve full-page illustrations by Thackeray.

DAMASCUS AND PALMYRA: A Journey to the East. . . . By Charles G. Addison, of the Inner Temple. . . . London: Richard Bentley, New Burlington Street. . . . 1838.

2 vols., 8vo, green cloth. The first 'issue' contains eighteen coloured plates by Thackeray; subsequent 'issues' only ten.

THE COMIC ALMANACK, for 1839: An Ephemeris in Jest and Earnest, containing 'All things fitting for such a work.' By Rigdum Funnidos Gent. Adorned with a dozen of 'righte merrie' cuts. . . . By George Cruikshank. London: Imprinted for Charles Tilt, Bibliopolist, in Fleet Street.

12mo, illustrated wrapper, blue type. Contains Thackeray's *Stubbs's Calendar: or, The Fatal Boots*, with twelve illustrations by Cruikshank.

THE COMIC ALMANACK, for 1840: (remainder of title as above).

12mo, illustrated wrapper, brown type. Contains Thackeray's *Barber Cox, and the Cutting of His Comb*, subsequently reprinted in the *Works* as *Cox's Diary*, with twelve illustrations by Cruikshank.

THE EXQUISITES: A Farce in Two Acts. . . . For private circulation only: London: 1839.

12mo, boards. Written by John Barrow, with four illustrations by Thackeray.

HEADS OF THE PEOPLE: or, Portraits of the English. Drawn by Kenny Meadows. With original essays by distinguished writers. London: Robert Tyas, 50 Cheapside. MDCCCXL.

2 vols., 8vo, bound up from the monthly parts, twenty-six in twenty-three, issued during 1840-41. Meadows's plates were engraved by Orrin Smith, who, according to Vizetelly, was the publisher's partner in the enterprise. Thackeray contributed *Captain Rook and Mr. Pigeon. By William Thackery (sic)*; *The Fashionable Authoress. By William Thackeray*; and *The Artists. By Michael Angelo Titmarsh.*

GEORGE CRUIKSHANK'S OMNIBUS. Illustrated with one hundred engravings on steel and wood. Edited by Laman Blanchard, Esq. Messrs. Tilt & Bogue, London, 1841-42.

Issued in nine monthly parts, 8vo wrappers, from May 1841 to January 1842. No. 6 contains *Little Spitz*, and No. 8 *The King of Brentford's Testament* (cf. *Fraser* for June 1834), both by Michael Angelo Titmarsh. There are twenty-two etchings and seventy-eight woodcuts.

GEORGE CRUIKSHANK'S TABLE BOOK. Edited by Gilbert Abbott à Beckett. London, published at the Punch Office, 1845.

8vo, wrappers, issued in twelve monthly parts, January to December 1845. Seven numbers, June-December, contain *A Legend of the Rhine, by Michael Angelo Titmarsh*, with fourteen woodcuts. There are twelve steel engravings and one hundred and ten woodcuts.

FISHER'S DRAWING ROOM SCRAP-BOOK. MDCCCXLVII. By The Hon. Mrs. Norton. (*Seven lines of verse by L. E. L.*) Fisher, Son, & Co. The Caxton Press, Angel Street, St. Martin's-le-Grand, London: H. Mandeville, Rue Neuve Vivienne, Paris.

4to, light brown cloth, lavishly decorated gilt, 84 pp. The printed title is preceded by one engraved by J. C. Varrall from a design by A. E. Chalon, R.A. Contains, on pp. 38-39, *The Anglers. By W. M. Thackeray, Esq.*, illustrated by a full-page plate, 'The Anglers.' These verses were reprinted for the first time in *Ballads*, the first volume of *Miscellanies* issued by Bradbury & Evans in 1855, as *Piscator and Piscatrix*, since when they have always been reprinted under the latter title, except in *The Princess Alexandra Gift Book*, edited by John Sherer, London, 1868.

PUNCH'S POCKET BOOK for 1847. London, Punch Office, 1847.

16mo, limp sheepskin, with flap and folding frontispiece in colour. Contains *An Eastern Adventure of the Fat Contributor*, with an illustration by John Leech.

THE KEEPSAKE. Edited by the Countess of Blessington. London, David Bogue, 86 Fleet Street, 1849.

8vo, cloth, g.e. Contains *An Interesting Event*, by Mr. Titmarsh.

THE KEEPSAKE. Edited by Miss Marguerite Power (niece of the Countess of Blessington). London, David Bogue, 1851.

8vo, red cloth, g.e. Contains *Voltigeur. By W. M. Thackeray, Esq.*

THE KEEPSAKE. Edited by Miss Power. London, David Bogue, 1853.

8vo, red cloth, g.e. Contains *The Pen and the Album*, by W. M. Thackeray.

THE KEEPSAKE. Edited by Miss Power. London, David Bogue, 1854.

8vo, red cloth, g.e. Contains *Lucy's Birthday*, by W. M. Thackeray, dated New York, April 15.

SAND AND CANVAS: A Narrative of Adventures in Egypt, With a Sojourn Among the Artists in Rome. By Samuel Bevan. London: Charles Gilpin, 5 Bishopsgate Street Without. MDCCCXLIX.

8vo, cloth, with seven full-page woodcuts and five in the text. Contains Thackeray's ballad, *The Three Sailors*, afterwards called *Little Billee*.

THE IDLER: Magazine of Fiction, Belles Lettres, News and Comedy. Edited by Edward Wilberforce.

Six monthly numbers, 8vo, yellow wrappers, January-June 1856. No. 3 contains *The Idler*, by Thackeray.

RIVAL RHYMES in Honour of Burns, with curious illustrative matter. Collected and Edited by Ben Trovato. . . . London: Routledge, Warne & Routledge, Farringdon Street. New York: 56 Walker Street, 1859.

12mo, cloth. Contains *Letter to the Directors of the Crystal Palace*, etc., signed 'W. M. T.'

THE VICTORIA REGIA: A Volume of Original Contributions in Poetry and Prose. Edited by Adelaide A. Procter. London: Printed and Published by Emily Faithfull and Co., Victoria Press (for the Employment of Women), Great Coram Street, W.C. 1861.

8vo, embossed cloth, g.e. Contains *A Leaf Out of a Sketch Book*, by Thackeray. There were afterwards printed '25 copies for the author's use,' bound in green paper wrappers.

POSTSCRIPT

ONE afternoon late in the autumn of 1860, lying on the truckle-bed in his spacious work-room at Onslow Square, Thackeray was reading a book. His elder daughter was busily writing at a table in the window. The light was failing. Turning on his side he glanced at her for a moment before shutting his book with a snap. She looked up inquiringly. Tapping the book with his forefinger, he said: 'Let there be nothing of this when I am gone!' And, with a gesture of contempt, he dropped the volume on the floor.

It was one of two ornately bound volumes, in embossed blue covers, with a crest and scroll emblazoned in gilt upon the fronts. The title-pages described them as *Memorials of Thomas Hood, collected, arranged, and edited by his daughter, with a preface and notes by his son. In two volumes. London. Edward Moxon & Co., 1860.*[1] It is the worst sort of memoir, scrappy, sketchy, ill-informed, sublimely careless of facts and dates, dishonestly concealing truth under a cloak of false candour, nauseating in the pomposity of its dutiful adulation, crude and impertinent in its fulsome tone of possessive vanity, of self-conscious dignity, of ostentatious glory in relationship to a man worth writing a book about—the type of ungainly tombstone which Victorian children loved to lay in dutiful piety upon the graves of literary fathers, crushing beneath its clumsy weight the struggling plant of posthumous reputation. Not only Hood, but Douglas Jerrold, Charles Reade, Charles Kingsley, Mortimer Collins, and countless smaller fry, suffered at the

[1] Cf. *On a Joke I once Heard from the late Thomas Hood,* in *Roundabout Papers.*

hands of well-intentioned but ill-inspired relatives. Dickens escaped by means of making John Forster his literary executor; so did Macaulay, who happened to have a gifted nephew, and Huxley, whose son chanced to have the instinct of a biographer; so did one or two more.

Sons and daughters, with few exceptions, make bad biographers. They commence with the handicap, overwhelmingly oppressive, of piety and partiality. They brood sentimentally over painful memories, and, on the principle of familiarity breeding contempt, ignore details of significance while exaggerating the importance of trifles. Frequently they adopt the attitude that the public is concerned solely with the public life of a public man, jealously preserving his private affairs as family property, forgetting that they thus stultify their own function and become mere commentators on the popular reference books. Even when approaching their task with sincerity, jealous tenderness of their subject's reputation suggests the suppression of some 'difficult' incident or detail, and having once compromised with conscience, they lose sight of truth and reason, committing the atrocity of Bowdlerising the life and character of their subject.

Thackeray foresaw the danger, especially apparent in his case, since his daughter manifested promising talent as a writer. She interpreted his injunction literally, steadfastly declining either to write a biography herself or to countenance an undertaking by others. If Thackeray could have foreseen the consequences of his prohibition, he would have retracted it with the eager contrition for a rash remark which he expressed to Tennyson for disparaging Catullus. He was too great a figure in literary history, too completely a national possession, for the public to rest content in ignorance of his private life and personality. Consequently, a succession of hopeful enthusiasts struggled against insuperable difficulties to supply a palpable deficiency in literary history, with results precisely such as Thackeray desired to avoid—half-truths, suppressions, omissions, discrepancies, accompanied by subterfuge and half-hearted apology. Aware of suppressions, the critics of 'vanity fair' conceived that there must be something objectionable or disgraceful to hide. His defenders did nothing to dispel the illusion by larding his memory with nauseating sentimentality—they only succeeded, being unable to introduce convincing evidence to the contrary, in supplying material for a charge of hypocrisy in addition to the popular imputation of snobbery, vanity, and arrogance.

Lady Ritchie realised the disastrous consequences of her father's injunction and sought to repair them, when she compromised with her resolution by writing the biographical introductions to his *Works*. Apart from that single remark, prompted by exasperation with the wretched *Memorials* of Hood, Thackeray never expressed any aversion to a biography of himself or anybody else. As a scholar he valued the art of biography as the mirror of history, and himself contemplated writing the life and editing the letters of Horace Walpole. He showed no inclination to reticence about his private feelings or affairs, for no writer introduced more autobiography into his novels, and the *Roundabout Papers* are full of personal reflections and reminiscences. FitzGerald, indeed, considered his habit of 'talking so of himself' a defect in his late work. Moreover, he more than once referred to himself as the subject of future biographers, notably in that letter to Mrs. Elliot and Miss Perry (cf. pp. 52-54 of *Letters of Anne Thackeray Ritchie*, ed. Hester Ritchie, 1924), from which is quoted the passage appearing on the title-page of this book, and Mrs. Brookfield preserved his letters with the intention either of publishing them—as she eventually did—or of offering them as material to his biographer, for she told him so in her own letters.

But in spite of the fact that Thackeray revealed himself with vivid clarity both in his works and the voluminous mass of letters which have been published from time to time in one form or another, he remains a figure of deeper mystery than any of his contemporaries. Books have been written about him—by John Camden Hotten (Theodore Taylor), Trollope, Herman Merivale and Frank T. Marzials, Mr. Lewis Melville, and General J. G. Wilson, besides countless magazine articles and slight monographs, like that by Charles Whibley—but no adequate portrait of his personality has yet appeared. It is the aim of this book to supply that deficiency, pending the appearance of that definitive biography which must, sooner or later, be written after consultation with all available documents, manuscripts, and letters. Here there are no pretensions to finality; the author's aim is to depict the personality of Thackeray against the background of his career, according to a conception derived from all printed material.

The main sources of this material, besides his own published works and the innumerable memoirs of contemporaries, both in books and magazine articles, are:—

(1) A COLLECTION OF LETTERS OF W. M. THACKERAY, 1847-1855. London, 1887.

These are the letters written to Mrs. Brookfield, who, in old age, faithfully carried out her avowed intention of publishing them. Before publication in volume form, the letters appeared serially in *Scribner's Magazine* from April to October 1887, and, according to a prefatory note, they were edited by the editor of the magazine, with the assistance of J. R. Lowell. They did their business abominably, for, except where Mrs. Brookfield was able to supply dates from memory, not a single letter of the series is accurately allocated. Consequently, the arrangement follows anything but the 'simple chronological order' modestly claimed by the editors. General J. G. Wilson justly described this volume as containing 'one of the best collections of epistolary literature published during the last century,' for Thackeray was a master in the art of letter-writing, and his letters to Mrs. Brookfield reflect his thoughts and actions during five most important years—1847 to 1851 inclusive—with the vivid fidelity of a mirror, but it badly needs re-editing. Meanwhile, reference to the present volume, in which extracts from the letters necessary for the present purpose are quoted, will supply a guide to check the errors of Lowell and his collaborator.

(2) LIBRARY OF THE LATE MAJOR WILLIAM H. LAMBERT OF PHILADELPHIA: PART II—THACKERAYANA. Metropolitan Art Association, New York.

The catalogue of the sale of Major Lambert's unique Thackeray collection, which was sold at New York on 25th, 26th, and 27th February 1914, contains extracts from the unpublished letters to Mrs. Brookfield, which she suppressed on Lowell's recommendation, though declaring her opinion that, if 'made public, without the slightest restriction, they would all the more redound to his (Thackeray's) honour.' Where necessary, quotations have been made from these letters, and, in one or two instances, from expurgated passages of letters appearing in the published collection. The catalogue contains also extracts from unpublished letters to Kate Perry, which will doubtless be included in some future edition of Thackeray's correspondence, and a variety of other useful material.

(3) THACKERAY'S LETTERS TO AN AMERICAN FAMILY. WITH AN INTRODUCTION BY LUCY W. BAXTER. London, 1904.

Contains letters written by Thackeray between 1852 and his death to members of the New York family of Baxter, with whom he became acquainted during his first American tour.

(4) THACKERAY IN THE UNITED STATES, by James Grant Wilson. 2 vols. London, 1904.

Besides detailed accounts of Thackeray's two American tours, these lavishly illustrated volumes contain a record of almost everything that every American whom Thackeray ever met had to say about him. An appendix contains an amazingly thorough bibliography by Frederick S. Dickson, comprising not only lists of American editions of Thackeray's works and the numerous works of reminiscence containing references to him, but also a laboriously complete enumeration of the countless periodical articles, directly and indirectly concerning him, issued by the American press over a period of sixty years. General Wilson had access to Major Lambert's library during the compilation of his work, and its value to the biographer is represented by numerous letters, either never previously published or reprinted from obscure magazine articles.

(5) LETTERS OF DR. JOHN BROWN, edited by his son and D. W. Forrest. London, 1907.

Contains a series of twenty letters written to Brown and his wife, whose acquaintance he made during his first lecturing tour in Scotland of December 1851.

(6) The Biographical Introductions to his *Works*, written by Lady Ritchie between 1897 and 1899, which include numerous letters and extracts from letters, mostly addressed to his mother, written at every epoch of his life from boyhood onwards, and furnishing the obvious and indispensable foundation to any account of his life.

(7) LETTERS OF ANNE THACKERAY RITCHIE: WITH FORTY-TWO ADDITIONAL LETTERS FROM HER FATHER, WILLIAM MAKEPEACE THACKERAY. Selected and Edited by her Daughter, Hester Ritchie. London, 1924.

To the authors, publishers, and present holders of any copyright in these works, I wish to make a general declaration of my indebtedness, while adding, in particular, my grateful thanks to the house of John Murray, the owners of the Thackeray copyrights, who have inspected the book in proof and kindly permitted me to quote from Thackeray's letters. Other works from which I have quoted are indicated in footnotes, though, to avoid an appearance of tiresome and cumbersome profusion, such indications are noted only on the first use of each work for the purpose of quotation; subsequent uses may be traced by reference to the Index.

Finally, I wish to acknowledge with gratitude the assistance received in the form of advice, introductions, and loans of books and other material, from Messrs. J. A. Waley Cohen, Albert M. Cohn, S. M. Ellis, Michael Sadleir, M. H. Spielmann, and A. J. A. Symons—above all, from Dr. Leonard Huxley, who not only allowed me to use the privately printed *House of Smith, Elder*, but tendered valuable advice both before and after reading the proofs of a book which, but for his courteous consideration and kindness, might not have attained its present degree of completeness.

MALCOLM ELWIN.

NORTH STOKE,
S. OXON.,
May 1932.

INDEX